FROM VIENNA TO CHICAGO AND BACK

FROM VIENNA TO CHICAGO AND BACK

Essays on Intellectual History and Political Thought
in Europe and America

GERALD STOURZH

THE UNIVERSITY OF CHICAGO PRESS
CHICAGO AND LONDON

Gerald Stourzh is professor emeritus at the University of Vienna. He is the author of several books in English and German, including *Benjamin Franklin and American Foreign Policy*, also published by the University of Chicago Press.

The University of Chicago Press, Chicago 60637
The University of Chicago Press, Ltd., London
© 2007 by Gerald Stourzh
All rights reserved. Published 2007
Printed in the United States of America

16 15 14 13 12 11 10 09 08 07   1 2 3 4 5

ISBN-13: 978-0-226-77636-1   (cloth)
ISBN-10: 0-226-77636-0   (cloth)

Library of Congress Cataloging-in-Publication Data

Stourzh, Gerald.
Vienna to Chicago and back : essays on intellectual history and political thought in Europe and America / Gerald Stourzh.
     p.   cm.
   Includes bibliographical references and index.
   ISBN-13: 978-0-226-77636-1 (cloth : alk. paper)
   ISBN-10: 0-226-77636-0 (cloth : alk. paper)   1. Political science—Europe.   2. Political science—United States.   I. Title.
JS84 .E9S75   2007
320.092—dc22

                                                              2006039090

TO

Thomas Angerer,
Birgitta Bader-Zaar,
Thomas Fröschl,

AND

Margarete Grandner,
my former doctoral students,
now companions in scholarship
and wonderful friends,
in gratitude.

CONTENTS

FOREWORD

It is a unique historian who can write with equal authority on Benjamin Franklin and Gustav Mahler, William Blackstone and Karl Kraus, Charles Beard and Alexis de Tocqueville, American constitutionalism and Austrian neutrality, and the meaning of human rights in both Anglo-America and continental Europe. Gerald Stourzh's scholarship in modern history, stretching over the full half-century after World War II, encompasses all of that, and more. His origins lay in his native Austria, where at the University of Vienna he came to occupy the premier professorship in modern history, but his first major publications—book-length studies of Franklin and Alexander Hamilton—were products of his research at the University of Chicago. As this collection of his papers shows so well, these early studies led him to a lifelong concern with the central issues of modern Anglo-American democracy, but his roots in central Europe were never neglected, and he continued over the years to probe the complexities of the multinational Austro-Hungarian empire and the modern state of Austria. His reach stretching from Hungary to London and from Bukovina to Philadelphia, he has transcended the parochial limitations—cultural-linguistic as well as political—that confine most historians' capacities, and offers the reader fresh insights into major issues of public life.

In all of this, Professor Stourzh is indeed unique. And there is a sense in which his scholarship is exemplary as well. One of the dominant developments in the historiography of the last half century has been the enlargement of the spheres of inquiry. Shortly after World War II the entire Mediterranean world emerged as a single historical subject. Since then the Atlantic world, the Pacific Rim, the Middle East, East Asia, the occident and the orient, ultimately the global world have all been seen as singular subjects. Professor Stourzh's history is equally broad, but analytic rather than descriptive and focused on certain key themes of western thought that thread through many nations' histories: constitutionalism, nationalism, ethnicity, equality and inequality, and the culture of rights. Anyone interested in these vital themes and in the major thinkers Professor Stourzh discusses will profit from viewing them from his distinctive point of view and from the penetration of his thought.

Bernard Bailyn
Harvard University

FOREWORD

Born in Vienna in 1929, Gerald Stourzh first studied at the University of Vienna, taking a doctorate with Heinrich Benedikt and Hugo Hantsch in 1951 with a dissertation on the political and constitutional history of the Austrian parliamentary system in the decades immediately after 1848. Rather than remain in post–war Austria, Gerald Stourzh accepted an invitation from Hans Morgenthau to come to the University of Chicago as a research assistant, where he was able to continue his studies in history and in political theory. Stourzh worked as a doctoral student and (intermittently) as a research associate at Chicago from 1951 to 1958, studying with such distinguished scholars as William T. Hutchinson, Friedrich von Hayek, Hans Rothfels, Leo Strauss, and Hans Morgenthau himself.

Although he could have remained in the United States and obtained a faculty position at a major research university, Stourzh decided to return to Europe and to make his career there. In 1962 he received his Habilitation from the University of Vienna, and in 1964 he was appointed Professor of History at the Free University of Berlin. In 1969 Stourzh was called back to the University of Vienna as Professor of Modern History.

During his stay at the University of Chicago Gerald Stourzh's primary research focused on American history and especially on American political and intellectual history during the Revolutionary period. This intellectual agenda was brought out with especial clarity and cogency in Stourzh's *Benjamin Franklin and American Foreign Policy* (1954), and in his later study on *Alexander Hamilton and the Idea of Republican Government* (1970). Stourzh came to these American subjects from another culture, bringing a rare blend of Central European learning and erudition and a freshness that enabled him to take a new look at scholarly problems that most American scholars thought were all too familiar.

Following his books on Franklin and Hamilton, Gerald Stourzh returned to the history of Central Europe, and particularly to the history of his own land, Austria, and of the Habsburg Empire. He brought to the study of Central Europe an interest in the relationship between articulated rights and liberties on the one hand and the formal structures of legislative and judicial power that can guarantee (or subvert) those rights on the other. His interest in Austrian legal and constitutional history is framed and informed by his interest in how politics shapes constitutions and how constitutions shape politics.

Stourzh's scholarship in Habsburg and Austrian history has encompassed a number of explorations. He is the author of several books that have had a decisive impact on the field of Habsburg and modern Austrian studies, especially his *Geschichte des Staatsvertrages 1945–1955: Österreichs Weg zur Neutralität* and *Die Gleichberechtigung der Nationalitäten in der Verfassung und Verwaltung Österreichs 1848–1918*. In the first book, recently republished in a much expanded, massive new edition,[1] Stourzh offered a brilliant analysis of the genesis of the Austrian State Treaty, demonstrating how international and domestic political factors in the first decade of the Cold War led to the reshaping of Austrian political self-understanding, producing a new consensus that allowed Austrian policy makers to take advantage of the break in Cold War relations that followed Stalin's death in 1953. This book explained the unique meshing of global and micro diplomacy that led to the voluntary departure of Soviet occupation forces and the remarkable emergence of the concept of Austrian neutrality (*immerwährende Neutralität*). Stourzh was one of the first to extend the field of contemporary history to encompass the history of the Second Republic and to insist on frank and resolute explorations of the complex political processes that led from the *NS-Zeit* to the State Treaty. The *Geschichte des Staatsvertrages* was thus of seminal import in legitimating and empowering a new field of post-war historiography that has made enormous progress in the last two decades.

In his book on *Die Gleichberechtigung der Nationalitäten*, Gerald Stourzh carefully reconstructed the powerful, yet up to that point little appreciated, role of the Austrian high courts in the mediation of ethnic conflicts in a multinational society where more overtly political mechanisms for conflict resolution had ceased to function. This book might be said to be the story of the unintended consequences of Austrian Liberalism

---

1. *Um Einheit und Freiheit. Staatsvertrag, Neutralität und das Ende der Ost-West-Besetzung Österreichs 1945–1955* (Böhlau, Vienna, 1998).

for although the German-speaking Liberals created a constitutional system in 1867 that accorded the various nationalities of the Empire extraordinary constitutional guarantees for their collective identity, they soon
became painfully aware of how exposed individual rights and liberties
could be against the truculent political energies that those collectivities
generated against each other and occasionally even against themselves.
In a constitutional system in which legislative decision-making was often immobilized, and in which collective ethnic identities were both politically irreducible and legally sacrosanct, state theorists were forced to
rely on the more indirect and mediated processes of administrative review
and appellate justice to render equity, if not harmony, among conflicting
interest groups and individuals in the multi-national Empire. Stourzh's
discovery of the powerful role of the *Verwaltungsgerichtshof* and *Reichsgericht* in trying to mediate these conflicts is of great importance for the
study of Austrian public administration, showing as it does how the continued presence of the post-Josephist administrative and judicial state
"saved" a powerful remnant of Liberalism in east central Europe, and thus
maintained the functional integrity and legitimacy of its governmental
processes.

In addition to these books, Stourzh has also authored a series of important essays on Austrian and Habsburg history, some of the most valuable
of which are contained in the present volume. These essays range from
insightful discussions of the origins of the national compromise in the
Austrian Crownland of Bukovina in 1909/10 and of the origins of Austrian
neutrality to stimulating contributions on Austrian nationality law, including its relation to the history of the Austrian Jews ("Ethnic Attribution in Late Imperial Austria: Good Intentions, Evil Consequences," "Max
Diamant and Diaspora Nationalism in the Bukovina 1909/10," and "The
Age of Emancipation and Assimilation: Liberalism and its Heritage." In
these latter essays Stourzh takes up the question as to whether the Jews
of Austria constituted an official nationality under the terms of the 1867
constitutional settlement. Not only does Stourzh reveal the complex range
of answers that Jews and non-Jews alike offered in response to this question, but he uses their answers to explore the political and moral dilemmas
faced by assimilated Austrian Jews in defending the promises of liberalism
and exploiting the opportunities of personal freedom in the late empire.
Gerald Stourzh was also at the center of a major debate about the way in
which scholars should understand the history of the Habsburg Monarchy
and its successor states as a part of the general history of Central Europe.
Reacting against Karl Dietrich Erdmann, who sought to embed the history

of Austria into the framework of a larger German political realm, Stourzh was one of the most articulate and forceful voices defending the historical memory of an Empire that contained more Slavic-speaking citizens than German speakers, and that represented social, cultural, and political traditions quite distinct from those of the Bismarckian *Reich* to the north. His essay "The Multinational Empire Revisited" reveals Stourzh's complex assessment of the longer term fate of the empire, but it should also be read in the context of his interventions about the integrity of Austrian history in the twentieth century.

Gerald Stourzh is one of the most important living Central European historians, and much of his training and his way of thinking about European and American history was influenced by his education at the University of Chicago. It is, therefore, fitting that the University of Chicago Press has republished these essays, all of which are remarkable and worth reading again.

John W. Boyer
University of Chicago

Traces of an Intellectual Journey

1. European Beginnings

On October 3, 1951, I set out from Vienna on a journey to Chicago—my first journey to the North American continent. After traveling in the old-fashioned manner—train from Vienna to Rotterdam, Atlantic passage (stormy) on the magnificent Dutch liner "Nieuw Amsterdam," passing the Statue of Liberty on the way into New York harbor, then again train from New York to Chicago—I arrived at my destination on October 14, 1951. The following day, a Monday, I began work in the Center for the Study of American Foreign Policy at the University of Chicago, headed by Hans J. Morgenthau; it was located in the Social Science Building. Only shortly before, on September 28, I had passed my final doctoral examinations in Vienna. The degree of Doctor of Philosophy in History was conferred on me, in absentia, on October 25, while I was already working in Chicago, whereupon my original appointment as Research Assistant was quickly changed to that of a Research Associate. I was 22 years old.

This transfer from Vienna to Chicago, with its decisive impact on my entire future life, was owing to Professor Morgenthau's sojourn in Austria in the spring of 1951. Morgenthau lectured at the Salzburg Seminar in American Studies and then went on to Vienna to write a report on Austria as a consultant to the U. S. Department of State. On this occasion he offered Research Assistantships at his newly established Center to three young members of the Student Section of the Austrian League for the United Nations, of whom I was one.

But what were the intellectual—and moral—prerequisites that I brought along from Europe to my new job in Chicago? Let me make the following six observations.

First, I grew up as the son of parents for whom writing was an important part of their lives. My mother, Helene Stourzh née Anderle, a specialist in obstetrics and gynecology, had received her M.D. in 1915. She was committed to lecturing and writing in the field of medical adult education, as well as to scholarly research.[1] My father, Herbert Stourzh, who held a Doctor of Philosophy in the field of philosophy, earned his bread as a mid-level civil servant. Not being a jurist, he was ineligible for higher ranks. By vocation, he was a philosophical writer. He wrote books and articles intended to reach a broadly educated public, notably in the field of ethics and increasingly in public affairs, until his writing was stopped by the Nazi takeover of Austria in 1938. Thus, I grew up full of respect for intellectual endeavor.

Second, I was profoundly marked by my parents' strongly anti-Nazi convictions. In his younger years, my father, born in 1889, was a non-religious, highly individualistic thinker,[2] who turned in his thirties to a rather undogmatic (Protestant) Christianity, based on the ethics of the Sermon on the Mount and the conviction of the equality of all human beings under God. He expressed his opposition against racist and notably National-Socialist thought in various publications. He criticized the racist basis of the organization of the student government at the University of Vienna of 1931.[3] As early as 1934 he castigated National Socialism literally as National Bestialism, and he denounced the ideology of National Socialism as intellectual barbarism ("geistiges Barbarentum").[4] His book *Humanität und Staatsidee,* was published in Switzerland under the pseudonym Karl Sturzenegger after the Nazi takeover of Austria.[5] On the basis of the Christian message of the brotherhood of all human beings, my father combated the propagators of the alleged higher dignity of the state (such as Othmar Spann), or of the master race (such as H. K. Günther). He sharply attacked such "bridge-builders" between Christianity and National Socialism as the Catholic bishop Alois Hudal. The Gestapo began investiga-

---

1. My mother published her first research article at the age of 24, while working for the noted anatomist Julius Tandler. Helene Anderle, Zur Lehre von der Querschnittstopographie der Nerven an der oberen Extremität, in *Zeitschrift für Angewandte Anatomie und Konstitutionslehre,* 1 (1914), pp. 397–425.

2. Herbert Stourzh, *Vom Sein und vom Soll,* Dresden/Leipzig 1922; idem, *Max Stirners Philosophie des Ich* (Berlin/Leipzig 1926).

3. Herbert Stourzh, Studentenrecht und Christentum, in *Menschheitskämpfer. Halbmonatsschrift der religiösen Sozialisten,* 6 (1932), No. 3, 5 February 1932, pp. 3–5. This racist student government was declared unconstitutional by the Austrian Constitutional Court.

4. Herbert Stourzh, Deutscher Mensch und deutscher Unmensch, in *Der christliche Ständestaat,* 1 (1933/34), No. 44, 7 October 1934, pp. 13–14.

5. Karl Sturzenegger (a pseudonym for Herbert Stourzh), *Humanität und Staatsidee* (Lucerne 1938).

tions against my father in 1940, and he was questioned twice. His early death from cancer at the age of 51 in August 1941 put an end to this.

Third, the Nazi takeover of Austria in 1938 brought about changes in my social environment which, together with the visible desperation of my parents, imparted to a nine-year-old boy the sense of unjust things happening. My pediatrician had to leave Vienna, as did my dentist; relatives as well as friends of the family left for England and France, respectively. My parents saw to it that I never did service in the Hitler Youth. As a fourteen-year-old boy I was allowed to secretly listen to BBC news, strictly forbidden by the Nazi regime, and the special BBC program for Austria during the War certainly had a part in my socialization as a conscious Austrian. I was not yet sixteen when Nazi rule and the Second World War were over. A lasting result of political upheavals witnessed early in life was a profound interest in things political, in the shape and shaping of the *res publica*. My lifelong interest in public affairs, political history, in constitutional history and the history of political thought as well as in the history of international relations, closely tied to interest in the fields of public law and political science, is rooted in my early experience of the primacy of politics. These interests have proved stronger and more enduring than the many "turns," not to mention fashions and fads within the discipline of history and the humanities in general to which I was witness in later years.

Fourth, to these interests awakened by the upheavals around me, there has to be added a certain talent for dealing with legal texts, particularly in the field of public law. Perhaps the fact that a grandfather on the paternal side as well as a great-grandfather on the maternal side were judges may have contributed to my interest in things legal and constitutional. During the War, at the age of about fourteen, I compiled the "Draft of a Republican Constitution" out of pocket book texts of various constitutions left by my father, including the American, Swiss, and Weimar Republic constitutions. I hid it in a stove (it is still extant). Later I more than once thought of studying the law in addition to history. Several of my works, notably the book on the Equality of Nationalities in the Constitution and Administration of Austria from 1848 to 1918 testify to these legal interests of mine; and I admit that the conferring of an honorary law degree by the University of Graz in 1989 filled me with great joy. If Jacques Le Goff has said that the law "is the historian's nightmare," it is not mine.[6] The reader

6. Jacques Le Goff, "Is Politics Still the Backbone of History?" In Felix Gilbert and Stephen R. Graubard, eds., *Historical Studies Today* (New York 1972), pp. 337–355, here p. 349. A volume

will find traces of these interests notably in Chapters 6, 8, 13, and 14 of the present volume. If I have been, all my life, a scholar more bent on the word as prime source of analysis and interpretation rather than on pictorial or other material sources, this may have to do with my *penchant* for the law. If I did employ pictorial sources, they often had to do with political and legal themes, like Ambrogio Lorenzetti's magnificent "buon governo" and "mal governo" in the Palazzo publico in Siena, whose interpretation often stood at the beginning of my classes on political thought. Yet in retrospect I think it possible to see much of my work as an ongoing examination of certain key words or key concepts such as "power," "republic," "constitution," "neutrality," "equal rights" and some more, always, to be sure, within historical contexts. I have never been willing to go along with the decontextualization trends of the late 20th century, and I share the critique of these phenomena brilliantly expressed by Carl Schorske.[7]

Fifth, in my university education, starting in 1947, a "western orientation" prevailed even before I arrived in America. I studied merely five semesters in Vienna; one semester I spent at the University of Clermont-Ferrand in France in 1949, and the academic year 1949–50 I spent at the University of Birmingham in England. There were additional vacation trips to France beginning in 1947. The opening toward the West, after the end of Nazi rule, was a great intellectual and even existential experience. My year in Birmingham, with the first exposure to Anglo-American habits of study—much more reading and writing than mere "listening" to lecturers—was a particularly valuable experience. Writing in my "essay class"—nothing of the sort existed in Vienna—included work on the development of religious toleration in England in the 17th century and on Max Weber and the spirit of Protestantism. I also wrote an essay on "The real Machiavelli"—work which encouraged me a couple of years later in Chicago to take a seminar on Machiavelli with Leo Strauss, where I reported on the history of Machiavelli interpretations. I gratefully recall my Birmingham tutor, John Stephens, a Quaker.

Sixth, during my university studies up to 1951, books were more important than teachers. I cannot say that I have been truly formed or profoundly influenced by a university teacher, though my two most important teachers in modern history in Vienna, Heinrich Benedikt (who had

---

of essays kindly dedicated to me on the occasion of my 70th birthday was appropriately titled by its editors *Geschichte und Recht*, ed. by Thomas Angerer, Birgitta Bader-Zaar and Margarete Grandner (Vienna 1999).

7. In his Scripps College lecture of 1988 on "History and the Study of Culture", printed in Carl Schorske, *Thinking with History* (Princeton 1998), pp. 219–232.

come back from emigration in England) and Hugo Hantsch (a Benedictine monk who for a while had been in Buchenwald concentration camp) were gifted historians with a great breadth of interests and of knowledge.[8]

I would single out six books—the majority of them not history books—which influenced me deeply before I got to Chicago. Some of them had an important impact on my work in Chicago, notably when writing the book on Benjamin Franklin. First, Friedrich Meinecke's *Die Idee der Staatsraison in der neueren Geschichte* impressed me by its discussion of the dilemmas of "reason of state," of "power imperatives" and the postulates of "ethical" conduct in public affairs.

Second, Josef Redlich, an Austrian, sometime Professor of Comparative Law at Harvard University, wrote a book titled *Das österreichische Staats- und Reichsproblem*, a magnificent exposition of the constitutional and political problems facing the "composite monarchy" of Habsburg Austria in the 19th century. Redlich, lawyer by training, historian by great talent, and political scientist by virtue of his incisive analytical power,[9] has been a great example for at least some of my writings, first on my Vienna doctoral dissertation on the development of bicameralism in the Austrian Constitution between 1848 and 1861, and above all for my book, already referred to, on the Equality of Nationalities in the Constitution and Administration of Austria from 1848 to 1918. Also, a more recent contribution on Austro-Hungarian Dualism between 1867 and 1918 may be placed in the Redlich tradition.[10] In the present volume, Chapters 5 and 6 come closest to this strand of my thought.

The third text, not really a book, which impressed me, was Max Weber's *Politik als Beruf* (Politics as a Vocation). This brief and famous text I read at the age of eighteen. Its juxtaposition of "Gesinnungsethik" (ethics of intention, the classic example being the ethics of the Sermon on the Mount, for Weber really an ethic for saints), and "Verantwortungsethik" (ethics of responsibility) implied for me criticism of my father's book on *Humanität und Staatsidee*, with its idealistic but, as I felt under Weber's

8. I have paid tribute to my Vienna teachers in two English language publications: Hugo Hantsch, in *Austrian History Yearbook* 9/10 (1973/74), pp. 507–514; Heinrich Benedikt (1886–1981), in *Austrian History Yearbook* 17/18 (1981/82), pp. 579–580.

9. Redlich also was the author of important, even classical works available in the English language, notably: *English Local Government* (1903), *The Procedure of the House of Commons* (1908), and *Austrian War Government* (1929).

10. Gerald Stourzh, "Der Dualismus 1867 bis 1918. Zur staatsrechtlichen und völkerrechtlichen Problematik der Doppelmonarchie," in Helmut Rumpler and Peter Urbanitsch, eds., *Die Habsburgermonarchie 1848–1918*, VII: *Verfassung und Parlamentarismus* (Vienna 2000), pp. 1177–1230.

impact, too simple postulate of putting political life under the guidance of the ethics of the Sermon on the Mount. The conflict between a (radically) Christian ethics of non-violence and the need to employ "power" when acting in the realm of the "ethics of responsibility" was something I attempted to settle by attributing to the Christian attitude of non-violence the role of a "purifying opposition" (*opposition purificatrice*) in political life. I expressed my view in a little piece on "Non-Violence and the Civil Community" written in French on the occasion of a meeting of pacifists organized or co-organized by the "International Fellowship of Reconciliation" in Le Chambon-sur-Lignon in France in the summer of 1949.[11]

A year later in England, I discovered and read three books which moved me greatly: Reinhold Niebuhr's *Moral Man and Immoral Society* of 1948, Herbert Butterfield's *Christianity and History* of 1949, and Hans J. Morgenthau's *Scientific Man vs. Power Politics* of 1946. Niebuhr, without apparently having been aware of Weber's text, also posited a "conflict between individual and social morality",[12] justifying the possible need for coercion to achieve social justice. Though being a theologian, he came down in favor of a kind of "ethics of responsibility." "We cannot build our individual ladders to heaven," he wrote, "and leave the total human enterprise unredeemed of its excesses and corruptions."[13]

Herbert Butterfield, the British historian, taught me to understand the phenomenon of "Hobbesian fear." Thus, before reading the *Leviathan* itself and before reading Leo Strauss on Hobbes, I had read Butterfield on Hobbes. For decades in my classes on the history of international relations I used his example of two persons closeted in one room with two pistols, each one full of good will "to disarm," yet each one finding it impossible to rid himself of his gun simultaneously with the other (because the other might throw away his gun a few seconds later or not at all, or the other might have hidden a second gun).[14]

Finally, I still think *Scientific Man vs. Power Politics* is Morgenthau's most original book. I was impressed by the radicalness of his views: "To

11. Gerald Stourzh, "La non-violence et la communauté civile," in *Fédéralisme et Non-violence* (Troisième Consultation fraternelle du Chambon), (Le Chambon-sur-Lignon 1949), pp. 37–40.

12. This is the title of the last chapter of Niebuhr's book. Reinhold Niebuhr, *Moral Man and Immoral Society* (New York/London 1948), pp. 257–277.

13. Ibid., p. 277.

14. In England I discovered and read an additional book which moved me deeply, though with less direct relation to my historico-political reflections: Simone Weil's *La pésanteur et la grâce*, with her note: "Those who take the sword, will perish by the sword. Those who do not take the sword will perish on the Cross."

the degree in which the essence and aim of politics is power over man, politics is evil; for it is to this degree that it degrades man to a means for other men." He who acts, Morgenthau quoted Goethe in a conversation with Eckermann, "is always unjust; nobody is just but the one who reflects." "The very act of acting destroys our moral integrity"—thus Morgenthau summed up his tragic view of social and political life.[15] The animus dominandi was a fundamental urge of man. At that time I did not know Nietzsche, and Morgenthau did not mention him anywhere, but in his polemic against Western rationalism Morgenthau acknowledged his intellectual debt to Niebuhr.[16] In any case, I was fascinated by Morgenthau's book—though later, in Chicago, I departed from those views and found the notion of the "security dilemma" in the sense of Butterfield's "Hobbesian fear" more convincing than the ubiquity of the lust for power.[17] What followed was really quite a fantastic story: The man whose book I had discovered in England in 1950, and which had fascinated me, came to Austria in 1951 and catapulted me to Chicago.

Intellectually, then, I did not arrive in Chicago from Europe empty-handed. In 1952 I put the gist of my discoveries and conclusions, truly a *confession de foi*, into the first lines of the first page of my first book, *Benjamin Franklin and American Foreign Policy*. It was more Weberian than Morgenthauian, but compared to my thoughts of 1949 in France I had gone over from "Gesinnungsethik" to "Verantwortungsethik"—though not without pain and regret and the continued yearning for Paradise on earth, before the Fall—or after Redemption:

"The fundamental problem of politics is the problem of coercion. Experience has taught man that he must restrain the freedom of action or sometimes even destroy the existence of some of his fellowmen in order to secure his own life and the life of others for whom he is responsible. But civilized man has ever yearned for a time when cooperation rather than competition,

15. Hans J. Morgenthau, *Scientific Man vs. Power Politics* (Chicago 1946), p. 189.
16. Ibid., pp. 40, 236.
17. I was—and continue to be—impressed by the arguments put forward by John H. Herz in his book *Political Realism and Political Idealism*, Chicago 1951, who also built on the Weberian dichotomy, yet in contrast to Morgenthau put the notion of security in the center of his theory, quoting from Spinoza's *Tractatus politicus*: "Liberality of spirit, or courage, is a private virtue; but the virtue of a state is security." Herz, *op. cit.*, p. 24. Herz, also a refugee from Nazi Germany, achieved less fame than Morgenthau. He first taught at Howard University in Washington, D.C., later at the City College of New York. I knew him personally and would like to preserve the memory of an excellent, moderate and modest scholar. One may ask whether I read Marx in those years? The answer is, with the exception of the Communist Manifesto, no. My readings of Marx, Engels and Hegel only date from the sixties and seventies.

love rather than fear and hatred, generosity rather than egotism, mercy rather than retaliation, and enlightened reason rather than selfish passion would govern the affairs of humanity. In the midst of horrors and trials of every kind, man has not given up the dream of a time when swords would be beaten into plowshares. In other words, man eternally strives to replace discord by harmony and present imperfection by lasting perfection." [18]

2. Chicago

Before continuing on Franklin and my research in Chicago, I turn to my impressions of the University of Chicago, and what I owe to it. Robert Hutchins was gone by the time I had arrived, yet the atmosphere at the University was vibrant and exhilarating. Two Europeans coming within the orbit of the University of Chicago a bit earlier than I did, yet sharing several experiences with me, including hearing Leo Strauss, have left accounts bursting with amazement and enthusiasm on having encountered the extraordinary and exceptional. George Steiner, scholar of comparative literature, in his autobiography *Errata*, has said of the U. of C. that a university which is worthy to attend is one where the student is brought into personal contact with "the aura and the menace of the excellent." When a young man or a young woman has been "exposed to the virus of the absolute," when he or she have seen, heard or "smelled" the fever of those who chase after disinterested truth, some after-gleam of this experience will remain even if he or she ends up living a quite average life, and it will protect them against emptiness.[19]

A wonderful declaration of love for the University of Chicago has come from the wife of the art historian Otto von Simson. Louise Alexandra von Simson, née Princess Schönburg-Hartenstein (1906–1976), of Austrian aristocratic origins, has written *Happy Exile* in 1961/62, privately printed by Otto von Simson in 1981. Her book culminates in the account of the 13 years from 1945 to 1958 when her husband was member of the Com-

---

18. Gerald Stourzh, *Benjamin Franklin and American Foreign Policy* (Chicago 1954), p. 1 (Second edition and paperback edition Chicago 1969, no change of pagination). The book was published in early spring 1954, but I wrote the first chapter in 1952.

19. Here rendered from the German edition: George Steiner, *Errata. Bilanz eines Lebens* (dtv pocket edition Munich 2002), pp. 60, 62. In the next few paragraphs I follow an unpublished lecture "History, Political Science and Social Thought at the University of Chicago Fifty Years Ago: Personal Experiences and their Transformation in an Austrian Academic Career" which I gave on 11 November 2004 at the University of Chicago within the framework of a symposium "Chicago-Vienna-Chicago: Urban Icons and the Transatlantic Relationship," co-organized by the College, The University of Chicago.

mittee on Social Thought. Her portraits of the colleagues in the Committee on Social Thought in the early '50s—such as its founder John U. Nef, Edward Shils, David Grene, Yves Simon, Peter von Blanckenhagen, Friedrich von Hayek, Robert Redfield and Frank Knight, and of other teachers at the University including Leo Strauss, should be obligatory reading for anyone interested in the history (and splendor) of the University around 1950. Louise Alexandra von Simson also had great respect for the pursuit and the love of knowledge for its own sake, which she detected in "average Americans" in the midst of downtown Chicago—a brilliant refutation of ignorant prejudices widespread, alas, in Europe. She taught ancient Greek at the U. of C. Downtown College, the Adult Education Center. One quotation shall suffice—it is a great compliment to the education offered by the University of Chicago and to its recipients —"average Americans":

"I had about 24 students and I taught the elements of Greek. . . . I had asked them in one of the first sessions why they wanted to learn Greek, and they all seemed to agree that they wanted to understand Plato and how could they even start to understand him without a knowledge of Greek. They worked as hard on it as I have ever seen anybody work and when we started painfully to decipher the first sentences of the Crito they did not seem disappointed with the results of their efforts. As I remember their faces, not very distinguished faces perhaps, a middle-aged couple who always sat on my right and helped each other with the translation, a broker always ahead of the others, a few young boys who had to earn their living and who could not go to College, a couple of secretaries, some others—I seem to hear the roar of the traffic on LaSalle Street and see us bent over our Greek text. We might have been in a lonely convent in some faraway country and if it is the destiny of man to find the truth, I have hardly ever seen people look for it with more dedication."[20]

Though employed as a Research Associate, I decided, with the approval of my boss Hans Morgenthau, to pursue doctoral studies, though I just had obtained my Doctor of Philosophy in Vienna. Why? An important motive was anxiety as to the future of Vienna, occupied by Soviet, American, British and French forces, and wholly surrounded by the Soviet zone of Austria. After all, this was 1951, when the Cold War in Europe was at its iciest, in Korea there was a hot war, and one could not know. . . .

20. Louise Alexandra von Simson, *Happy Exile*, privately printed 1981, pp. 101–102.

As a doctoral student, I branched out from traditional fields familiar to me like European history (Charles Mowat was an excellent teacher of British history, Louis Gottschalk very stimulating on the French Revolution) into fields unknown. These were American history and political science, then a discipline non-existent in Vienna; within the political science spectrum I concentrated on International Relations and Political Thought. I took classes with some extremely interesting and, in some cases, world renowned teachers. Apart from Hans Morgenthau, to whose brilliant intellect we owe one of the most influential textbooks of international relations, *Politics among Nations*,[21] I heard Quincy Wright, expert on International Law and on War Studies. He was author of the very well-known *A Study of War*, and I wrote for him a seminar paper on "Ideology and Foreign Policy." He looked like a gentleman of the old school, as if he just had stepped out of the Old State Department Building in Washington. My intellectual curiosity was most aroused by Political Thought and by American History. Political Thought from the 16th to the 19th century, from Machiavelli to Tocqueville, was then fairly new to me. It has remained one of the abiding interests of my life, and I had to come to Chicago to be confronted with Aristotle's Politics for the first time in my life. Attending Leo Strauss's Machiavelli-Seminar, his classes on early modern thought accompanied by the reading of his book on Hobbes and his then new *Natural Right and History*, were exciting experiences. His spellbinding speech has been described often. Though I did not become a "Straussian," Strauss more than anyone else opened my eyes on the fundamental differences between ancient and modern political thought, and notably the impact of his book on Hobbes has been important.[22] With Friedrich von Hayek, I took a seminar on 19th century liberalism, writing a paper on French Catholic liberalism—Lamennais and Montalembert. I also attended his seminar on Tocqueville. Hayek at that time was not teaching economic theory, but social and political thought, notably 18th and 19th centuries. He then worked on what was to become *The Constitution of Liberty*. Being allowed to live in his

21. In 1955, on the request of Hans Rothfels, also one of my teachers in Chicago, who was commuting between Chicago and Tübingen before definitively returning to Germany, and who in 1953 had been one of the co-founders of the first German review on contemporary history, I published a review essay on the most important authors of so-called "realism" in foreign policy literature (paying special attention to Niebuhr and Morgenthau), thereby also contributing to a transatlantic transfer of ideas. Cf. Gerald Stourzh, "Ideologie und Machtpolitik als Diskussionsthema der amerikanischen außenpolitischen Literatur," in *Vierteljahrshefte für Zeitgeschichte* 3 (1955), pp. 99–112.

22. Traces of what I learned from Strauss will be found in my book *Alexander Hamilton and the Idea of Republican Government* (Stanford CA 1970), pp. 130–133.

apartment on various occasions when he and his wife were away, I was able to make use of his magnificent private library, especially rich in 18th and 19th century English and Scottish thought.

As to United States History, I was fortunate to encounter Professor William T. Hutchinson. A scholar with not a very large list of publications, he was a brilliant teacher—the best I ever had. His two-quarter course on American Constitutional History has rightly been called a classic.[23] There I heard for the first time about the great cases of American Constitutional History, about *Marbury* vs. *Madison,* the Dred Scott case, etc.[24] Learning about them went well together with my existing interest in constitutional issues, and I was fascinated. The impact of this new knowledge has been double. On the one hand, in my teaching of American history after my return to Europe, both in Berlin and in Vienna, I was to pay close attention to these cases, particularly the civil rights cases. On the other hand, awareness of the American cases sharpened, if it did not awaken, my interest in constitutionally relevant cases in Austrian history. I was the first Austrian historian to make full use of archival material on judicial decision making in two of the highest Courts of imperial Austria, the "Reichsgericht" (Imperial Court, a kind of constitutional Court) and the "Verwaltungsgerichtshof" (High Administrative Tribunal). As John Boyer has pointed out in his Foreword, my book on The Equality of Nationalities in Austria between 1848 and 1918 is chiefly based on the analysis of law cases in the constitutionally sensitive field of ethnic and linguistic conflicts. Readers of the present volume will find examples of my analysis in this field in Chapters 6 and 8.

Hutchinson's teaching was important to me in a second field: I took a seminar with him on American historiography. There for the first time I heard about Carl L. Becker, Charles Beard, Francis Parkman, Frederick Jackson Turner, and others. I wrote a seminar paper on Beard's interpretations of U.S. foreign policy, and the reader of this volume may inspect the result of my work in Chapter 4. To sum up: For my subsequent teaching of American history both at the Free University of Berlin and at the University of Vienna, Hutchinson's teaching in Chicago has been essential. However, due to my return to Austria in 1958, I was not to complete my doctoral studies in Chicago.

23. Tribute by Professor James L. Cate on the occasion of the Memorial Service for W. T. Hutchinson on 21 January 1977. In University of Chicago Library, Special Collections, W. T. Hutchinson Papers.

24. Don Fehrenbacher, author of a magnificent book on the Dred Scott case, had been a student of Hutchinson in Chicago.

In addition to interesting teachers, there were visitors coming to the University of Chicago whom I never might have heard or encountered in Vienna. I met Raymond Aron and Walter Lippmann in the house of Hans Morgenthau, Reinhold Niebuhr in the house of Kenneth W. Thompson, Karl Menger (who actually was teaching at another university in Chicago), Eric Voegelin in the house of Friedrich Hayek. I listened to lectures by Hannah Arendt, Karl Löwenstein, Jacques Maritain, Kurt Riezler, and Arnold Toynbee.

One of the great impressions of the Chicago years was both the number and intellectual significance of scholars from Europe at the University of Chicago—most, though not all, refugees from Nazism (Hayek, for one, had left Austria for England without any threat). Many of these scholars have been mentioned already. Both Friedrich von Hayek and I were interested in and impressed by the numbers of scholars from Austria in the United States, and jointly we began compiling a list, enriched by numerous answers to letters which we sent out in 1957. By December 1958—I had in the meantime returned to Austria—we sent the final version of this "List of scholars and scientists of Austrian origin in the United States"—to various institutions and libraries in America and Austria.

My main task in Chicago, however, was research and writing. Work first on Benjamin Franklin, and in the later years on Alexander Hamilton, truly opened a new world. Though some of my essays written in England pointed toward North America as well, my main work in Vienna, the doctoral dissertation, had been on 19th century Austrian history. In Chicago I made two great discoveries: first, American history, chiefly of the 18th century and more particularly of the Age of the American Revolution, the War of Independence and the period of constitution-making; second, the discovery of the Enlightenment, both European and American. This was a wonderful intellectual adventure, quite intoxicating. I recall reading for the first time Carl Becker's *Heavenly City of the Eighteenth Century Philosophers*, Ernst Cassirer's *Philosophy of the Enlightenment*, Arthur Lovejoy's *Great Chain of Being*, and many other works. Chapter 1 of the present volume will tell the reader the nature of my discoveries about the Enlightenment.

Out of these two discoveries there came a third one: the unity of the North Atlantic world in the 18th century. The Atlantic Ocean, intellectually seen, was an inland lake! Franklin, who crossed the North Atlantic no less than eight times, became for me the symbol of this phenomenon. Perhaps it's worth calling this to our attention at a time when the Atlantic between Europe and America seems to be getting wider and wider in spite of the available means of communication.

Working on Franklin, and later on Hamilton and on the Age of Revolution and Constitution-making, meant research trips to the East—chiefly to the Library of Congress; to the American Philosophical Society in Philadelphia; to New York; to Hartford, Connecticut; to Boston; and Cambridge, Massachusetts. The results of research in Charleston, South Carolina—pursued not during my Chicago years, but on the occasion of a later stay at the Institute for Advanced Study in Princeton in 1967–68—may be seen in Chapter 2 of the present volume. Research trips, as well as participation in professional conventions, brought me in personal contact—gratefully remembered!—with a generation of scholars who by now have become part of American historiography, like Douglass Adair, Carl Bridenbaugh, Lester Cappon, Gilbert Chinard, Verner Crane, Felix Gilbert (who became a close friend whose memory I treasure with fondness), Clinton Rossiter, and others. In later years, on the occasion of frequent trips to the United States and sometimes meetings in Europe, my circle of contacts widened to include scholars like Joyce Appleby, Bernard Bailyn, Jack Greene, Michael Kammen, Richard Morris, Stanley Katz, Robert R. Palmer, J.G.A. Pocock, Jack Rakove (I worked with his father, Milton Rakove, in Morgenthau's Center), and Gordon Wood. To the memory of Douglass Adair, a wonderful friend, I have dedicated my book *Alexander Hamilton and the Idea of Republican Government* (1970). Nor should I, or will I, forget political scientists, many first met in Chicago, notably among students of Leo Strauss, like the late Martin Diamond and the late Herbert Storing, as well as Robert Goldwin and Richard Cox. University of Chicago Professor Ralph Lerner has become a lifelong close friend, and Chapter 14 of this book—the essay on Tocqueville—is dedicated to him. He and I first met in 1957 when we were both Research Associates at the American Foundation of Political Education with offices on LaSalle Street in Chicago.

Work done in Chicago included the book *Benjamin Franklin and Foreign Policy* (1954, second and paperback edition 1969, published by the University of Chicago Press). In 1955 it won the prize for the best book in Early American history awarded by the Institute of Early American History and Culture. I may be allowed to reproduce from the citation giving the reasons for the award those sentences that relate to the theme of this book – intellectual journeys across the Atlantic:

"Although Franklin holds something of himself reserved from us all, you have given us his wisdom where he would most want us to have it, in our relation with the rest of the world. It is fitting that you, born and educated in Austria, should have crossed the Atlantic to teach this lesson. In doing so you have demonstrated what Franklin himself exemplified, that

national boundaries are but a feeble barrier against the power of ideas."
(Citation read in Williamsburg, Va. on May 7, 1955.)

Additional work produced in Chicago included the extended article on
Charles Beard already referred to. It included, during employment as Research Associate at the American Foundation for Political Education, work
as a co-editor on a series of readers. With Ralph Lerner I did *Readings in
American Democracy*. I cooperated with Robert Goldwin and Ralph Lerner editing *Readings in World Politics* and *Readings in American Foreign
Policy*, and with Robert Goldwin and Marvin Zetterbaum on *Readings
in Russian Foreign Policy*. The most important second work originating
in Chicago was a book manuscript on Alexander Hamilton. Working on
Hamilton, I became more and more fascinated with the question as to
the meaning of the term "republican government"—a question that had
not really concerned me when I had worked on Franklin. I now explored,
successively, the "meaning," the "springs," and the "foreign policy" of republican government. The "Federalist", read and re-read, became my constant companion, and I took special care of the little green Modern Library
edition with many pencilled annotations when I returned to Europe. At
the turn of 1957–58 I had decided to return to Austria to take up a position opening up in Vienna rather than pursuing an academic career in the
States, though there were promising prospects (an excellent offer from the
University of California, Berkeley) at that time. That decision had been
maturing for some time (since about 1955). I had been impressed by the
failed return from America to Austria of a prominent historian very well
known to me. Therefore the risk of missing the chance to return to my native Austria, which I was firmly set to do, seemed too great if postponed for
very long. A first version of the Hamilton book had been completed when
I returned to Vienna at the end of June 1958. The publisher, faced with
one excellent and one very critical report (by an ardent Jeffersonian), decided not to go ahead with publication plans. Returning to Vienna meant
that the Hamilton project had to be put aside for several years. The book
Alexander Hamilton and the Idea of Republican Government was to be
published by Stanford University Press in 1970.

3. Europe Again: Vienna—Berlin—Vienna

In Vienna, my task was to build up a new Foreign Policy Association. Having been associated with one of the best known representatives of the discipline of International Relations—Hans J. Morgenthau—was certainly an
excellent recommendation. My work at this new institution was chiefly

organizational—which I enjoyed—but to this were added interesting intellectual challenges. I prepared the launch of a new Austrian Foreign Policy Journal, of which I became the first editor.[25] Invitations for lectures induced me to publish articles in a field then new to me, the development of Austria's international position in the post-war decade 1945–1955, leading to the termination of the four-power occupation of Austria, the Austrian State Treaty of 1955 and the establishment of Austria's neutrality. These were the modest beginnings of a research interest that would intensively occupy me in subsequent decades.

Also, I prepared my "Habilitation" at the University of Vienna—obtaining the *venia legendi* or the right to lecture at the University as *Dozent*. The procedure required the submission of one book, the *Habilitationsschrift*, and I was in the happy position to be able to submit my *Benjamin Franklin and American Foreign Policy*. A "trial lecture" was also required as part of these proceedings, and I spoke in May 1962 on the "Political Theory of the American Revolution." My first regular lecture course at the University of Vienna in 1963 was on "The Political Ideas of the American Revolution and the Formation of the Constitution 1763–1789." Clearly, knowledge acquired in Chicago stood me in good stead in Vienna. It stood me in good stead a second time, in Berlin, when after an interesting interlude of slightly more than two years in the Austrian Foreign Office[26] I was appointed in 1964 to the newly created chair of Modern History with particular emphasis on American History at the Free University of Berlin. Simultaneously, I was appointed Director of the History Department of the John F. Kennedy Institute of American Studies at that University. I remained in Berlin from 1964 to 1969.

The Berlin years brought a renewal of work in American history, through my classes, through the supervising of theses for the state examination and doctoral dissertations, and through scholarly publications. I again took up the investigation of the meaning of "republican government." A German article published in January 1965 titled "The Virtuous Republic: Montesquieu's Notion of 'Vertu' and the Beginnings of the

25. *Österreichische Zeitschrift für Aussenpolitik*, appearing six times a year. The first issue was published in October, 1960.

26. Working in the Foreign Office—my domain was the Council of Europe—taught me a great deal about the "physiology" of bureaucratic proceedings, and subsequently I looked with different eyes on the archival records of diplomatic negotiations and their preparation. I have pity for all young students who are confronted with such archival materials without ever having had the opportunity to observe bureaucracy or diplomacy "in action", and I tried to make good use of my—limited —insights when teaching and writing diplomatic history.

United States of America" had no impact at all in the United States.[27] At
the same time, I now was able to revise my book manuscript on Hamilton,
helped by a research sojourn at the Institute of Advanced Study in Princeton in 1967–68.[28] As mentioned before, the book was published in 1970;
it was integrated, as it were, into the American "republicanism" debate,
then in full force, through J. G. A. Pocock's joint review of Gordon Wood's
The Creation of the American Republic and my *Alexander Hamilton and
the Meaning of Republican Government* in 1972–73.[29] In this book I emphasized the need to distinguish between two strands of political thought:
one concerned with the principles of political obligation and their origin,
whether theological, philosophical, or juridical, the other inquiring em-
pirically and comparatively into specific forms of government, into the
domestic institutions, foreign policies and moral properties of societies.
I found an excellent statement to this effect by a well-known member of
the revolutionary generation, Benjamin Rush: "It is one thing to understand the *principles*, and another thing to understand the *forms* of government. . . . Mr. Locke is an oracle as to the *principles*, Harrington and
Montesquieu are oracles as to the *forms* of government."[30] I wrote that
the Founders (including Hamilton), according to the necessities of the
situation, first had to deal with the principles of political obligation and
disobedience, notably with "rights", whether natural or constitutional—
therefore the recurrence to Locke or Blackstone—and then with forms
of government, specifically with the republican form of government—
therefore the recurrence to Montesquieu, sometimes to Harrington and (by
Madison and Hamilton) to Hume.[31] The "republican" paradigm so strong

27. Gerald Stourzh, "Die tugendhafte Republik. Montesquieu's Begriff der 'vertu' und
die Anfänge der Vereinigten Staaten," in *Österreich und Europa. Festgabe für Hugo Hantsch
zum 70. Geburtstag*, ed. by Institut für Österreichische Geschichtsforschung and Wiener
Katholische Akademie, Graz/Vienna/Cologne 1965, pp. 247–267.

28. To this sojourn I owe the acquaintance with Carl Schorske, who was to become the
great interpreter of Vienna's *fin de siècle*, and also a lifelong generous friend whose ideas have
enriched me enormously. I am happy that the present volume includes a contribution to the *fin
de siècle* theme, the essay on Gustav Mahler and Karl Kraus (Chapter 10).

29. J. G. A. Pocock, "Virtue and Commerce in the Eighteenth Century," in *Journal of
Interdisciplinary History* 1 (1972/73), pp. 119–134. Cf. also idem, *Virtue, Commerce and History*, Cambridge, England 1985, p. 140.

30. Quoted in Gerald Stourzh, *Alexander Hamilton and the Meaning of Republican Government* (Stanford CA 1970), p. 4. The comparative tradition here symbolized by the names
of Harrington and Montesquieu is of course a much wider one, reaching from Aristotle and
Machiavelli to Montesquieu and Tocqueville.

31. For a discussion of these two strands of political thought cf. ibid., pp. 3–6. On the influence of Hume on Hamilton see ibid., pp. 117–119.

in American historiography from the late sixties to the eighties of the 20th century underestimated the place of the "liberal" quest for the principles of political obligation and rights based on these principles. The "liberal" interpretation perhaps did not do full justice to the originality of the long neglected quest for the meaning of "republican" government.[32]

In Berlin I also encouraged my most promising doctoral student and research assistant, Willi Paul Adams, to investigate the "republicanism" theme in the early American State constitutions between 1776 and 1780. This Adams did most successfully. His *summa cum laude* doctoral dissertation was submitted in 1968. Out of this grew a first rate book in German (1973),[33] but only the American translation in 1980 brought this work to the attention of the American specialists in the field.[34]

Willi Paul Adams was very much aware, as I was, of a dilemma with which teachers and writers of American history outside the English-speaking world are confronted: On the one hand, they need and wish to write in their own language, reaching the students and the reading public of their own country. This means, however, that they cut themselves off from the attention of their peers in America who often do not have the linguistic skills to read on American history in a foreign language. If, on the other hand, scholars in the field of American history decide to write in the English language and to publish in American or, at least, anglophone journals, he or she risks cutting themselves off from the reading public of their own social environment. To put it paradoxically: parochialism is a ubiquitous phenomenon and menace to the practitioners of the discipline of history. Adams published interesting reflections on what for him was an existential question, and he also tried through a variety of initiatives to improve the situation.[35] The premature death in 2002 of this most gifted of

32. The impact of the "republican" paradigm owed much to the work of J. G. A. Pocock. On my respectfully critical position with regard to Pocock's overemphasis on republicanism and civic humanism, see Gerald Stourzh, *Fundamental Laws and Individual Rights in the 18th Century Constitution* (Claremont CA 1984), p. 10.

33. Willi Paul Adams, *Republikanische Verfassung und bürgerliche Freiheit. Die Verfassungen und politischen Ideen der amerikanischen Revolution* (collection "Politica," vol. 37), Darmstadt/Neuwied 1973. One section of this work had come out in English, in Adams' article "Republicanism in Political Rhetoric before 1776," in *Political Science Quarterly*, 85 (1970), pp. 397–421.

34. Idem, *The First American Constitutions: Republican Ideology and the Making of the State Constitutions in the Revolutionary Era* (Chapel Hill NC 1980). A second edition came out 21 years later (Lanham MD, 2001)—a great compliment for the solidity and durability of Adams' work.

35. Cf. Willi Paul Adams, "American History Abroad: Personal Reflections on the Condition of Scholarship in West Germany," in *Reviews in American History*, 14 (1986), pp. 557–568.

my Berlin students in the American field was followed only a few months later by the death of his wife, Angela Meurer Adams, also a Berlin student of mine and close collaborator of her husband, most notably on their joint German translation and edition of *The Federalist*.[36] These were most painful losses.[37]

I would like to evoke the memory of one personality whose intellectual and moral stature impressed me greatly during my Berlin years. This was Ernst Fraenkel (1898–1975), Professor of Comparative Government at the Free University. Fraenkel was a man of intellectual brilliance and tremendous energy, and an intrepid fighter against injustice and meanness. He was trained as a lawyer and became a Social Democrat. He was Jewish, yet having fought in the First World War, he was admitted in the first years of Nazi rule as an attorney. He defended persons (chiefly workers) persecuted by the Nazis until his flight from Berlin in 1938. He took refuge in the United States, went at the age of 40 again through Law School (in Chicago), while his wife earned money as a household aid. Fraenkel then worked for the U.S. Government and went for a few years as legal adviser to the American forces in South Korea. In 1951, he was called back to West-Berlin to assume a professorship at the "Deutsche Hochschule für Politik", soon to be integrated into the Free University. He also was the founder of the multi-disciplinary John F. Kennedy Institute for American Studies. His most original book was *The Dual State*, based on his experiences as Jewish lawyer in Nazi Germany and published in the United States in 1941.[38] It was an analysis of the Nazi system of government which availed itself of the existing legal rules in a most bureaucratic manner and simultaneously set measures of repression above and beyond all

---

Adams was instrumental, jointly with David P. Thelen, in "internationalizing" the *Journal of American History*. On this see David P. Thelen, "What I learned from Willi Paul Adams and Internationalization of the Journal of American History," in A. Etges/U. Lehmkuhl, eds., *Atlantic Passages. Constitution—Immigration—Internationalization. In memoriam Willi Paul Adams*, Berlin 2006, pp. 133–139.

36. Willi Paul Adams and Angela Meurer Adams eds., *Alexander Hamilton/James Madison/John Jay, Die Federalist-Artikel. Politische Theorie und Verfassungskommentar der amerikanischen Gründerväter*, Paderborn 1994.

37. Cf. Gerald Stourzh, "Willi Adams, 1940–2002," in: *Historische Zeitschrift*, vol. 276 (2003), pp. 548–551, and idem, "'Members Only': Willi Adams and Equality in Revolutionary America—Some Lessons for the Understanding of American Constitutionalism," in Etges/ Lehmkuhl, eds., *Atlantic Passages* (supra note 35), pp. 33–44.

38. Ernst Fraenkel, *The Dual State* (New York 1941) (reprint 1949). The German edition with an important autobiographical Foreword is *Der Doppelstaat* (Frankfurt on Main/ Cologne 1974).

legal rules.[39] I owe to Fraenkel's *Dual State* my knowledge of one of the most sinister law cases in Nazi history, dated as early as 1936, destroying the liberal doctrine of the equal rights of all citizens.[40]

In 1969, I assumed a Professorship of Modern History at the University of Vienna, following Friedrich Engel-Janosi, 36 years my senior, who was driven out of Austria by the Nazis and taught for many years at the Catholic University of America.[41] I was to remain in this position until entering the status of *emeritus* in 1997. My inaugural lecture was on an Anglo–American theme of the 17th and 18th centuries: "From the Right to Resistance to Judicial Review: The Problem of Unconstitutionality in the 18th Century". It has been published twice in German, but no English translation is available.[42] I started with the legitimation of the right to resistance by John Locke, who did not know of any judge in case of a conflict between the legislator and the people—except God, or the people themselves exercising the right to resistance. I also pointed out how on several occasions in English history in the 18th century the fact of an unconstitutional situation has been diagnosed, without a regular remedy available. I also had found out how during the debates surrounding the Stamp Act crisis, the word "unconstitutional," introduced into political discourse by Bolingbroke, yet rarely employed up to that time, suddenly sprang up—first in Rhode Island[43]—and mushroomed, as it were, in the subsequent polemics against Parliament in London. I then discussed the "State precedents" for judicial review and led the story up to Marbury vs. Madison, showing how judicial review had become a substitute for the right of resistance.

39. It was the dualism (or parallelism) of "Normenstaat" and "Maßnahmenstaat" (state of norms and state of—arbitrary—"measures")

40. See below chapter 14. I have paid tribute to Fraenkel in a necrologue: In memoriam Ernst Fraenkel, in *Amerikastudien/American Studies*, vol. 20, 1975, pp. 207–208.

41. Friedrich Engel-Janosi has written an autobiography well worth reading, covering his life and professional work on two continents: . . . *aber ein stolzer Bettler* (Graz 1974). I have paid tribute to my predecessor in: Friedrich Engel Janosi. Nachruf, in *Almanach der Österreichischen Akademie der Wissenschaften* 128 (1978), pp. 358–369.

42. Gerald Stourzh, *Vom Widerstandsrecht zur Verfassungsgerichtsbarkeit: Zum Problem der Verfassungswidrigkeit im 18. Jahrhundert* (Graz 1972), reprinted in idem, *Wege zur Grundrechtsdemokratie. Studien zur Begriffs- und Institutionengeschichte des liberalen Verfassungsstaats* (Vienna/Cologne 1989), pp. 37–74. Some of the source materials analysed there are also presented, more briefly, in chapter 13 of this volume.

43. Cf. ibid., p. 52. The word "unconstitutional" was first used during the Stamp Act crisis in a pamphlet written by Governor Stephen Hopkins of Rhode Island, "The Rights of Colonies Examined," in Bernard Bailyn, ed., *Pamphlets of the American Revolution 1750–1776*, vol. I (Cambridge, Mass. 1965), p. 521.

In Vienna, too, I pursued American themes in lectures, in the assignment or suggestion of topics for dissertations, and in research. An Overseas Fellowship at Churchill College in Cambridge in 1976 enabled me to do research on British 16th and 17th century sources on the term "constitution." The Vice-Master of Churchill was then Jack Pole, the foremost British expert on early American history who became a good friend, and to whose masterful *The Pursuit of Equality in American History*[44] I am much indebted. There were also trips to the United States, starting again in about 1973 and becoming particularly frequent in the '80s in view of the bicentennial of the American Constitution.[45] One trip to America in the spring of 1987 was occasioned by a meeting of the Conference on Political Thought in the Folger Library in Washington, D.C. where, with John Pocock presiding, I gave a paper on the changing meanings of the term "constitution" in England and North America in the 17th and 18th centuries. This paper resulted chiefly from my research in Cambridge in 1976; it is included in this volume as Chapter 3. A deeply moving experience was an invitation to the University of Chicago in 1992, where the honorary degree of Doctor of Humane Letters was conferred on me on the occasion of the University's centennial commemorations.

Looking back over the 37 years that have elapsed since my return from Berlin to Vienna, I would like to make two comments on my teaching experience in Austria, in the perspective of my knowledge of the American university system.

First: I have suffered—the word is not too strong—from the marked heterogeneity of the quality of students encountered in one and the same class. One hardly can escape the dilemma of being either unjust to the highly qualified minority by chiefly catering to the less qualified majority, or to the majority by giving too much attention to the qualified minority. American (and Canadian) universities have the advantage of having a much more homogeneous student body. This homogeneity is the result of the application and interview system; it may of course exist on the basis of very high or somewhat less high standards. But there is a spectrum from high excellence to more modest requirements, and most applicants will find the place that is appropriate to their qualifications. Heterogeneity, on

---

44. First edition Berkeley, Calif. 1978, Revised edition 1993.

45. These trips included some memorable occasions, like a black-tie dinner in 1983 given by the Supreme Court of the United States on the premises of the Court, followed by a guided tour led by Chief Justice Warren Burger, or in 1987 the bicentennial commemoration of the Smithsonian Institution, where I presented the opening paper in Jefferson's rotunda at the University of Virginia in Charlottesville.

the other hand, is the result of a very open access to the universities, when as in Austria (with very few recent exceptions) access does not depend on the receiving university.

Second: In most European countries, as opposed to North America, the age for selecting studies leading to a professional career is too young. In most European countries including Austria, young people at the age of 18 or 19 are to decide whether to enter medical school, law school, business school, etc. In North America, the institution of the college offers a transitional and preparatory period of a few years preceding the choice (if any) of a graduate school. Thus young people do not enter professional schools like medicine or the law before the age of 21 or 22. The wasteful consequences of entering professional school at too young an age often are high drop out rates and long sequences of study. Though aware of the financial aspects involved, I nevertheless have concluded that the North American system is superior to the one in Europe.

As far as research and writing after my definitive return to Vienna in 1969 are concerned, I would like to identify (apart from my repeated return to North American topics) six major themes.

First, beginning in the mid-1960s, and considerably enlarging research in the '70s, I studied the legal and constitutional means by which linguistic and ethnic conflicts in the Habsburg Empire in the era 1848–1918 had been dealt with. My early interest in Austrian constitutional history in the post–1848 era and Josef Redlich's interpretation of it were now combined with insights I had gained in Chicago through my encounter with the great law cases of American history. Out of this combination arose my research on judicial conflict resolution on the basis of the constitutional provision for the equal rights ("Gleichberechtigung") of nationalities and their languages by the *Reichsgericht* and the *Verwaltungsgerichtshof.* It was first published in 1980 in a collective volume on the Habsburg Monarchy and was enlarged as a book in 1985. As to the present volume, I refer to Chapters 5, 6, 7, 8, and 9, where diverse aspects of the theme of equal rights or the nationalities are discussed. From then on, the notion of equal rights—the English language has no noun exactly corresponding to the German term "Gleichberechtigung"—has steadily and increasingly become one of my chief themes of interest. This interest was reinforced by the fact that my wife Christiane—we had been married in 1962—was a jurist and was much committed to the cause of equal rights for women.

Second, there was the theme of Austria's international position after World War II which, after several smaller publications, found expression in my history of the Austrian State Treaty, first published in 1975 and republished, under varying titles in new editions of growing size, when slowly and in a piecemeal manner archival materials became available. I looked for such archival sources in a variety of places, reaching from Abilene, Kansas, via Independence, Missouri, and Washington, D.C., to London, Paris, Bonn, Bern, Vienna, and, after 1990, to Berlin (GDR materials) and even to Moscow. The reader of this volume will find in Chapter 11 an example of my work in this field.[46]

Third, I encouraged work on social policies and social legislation from the late 19th to the early 20th centuries among my students, finding that the history of "Sozialpolitik" as well as the development of collective bargaining and of the integration of trade unions in the institutional fabric of the modern state were rather underdeveloped at the time; I also contributed a piece on the institutional history of labor relations and of social security to a volume I co-edited with my former doctoral student and long-time associate Margarete Grandner.[47] Writing on institutional history, I was much impressed by a type of historical writing more developed in French than in Anglo-American scholarship, and I would like to single out the impact of a masterpiece of French institutional history—Jacques Godechot's history of institutions during the French Revolution and the Napoleonic Empire.[48]

Fourth, time and again I contributed to the debate on "Austrian identity." In the mid-1980s I took a stand against the efforts of the German historian Karl Dietrich Erdmann to speak of "three German states"—Federal Republic of Germany, German Democratic Republic, and Austria.[49] I also discussed, in a historiographical paper devoted to changing interpretations of Austrian history by noted Austrian historians of the 19th and 20th centuries, the problems arising out of the great divergences connected with the name of Austria, as the name of a "House" as well as of territorial units of changing size in the course of modern and contemporary history.[50]

46. Cf. the bibliographical appendix to this volume.
47. Gerald Stourzh and Margarete Grandner, eds., *Historische Wurzeln der Sozialpartnerschaft* (Wiener Beiträge zur Geschichte der Neuzeit, vol. 12/13) (Vienna 1986).
48. Jacques Godechot's *Les institutions de la France sous la Révolution et l'Empire* must be consulted in its second edition (Paris 1968), vastly enlarged vis-à-vis the first edition of 1951. The work of another great French historian of institutions, Roland Mousnier, is available in English: *The Institutions of France under the Absolute Monarchy 1598–1789* (Chicago 1979). In German scholarship, the work of Otto Hintze has been important to me in this respect.
49. Gerald Stourzh, *Vom Reich zur Republik. Studien zum Österreichbewußtsein im 20. Jahrhundert* (Vienna 1990), particularly pp. 10–20.
50. Idem, "Der Umfang der österreichischen Geschichte," in Herwig Wolfram and Walter Pohl, eds., *Probleme der Geschichte Österreichs und ihrer Darstellung* (Vienna 1991), pp. 3–27.

Fifth: Taking my point of departure from the constitutional postulate of "equal rights," but also having been aware since 1938 of the experience of discrimination and persecution of people within my social environment, I examined various aspects of the position of the Jewish population of imperial Austria, including the rather special problems of Jewish Diaspora nationalism in the Bukovina, Austria's easternmost province. I also discussed aspects of emancipation and assimilation after the achievement of constitutional "Gleichberechtigung" in 1867; Chapters 7, 8, and 9 deal with one or the other of the aspects just mentioned. I also studied the problem of conversion, more important in Austria than elsewhere because marriage contracts between Christians and non-Christians were prohibited by the Austrian Civil Code of 1811. Among the many famous converts of *fin de siècle* Vienna, I was particularly fascinated by the biographies of Gustav Mahler and Karl Kraus, as the reader will see in Chapter 10. The horrible fate of Jews under Nazi rule from discrimination to extermination was a central theme of my valedictory lecture at the University of Vienna in 1997, "Human Rights and Genocide," not available in English.[51]

Sixth, having observed before that the theme of equal rights increasingly became one of my main interests from the 1970s onward, I ought to add that this interest was and is not limited to one or two countries, such as the United States or Austria, but pertains to Western history in general in attempts at comparative analysis, most advanced perhaps in Chapter 13 below.[52] I would like to identify as the "Tocquevillian Moment" in Western history the transition from the gradated order of *ancien régime* societies to societies where, in the midst of all imaginable social, economic, or health inequalities, the standard of legal equality has replaced earlier hierarchical status differences.[53] It is not nature that makes human beings

51. Idem, Menschenrechte und Genozid, in Heinz Schäffer et al., eds., *Staat—Verfassung— Verwaltung. Festschrift for Friedrich Koja* (Vienna/New York 1998), pp. 135–159. The theme of the Shoa is also reflected in the author's article Fünf Thesen zu "Holocaust," in the Austrian weekly *Die Furche*, No. 10/1979 (7 March 1979), p. 5, and in his booklet *Begründung und Bedrohung der Menschenrechte in der europäischen Geschichte* (Vienna 2000).

52. An early master in the field of comparative history was Robert R. Palmer, whose work on *The Age of Democratic Revolution. A Political History of Europe and America, 1760 to 1800* came out in Princeton in 1959 and 1964, respectively. The broad sweep of his Volume I, "The Challenge," for the period from about 1760 to 1789 particularly impressed me, and I have also used it much in teaching.

53. The phrase "Tocquevillian Moment" is inspired by John Pocock's well-known book *The Machiavellian Moment*. There exists also an issue of the French review *Raisons politiques* (new series No. 1, February 2001), entitled "Le moment tocquevillien"; this refers however to the renaissance of Tocqueville-centered political and historical writing in France in the nineties of the 20th century, and not to what I consider the historical "Tocquevillian

equal, but the law, as has been rightly said.[54] Chapters 12, 13, and 14 are thus grouped together under this title. Tocqueville is the great analyst of this transition, and my interest in Tocqueville has grown over the years ever since I first read "Democracy in America" in September 1954 aboard the "Andrea Doria" traveling from Genoa to New York. It is fitting that the last historical essay in this volume should be dedicated to an analysis of Tocqueville's thought, whose work so closely has tied together America and Europe.

The concluding short piece on Albert Camus, though published in 1961, was written in the first half of 1958 in Chicago.[55] It should testify to my conviction that historical, political or legal analyses surely cannot as adequately reflect the human condition as great works of literature. Camus' La chute, I thought then and still think now, is one of them.

Looking back at the age of 77, what might be said of satisfactions, regrets, and unfinished business? I have derived great satisfaction from writing, or in other words, working with language—in my case working with two (sometimes three, with French included) languages, which has been a cause of immense enrichment. Though I have derived greater satisfaction from writing than from teaching, the supervision of doctoral students has been the greatest joy of my academic life, and I confidently assert that there are about a dozen or so among my doctoral students whose dissertations surely would have found acceptance among America's top ten universities, or in "Oxbridge," for that matter.

Regrets: mistakes and oversights, of course. Regrets that I have not written one or two books more (and perhaps a few articles less). Also, regrets that I have not sufficiently exploited a certain talent for foreign languages to achieve mastery in a Slavic language. Several Slavic languages, notably the Czech language (and in addition to Slavic languages, of course, the Magyar language), are important for the advanced study of many aspects of Habsburg history, and I am quite conscious of this deficiency. I have been able, rather late in life, to acquire rudiments of the Russian language, but the satisfaction of having advanced into new and fascinating

---

moment" the transformation of hierarchical societies into those based (in principle at least) on the notion of equal rights.

54. Karl Renner, Das Selbstbestimmungsrecht der Nationen in besonderer Anwendung auf Österreich, 1. Teil: Nation und Staat (Leipzig/Vienna 1918), p. 148.

55. I sent the manuscript to Albert Camus in France. His response consisted in the gift of his book L'envers et l'endroit, with a dedication: "à M. Gerald Stourzh en reconnaissant hommage Albert Camus." I treasure it.

territory is balanced by the regret that it was too late to achieve fluency at least in reading.

Unfinished business: I wish to advance further in the description and analysis of what I have called above the Tocquevillian moment of Western history, in other words: the replacement of the paradigm of a gradated society by the paradigm of equal rights for all human beings, a paradigm that continues to be valid in spite of various powerful enemies working against it since its breakthrough in the foundational texts of the American and French Revolutions and its globalization in the Universal Declaration of Human Rights. Unfinished business so far, indeed. Yet I believe in the regenerative power of writing, until that very moment when the pen—or now the computer—will be taken out of my hands.

The papers assembled in this volume have been substantially left as originally published between 1953 and 2006. All of them with one exception (Chapter 7, which was translated) I wrote in English. The essays are meant to show the author's awareness of the state of the art at the time of writing. Addenda—clearly marked as such!—have been supplied to six essays, they will be found in Chapters 5, 8, 9, 10, 11, and 13. Some minor errors have been corrected; a few linguistic deficiencies have been repaired. A few small cuts have been made in order to avoid repetitions; where they occur, the author felt that further cuts would endanger the structure of the individual essays, and the reader is kindly asked to bear with them understandingly.

I am most grateful to Professors Thomas Fröschl, Margarete Grandner, and Dr. Birgitta Bader-Zaar of the University of Vienna as well as to Professor Ralph Lerner of the University of Chicago for their precious advice. Ralph Lerner felicitously suggested the phrase "Traces of an Intellectual Journey", which has become the title of this Introduction. Both to Dean John Boyer and to Ralph Lerner I am most obliged for their unremitting efforts on behalf of the publication of this book. My sincere thanks go to Professor Bernard Bailyn of Harvard University and again to Dean John Boyer for their kind and generous introductory remarks. I am grateful to Dr. Bernhard Stillfried and to the Austrian Ministry of Science and Research for their support on behalf of the publication of this book. Finally, the cooperation with the University of Chicago Press has been excellent, combining efficiency and speed with great friendliness and understanding. My warmest thanks go to the acquisitions editor Robert Devens, to Elizabeth Branch Dyson, Kate Frentzel, and Megan Marz.

Gerald Stourzh
Vienna, Austria, January 2007

PART I

Anglo-American History

CHAPTER ONE

Reason and Power in Benjamin Franklin's Political Thought*

Perhaps no period of modern history has been more a victim of generalization than the Age of Enlightenment. The worship of reason and progress and belief in the essential goodness and perfectibility of human nature are most commonly associated with the 18th century climate of opinion. Many of the stereotypes which have been applied to it have automatically been transferred to Benjamin Franklin. Already to contemporaries of his old age, Franklin seemed the very personification of the Age of Reason. Condorcet, who had known Franklin personally, summed up his description of Franklin's political career as follows: "In a word, his politics were those of a man who believed in the power of reason and the reality of virtue."[1] In Germany, an admirer was even more enthusiastic: "Reason and virtue, made possible through reason alone, consequently again reason and nothing but reason, is the magic with which Benjamin Franklin conquered heaven and earth."[2] This is also the judgment of posterity. F. L. Mott and Chester E. Jorgensen, who have so far presented the most acute analysis of Franklin's thought and its relationship to the intellectual history of his time, do not hesitate to call him "the completest colonial representative" of the Age of Enlightenment.[3]

---

* First published in *The American Political Science Review,* Vol. 47, no. 4, December 1953, pp. 1092–1115. The permission to reprint was gracefully granted by Cambridge University Press.

 1. *Oeuvres du Marquis de Condorcet,* eds. A. Condorcet O'Connor and M. F. Arago, 2nd ed., 12 vols. (Paris, 1847–49), Vol. 3, p. 420.

 2. Georg Forster, "Erinnerungen aus dem Jahre 1790," in "Kleine Schriften," *Georg Forsters saemmtliche Schriften,* ed. by his daughter, 9 vols. (Leipzig, 1843), Vol. 6, p. 207.

 3. Benjamin Franklin, *Representative Selections with Introduction, Bibliography, and Notes,* eds. F. L. Mott and Chester E. Jorgenson (New York, 1936), p. xiii.

Unanimous agreement seems to exist that Franklin was "in tune with his time."[4]

This essay will attempt to show that these generalizations, instead of illuminating the essence of Franklin's moral and political philosophy, tend rather to obscure some of the mainsprings of his thought and action. Our investigation rests upon the assumption that man's understanding of politics is inseparable from his conception of human nature. Consequently, this reappraisal of Franklin's political thought will subject his views on human nature to close scrutiny; it is hoped that this procedure may lead to a rejection of some of the clichés to which he has fallen victim.

I. The "Great Chain of Being"

Many of the notions which are commonly applied to the 18th century, such as the belief in progress and in the perfectibility of human nature, are significant chiefly with respect to the currents of thought and action related to the American and French Revolutions, and do little to deepen our understanding of earlier developments. So it is to the first half of the 18th century that we must now turn. We are prone to overlook the extraordinary difference in age which separated Franklin from the other Founding Fathers of the Republic. Franklin was born in 1706, twenty-six years before Washington, twenty-nine years before John Adams, thirty-seven years before Jefferson, thirty-nine years before John Jay, forty-five years before James Madison, and fifty-one years before Alexander Hamilton.

Franklin's fame as a social and natural philosopher rests mainly on the achievements of his middle and late years. One needs to remember, however, that he was a moral philosopher long before he became a natural philosopher and before he advised his fellowmen how to acquire wealth.[5] At the age of twenty-two, he formed a "club for mutual improvement,"[6] the Junto, where great emphasis was laid on moral or political problems.

---

4. Carl Becker, review of the Franklin Institute's *Meet Dr. Franklin*, in *American Historical Review*, Vol. 50, p. 142 (Oct., 1944). Cf. Henry Steele Commager's statement that it was the faith in reason which gave unity to Franklin's life. "Franklin, the American," review of Carl Van Doren's *Benjamin Franklin*, in the *New York Times Book Review*, Oct. 9, 1938, p. 1. Charles A. Beard explicitly referred to Franklin as an outstanding example of American writers on Progress. Introduction to J. B. Bury, *The Idea of Progress* (New York, 1932), p. xxxvii.

5. Even after having achieved world-wide fame as a natural philosopher, he observed that we deserve reprehension if "we neglect the Knowledge and Practice of essential Duties" in order to attain eminence in the knowledge of nature. *The Writings of Benjamin Franklin*, ed. Henry Albert Smyth, 10 vols. (New York, 1905–1907), Vol. 4, p. 22. (Hereafter cited as *Writings*.)

6. *Autobiography, Writings*, Vol. I, p. 22.

Whether self-interest was the root of human action, whether man could attain perfection, whether "encroachments on the just liberties of the people"[7] had taken place—all these things were matters of discussion at 'Franklin's club. Already at the age of nineteen, during his first stay in London, he had printed his first independent opus, *A Dissertation on Liberty and Necessity, Pleasure and Pain*.[8] This piece showed that no trace was left of his Presbyterian family background. The secularization of his thought had been completed.[9] Gone were the Puritan belief in revelation and the Christian conception of human nature which, paradoxically, included the notion of the depravity of man, as well as of his uniqueness among all created beings.[10] Franklin's *Dissertation* shows that he was thoroughly acquainted

7. James Parton, *Life and Times of Benjamin Franklin*, 2nd ed., 2 vols. (Boston, 1897), Vol. 1, p. 160. See also *Writings*, Vol. 2, p. 89. The authors who so far have most closely scrutinized Franklin's political thought do not see the relevance of many of the younger Franklin's remarks on human nature, arbitrary government, or the nature of political dispute to his concept of politics. See M. R. Eiselen, *Franklin's Political Theories* (Garden City, NY, 1928), p. 13; R. D. Miles, "The Political Philosophy of Benjamin Franklin," unpub. diss. (Univ. of Michigan, 1949), p. 36; Benjamin Franklin, *Representative Selections* (cited in note 3), p. lxxxii. The most recent work in this field, Clinton Rossiter's "The Political Theory of Benjamin Franklin," *Pennsylvania Magazine of History and Biography*, Vol. 76, pp. 259–93 (July, 1952), pays no attention to Franklin's conception of human nature and his attitude towards the problem of power and the ends of political life. Rossiter's contention (p. 268) is that Franklin "limited his own thought process to the one devastating question: *Does it work?* or more exactly, *Does it work well?*" Franklin, however, like everybody else, had certain ends and goals in view, and the question "Does it work?" is meaningless without the context of certain basic desiderata.

8. This little work has been omitted in the Smyth edition of Franklin's writings, because "the work has no value, and it would be an injury and an offence to the memory of Franklin to republish it." *Writings*, Vol. 2, p. vi. It is, however, reprinted as an appendix to Parton, *op. cit.*, Vol. 1, and has since been republished independently with a bibliographical note by Lawrence C. Wroth (New York, 1930).

9. See Herbert Schneider, "The Significance of Benjamin Franklin's Moral Philosophy," *Columbia University Studies in the History of Ideas*, Vol. 2, p. 298 (1918).

10. In his *Autobiography*, Franklin acknowledges his debt to Shaftesbury and Collins for becoming "a real doubter in many points of our religious doctrine." *Writings*, Vol. 1, p. 244. The question of Franklin's attitude toward the great moral philosophers and of their influence upon him is considerably more difficult to determine than the same question with regard to John Adams or Thomas Jefferson. With the exception of authors named in the *Autobiography*, comments on books Franklin read are extremely rare. His library has not been preserved; there is, however, a list of books known to have been in Franklin's library at the time of his death (compiled by Dr. George Simpson Eddy in Princeton University; photostat in the library of the American Philosophical Society in Philadelphia). See also Mr. Eddy's article, "Dr. Benjamin Franklin's Library," *Proceedings of the American Antiquarian Society*, new series, Vol. 34, pp. 206–26 (Oct., 1924). Except for comments in some English pamphlets, there exists nothing like the voluminous marginal notes of John Adams and Jefferson. Also he was not able to keep up a correspondence like Adams' or Jefferson's, discussing great problems from the perspective of a long life in retirement after the great events of their lives had taken place. Immersed in public business almost until his death, Franklin does not seem to have had much

with the leading ideas of his time. The early decades of the 18th century were characterized by the climate of opinion which has been aptly called "cosmic Toryism."[11] Pope's *Essay on Man* and many pages of Addison's *Spectator*—both of which Franklin admired—most perfectly set forth the creed of a new age. Overshadowing everything else, there was joy about the discoveries of the human mind, which had solved the enigma of creation:

> Nature and Nature's Laws lay hid in Night:
> GOD said, *Let Newton be!* and all was Light.[12]

The perfection of that Great Machine, the Newtonian universe, filling humanity with admiration for the Divine Watchmaker, seemed to suggest that this world was indeed the best of all possible worlds. Everything was necessary, was good. Pope's "Whatever is, is right," is the key phrase of this period. The goodness of the Creator revealed itself in His giving existence to all possible creatures. The universe "presented the spectacle of a continuous scale or ladder of creatures, extending without a break from the worm to the seraph."[13] Somewhere in this "Great Chain of Being," to use a favorite phrase of the period,[14] there must be a place for Man. Man, as it were, formed the "middle link" between lower and higher creatures. No wonder, then, that Franklin chose as a motto for his *Dissertation* the following lines of Dryden:

> Whatever is, is in its Causes just,
> Since all Things are by Fate; but purblind Man

---

time left over for reading. Benjamin Rush told John Adams that "Dr. Franklin thought a great deal, wrote occasionally, but read during the middle and later years of his life very little." October 31, 1807, in Benjamin Rush, *The Letters of Benjamin Rush*, ed. L. H. Butterfield, 2 vols. (Princeton, 1951), Vol. 2, p. 953. For a compilation of the authors with whom Franklin was acquainted, see Lois Margaret MacLaurin, *Franklin's Vocabulary* (Garden City, NY, 1928), Ch. 1, and Benjamin Franklin, *Representative Selections* (cited in note 3), p. lv.

11. Basil Willey, *The Eighteenth Century Background* (London, 1940), Ch. 3, *passim.*

12. Pope's epitaph intended for Newton's tomb.

13. Willey, *op. cit.*, pp. 47–48.

14. See A. O. Lovejoy, *The Great Chain of Being* (Cambridge, MA, 1936). This brilliant analysis of that complex of ideas has been applied to Franklin only once, although it offers important clues for an understanding of Franklin's conception of human nature. Arthur Stuart Pitt in "The Sources, Significance, and Date of Franklin's 'An Arabian Tale,'" *Publications of the Modern Language Association*, Vol. 57, pp. 155–68 (March, 1942), applies Lovejoy's analysis to one piece of Franklin's and does not refer to relevant writings of Franklin's youth in which this idea may also be found. Pitt's article is valuable in pointing out the sources from which Franklin could have accepted the idea directly, namely Locke, Milton, Addison, and Pope.

Sees but a part o' th' Chain, the nearest Link,
His Eyes not carrying to the equal Beam
That poises all above.[15]

The consequences of the conception of the universe as a "Great Chain of Being" for Franklin's understanding of human nature are highly significant. To be sure, man had liberated himself from the oppression of Original Sin, and in his newly established innocence he hailed the Creator and praised the Creation. But if the depravity of human nature had been banished, so had man's striving for redemption, man's aspiration for perfection. There was nothing left which ought to be redeemed. Indeed, in the new rational order of the universe, it would not seem proper to long for a higher place in the hierarchy of beings. Man's release from the anguish of Original Sin was accompanied by a lowering of the goals of human life. "The imperfection of man is indispensable to the fullness of the hierarchy of being." Man had, so to speak, already attained the grade of perfection which belonged to his station. From the point of view of morality, then, what this amounted to was a "counsel of imperfection—an ethics of prudent mediocrity." [16]

Quiet contentment with, and enjoyment of, one's place in the Great Chain of Being must have been a comforting creed for the wealthy and educated classes of the Augustan Age:

Order is Heav'n's first law; and this confest,
Some are, and must be, greater than the rest,
More rich, more wise.[17]

This was not the optimism of progress, which we usually associate with the eighteenth century. It was an optimism of acceptance;[18] for the rich and complacent, the real and the good seemed indeed to coincide.

Not so for Benjamin Franklin. Late in his life, in 1771, he referred to "the poverty and obscurity in which I was born and bred." His innate desire for justice and equality, his keen awareness of existing conditions of injustice and inequality, finally his own experience of things which he could not possibly call just or good—for instance, he tells us that his brother's "harsh

15. Parton, *Life and Times of Benjamin Franklin* (cited in note 7), Vol. 1, p. 605.
16. Lovejoy, *op. cit.*, pp. 199, 200.
17. Alexander Pope, "An Essay on Man," Epistle 4, in *Selected Works,* Modern Library ed. (New York, 1948), p. 127.
18. Willey, *op. cit.*, p. 56.

and tyrannical treatment of me might be a means of impressing me with that aversion to arbitrary power that has stuck to me through my whole life"[19]—all this contravened the facile optimism of the Augustan Age.

Franklin, indeed, accepted the cosmological premises of his age (as witness the above quoted motto of the *Dissertation*). But his conclusions make the edifice of "cosmic Toryism"—so imposing in Pope's magnificent language—appear a mockery and an absurdity. Franklin's argumentation was simple enough: God being all-powerful and good, man could have no free will, and the distinction between good and evil had to be abolished. He also argued that pain or uneasiness was the mainspring of all our actions, and that pleasure was produced by the removal of this uneasiness. It followed that *"No State of Life can be happier than the present, because Pleasure and Pain are inseparable."* The unintentional irony of this brand of optimism cannot be better expressed than in young Franklin's conclusion:

> I am sensible that the Doctrine here advanc'd, if it were to be publish'd, would meet with but an indifferent Reception. Mankind naturally and generally love to be flatter'd: Whatever sooths our Pride, and tends to exalt our Species above the rest of the Creation, we are pleas'd with and easily believe, when ungrateful Truths shall be with the utmost Indignation rejected. "What! bring ourselves down to an Equality with the Beasts of the field! With the *meanest* part of the Creation! 'Tis insufferable!" But, (to use a Piece of *common* Sense) our *Geese* are but *Geese* tho' we may think'em *Swans*; and Truth will be Truth tho' it sometimes prove mortifying and distasteful.[20]

The dilemma which confronted him at the age of nineteen is characteristic of most eighteenth-century philosophy: "[I]f nature is good, then there is no evil in the world; if there is evil in the world, then nature so far is not good."[21]

Franklin cut this Gordian knot by sacrificing "Reason" to "Experience." He turned away from metaphysics for the quite pragmatic reason that his denial of good and evil did not provide him with a basis for the attainment of social and individual happiness:

---

19. *Autobiography, Writings*, Vol. 1, pp. 226, 247 (n.1).

20. Parton, *op. cit.*, Vol. 1, p. 617.

21. Carl Becker, *The Heavenly City of the Eighteenth Century Philosophers* (New Haven, 1932), p. 69.

Revelation had indeed no weight with me, as such; but I entertain'd an opinion that, though certain actions might not be bad *because* they were forbidden by it, or good *because* it commanded them, yet probably these actions might be forbidden *because* they were bad for us, or commanded *because* they were beneficial to us. . . .[22]

To achieve useful things rather than indulge in doubtful metaphysical speculations, to become a doer of good—these, then, became the principal aims of Franklin's thought and action.[23]

This fundamental change from the earlier to the later Enlightenment— from passive contemplation to improvement, from a static to a dynamic conception of human affairs—did contribute to the substitution of the idea of human perfectibility for the idea of human perfection—a very limited kind of perfection, as we have seen; but it was by no means sufficient to bring about the faith in the perfectibility of human nature. Something else was needed: proof that "social evils were due neither to innate and incorrigible disabilities of the human being nor the nature of things, but simply to ignorance and prejudices."[24] The associationist psychology, elaborating Locke's theory of the malleability of human nature, provided the basis for the expansion of the idea of progress and perfectibility from the purely intellectual domain into the realm of moral and social life in general. The Age of Reason, then, presents us with a more perplexing picture than we might have supposed.

Reason, after all, may mean three different things: reason as a faculty of man; reason as a quality of the universe; and reason as a temper in the conduct of human affairs.[25] We might venture the generalization that the earlier Enlightenment stressed reason as the quality of the Newtonian universe, whereas the later Enlightenment, in spite of important exceptions, exalted the power of human reason to mold the moral and social life of mankind.[26] Franklin's "reason," as we shall see presently, is above all a temper in the conduct of human affairs.

22. *Autobiography, Writings*, Vol. 1, p. 296. See also *Writings*, Vol. 7, p. 412.

23. See *Writings*, Vol. 1, p. 341; Vol. 2, p. 215; Vol. 3, p. 145; Vol. 9, p. 208; Vol. 10, p. 38.

24. Bury, *The Idea of Progress* (cited in note 4), p. 128.

25. This distinction is Roland Bainton's. See his "The Appeal to Reason and the American Revolution," in *The Constitution Reconsidered*, ed. Conyers Read (New York, 1938), p. 121.

26. Cf. A. O. Lovejoy's statement: "The authors who were perhaps the most influential and the most representative in the early and mid-eighteenth century, made a great point of reducing man's claims to 'reason' to a minimum." " 'Pride' in Eighteenth Century Thought," in *Essays in the History of Ideas* (Baltimore, 1948), p. 68.

This discussion is important for a correct understanding of Franklin's position in the center of the cross-currents of the Age of Enlightenment. The fact that the roots of his thought are to be found in the early Enlightenment is not always realized, or, if realized, not always sufficiently explained. Julian P. Boyd, in his introduction to Carl Becker's biographical sketch of Franklin, states that Franklin and Jefferson believed "that men would be amenable to rational persuasion, that they would thereby be induced to promote their own and their fellows' best interests, and that, in the end, perfect felicity for man and society would be achieved."[27] These ideas are certainly suggestive of the later Enlightenment, and appear to be more applicable to Jefferson than to Franklin. Carl Becker himself asserts, somewhat ambiguously and with undue generalization, that Franklin "was a true child of the Enlightenment, not indeed of the school of Rousseau, but of Defoe and Pope and Swift, of Fontenelle and Montesquieu and Voltaire."[28] There is little evidence that this school prophesied the achievement of perfect felicity for man and society.

Bernard Mandeville, a personal acquaintance of Franklin, joined the chorus of those who proclaimed the compatibility of human imperfection and the general harmony. "Private Vices, Public Benefits" was the subtitle of his famous *Fable of the Bees*, which Franklin owned and probably read. Mandeville's paradoxical doctrines must have been a powerful challenge to Franklin's young mind. "The Moral Virtues," Mandeville asserted in terms reminiscent of Machiavelli, "are the Political Offspring which Flattery begot upon Pride." While arguing that men are actuated by self-interest and that this self-interest promotes the prosperity of society as a whole, Mandeville maintains a rigorous standard of virtue, declaring those acts alone to be virtuous "by which Man, contrary to the impulse of Nature, should endeavour the Benefit of others, or the Conquest of his own Passions out of a Rational Ambition of being good."[29]

By making ethical standards so excessively rigorous, Mandeville rendered them impossible of observance, and indirectly (though intentionally) pointed out their irrelevance for practical life. The very rigor of his ethical demands in contrast to his practical devices suggests that Mandeville lacked "idealism." This was not the case with Franklin. The consciously

27. Carl Becker, *Benjamin Franklin* (Ithaca, 1946), p. ix.

28. Ibid, p. 31.

29. Bernard Mandeville, *The Fable of the Bees*, ed. F. B. Kaye, 2 vols. (Oxford, 1924), Vol. 1, pp. 48–49, 51. Franklin owned Mandeville's work, according to a list in the Mason-Franklin Collection of the Yale University Library. He was introduced to Mandeville during his first stay in London. *Writings*, Vol. 1, p. 278.

paradoxical Mandeville could offer no salvation for the young Franklin caught on the horns of his own dilemma. Shaftesbury, Mandeville's bête noire—whose works were already familiar to Franklin—had a more promising solution. In his *Inquiry Concerning Virtue or Merit* (1699), Shaftesbury had asserted that man by nature possesses a faculty to distinguish and to prefer what is right—the famous "moral sense."

Franklin's option for Shaftesbury was made clear from his reprinting two dialogues "Between Philocles and Horatio, . . . concerning Virtue and Pleasure" from the *London Journal* of 1729 in the *Pennsylvania Gazette* of 1730. In the second dialogue, reason was described as the chief faculty of man, and reasonable and morally good actions were defined as actions preservative of the human kind and naturally tending to produce real and unmixed happiness. These dialogues until recently have been held to be Franklin's own work; however, a reference in the *Autobiography* to a "Socratic dialogue" and "a discourse on self-denial," traditionally interpreted as concerning the two dialogues between Philocles and Horatio, recently has been shown to concern two pieces published in the *Pennsylvania Gazette* of 1735. The first piece is a dialogue between Crito and Socrates, never before correctly attributed to Franklin, in which he asserted that the "SCIENCE OF VIRTUE" was "of more worth, and of more consequence" to one's happiness than all other knowledge put together; in the second piece, a discourse on self-denial, Franklin combated the (Mandevillean) idea that "the greater the *Self-Denial* the greater the Virtue." Thirty-three years later, Franklin was still following Shaftesbury when he exhorted: "Be in general virtuous, and you will be happy." However, we shall see later that Franklin, in the last analysis, was not as far removed from Mandeville's pessimism as there cheerful views would suggest. His was a sort of middle position between Mandeville's "realism" and Shaftesbury's "idealism."[30]

II. The Idea of Progress

The restraining influence of the idea of the Great Chain of Being retained its hold on Franklin after his return to a more conventional recognition of

---

30. The proof that the two dialogues between Philocles and Horatio were not written by Franklin and the identification of the two other pieces have been furnished by Alfred O. Aldridge, "Franklin's 'Shaftesburian' Dialogues Not Franklin's: A Revision of the Franklin Canon," *American Literature*, Vol. 21, pp. 151–59 (May, 1949). See also *Writings*, Vol. 1, p. 343; Vol. 2, pp. 168–69. The discourse on self-denial is printed in *The Complete Works of Benjamin Franklin*, ed. John Bigelow, 10 vols. (New York, 1887–88), Vol. 1, pp. 414–17. The last quote, written in 1768, is in *Writings*, Vol. 5, p. 159.

good and evil. In his "Articles of Belief" of 1728 he said that "Man is not
the most perfect Being but one, rather as there are many Degrees of Beings his Inferiors, so there are many Degrees of Beings superior to him."[31]
Franklin presented the following question and answers to the discussions
in the Junto:

> Can a man arrive at perfection in his life, as some believe; or is it im-
> possible, as others believe?
> *Answer.* Perhaps they differ in the meaning of the word *perfection.* I
> suppose the perfection of any thing to be only the greatest the nature
> of the thing is capable of. . . .
>
> [I]f they mean a man cannot in this life be so perfect as an angel,
> it may be true; for an angel, by being incorporeal, is allowed some
> perfections we are at present incapable of, and less liable to some
> imperfections than we are liable to. If they mean a man is not ca-
> pable of being perfect here as he is capable of being in heaven, that
> may be true likewise. But that a man is not capable of being so per-
> fect here, is not sense. . . . In the above sense, there may be a per-
> fect oyster, a perfect horse, a perfect ship; why not a perfect man?
> That is, as perfect as his present nature and circumstance admit.[32]

We note here the acknowledgment of man's necessarily "imperfect"
state of perfection. However, it is striking to see that Franklin refused
to employ this theory as a justification of the status quo. Within certain
bounds, change, or progress for the better, was possible. Many years later,
Franklin was to use exactly the same argument in the debate on the status
of America within the British Empire. A pro-English writer had presented
the familiar argument of "cosmic Toryism" (and of conservatism in general, of course): "To expect perfection in human institutions is absurd."
Franklin retorted indignantly: "Does this justify any and every Imperfection that can be invented or added to our Constitution?"[33]

This attitude differs from the belief in moral progress and perfectibility. There are, however, some passages in Franklin's later writings, better known than the preceding ones, which seem to suggest his agreement

---

31. *Writings,* Vol. 2, p. 92; see also Vol. 10, p. 124 and note 14, above.

32. *The Works of Benjamin Franklin,* ed. Jared Sparks, 10 vols. (Boston, 1836–40), Vol. 2,
p. 554.

33. Franklin's marginal notes in [Matthew C. Wheelock], *Reflections Moral and Political
on Great Britain and the Colonies* (London, 1770), p. 48. Franklin's copy in the Jefferson Collection of the Library of Congress.

with the creed of moral progress and perfectibility. Two years before his death, looking with considerable satisfaction upon the achievements of his country and his own life, he explained to a Boston clergyman his belief in "the growing felicity of mankind, from the improvements in philosophy, morals, politics"; he also stressed "the invention and acquisition of new and useful utensils and instruments" and concluded that "invention and improvement are prolific. . . . The present progress is rapid." However, he immediately added: "I see a little absurdity in what I have just written, but it is to a friend, who will wink and let it pass."[34]

There remains, then, a wide gulf between this qualified view of human progress and the exuberant joy over the progress of man's rational and moral faculties so perfectly expressed in the lines of a good friend of Franklin's, the British non-conformist clergyman and philosopher, Joseph Priestley:

> Whatever was the beginning of this world, the end will be glorious and paradisiacal beyond what our imaginations can now conceive. Extravagant as some people may suppose these views to be, I think I could show them to be fairly suggested by the true theory of human nature and to arise from the natural course of human affairs.[35]

Franklin himself was well aware of this gulf. He distinguished sharply between man's intellectual progress and the steadily increasing power of man over matter, on the one hand, and the permanency of moral imperfection, on the other. He wrote to Priestley in 1782:

> I should rejoice much, if I could once more recover the Leisure to search with you into the works of Nature; I mean the *inanimate*, not the *animate* or moral part of them, the more I discover'd of the former, the more I admir'd them; the more I know of the latter, the more I am disgusted with them. Men I find to be a Sort of Beings very badly constructed, as they are generally more easily provok'd than reconcil'd, more disposed to do Mischief to each other than to make Reparation, much more easily deceiv'd than undeceiv'd, and having more Pride and even Pleasure in killing than in begetting one another.

He had begun to doubt, he continued, whether "the Species were really worth producing or preserving. . . . I know, you have no such Doubts

---

34. *Writings*, Vol. 9, p. 651. See also Vol. 9, pp. 489, 530; Vol. 1, p. 226.
35. Quoted by Bury, *The Idea of Progress* (cited in note 4), pp. 221–22.

because, in your zeal for their welfare, you are taking a great deal of pains to save their Souls. Perhaps, as you grow older, you may look upon this as a hopeless Project."[36]

One is struck by the remarkable constancy of Franklin's views on human nature. In 1787 he tried to dissuade the author of a work on natural religion from publishing it. In this famous letter, we may find the quintessence of Franklin's concept of human nature. There is little of the trust in human reason which is so generally supposed to be a mark of his moral teachings:

> You yourself may find it easy to live a virtuous Life, without the Assistance afforded by Religion; you having a clear perception of the Advantages of Virtue, and the Disadvantages of Vice, and possessing a Strength of Resolution sufficient to enable you to resist common Temptations. But think how great a Proportion of Mankind consists of weak and ignorant Men and Women, and of inexperienc'd, and inconsiderate Youth of both Sexes, who have need of the Motives of Religion to restrain them from Vice, and Support their Virtue, and retain them in the Practice of it till it becomes *habitual*, which is the Great Point for its Security. . . . If men are so wicked as we now see them *with religion*, what would they be *if without it?*[37]

One is reminded of Gibbon's approval of conditions in the Rome of the Antonines, where all religions were considered equally false by the wise, equally true by the people, and equally useful by the magistrates.

III. The Belief in "Reason"

Reason as a temper in the conduct of human affairs counted much with Franklin, as we shall see later. However, reason as a faculty of the human mind, stronger than our desires or passions, counted far less. Often Franklin candidly and smilingly referred to the weakness of reason. In his *Autobiography*, he tells us of his struggle "between principle and inclination" when, on his first voyage to Philadelphia, his vegetarian principles came into conflict with his love of eating fish. Remembering that greater fish ate the smaller ones, he did not see any reason why he should not eat fish:

36. *Writings*, Vol. 8, pp. 451–52.
37. *Writings*, Vol. 9, pp. 521–22. See also Vol. 2, pp. 203, 393, and Vol. 9, pp. 600–601.

"So convenient a thing it is to be a *reasonable creature*, since it enables one to find or make a reason for every thing one has a mind to do."[38]

Reason as a guide to human happiness was recognized by Franklin only to a limited degree.

> Our Reason would still be of more Use to us, if it could enable us to *prevent* the Evils it can hardly enable us to *bear*. But in that it is so deficient, and in other things so often misleads us, that I have sometimes been almost tempted to wish we had been furnished with a good sensible Instinct instead of it.[39]

Trial and error appeared to him more useful to this end than abstract reasoning. "We are, I think, in the right Road of Improvement, for we are making Experiments. I do not oppose all that seem wrong, for the Multitude are more effectually set right by Experience, than kept from going wrong by Reasoning with them." Another time he put it even more bluntly: "What assurance of the *Future* can be better founded than that which is built on Experience of the *Past?*"[40] His scepticism about the efficacy of "reason" also appears in his opinion that "happiness in this life rather depends on internals than externals; and that, besides the natural effects of wisdom and virtue, vice and folly, there is such a thing as a happy or an unhappy constitution."[41]

There remains one problem with regard to Franklin's rather modest view of the power of human reason in moral matters: his serenity—some might call it complacency—in spite of his awareness of the disorder and imperfection of human life. Sometimes, it is true, he was uneasy:

> I rather suspect, from certain circumstances, that though the general government of the universe is well administered, our particular little affairs are perhaps below notice, and left to take the chance of human

---

38. *Writings*, Vol. 1, p. 267. See also Vol. 5, p. 225, and Vol. 9, p. 512.

39. *The Letters of Benjamin Franklin & Jane Mecom*, ed. Carl Van Doren (Princeton, 1950), p. 112.

40. *Writings*, Vol. 9, p. 489, and Vol. 4, p. 250. On another occasion Franklin acknowledged the weakness of reason by the use of a pungent folk saying: "An Answer now occurs to me, for that Question of Robinson Crusoe's Man Friday, which I once thought unanswerable, *Why God no kill the Devil?* It is to be found in the Scottish Proverb, 'Ye'd do little for God an the Dell' were dead.'" To John Whitehurst, New York, June 27, 1763. Unpubl. letter in the Mason-Franklin Collection of the Yale University Library. Cf. also Vol. 3, pp. 16–17, Vol. 4, p. 120, and Vol. 6, p. 424.

41. *Writings*, Vol. 3, p. 457. See also Vol. 9, p. 548.

prudence or imprudence, as either may happen to be uppermost. It is, however, an uncomfortable thought, and I leave it.[42]

But on another occasion Franklin felt obliged to quiet the anxieties of his sister, who had been upset by his remark that men "are devils to one another":

> I meant no more by saying Mankind were Devils to one another, than that being in general superior to the Malice of the other Creatures, they were not so much tormented by them as by themselves. Upon the whole I am much disposed to like the World as I find it, & to doubt my own Judgment as to what would mend it. I see so much Wisdom in what I understand of its Creation and Government, that I suspect equal Wisdom may be in what I do not understand: And thence have perhaps as much Trust in God as the most pious Christian.[43]

Indeed, Franklin's pessimism does not contain that quality of the tragic sense of life which inevitably presents itself wherever a recognition of the discrepancy between man's actual depravity and the loftiness of his aspirations exists.

We suggest a threefold explanation for this phenomenon: first of all, as we have pointed out, the complex of ideas associated with the concept of the "Great Chain of Being," predominant at the time of Franklin's youth, worked in favor of bridging this gulf by lowering the goals of human endeavor. Secondly, the success story of his own life taught him that certain valuable things in human life can be achieved. Thirdly, we cannot help thinking that Franklin himself was endowed with that "happy constitution" which he deemed a requisite for true happiness in this life.

IV. The Passion of Pride

Having discovered that Franklin acknowledged the imperfection of human reason and consequently the existence and importance of the passions to a greater degree than one might have supposed, let us specify in greater

---

42. Rev. L. Tyerman, *Life of the Rev. George Whitefield*, 2 vols. (London, 1876), Vol. 2, pp. 540–41, quoted *in Benjamin Franklin, Representative Selections* (cited in note 3), p. cxxxvi.

43. *The Letters of Benjamin Franklin & Jane Mecom* (cited in note 39), pp. 124, 125–26. See also *Writings*, Vol. 2, p. 61; Vol. 4, p. 388; Vol. 9, p. 247.

detail his insight into the nature of the two outstanding passions of social life, the desire for wealth and the desire for power—avarice and ambition. "That I may avoid Avarice and Ambition . . .—Help me, O Father," was Franklin's prayer in the "Articles of Belief" of 1728.[44]

The universal fame of Poor Richard and the description of Franklin's own "way to wealth" in his *Autobiography* (Franklin's account of his life ends with his arrival in London in 1757 for the first of his three great public missions in Europe) have led many people to see in Franklin only the ingenious businessman pursuing thrift for thrift's sake and money for money's sake. Nothing could be further from the truth than this conception. To be sure, he recognized the existence and the nature of avarice in unequivocal terms: "The Love of Money is not a Thing of certain Measure, so as that it may be easily filled and satisfied. Avarice is infinite; and where there is not good Œconomy, no Salary, however large, will prevent Necessity."[45] He denied, however, that desire for more wealth actuated his work. His early retirement from business (1748) to devote himself to the higher things of life—chiefly to public service and scientific research—seems to prove this point.

Franklin considered wealth essentially as means to an end. He knew that it was not easy "for an empty sack to stand upright." He looked upon his fortune as an essential factor in his not having succumbed to corruption.[46] In a famous and often quoted letter to his mother, Franklin said that at the end of his life he "would rather have it said, *He lived usefully* than *He died Rich.*" At about the same time (two years after his retirement) he wrote to his printer friend William Strahan in England: "London citizens, they say, are ambitious of what they call *dying worth* a great sum. The very notion seems to me absurd."[47]

On the other hand, the motive of power and prestige found much earlier recognition in Franklin's writings; he even confessed candidly that he himself was not free from this desire and from the feeling of being superior to his fellowmen. At the age of sixteen, in his first secret contributions to his brother's *New-England Courant* (he wrote under the pseudonym Mrs. Dogood), he gave a satisfactory definition of what we nowadays

44. *Writings*, Vol. 2, p. 99.
45. *Writings*, Vol. 5, p. 325.
46. *The Letters of Benjamin Franklin & Jane Mecom* (cited in note 39), p. 123.
47. *Writings*, Vol. 3, pp. 5, 6. Cf. Benjamin Rush to John Adams: "The Doctor was a rigid economist, but he was in every stage of his life charitable, hospitable, and generous." August 19, 1811, in *Letters of Benjamin Rush* (cited in note 10), Vol. 2, p. 1093.

would call lust for power, and what was in the eighteenth century called Pride:

> Among the many reigning Vices of the Town which may at any Time come under my Consideration and Reprehension, there is none which I am more inclin'd to expose than that of *Pride*. It is acknowledged by all to be a Vice the most hateful to God and Man. Even those who nourish it themselves, hate to see it in others. The proud Man aspires after Nothing less than an unlimited Superiority over his Fellow-Creatures.[48]

As Arthur O. Lovejoy has pointed out, the idea of Pride was frequently contemplated during the earlier half of the eighteenth century.[49] There are two different, though not unrelated, conceptions of Pride. First of all, it means "the most powerful and pervasive of all passions," which manifests itself in two forms: self-esteem and desire for the admiration of others. The second conception is closely connected with the idea of the Scale of Being; it means the generic Pride of man as such, the sin against the laws of order, of gradation, the revolt of man against the station which has been allotted to him by the Creator.

These different conceptions of Pride are indeed inseparable. In Franklin's own writings, the accent is on the first rather than on the second meaning. This topic runs through his work like a red thread. In 1729, at the age of 23, he wrote that "almost every Man has a strong natural Desire of being valu'd and esteem'd by the rest of his Species."[50] Observations in a letter written in 1751 testify to his keen psychological insight:

> What you mention concerning the love of praise is indeed very true; it reigns more or less in every heart, though we are generally hypocrites, in that respect, and pretend to disregard praise. . . . Being forbid to praise themselves, they learn instead of it to censure others; which is only a roundabout way of praising themselves. . . . This fondness for ourselves, rather than malevolence to others, I take to be the general source of censure. . . .[51]

48. *Writings*, Vol. 2, pp. 18–19.
49. Lovejoy, "'Pride' in Eighteenth Century Thought," (cited in note 26), pp. 62–68.
50. *Writings*, Vol. 2, p. 108.
51. *Writings*, Vol. 3, pp. 54–55.

Quite revealing with regard to our discussion is Franklin's well-known account of his project of an "Art of Virtue." His list of virtues to be practiced contained at first only twelve: "But a Quaker friend having kindly informed me that I was generally thought proud . . . I added *Humility* to my list. . . . I cannot boast of much success in acquiring the *reality* of this virtue, but I had a good deal with regard to the *appearance* of it."[52] His account of his rise in Pennsylvania's public life and politics reflects his joy and pride about his career. In 1737 he was appointed Postmaster of Philadelphia and Justice of the Peace; in 1744 he established the American Philosophical Society; in 1748 he was chosen a member of the Council of Philadelphia; in 1749 he was appointed Provincial Grandmaster of the Colonial Masons; in 1750 he was appointed one of the commissioners to treat with the Indians in Carlisle; and in 1751 he became a member of the Assembly of Pennsylvania. He was particularly pleased with this last appointment, and he admitted candidly that his ambition was "flatter'd by all these promotions; it certainly was; for, considering my low beginning, they were great things to me."[53]

There is no change of emphasis with respect to Pride during his long life. The old man of 78 denounces the evil of Pride with no less fervor, though with more self-knowledge, than the boy of 16:

In reality, there is, perhaps, no one of our natural passions so hard to subdue as *pride*. Disguise it, struggle with it, beat it down, stifle it, mortify it as much as one pleases, it is still alive, and will every now and then peep out and show itself; you will see it, perhaps, often in this history; for even if I could conceive that I had compleatly overcome it, I should probably be proud of my humility.[54]

Furthermore, the experience of English political life which he acquired during his two protracted stays in England (from 1757 to 1762, and from 1765 to 1775) made an indelible impression on his mind. The corruption and venality in English politics and the disastrous blunders of English politicians which Franklin traced back to this cause[55] probably were the main reasons why he advocated at the Federal Convention of 1787 what

52. *Writings*, Vol. 1, p. 337.
53. *Writings*, Vol. 1, p. 374. For Franklin's acknowledgment of his own political ambition, see *Writings*, Vol. 5, pp. 148, 206, 357; Vol. 9, pp. 488, 621.
54. *Autobiography* (end of the part written in Passy, France, 1784), *Writings*, Vol. 1, p. 339.
55. *Writings*, Vol. 10, p. 62. See also Vol. 5, pp. 100, 112, 117, 133. See also *Benjamin Franklin's Letters to the Press, 1758–1775*, ed. Verner W. Crane (Chapel Hill, 1950), pp. 59, 164, 232.

he himself said some might regard as a "Utopian Idea": the abolition of salaries for the chief executive. The reason he gave for advocating such a step has hitherto not been appreciated as being of crucial importance for an understanding of his political thought:

> There are two Passions which have a powerful Influence in the Affairs of Men. These are *Ambition* and *Avarice;* the Love of Power and the Love of Money. Separately, each of these has great Force in prompting Men to Action; but when united in View of the same Object, they have in many minds the most violent Effects. Place before the Eyes of such Men a Post of *Honour,* that shall at the same time be a Place of *Profit,* and they will move Heaven and Earth to obtain it.[56]

It has never been pointed out that this scheme of what might be called the "separation of passions" had been ripening in Franklin's mind for several years. The first expression of it is to be found early in 1783.[57] In 1784 he mentioned it several times, and it is in these statements that we find one of the few allusions to the concept of checks and balances in Franklin's thought. He recommended: "Make every place of *honour* a place of *burthen.* By that means the effect of one of the passions above-mentioned would be taken away and something would be added to counteract the other."[58]

V. The Nature of Politics

Franklin's frequent praise of the general welfare did not blind him to the fact that most other people had a much narrower vision than his own. "Men will always be powerfully influenced in their Opinions and Actions by what appears to be their particular Interest," he wrote in his first tract on political economy, at the age of twenty-three.[59] Fortunately, one of the very few memoranda and notes dealing with the studies and discussions of young Franklin which have come to our knowledge directly concerns this problem. Franklin himself, in his *Autobiography,* gives us the text of "*Observations* on my reading history, in Library, May 19th, 1731" which, in his words, had been "accidentally preserv'd":

56. *Writings,* Vol. 9, p. 591.
57. *Writings,* Vol. 9, p. 23.
58. *Writings,* Vol. 9, p. 170. See also ibid., pp. 172 and 260.
59. *Writings,* Vol. 2, p. 139.

That the great affairs of the world, the wars, revolutions, etc., are carried on and affected by parties.

That the view of these parties is their present general interest, or what they take to be such.

That the different views of these different parties occasion all confusion.

That while a party is carrying on a general design, each man has his particular private interest in view.

That as soon as a party has gain'd its general point, each member becomes intent upon his particular interest; which, thwarting others, breaks that party into divisions, and occasions more confusion.

That few in public affairs act from a mere view of the good of their country, whatever they may pretend; and, tho' their actings bring real good to their country, yet men primarily considered that their own and their country's interest was united, and did not act from a principle of benevolence.

That fewer still, in public affairs, act with a view for the good of mankind. . . .[60]

These lines do not mirror Shaftesbury's benevolent altruism; Franklin's contention that men act primarily from their own interest "and . . . not . . . from a principle of benevolence," "tho' their actings bring real good to their country," strongly suggests the general theme of Mandeville's work: "Private vices, public benefits."

Many decades after the foregoing observations, the contrast between Franklin's views on politics and those of the enlightened rationalism of contemporary France is clearly expressed in a discussion with the French physiocrat Dupont de Nemours. Dupont had suggested that the Federal Convention be delayed until the separate constitutions of the member states were corrected—according to physiocratic principles, of course. Franklin mildly observed that "we must not expect that a new government may be formed, as a game of chess may be played." He stressed that in the game of politics there were so many players with so many strong and various prejudices, "and their particular interests, independent of the general, seeming so opposite," that "the play is more like *tric-trac* with a box of dice."[61] In public, and when he was propagandizing for America in Europe, Franklin

60. *Writings*, Vol. 1, pp. 339–40. Cf. also Vol. 2, p. 196, and Vol. 4, p. 322.
61. *Writings*, Vol. 9, p. 659; see also p. 241.

played down the evils of party strife: after the end of the War of Independence he conceded somewhat apologetically that "it is true, in some of the States there are Parties and Discords." He contended now that parties "are the common lot of Humanity," and that they exist wherever there is liberty; they even, perhaps, help to preserve it. "By the Collision of different Sentiments, Sparks of Truth are struck out, and Political Light is obtained."[62]

In private, Franklin did not conceal his suspicion that "unity out of discord" was not as easily achieved as his just quoted method of obtaining "political light" might suggest. But he certainly did not believe that passions and prejudices always, or even usually, overrule enlightened self-interest. He held that "there is a vast variety of good and ill Events, that are in some degree the Effects of Prudence or the want of it."[63] He believed that "reasonable sensible Men, can always make a reasonable scheme appear such to other reasonable Men, if they take Pains, and have Time and Opportunity for it . . ." However, this dictum is severely limited by the conclusion: ". . . unless from some Circumstance their Honesty and Good Intentions are suspected."[64] That Franklin thought those circumstances to exist frequently, we learn from a famous message to George Washington, written in France in 1780. He told Washington how much the latter would enjoy his reputation in France, "pure and free from those little Shades that the Jealousy and Envy of a Man's Countrymen and Cotemporaries are ever endeavouring to cast over living Merit."[65]

Although Franklin himself talked so much about "common Interests," he could be impatient when others built their arguments on this point. He observed that "it is an Insult on common sense to affect an Appearance of Generosity in a Matter of obvious Interest."[66] This belief in self-interest as a moving force of politics appears with rare clarity in marginal notes in a pamphlet whose author argued that "if the Interests of Great Britain evidently raise and fall with those of the Colonies, then the Parliament of Great Britain will have the same regard for the Colonists as for her own People." Franklin retorted:

All this Argument of the Interest of Britain and the Colonies being the *same* is fallacious and unsatisfactory. Partners in Trade have a *com-*

62. *Writings*, Vol. 10, pp. 120–21. See also Vol. 4, p. 35.

63. *Writings*, Vol. 7, p. 358.

64. *Writings*, Vol. 3, pp. 41–42.

65. *Writings*, Vol. 8, p. 28. Cf. the expression of the same idea 36 years earlier in *Writings*, Vol. 2, p. 242.

66. *Benjamin Franklin's Letters to the Press* (cited in note 55), p. 183.

mon Interest, which is the same, the Flourishing of the Partnership Business: But they may moreover have each a *separate* Interest; and in pursuit of that *separate* Interest, one of them may endeavour to impose on the other, may cheat him in the Accounts, may draw to himself more than his Share of the Profits, may put upon the other more than an equal Share of the Burthen. Their having a common Interest is no Security against such Injustice. . . .[67]

VI. Democracy

It is fair to ask how Franklin's views on the above matters square with his avowal of radically democratic notions after 1775. In view of the foregoing, Franklin would not, it seems, agree with the underlying assumptions of Jeffersonian democracy, stated by Jefferson himself: "Nature hath implanted in our breasts a love of others, a sense of duty to them, a moral instinct, in short, which prompts us irresistibly to feel and to succor their distresses . . ." It was also Jefferson who believed "that man was a rational animal, endowed by nature with rights, and with an innate sense of justice."[68] On this faith in the rationality and goodness of man, the theory of Jeffersonian democracy has been erected. Vernon L. Parrington said of Franklin that "he was a forerunner of Jefferson, like him firm in the conviction that government was good in the measure that it remained close to the people."[69] Charles A. Beard, discussing the members of the Federal Convention, tells us that Benjamin Franklin "seems to have entertained a more hopeful view of democracy than any other member of that famous group."[70] All this must seem rather strange in view of the none too optimistic conception of human nature which we have found in Franklin. His radically democratic views after 1775—before that time his outlook seemed essentially conservative—baffled contemporary observers as it has later students.

There is, as a matter of fact, plenty of evidence of Franklin's sincere devotion to monarchy during the greater part of his life. It was the most

---

67. Marginal comments in *Good Humour, or, A Way with the Colonies* (London, 1766), pp. 26–27. Franklin's copy is in the library of the Historical Society of Pennsylvania, Philadelphia. This comment is reprinted in *A Collection of the Familiar Letters and Miscellaneous Papers of Benjamin Franklin*, ed. Jared Sparks (Boston, 1833), p. 229.

68. Jefferson to Thomas Law, June 13, 1814, and to Judge William Johnson, June 12, 1823, quoted by Adrienne Koch, *The Philosophy of Thomas Jefferson* (New York, 1943), pp. 19, 139.

69. Vernon L. Parrington, *Main Currents in American Thought*, 3 vols. (New York, 1930), Vol. I, pp. 176–77.

70. Charles A. Beard, *An Economic Interpretation of the Constitution* (New York, 1913), p. 197.

natural thing for him to assure his friend, the famous Methodist preacher
George Whitefield, that a settlement of colonies on the Ohio would be
blessed with success "if we undertook it with sincere Regard to . . . the
Service of our gracious King, and (which is the same thing) the Publick
Good."[71] Franklin loved to contrast the corruption of Parliament and the
virtues of George III. To an American friend, he said that he could "scarcely
conceive a King of better Dispositions, of more exemplary virtues, or more
truly desirous of promoting the Welfare of all his Subjects."[72]

Another "conservative" aspect of Franklin which cannot be glossed
over lightly is his acceptance of the Puritan and mercantilistic attitude
towards the economic problems of the working class. Throughout his life
he was critical of the English Poor Laws. He deplored "the proneness of
human nature to a life of ease, of freedom from care and labour," and he
considered that laws which *compel the rich to maintain the poor* might
possibly be "fighting against the order of God and Nature, which perhaps
has appointed want and misery as the proper punishments for, and cau-
tions against, as well as necessary consequences of, idleness and extrava-
gance."[73] This was written in 1753. But as late as 1789, long after he had
come out for the political equality of the poor and for a radical theory of
property, he still confirmed to an English correspondent that "I have long
been of your opinion, that your legal provision for the poor is a very great
evil, operating as it does to the encouragement of idleness."[74]

Franklin's endorsement of democracy is most emphatically revealed in
his advocacy of a unicameral legislature for the Commonwealth of Pennsylvania, as well as for the federal government. The issue of unicameral
versus bicameral legislative bodies—an issue much discussed in the latter decades of the eighteenth century—reflected faithfully, as a rule, the
clash of views of two different theories of human nature and of politics.
The bicameral system was based on the principle of checks and balances;
a pessimistic view of human nature naturally would try to forestall the
abuse of power in a single and all-powerful assembly. On the other hand,
most of those who trusted in the faculties of human reason did not see the

71. *Writings*, Vol. 3, p. 339. See also Vol. 2, pp. 377–78; Vol. 4, pp 94, 213.

72. *Writings*, Vol. 5, p. 204. See also Vol. 5, p. 261. Another sign of Franklin's antiradical
attitude during his stay in England is his disgust with the Wilkes case. See *Writings*, Vol. 5,
pp. 121, 133, 134, and 150. Also *Letters and Papers of Benjamin Franklin and Richard Jackson,
1753–1785*, ed. Carl Van Doren (Philadelphia, 1947), p. 139.

73. *Letters and Papers of Benjamin Franklin and Richard Jackson, op. cit.*, pp. 34, 35.

74. *Writings*, Vol. 10, p. 64. See for an elaboration of his arguments "On the Labouring
Poor," *Writings*, Vol. 5, pp. 122–27, and "On the Price of Corn, and Management of the Poor,"
Writings, Vol. 5, pp. 534–39.

necessity for a second chamber to check and harass the activities of a body of reasonable men.

In the case of Franklin, however, this correspondence of political convictions with views on human nature is lacking. He was the president of the Pennsylvania Convention of 1776 which—almost uniquely among the American states—set up a unicameral system. This, of course, filled many of the French *philosophes* with great joy. Franklin, they supposed, had secured a triumph of enlightened principles in the new world. Condorcet, in his "Éloge de Franklin," had this to say:

> Franklin's voice alone decided this last provision. He thought that as enlightenment would naturally make rapid progress, above all in a country to which the revolution had given a new system, one ought to encourage the devices of perfecting legislation, and not to surround them with extrinsic obstacles. . . . The opinion contrary to his stands for that discouraging philosophy which considers error and corruption as the habitual state of societies and the development of virtue and reason as a kind of miracle which one must not expect to make enduring. It was high time that a philosophy both nobler and truer should direct the destiny of mankind, and Franklin was worthy to give the first example of it.[75]

As a matter of fact, it has since been shown that Franklin, who at the time of the Pennsylvania Convention also served in the Continental Congress, played a minor role in the adoption of the unicameral system. The unicameral legislature was rooted in the historical structure of Pennsylvania's proprietary government.[76] This, however, is irrelevant from our point of view, since Franklin endorsed and defended the unicameral system in his "Queries and Remarks respecting Alterations in the Constitution of Pennsylvania," written in November, 1789.[77]

In the opposition to checks and balances and a second chamber, Franklin's most famous companion was Thomas Paine, author of *The Age of Reason*. This similarity of views between Franklin and one of the most vocal spokesmen of the creed of reason and the perfectibility of man perhaps contributes to the misinterpretation of Franklin's position among the

75. *Oeuvres de Condorcet* (cited in note 1), Vol. 3, pp. 401–402 (my translation).

76. See J. Paul Selsam, *The Pennsylvania Constitution of 1776* (Philadelphia, 1926), and Charles M. Andrews, *The Colonial Period of American History*, 4 vols. (New Haven, 1934–38), Vol. 3, p. 320.

77. *Writings*, Vol. 10, pp. 54–60.

eighteenth-century philosophers. Paine's arguments against the system of checks and balances and for a single house were characteristic of the later Enlightenment:

> Freedom is the associate of innocence, not the companion of suspicion. She only requires to be cherished, not to be caged, and to be beloved is, to her, to be protected. Her residence is in the undistinguished multitude of rich and poor, and a partisan to neither is the patroness of all.[78]

This argument, of course, presupposes the rationality and goodness of human nature. We might perhaps agree with Paine that "no man was a better judge of human nature than Franklin,"[79] but Paine certainly did not have Franklin's conception of human nature.

The reasons for Franklin's almost radical attitude in 1776 and 1787 appear in his own writings. One thing seems certain: belief in the goodness and the wisdom of the people is not at the root of his democratic faith. This idea is quite foreign to Franklin. Discussing the Albany Plan of Union in 1754, he thought that "it is very possible, that this general government might be as well and faithfully administered without the people, as with them."[80] Nor did he fundamentally change his view in the last years of his life: "Popular favour is very precarious, being sometimes lost as well as gained by good actions." In 1788, he wrote publicly that "popular Opposition to a public Measure is no Proof of its Impropriety."[81] What a strange democrat it was who told the Federal Convention that "there is a natural Inclination in Mankind to kingly Government."[82] The most plausible and popular reason for belief in democracy, then, is eliminated.

On the other hand, Franklin did not believe in the intrinsic goodness of the wealthy or the wisdom of the powerful; he had no liking for aristocratic government, be it by an aristocracy of wealth or an aristocracy of birth. He was scornful of the House of Lords and thought "Hereditary

78. "A Serious Address to the People of Pennsylvania on the Present Situation of their Affairs" (Dec., 1778), in *The Complete Writings of Thomas Paine*, ed. Philip S. Foner, 2 vols. (New York, 1945), Vol. 2, p. 284.
79. "Constitutional Reform" (1805), ibid., pp. 998–99.
80. *Writings*, Vol. 3, p. 231. See also p. 309.
81. *Writings*, Vol. 9, pp. 564, 702. In 1788, Franklin repeatedly said that there was at present the "danger of too little obedience in the *governed*," although in general the opposite evil of "giving too much power to our *governors*" was more dreaded. *Writings*, Vol. 9, p. 638; and Vol. 10, p. 7
82. *Writings*, Vol. 9, p. 593.

Professors of Mathematicks" preferable to hereditary legislators because they could do less mischief.[83]

It is noteworthy that in the whole of Franklin's work only one reference to Montesquieu can be found; and that concerns his ideas on criminal law. Separation of powers, the role of the aristocracy in a healthy society—these are doctrines which never took possession of Franklin's mind.

The antithesis between Adams, under the influence of Harrington, and Franklin, chiefly influenced by his own experience, is remarkably complete. Adams wrote:

> It must be remembered that the rich are *people* as well as the poor; that they have rights as well as others; they have as clear and as *sacred* a right to their large property as others have to theirs which is smaller; that oppression to them is as possible and wicked as to others. . . .[84]

Franklin mounts a formidable counterattack:

> And why should the upper House, chosen by a Minority, have equal Power with the lower chosen by a majority? Is it supposed that Wisdom is the necessary concomitant of Riches . . . and why is Property to be represented at all? . . . The Combinations of Civil Society are not like those of a Set of Merchants, who club their Property in different Proportions for Building and Freighting a Ship, and may therefore have some Right to Vote in the Disposition of the Voyage in a greater or less Degree according to their respective Contributions; but the important ends of Civil Society, and the personal Securities of Life and Liberty, these remain the same in every member of the Society; and the poorest continues to have an equal Claim to them with the most opulent. . . .[85]

---

83. *Writings*, Vol. 6, pp. 370–71. For other attacks on the principle of hereditary honors and privileges, in connection with the Order of the Cincinnati, see *Writings*, Vol. 9, pp. 162, 336.

84. Quoted by Zoltán Haraszti, *John Adams and the Prophets of Progress* (Cambridge, MA, 1952), p. 36.

85. "Queries and Remarks." *Writings*, Vol. 10, pp. 58–61. For Franklin's disagreement with the bicameral system of the United States Constitution, see *Writings*, Vol. 9, pp. 645, 674. The paradox of Franklin's attitude is thrown into relief if one considers that even Jefferson, in his *Notes on Virginia*, raised his voice against the dangers of an "elective despotism," and exalted "those benefits" which a "proper complication of principles" would produce. *The Works of Thomas Jefferson*, ed. Paul Leicester Ford (New York and London, 1904–1905), Vol. 4, p. 19.

It is this strong objection against the attempt to use—openly or
covertly—a second chamber as a tool of class rule which seems to under-
lie Franklin's disapproval of the bicameral system. Franklin, it should be
pointed out, was aware of the necessity and inevitability of poises and
counter-poises. This is shown by his attempt, referred to above, to create
a sort of balance of passions, checking avarice with ambition. There exist
some, though quite rare, allusions to a balance of power concept in his
utterances on imperial and international relations. The most pointed and
direct reference to the idea of checks and balances, however, may be found
in an unpublished letter to a well-known figure of Pennsylvania politics,
Joseph Galloway, in 1767. Franklin discussed and welcomed a new Circuit
Bill for the judges of Pennsylvania. He suggested and encouraged an increase in the salaries to be granted by the Assembly for the judges to offset
the nominating and recalling powers of the Proprietor: "From you they
should therefore receive a Salary equal in Influence upon their Minds, to
be held during your Pleasure. For where the Beam is *moveable*, it is only
by equal Weights in opposite scales that it can possibly be kept even."[86]

Consequently, the arguments of Thomas Paine or the French *philosophes*, which derive their validity from assumptions about the goodness or
rationality of human nature, do not hold in the case of Franklin. In a brilliant recent essay Louis Hartz has suggested that "despite the European flavor of a Jefferson or a Franklin, the Americans refused to join in the great
Enlightenment enterprise of shattering the Christian concept of sin, replacing it with an unlimited humanism, and then emerging with an earthly
enterprise as glittering as the heavenly one that had been destroyed."[87] As
far as Franklin is concerned, however, the alternatives of Calvinist pessimism and the "unlimited humanism" of the European Enlightenment
do not really clarify the essential quality of his political thought. His
thought is rooted in a climate of opinion which combined the rejection of
the doctrine of original sin with a rather modest view of human nature.

It seems, then, that the desire for equality, rather than any rationalistic
concepts, offers the clue to an adequate understanding of those elements in
Franklin's political thought which at first sight appear inconsistent with his
not too cheerful view of human goodness. His striving for equality also suggests a solution to the thorny problem of reconciling his democratic views
after he had decided for American independence with his faithful loyalty

86. April 14, 1767, in the William L. Clements Library, Ann Arbor, Michigan.
87. Louis Hartz, "American Political Thought and the American Revolution," *American
Political Science Review*, Vol. 46, pp. 321–42, at p. 324 (June, 1952).

to the Crown before that date. The American interest obliged him to fight against Parliament—an aristocratic body in those days—while remaining loyal to the King; in recognizing the King's sovereignty while denying the Parliament's rights over the Colonies, Franklin by necessity was driven into a position which—historically speaking—seemed to contradict his Whig principles. The complaining Americans spoke, as Lord North rightly said, the "language of Toryism."[88] During the decade before 1775 Franklin fought for the equal rights of England and the Colonies under the Crown. But his desire for equality went deeper than that. In his "Some good Whig Principles," while conceding that the government of Great Britain ought to be lodged "in the hands of King, Lords of Parliament, and Representatives of *the whole Body* of the freemen of this realm," he took care to affirm that "*every man* of the commonalty (excepting infants, insane persons, and criminals) is, of common right, and by the Laws of God, a *freeman*" and that "the poor man has an *equal* right, but *more* need, to have representatives in the legislature than the rich one."[89] It has not been widely known that Franklin, in a conversation with Benjamin Vaughan, his friend and at the same time emissary of the British Prime Minister Lord Shelburne during the peace negotiations of 1782, has confirmed this view. Vaughan reported to Shelburne that "Dr. Franklin's opinions about *parliaments* are, that people should not be rejected as electors because they are at *present* ignorant"; Franklin thought that "a statesman should meliorate his people," and Vaughan supposed that Franklin "would put this, among other reasons for extending the privilege of election, that it *would* meliorate them." It was Franklin's opinion, Vaughan thought, "that the lower people are as we see them, because oppressed; & then their situation in point of manners, becomes the reason for oppressing them."[90] The fact is that Franklin's overriding concern for equality foreshadows the attacks of the socialism of later generations on the absolute sanctity of private property:

All the Property that is necessary to a Man, for the Conservation of the Individual and the Propagation of the Species, is his natural Right, which none can justly deprive him of: But all Property superfluous to such purposes is the Property of the Publick, who, by their Laws, have

88. Quoted by G. H. Guttridge, *English Whiggism and the American Revolution* (Berkeley, 1942), p. 62.

89. *Writings*, Vol. 10, p. 130.

90. Benjamin Vaughan to Lord Shelburne, November 24, 1782. Benjamin Vaughan Papers in the American Philosophical Society, Philadelphia. Photostat in the Benjamin Vaughan Collection in the William L. Clements Library, Ann Arbor, Michigan.

created it, and who may therefore by other Laws dispose of it, whenever
the Welfare of the Publick shall demand such Disposition.[91]

Franklin's previously quoted speech in the Federal Convention provides us with an essential insight: he expressed belief in "a natural Inclination in Mankind to kingly Government." His reasons are revealing: "It
sometimes relieves them from Aristocratic Domination. They had rather
one Tyrant than 500. It gives more of the Appearance of Equality among
Citizens; and that they like."[92] Equality, then, is not incompatible with
monarchy.

From all this a significant conclusion may be drawn. It is an oversim-
plification to speak of Franklin's "conservatism" before 1775 and of his
"radicalism" after 1775. Professor MacIver illustrates the conservative
character of the first stage of American political thought preceding the
appeal to natural rights by reference to Franklin, who, in spite of his later
attacks on the Order of the Cincinnati, "nevertheless clung to the principle of a hereditary, though constitutional monarchy, until the tide of
revolution rendered it untenable."[93] The term "conservative" does not do
justice to the possibility of paying faithful allegiance to a monarchy and
still disliking aristocracies of heredity or wealth. Because of his innate
desire for equality, as well as his defense of the American cause against
the encroachments of Parliament, Franklin found it much easier to be a
monarchist. Monarchy, rather than aristocracy, was compatible with those
elements of his thought which after 1775 made him a democrat.

Another of the factors which, while not incompatible with monarchical feelings, contributed greatly to Franklin's acceptance of democracy, is
the belief which he shared with Hume that power, in the last analysis, is
founded on opinion. "I wish some good Angel would forever whisper in
the Ears of your great Men, that Dominion is founded in Opinion, and
that if you would preserve your Authority among us, you must preserve
the Opinion we us'd to have of your Justice."[94] He thought that "Government must depend for its Efficiency either on Force or Opinion." Force,
however, is not as efficient as Opinion: "Alexander and Caesar . . . received
more faithful service, and performed greater actions, by means of the love

91. *Writings*, Vol. 9, p. 138 (written in 1783). See also Vol. 10, p. 59.

92. *Writings*, Vol. 9, p. 539.

93. R. M. MacIver, "European Doctrines and the Constitution," in *The Constitution Reconsidered* (cited in note 25), p. 55.

94. *Letters and Papers of Benjamin Franklin and Richard Jackson* (cited in note 72), p. 145
(written in 1764). See also *Writings*, Vol. 6, p. 129; Vol. 9, p. 608.

their soldiers bore them, than they could possibly have done, if, instead of being beloved and respected, they had been hated and feared by those they commanded." Efficiency, then, became an argument for democracy. "Popular elections have their inconvenience in some cases; but in establishing new forms of government, we cannot always obtain what we may think the best; for the prejudices of those concerned, if they cannot be removed, must be in some degree complied with."[95]

It has rarely been noticed how detached Franklin, the greatest champion of democracy in the Federal Convention, was from the problem of the best government. His speech at the conclusion of the deliberations of the Constitutional Convention may give us a clue to the perplexing problem of why he gave comparatively little attention to the theoretical questions of political philosophy and devoted almost all his time to the solution of concrete issues. He stated his disagreement with several points of the Constitution, nevertheless urging general allegiance and loyalty to its principles. Asking his colleagues to doubt a little their feeling of infallibility, Franklin summed up the experience of his life: "I think a general Government necessary for us, and there is no *form* of government but what may be a blessing to the people, if well administered."[96] Perhaps in speaking these words he was thinking of one of the favorite writers of his younger days, Alexander Pope:

> For Forms of Government let fools contest;
> Whate'er is best administer'd is best.[97]

VII. The Duality of Franklin's Political Thought

There are two outstanding and sometimes contradictory factors in Franklin's political thought. On the one hand, we find an acute comprehension of the power factor in human nature, and, consequently, in politics. On the other hand, Franklin always during his long life revolted in the name of equality against the imperfections of the existing order. He himself stated the basic antithesis of his political thought: Power versus Equality.

Fortunately, Franklin's notes on the problem at hand have been preserved; they are to be found in his marginal comments to Allen Ramsay's

95. *Benjamin Franklin's Letters to the Press* (cited in note 55), p. 193; *Writings*, Vol. 2, p. 56; Vol. 3, p. 228. See also Vol. 3, 231; Vol. 5, p. 79.

96. *Writings*, Vol. 9, p. 607.

97. Pope, "Essay on Man," *Epistle 3, Selected Works* (cited in note 17), p. 124.

pamphlet, *Thoughts on the Origin and Nature of Government*, which presents the straight view of power politics. Franklin rebelled against the rationalization and justification of the power factor. "The natural weakness of man in a solitary State," Ramsay proclaimed, "prompts him to fly for protection to whoever is able to afford it, that is to some one more powerful, than himself; while the more powerful standing equally in need of his Service, readily receives it in return for the protection he gives." Franklin's answer is unequivocal: *"May not Equals unite with Equals for common Purposes?"* [98]

In the last analysis, Franklin looked upon government as the trustee of the people. He had stated this Whig principle in his very first publication as a sixteen-year-old boy [99] and he never deviated from it. So in opposition to Ramsay's doctrine, according to which the governed have no right of control whatsoever, once they have agreed to submit themselves to the sovereign, Franklin declared the accountability of the rulers:

> If I appoint a Representative for the express purpose of doing a business for me that is for *my Service* and that of others, & to consider what I am to pay as my Proportion of the Expense necessary for accomplishing that Business, I am then tax'd by my own Consent.—A Number of Persons unite to form a Company for Trade, Expences are necessary, Directors are chosen to do the Business & proportion those Expences. They are paid a Reasonable Consideration for their Trouble. Here is nothing of weak & Strong. Protection on one hand, & Service on the other. The Directors are the Servants, not the Masters; their Duty is prescrib'd, the Powers they have is from the members & returns to them. The Directors are also accountable. [100]

Franklin refused to recognize that power alone could create right. When Ramsay declared that according to nature's laws every man "in Society shall rank himself amongst the Ruling or the Ruled, . . . all Equality and Independence being by the Law of Nature strictly forbidden. . . ," Franklin rejoined indignantly, "I do not find this Strange Law among those of Nature. I doubt it is forged. . . ." He summarized Ramsay's doctrine as meaning that

---

98. [Allen Ramsay], *Thoughts on the Origin and Nature of Government* (London, 1769), p. 10. Franklin's copy in the Jefferson Collection of the Library of Congress. (My italics.)

99. "Dogood Papers," *Writings*, Vol. 2, p. 26. Cf. *Benjamin Franklin's Letters to the Press* (cited in note 55), p. 140.

100. Marginal notes to Ramsay, *op. cit.*, pp. 33–34.

"He that is strongest may do what he pleases with those that are weaker," and commented angrily: "A most Equitable Law of Nature indeed." [101]

On the other hand, Franklin's grasp of the realities of Power inevitably involved him in moral and logical ambiguities of political decision. At times he expressed the tragic conflict of ethics and politics. Characteristic of the peculiar contradiction within his political thought was this statement three years before the Declaration of Independence on England's prospects in the Anglo-American conflict: "Power does not infer *Right*; and, as the *Right* is nothing, and the *Power*, by our Increase, continually diminishing, the one will soon be as insignificant as the *other*." [102] In this instance, obviously, he was trying to make the best of both worlds. But there were times when he was only too well aware of the conflict of these two worlds. In a passage which seems to have escaped the notice of most students of his political thought, Franklin observed that *"moral and political Rights sometimes differ, and sometimes are both subd'd by Might."* [103]

The measured terms of Franklin's political thinking present a striking contrast to the optimism and rationalism which we usually associate with the Age of Enlightenment. Franklin's insight into the passions of pride and power prevented him from applying the expectation of man's scientific and intellectual progress to the realm of moral matters. To be sure, he would not deny the influence of scientific insights upon politics, and he thought that a great deal of good would result from introducing the enlightened doctrines of free trade and physiocracy into international politics. But Franklin, unlike many of his friends in France, was never inclined to consider these and other ideas as panaceas. The mutual adjustment of interests would always remain the chief remedy of political evils. It was in this domain that reason, as a temper in the conduct of human affairs, made its greatest contribution to his political thought. Moderation and equity, so he had been taught by his experience (rather than by abstract reasoning) were true political wisdom. His belief that the rulers ought to be accountable, together with his more pragmatic conviction that force alone, in the long run, could not solve the great problems of Politics, brought forth his declaration of faith that "Government is not establish'd merely by *Power*; there must be maintain'd a general Opinion of its *Wisdom* and *Justice* to make it firm and durable." [104]

101. Ibid., pp. 12, 13.

102. *Writings*, Vol. 6, p. 87.

103. *Writings*, Vol. 8, p. 304. (My italics.)

104. *Benjamin Franklin's Autobiographical Writings*, ed. Carl Van Doren (New York, 1945), pp. 184–85. Cf. *Writings*, Vol. 4, p. 269; Vol. 7, p. 390.

CHAPTER TWO

William Blackstone:
Teacher of Revolution*

In this paper I would first like to throw some light on a little known aspect of Revolutionary newspaper and pamphlet warfare in South Carolina in the years from 1769 to 1776. The tale to be told may add merely details to our knowledge of Revolutionary political thought; yet it will raise some broader questions as to the type of argument applied by at least some of the Revolutionaries to the predicament in which they found themselves. It will also focus attention, as the title indicates, on a feature of William Blackstone's constitutional thought which has been obscured by his championship of parliamentary sovereignty.

The story unfolds in the second half of 1769 in Charleston, S. C. The efforts to execute the non-importation association—a reaction against the Townshend legislation of 1767—had run into some opposition. The subscribers of the non-importation agreement had threatened boycott measures against non-subscribers; advocates and opponents of the association were locked in battle in Peter Timothy's *South Carolina Gazette* between August and December of that year. The protagonist—though not the only contributor—on the side of the non-importation fighters was Christopher Gadsden, from the days of the Stamp Act Crisis one of the leaders of what was to become the American Revolution in South Carolina. He was opposed by a young and wealthy Charlestonian, William Henry Drayton, seconded by a planter by the name of William Wragg.

The battle of invectives as well as arguments that raged in Charleston at that time has early been noticed by the historian of colonial South Carolina, Edward McCrady, though his judgment that these articles contained "long and tiresome disquisitions" and "do not afford pleasant reading"

* First published in *Jahrbuch für Amerikastudien* (Heidelberg), Vol. 15 (1970), pp. 184–200.

may not be shared by a generation of historians that has rediscovered how fascinating the pamphlet literature of the American Revolution turns out to be on closer inspection.[1]

The significance of this newspaper debate within the larger framework of the American Revolution was seen by Arthur Schlesinger, Sr. in his great study on the *Colonial Merchants and the American Revolution* in 1918. Schlesinger was impressed how radically Gadsden reacted to Drayton's charge that the association was punishable by law as a "confederacy" (in the sense of conspiracy) to the detriment of third parties:

> Gadsden now advanced to a truly revolutionary position. Passing over the charges of the illegal character of the association, and citing the history of England as his best justification, he affirmed that, whenever the people's rights were invaded in an outrageous fashion by a corrupt Parliament or an abandoned ministry, mankind exerted "those *latent,* though *inherent* rights of SOCIETY, which *no climate, no time, no constitution, no contract,* can ever destroy or diminish."[2]

Schlesinger again referred to Gadsden and this passage in his later study on the Newspaper War against Britain from 1764 to 1776.[3]

A few years after Schlesinger, another historian of the American Revolution, Claude Van Tyne, asked what Christopher Gadsden meant by the allusion to those "*latent,* though *inherent* rights," and commented that "to a mind that venerated the Constitution such ideas were poisonous, and pointed plainly to anarchy."[4] More recently, Clinton Rossiter has also adduced these words of a "south Carolinian"—"probably Christopher Gadsden"—as testimony for the growth of revolutionary thought.[5]

At this point, two clarifications are in order: First, the article referred to by Schlesinger, Van Tyne, and Rossiter was not written by Gadsden, but by a virtually forgotten man, John McKenzie. Second, the statement which Schlesinger has qualified as a "truly revolutionary position," the words which for Van Tyne were "poisonous" to a mind that "venerated the

1. E. McCrady, *The History of South Carolina under the Royal Government, 1719–1776* (New York, 1899), p. 657.

2. A. M. Schlesinger, *The Colonial Merchants and the American Revolution 1763–1776* (New York, 1918, new ed. New York, 1957), p. 205, quoting from *South Carolina Gazette,* Oct. 18, 1769, "A Member of the General Committee."

3. Idem, *Prelude to Independence: The Newspaper War on Britain 1764–1776* (New York, 1958), p. 128.

4. C. Van Tyne, *The Causes of the War of Independence* (Boston, 1922), p. 237.

5. C. Rossiter, *Seedtime of the Republic* (New York, 1953), pp. 393 and 532n. 167.

Constitution," were bodily taken out of William Blackstone's *Commentaries on the Laws of England*, Book I, ch. 7, "Of the King's Prerogative."

Though I shall return to Blackstone's South Carolina plagiarizer, John McKenzie, I would first like to clarify the context of the revolutionary talk by one of the most celebrated conservatives of 18th century England.

Examining the royal prerogative, Blackstone addressed himself to the question as to whether the subjects of England were totally destitute of remedy in case the crown should invade their rights either by private injuries or "public oppressions."[6] We must leave aside the question of private injuries, and turn to his answer concerning public oppressions. To the maxim that the king can do no wrong, Blackstone replied that in cases of "ordinary public oppression, where the vitals of the constitution are not attacked," the law had assigned as remedy the possibility of indicting or impeaching the king's evil counselors. Much more remarkable, however, was Blackstone's advice for public oppressions of more than ordinary character, for "such public oppressions as tend to dissolve the constitution, and subvert the fundamentals of government." In those cases the law, Blackstone said, "feels itself incapable of furnishing any adequate remedy." Such oppressions were necessarily "out of the reach of any *stated rule,* or *express legal* provision." From law, Blackstone referred his readers to prudence: if ever such oppressions "unfortunately happen, the prudence of the times must provide new remedies upon new emergencis." But he did not leave it at that. Prudence should be informed by experience. It was found by experience, Blackstone proclaimed,

> that whenever the unconstitutional oppressions, even of the sovereign power, advance with gigantic strides and threaten desolation to a state, mankind will not be reasoned out of the feelings of humanity; nor will sacrifice their liberty by a scrupulous adherence to those political maxims, which were originally established to preserve it.

This sentence seemed striking enough to our South Carolina polemicist to be used in his defense of the non-importation association; slightly abridged, but substantially correct, we read in the *South Carolina Gazette* of Oct. 18, 1769: "When oppression threatens desolation to a state, mankind will not be reasoned out of the feelings of humanity; nor will they strictly adhere

---

6. William Blackstone, *Commentaries on the Laws of England,* 1st ed. (London, 1765), I, p. 238. Henceforth cited as "Blackstone, I."

to those political maxims which were intended to preserve it." Blackstone did not content himself with such generalities. Experience furnishes us, he said, "with a very remarkable case," wherein, though the positive laws were silent, "nature and reason prevailed." This case was, of course, the Glorious Revolution. "When king James the second invaded the fundamental constitution of the realm, the convention declared an abdication, whereby the throne was rendered vacant, which induced a new settlement of the crown." With a lawyer's precision, Blackstone now stated the consequences of this remarkable case: "And so far as this precedent leads, and no farther, we may now be allowed to lay down the *law* of redress against public oppression." If a future prince should

> endeavour to subvert the constitution by breaking the original contract between king and people, should violate the fundamental laws, and should withdraw himself out of the kingdom; we are now authorized to declare that this conjunction of circumstances would amount to an abdication, and the throne would be thereby vacant.

Out of the precedent of the Glorious Revolution, Blackstone distilled what he himself called "the *law* of redress against public oppression." The interesting question arises, of course, what kind of "law" this law of redress against public oppression was. It was not positive law in a sense in which we would understand that term and which Blackstone seems to have thought of when he said that such public oppressions were out of the reach of any "stated rule, or express legal provision." But it was more specific, more precise than a simple reference to the law of nature and of reason, to a generalized right of resistance. That it was more precise emerges from what follows: It is not for him to say, Blackstone adds, if merely any one or two of the ingredients which all jointly were present at the case just mentioned—the Glorious Revolution—would amount to such a situation: "for there our precedent would fail us." It is only now, as it were, that Blackstone is prepared to go all the way, in direction of a natural right to revolution. He does so, however, with a remarkable sense of the limitations of the legal method, of the limitations of the advice he can tender, with a remarkable sense of proportion. In circumstances which did not correspond to his precedent, in circumstances,

> which a fertile imagination may furnish, since both law and history are silent, it becomes us to be silent too; leaving to future generations, whenever necessity and the safety of the whole shall require it,

the exertion of those inherent (though latent) powers of society, which no climate, no time, no constitution, no contract, can ever destroy or diminish.[7]

And here we are back in Charleston, S. C., October 18, 1769. Merely four years after the appearance of the first volume of Blackstone's *Commentaries*, at least one American, joined in a non-importation association to defy what he and his fellows regarded as a public oppression emanating from the Parliament of Great Britain, found the circumstances apt to take his cue from Blackstone: "Under such circumstances mankind will exert those latent, though inherent rights of society, which no climate, no time, no constitution, no contract, can ever destroy or diminish." A bit briefer than Blackstone's original sentence, but again substantially accurate, even though the South Carolinian substituted "rights" for "powers." While Blackstone spoke of "those inherent (though latent) powers of society," John McKenzie threatened exerting "those latent, though inherent rights of society." "Powers" was the more technical expression, "powers" in the sense of "competence"; "rights" was the word which would have the wider resonance among Americans who at least since the crisis around the Sugar and Stamp Acts had become accustomed to appeal to their rights, natural as well as constitutional.[8]

7. Blackstone, I, pp. 237–38 (all quotations since previous note).
8. For the following: the left column is taken from Blackstone, I, p. 238; the right column from McKenzie's article reprinted in *The Letters of Freeman, &c.* (see below, note 9), pp. 111–12. All italics are mine, to make clear the extent of McKenzie's debt to Blackstone, with the exception of *law* in Blackstone's text, and *Hume, Scotch, Stuarts,* and *England* in McKenzie's text.

Blackstone	McKenzie
"Indeed, it is found by experience, that *whenever* the unconstitutional *oppressions*, even of the sovereign power, advance with gigantic strides and *threaten desolation to a state, mankind will not be reasoned out of the feelings of humanity; nor will* sacrifice their liberty *by a scrupulous adherence to those political maxims, which were* originally *established to preserve it.* And therefore, though the positive laws are silent, experience will furnish us with a very remarkable case, wherein nature and reason prevailed. When king James the second invaded the fundamental constitution of the realm, the convention declared an abdication,	"*When oppression threatens desolation to a state, mankind will not be reasoned out of the feelings of humanity; nor will they strictly adhere to those political maxims which were intended to preserve it.* Hume, the *Scotch* apologist for the *Stuarts,* who has spent his whole life in destroying the principles of civil liberty and revealed religion, is obliged to declare, that in the most absolute government, there is a degree of tyranny, beyond which mankind will never be brought to submit; and from this natural disposition to liberty, it sometimes happens, that even in *Turkey,* the sultan is now and then dispatched with a silken cord: and the history of *England*

Who was this South Carolinian who knew his Blackstone well, having read further than the Introduction with its famous, but much vaguer incantations of the Law of Nature? The author of this interesting article in the *S. C. Gazette* used the pseudonym of "Member of the General Committee"; in earlier contributions he had signed as "Libertas et Natale Solum." Christopher Gadsden signed his articles partly "C. G.," partly "Member of Assembly, and Signer of the Resolution." On the opposite side, there stood William Henry Drayton as "Freeman," while his fellow loyalist William Wragg used his full name. None of the contemporaries in Charleston were deceived about the real participants in the debate. For posterity, the authors were identified by one of the protagonists themselves. W. H. Drayton, having been forced to leave Charleston by the pressure of his enemies, went to London, where he collected and republished this whole newspaper battle in 1771 in a little book *The Letters of Freeman, &c.* In the preface dated January 26, 1771, Drayton revealed the attributions of the various articles. This octavo volume of 244 pages is unfortunately not listed in Thomas R. Adams' bibliographical study *American Independence*. The criteria used

whereby the throne was rendered vacant, which induced a new settlement of the crown. And so far as this precedent leads, and no farther, we may allowed to lay down the *law* of redress against public oppression. If therefore any future prince should endeavour to subvert the constitution by breaking the original contract between king and people, should violate the fundamental laws, and should withdraw himself out of the kingdom; we are now authorized to declare that this conjunction of circumstances would amount to an abdication, and the throne would be thereby vacant. But it is not for us to say, that anyone, or two, of these ingredients would amount to such a situation; for there our precedent would fail us. In these therefore, or other *circumstances*, which a fertile imagination may furnish, since both law and history are silent, it becomes us to be silent too; leaving to future generations, whenever necessity and the safety of the whole shall require it, *the exertion of those inherent (though latent) powers of society, which no climate, no time, no constitution, no contract, can ever destroy or diminish."*

shews, beyond that of any other country in the world, whenever a corrupt parliament or an abandoned ministry invaded, in an outrageous manner, the privileges of the people, that they never rested, until they had reduced the powers of government to its first principles. *Under such circumstances, mankind will exert those latent, though inherent rights of society, which no climate, no time, no constitution, no contract, can ever destroy or diminish."*

there do not permit including pamphlets written by Americans but printed in England; and the book was never reprinted in America.[9]

Our curiosity concerns chiefly the man who used Blackstone so aptly for revolutionary purposes, the author of the *South Carolina Gazette* article of October 18, 1769. John McKenzie, of Broom-Hall in the parish St. James's Goose-creek, was born in 1737 or 1738. Like many sons of wealthy South Carolina planter families, he was sent to England. He studied in Cambridge,[10] was admitted to the Middle Temple, returned to South Carolina and served in the Commons House in Charleston from 1762 to 1765 and 1769 to 1771. He married in 1769 and died two years later, without leaving children, at the age of 33 or 34. Biographical material about this young planter-lawyer-politician is extremely scanty.[11] His intellectual and cultural interests must have been considerable. In his will, he left a sum of 1000 Pound Sterling for the establishment of a College in South Carolina.[12]

9. Thomas R. Adams, *American Independence. The Growth of an Idea* (Providence, RI, 1965), p. xiii. Nor is it listed in J. Sabin, *A Dictionary of Books Relating To America*, 29 vols. (New York, 1868–1936) and Ch. Evans, *A Chronological Dictionary of All Books, and Periodical Publications Printed in the United States of America From the Genesis of Printing in 1639 Down to and Including the Year 1820*, 12 vols. (New York, 1903–1934). L. H. Gipson's *A Bibliographical Guide to the History of the British Empire, 1748–1776* (New York, 1969) likewise makes no mention of Drayton's collection. A brief reference to Drayton's collection in Hennig Cohen, *The South Carolina Gazette 1732–1775* (Columbia, SC, 1953), p. 224, more details in W. M. Dabney and M. Dargan, *William Henry Drayton and the American Revolution* (Albuquerque, NM, 1962), pp. 37–38. Dabney and Dargan, too, speak of McKenzie's "revolutionary position" with reference to the passage quoted above actually taken out of Blackstone, but connected by the authors merely with "Lockian doctrine," ibid., p. 35.

10. This provided Lieutenant Governor Bull with the opportunity of complaining that McKenzie's "education at Cambridge ought to have inspired him with more dutiful sentiments of the Mother Country." Richard Walsh, *Charleston's Sons of Liberty—A Study of the Artisans* (Columbia, SC, 1959), p. 48 (from a report of Bull to Hillsborough of December 5, 1770, *Records Relating to South Carolina in the Public Record Office*, XXXII (London), 416, Transcripts in the S. C. Archives Dept.). McKenzie seems to have been admitted to Trinity Hall in Cambridge on February 1, 1755, but no graduation date is listed. See *Alumni Cantabrigienses*, Part II (1752–1900) (Cambridge, 1951), IV, p. 271.

11. He married Sarah Smith, daughter of Thomas Smith of Broad Street. On the politically influential family of McKenzie's wife see George C. Rogers, Jr., *Evolution of a Federalist—William Loughton Smith of Charleston (1758–1812)* (Columbia, SC, 1962); on McKenzie pp. 28, 58–59, 403. For some of the biographical information I am grateful to Mr. Robert M. Weir, of the Dept. of History of the University of South Carolina, Columbia, SC, in a letter to the author of March 5, 1968. McKenzie's death notice from the *South Carolina Gazette* of May 30, 1771, is reprinted in *South Carolina Historical and Genealogical Magazine*, XXXIV (1933), 149–50.

12. The will of McKenzie was procured from the South Carolina Archives Department, Columbia, SC. The sum of 7000 pounds mentioned in various studies, e.g. F. P. Bowes, *The Culture of Early Charleston* (Chapel Hill, NC, 1942) p. 49; Carl Bridenbaugh, *Cities in Revolt—Urban Life in America 1743–1776* (New York, 1955), p. 379, is erroneous, though the legacy

Of his library, he left the Parliamentary History and the Collection of Debates of the British House of Commons and House of Lords to the S. C. House of Assembly, and the remaining part to the Charleston Library Society for future use in a College. This library, of which only a few volumes are extant after a fire in 1778, seems to have been, on the basis of a printed catalogue, one of the most magnificent private colonial libraries of which we know. McKenzie possessed as diverse titles as Bacon, Bayle, Clarendon, Hobbes' works, the *Oeuvres de Racine*, Edmund Burke's *Dissertation on the Sublime and the Beautiful*, Adam Smith's *Theory of Moral Sentiments*, Voltaire's *History of Charles XII*, many authors of what Caroline Robbins has called the "Whig canon" like Molesworth's *Account of Denmark*, Algernon Sidney's *Discourses*, *Cato's Letters* and Gordon's *Tacitus*, Catherine Macaulay's *History of England*, but we find rarer works as well: Machiavelli's *Discorsi* as well as an astonishing number of Rousseau's writings: The *Discours sur l'origine de l'inégalité parmi les hommes* (in French), the *Nouvelle Heloise*, *Émile*, and the *Social Contract* in English. Montesquieu was represented not merely by the *Esprit des lois*, but also by the *Causes de la grandeur des Romains et de leur décadence*. Among many law writers, like Coke, Hale, Jean Domat, there were Blackstone's *Law Tracts* of 1762 as well as a 1770 Oxford edition of the *Commentaries*. This means, incidentally, that McKenzie in composing his essays for the *South Carolina Gazette* in 1769 must have used an earlier edition, and indeed the Charleston Library Society possessed a 1768 edition of the *Commentaries* (the first American edition came out in Philadelphia only in 1771).[13]

There are two peculiar things to be noticed about John McKenzie's use of Blackstone. First, the comparison of the pertinent texts shows that McKenzie took from Blackstone's paragraph on the law of redress against public oppression the beginning and the end—Blackstone's most radical

---

of 1000 pounds, when the balance was finally secured by the College after litigation about 60 years later, by then had produced 7000 pounds. Details in J. H. Easterby, *A History of the College of Charleston* (Charleston, 1935), pp. 13, 69, 84, 340–41.

13. See *A Catalogue of Books, given and devised by John Mackenzie Esquire, to the Charleston Library Society, for the Use of the College when erected* (Charleston, 1772). A selection of the titles is found in H. Trevor Colbourn, *The Lamp of Experience* (Chapel Hill, NC, 1965), p. 222. The 1768 edition of Blackstone's *Commentaries* is listed in *A Catalogue of Books belonging to the Incorporated Charleston Library Society . . .* (Charleston, 1770). The inventory of McKenzie's personal estate, which was procured from the S. C. Archives Dept. in Columbia, SC, lists the value of "The Liberary of Books" [sic] with £ 21000. I would gratefully like to acknowledge the help accorded me by the staffs of the Charleston Library Society, the Library of the College of Charleston and the South Carolina Historical Society, respectively, on the occasion of my research in Charleston in December, 1967.

phrases—while he omitted the middle—the reference to the "abdication" of James II. For Blackstone's specific precedent McKenzie substituted instead rather general warnings drawn from experiences of history, about tyranny and resistance to it. The most plausible explanation would seem that at the juncture of the non-importation debate of 1769, the break with the king was not yet at issue. In other words, it was more opportune for McKenzie to assert, with Blackstone's help, a right of resistance in extreme emergencies, without referring to the deposition—styled "abdication"—of James II.[14] Had he done that, he would have raised the specter of the deposition of George III—and that moment was, as yet, far away. My explanation would seem to be supported by the way a far more famous American had handled the right of resistance less than two years earlier. John Dickinson's celebrated "Pennsylvania Farmer" Letters, also occasioned by the Townshend legislation, presented an interesting plan of "escalation" for the redress of grievances, culminating in the right of resistance by force, avoiding, however, any specific reference to the deposition of James II. Dickinson observed that if "an inveterate resolution is formed to annihilate the liberties of the governed, the *English* history affords frequent examples of resistance by force. What particular cicumstances," Dickinson concluded in rather general terms, "will in any future case justify such resistance, can never be ascertained, till they happen."[15]

My second point may well be related to the first. This point is that MacKenzie did not reveal his loan from Blackstone, while in the same article freely giving credit to Swift or Hume for arguments or examples he took from them. Revealing Blackstone, he would have revealed Blackstone's context, the abdication of James II. It was one thing to speak, as the colonists frequently did, of "Revolution principles;"[16] but it was perhaps another thing, at that juncture, seeming to suggest the repetition of the events of 1688. McKenzie, too, invoked the formula of "Revolution principles"—a formula that shows how basic the Glorious Revolution was to the colonists'

14. James Otis once wrote indignantly that "the Scots rightly called it a forfeiture of the crown, and this in plain English is the sense of the term *abdication* as by the Convention and every Parliament since applied." "The Rights of the British Colonies Asserted and Proved," (1764) in Bernard Bailyn, ed., *Pamphlets of the American Revolution* (Cambridge, MA, 1965), I, p. 421. Henceforth quoted as Bailyn, *Pamphlets.*

15. "Letters From a Farmer in Pennsylvania to the Inhabitants of the British Colonies," Letter III, Dec. 14, 1767, in P. L. Ford, ed., *The Writings of John Dickinson,* vol. I, *Political Writings 1764–1774* (Philadelphia, 1895), p. 325.

16. E.g., a reference to the "British Constitution as it at present stands, on Revolution principles." Stephen Hopkins, "The Rights of Colonies Examined," (1765) in Bailyn, *Pamphlets,* p. 507.

constitutional thinking. The Glorious Revolution was the respectable revolution, quite different from the dark memories of the Civil War. It was respectable to base one's arguments on "Revolution principles." This clearly emerges from McKenzie's remark in an earlier article in the *S. C. Gazette:*

> In every free state, when government cannot, or will not, protect the people, they have a right to fall upon such measures as they may think conducive to their own preservation. This is a truth, founded on revolution principles, which a man need not be ashamed or afraid to avow.[17]

Here we must take leave, however, of John McKenzie, whose contribution to "the Growth of an Idea"—to use the subtitle of Thomas Adams' bibliographical study of the American Revolution—has been obscured too long. His death at an early age—33 or 34—and at an early stage of the Revolution—in 1771—seems to have cut short a remarkable, so far little noticed career. He deserves recognition as that man who indeed "advanced to a truly revolutionary position," as Schlesinger said fifty years ago mistakenly about Gadsden. And he deserves recognition as a writer who knew to find the most telling phrases in unexpected quarters—eminently conservative quarters, that is—and put them to good use. McKenzie thus deserves a rather special place in a story that has not yet been written, the story of William Blackstone's significance for American Revolutionary thought. I shall soon return to this implication of my paper.

Though we take leave of McKenzie, we do not yet leave South Carolina. McKenzie's ideas, based on "Revolution principles," had a peculiar fortune. I have mentioned before that McKenzie's and Gadsden's chief opponent, W. H. Drayton, was forced to leave for England, where he published the Charleston newspaper battle as a little book. His biographers suspect that he may have hoped to attract the attention of the British ministry to his loyalty to the Crown during the non-importation controversy, and in this effort he did have some success.[18] Without going into biographical details, we must know that Drayton returned to South Carolina and joined the Whig cause. As an ardent, though socially conservative Whig he published in August 1774 *A Letter From Freeman Of South-Carolina, To The Deputies of North-America, Assembled in the High Court of Congress At Philadelphia.* Drayton, that is, used as a Whig in 1774 the same pseudonym that he had employed as a loyalist in 1769. Though he kept his

17. *Letters of Freeman, &c.,* p. 42.
18. Dabney and Dargan, *W. H. Drayton,* p. 38.

pen-name, he adopted his erstwhile opponent's phraseology in an important particular: In a draft for a Declaration of Rights Drayton asserted: "That the Americans, are of natural right entitled, to all and singular those inherent though latent powers of Society, necessary for the safety, preservation and defence of their just claims, rights and liberties herein specified; which no contract, no constitution, no time, no *climate* can destroy or diminish."[19] The phrasing sounds familiar by now. Drayton in 1774 did what McKenzie in 1769 had avoided, in a footnote he gave credit to Blackstone; his reference is correct. It seems legitimate to conjecture, however, that Drayton, picking just these words for asserting the natural rights of Americans, may have been impressed by them when he read McKenzie's article of 1769 which he included in his collection of 1771.

The interest of Drayton's *Letter from Freeman* for our inquiry does not end here. In his defence of American rights, Drayton displayed a sensitivity for precedent which seems to me to go even beyond the major political pamphlets of 1774 and 1775. His great precedent is, of course, the respectable, the Glorious Revolution. Drayton suggested to the Deputies of the First Continental Congress about to assemble in Philadelphia a Declaration of Rights patterned on the Declaration of Rights of February,1689. Like the Declaration of 1689, Drayton's Declaration contains a catalogue of grievances, a catalogue of rights, and a catalogue of resolves.[20]

---

19. *A Letter From Freeman* . . . (Charleston, 1774), pp. 13–14.

20. Drayton patterns his formula concluding the catalogue of rights and introducing the catalogue of resolves from the document of 1689:

Decl. of Rights, 1689	Drayton, 1774
"To which demand of their rights they are particularly encouraged by the declaration of his highness the prince of Orange, as being the only means for obtaining a full redress and remedy therein."	"To which demand of their rights, they are particularly encouraged by a reliance on the Virtues of their Sovereign Lord George; convinced that this their demand, is the most peaceable means they have to obtain a full redress and remedy therein . . ."
"Having therefore an entire confidence, That his said highness the Prince of Orange will perfect the deliverance so far advanced by him, and will still preserve them from the violation of their rights, which they have here asserted, and from all other attempts upon their rights, and liberties.	"Having therefore an entire confidence, that the Crown of Great-Britain will preserve them from the Violation of their Rights, which they have here asserted; and from all other attempts upon their Rights and Liberties; the said People of America by their Deputies aforesaid, do resolve . . ."
The said lords spiritual and temporal, and commons, assembled at Westminster, do resolve . . ."	

Text of Declaration of Rights of 1689 in E. N. Williams, ed., *The Eighteenth Century Constitution* (Cambridge, 1965), p. 29; Drayton's draft in *Letter from Freeman*, p. 14.

The actual Declaration of the First Continental Congress adopted on October 14, 1774, did not go as far as Drayton in imitating the formulas of the Declaration of 1689; but the threefold pattern of grievances stated, rights declared and resolves adopted will be found in that Declaration as well, and also certain formulas like the conclusion of the catalogue of rights. Americans discussing the Declaration of the Continental Congress were aware of that pattern or precedent. John Adams in December 1774 wrote about "our bill of rights," and Joseph Galloway spoke ironically, since by February 1775 he had gone into opposition, of "this famous American bill of rights, this pillar of American liberties."[21]

But we must return once more to William Henry Drayton in South Carolina. His quest for fitting the American Revolution into the pattern of the Glorious Revolution culminated in a charge to the Grand Jury in Charleston on April 23, 1776, in his capacity of Chief Justice of the revolutionary government of South Carolina. Drayton wanted to explain "the principal causes leading to the late revolution of our government—the law upon the point—and the benefits resulting from that happy and necessary establishment."[22]

Drayton justified the revolutionary government of South Carolina in words patterned after the Resolution of Lords and Commons in Convention of February 7, 1689, declaring James' II abdication:[23]

Convention, February *1689*	Drayton, April *1776*
"King James the Second, having endeavoured to subvert the Constitution of the Kingdom, by breaking the original Contract between King and People, and, by the advice of Jesuits, and other wicked Persons, having violated the fundamental Laws, and having withdrawn himself out of this	"The king's judges in this country refused to administer justice; and the late governor, lord William Campbell, acting as the king's representative for him, and on his behalf, having endeavoured to subvert the constitution of this country, by breaking the original contract between king and people,

21. J. Adams to Edward Biddle, Dec. 12, 1774, in E. C. Burnett, ed., *Letters of Members of the Continental Congress* (Washington, 1921), I, p. 87; J. Galloway, "A Candid Examination of the Mutual Claims of Great Britain and the Colonies" in Merrill Jensen, ed., *Tracts of the American Revolution 1763–1776* (Indianapolis, 1967), p. 374.

22. This charge is reprinted in Dabney and Dargan, *W. H. Drayton*, pp. 178–92. The significance of political charges is well discussed by Ralph Lerner, "The Supreme Court as Republican Schoolmaster," in Philip B. Kurland, ed., *The Supreme Court Review* (1967), pp. 127–80, with references to Drayton pp. 132, 142, 154.

23. Blackstone, I, p. 204; Dabney and Dargan, *W. H. Drayton*, p. 183.

Kingdom, has abdicated the Government, and that the Throne is thereby become vacant." attacking the people by force of arms; having violated the fundamental laws; having carried off the great seal, and having withdrawn himself out of this colony, he abdicated the government."

Drayton himself referred to the precedent and added the indictment of James' II misdeeds from the Declaration of Rights. He went on to say that it was laid down in the best law authorities, "that protection and subjection are reciprocal; and that these reciprocal duties form the original contract between king and people." Here Drayton quite obviously referred to Blackstone's chapter "Of the King's Duties."[24] Drayton then launched into a rhetorically highly effective, point for point comparison of James' II and George's III misdeeds. The most important of these was perhaps that King James broke the original contract by not affording due protection to his subjects, although he was not charged with having seized their towns and with having held them against the people—or with having laid them in ruins by his arms—or with having seized their vessels . . . etc. etc. "But George the third hath done all those things against America; . . . wherefore if James the second broke the original contract, it is undeniable that George the third has also broken the original contract between king and people."

The punishment must fit the crime. And Drayton was after all addressing a Grand Jury. "Treating upon this great precedent in constitutional law, the learned judge Blackstone declares," so Drayton informed the Grand jury, that the result of the facts charged against James amounted "to an abdication of the government."[25] Fortified by what the "best authorities" had made "evident," Drayton now felt himself to be authorized by the law of the land to declare that George III had abdicated, that the throne was vacant, that he had "NO AUTHORITY OVER US, and WE OWE NO OBEDIENCE TO HIM."[26]

Drayton, to be sure, turned out to be a great stickler for precedent. Reading his charge to the Charleston Grand Jury in April, 1776, one gets

---

24. Blackstone, I, p. 226: ". . . it being a maxim in the law, that protection and subjection are reciprocal. And these reciprocal duties are what, I apprehend, were meant by the convention in 1688, when they declared that king James had broken the *original contract* between king and people."

25. Drayton quoted Blackstone, I, p. 205 (in the chapter "Of the King, and his Title").

26. Dabney and Dargan, *W. H. Drayton*, pp. 188–89.

the feeling that he was trying very hard indeed to live up to Blackstone's exhortation that the law of redress against public oppression went only as far as the precedent of 1689. But there are other sources to show that he was by no means alone in his reference to the precedent of 1689. An example is furnished by James Wilson's and John Dickinson's "Address to the Inhabitants of the Colonies" (February, 1776), where they attempted to prove the constitutionality of the Continental Congress on the grounds of analogy to the "assembly of the barons at Runningmede, when Magna Charta was signed, the Convention Parliament that recalled Charles II, and the Convention of Lords and Commons that placed King William on the throne." If Bernard Bailyn refers to this document as a "forceful invocation of the Lockean notion of active consent at the moment of rebellion," I would disagree with him and would say that it is an example of Blackstonian rather than Lockean, of legal or constitutional rather than philosophical reflection.[27] Locke, too, of course, was linked to the precedent of 1688/89. But there is a difference, I suggest, between the Glorious Revolution as explained or justified by Locke (disregarding the question of the actual origin of the Second Treatise—for the Revolutionaries of 1776 it *was* tied to the Glorious Revolution), and the Glorious Revolution as it was embodied in constitutional documents like the Convention's abdication resolution, or the Declaration of Rights, or even the constitutional interpretation of these documents by a man like Blackstone. My suggestion is that, on the whole, this latter way of looking at the Glorious Revolution was more important in 1775/76 than the former. I would like to mention three additional points in support of my suggestion.

In January 1775, James Wilson argued the case for resistance against England on the principle that it was not directed against the king. He invoked the constitutional principle that the king can do no wrong, that oppression sprang from the ministers of the throne, not from the throne itself. Yet Wilson added a threat: "Resistance, both by the letter and spirit of the British constitution, may be carried farther, when necessity requires

---

27. B. Bailyn, *Ideological Origins of the American Revolution* (Cambridge, MA, 1967), p. 173n. 13, quoting from *Journals of the Continental Congress*, IV, 137. Wilson seems to have been the main, if not the sole author. Cf. Journals, IV, 146, note. I also found these three precedents (Magna Charta, recall of Charles II, and placing of William III on the throne) in much the same phrasing in Wilson's speech in the Pennsylvania Convention in January 1775 [sic!]. See Robert G. McCloskey, ed., *The Works of James Wilson*, 2 vols. (Cambridge, MA, 1967), II, p. 751.

it, than I have carried it. Many examples in the English history might be adduced," Wilson continued,

> and many authorities of the greatest weight might be brought, to show, that when the king, forgetting his character and his dignity, has stepped forth, and openly avowed and taken a part in such iniquitous conduct as has been described; in such cases, indeed, the distinction above mentioned, wisely made by the constitution for the security of the crown, could not be applied; because the crown had unconstitutionally rendered the application of it impossible. What has been the consequence? The distinction between him and his ministers has been lost: but they have not been raised to his situation: he has sunk to theirs.[28]

Wilson's argument here closely resembles Blackstone's argument on redress against public oppression presented earlier, and it is most likely that by referring to "many authorities of the greatest weight" Wilson thought particularly of Blackstone.

In the same speech, Wilson referred to "the great compact between the king and his people," to an "original contract" which "to prove . . . in our constitution" was since the Revolution of 1688 "the easiest thing imaginable."[29] That illustrates my second point: The material I have examined myself as well as that assembled, for instance, by Thad Tate in his work on the "Theory of the Social Contract in the American Revolution" would seem to show that the kind of contract referred to most often, whose violation was charged most often, was the governmental contract between ruler and ruled. However, this contract is not part of Locke's system. It is, on the other hand, part of the formula the Convention of 1689 found for declaring the abdication of James II and the vacancy of the throne. And it is part of Blackstone's "official," as it were, interpretation of the Revolu-

---

28. "Speech Delivered in the Convention for the Province of Pennsylvania Held at Philadelphia, in January, 1775," *Works of James Wilson*, II, p. 758. In his law lectures in the winter of 1790/91, Wilson explicitly referred to Blackstone's interpretation of the Glorious Revolution, that it would fail as precedent if not the same conjunction of circumstances were present, and proudly added: "But we have thought, and we have acted upon revolution principles, without offering them up as sacrifices at the shrine of revolution precedents." In January 1775, however, Wilson was rather keen on suitable precedents! Wilson in 1790/91 also quoted Blackstone's passage on the "inherent, though latent powers of society" and commented: "But what does this prove? not that revolution principles are, in his opinion, recognized by the English constitution; but that the English constitution, whether considered as a law, or as a contract, cannot destroy or diminish those principles." Ibid., I, pp. 78–79.

29. Ibid., II, pp. 754, 753.

tion.[30] The Blackstonian, rather than the Lockean model of the contract and of the justification of resistance is particularly visible in Alexander Hamilton's revolutionary pamphlets of 1774 and 1775, which I am discussing elsewhere.[31]

My final point concerns Jefferson and the Declaration of Independence. Jefferson, we know, wrote an introductory catalogue of George's III misdeeds for his drafts of the Virginia Constitution, and this catalogue has actually entered the Virginia Constitution of 1776. This catalogue has been, of course, an important source for the similar catalogue in the Declaration of Independence. I shall limit myself to one single sentence in each of these lists of misdeeds. In the Virginia drafts, and in the final Constitution as well, we read: ". . . and finally, by abandoning the Helm of Government, and declaring us out of his Allegiance and Protection."[32] The verb "abandon" does not occur in the constitutional texts of 1689; it does, however, occur in Locke's second Treatise, section 219, where Locke deals with the dissolution of government in the case "when he who has the supreme executive power neglects and abandons that charge . . ."[33] In the Declaration of Independence, Jefferson does not speak of the king abandoning the helm of government. He now wrote in his "original rough draft": "he has abdicated government here, withdrawing his governors, & declaring us out of his allegiance & protection."[34] The word "abdicated" occurs, of course, in the Convention's resolution of February 7, 1689 and in

30. Thad. W. Tate, "The Theory of the Social Contract in the American Revolution 1776–1787," (Doctoral Dissertation, Brown University, 1960), p. 71, refers to W. H. Drayton's use of the precedent of 1689. Also *idem*, "The Social Contract in America, 1774–1787— Revolutionary Theory as a Conservative Instrument," *William and Mary Quarterly*, 3rd ser., XXII (July, 1965), 378. There is no reference to Drayton's use of Blackstone. An interesting passage, combining the "un-Lockean" use of the governmental contract with the newly developed "Commonwealth" Theory of the British empire is John Adams' "Novanglus" essay No. VII: "It ought to be remembered that there was a revolution here, as well as in England, and that we, as well as the people of England, made an original, express contract with King William." Charles F. Adams, ed., *Works of John Adams* (Boston, 1851), IV, p. 114.

31. Gerald Stourzh, *Alexander Hamilton and the Idea of Republican Government* (Stanford, 1970), ch. I, "'Resort to First Principles'—Blackstone, Hamilton and the Natural Right to Revolution," pp. 9–37.

32. Julian Boyd, ed., *The Papers of Thomas Jefferson* (Princeton, 1952), I, p. 339, also pp. 378, 419.

33. To this passage, in Locke's chapter on the Dissolution of Government, reference has been made by E. Dumbauld, *The Declaration of Independence and What it Means Today* (Norman, OK, 1950), p. 142n. 6; however, the section is erroneously given as 227. Dumbauld also stresses how close the Glorious Revolution was to the men of 1776. Ibid., pp. 21–22.

34. Boyd, *Papers*, I, p. 425. The final text ran as follows: "He has abdicated Government here, by declaring us out of his Protection and waging War against us." Ibid., p. 431.

the Declaration of Rights of 1689. Whatever the motives for this change, there seems to be no question that the second formulation came close to historical, constitutional precedent.

Is it permissible to speak of a "constitutional" precedent for an event which involved the dissolution of constitutional ties? Charles H. Mcllwain would seem to deny it when he said that the last *constitutional* phase of the controversy between colonies and mother country was the argument on the constitution of the empire as asserted in the Declaration of October, 1774. "Then followed revolution and the final, political, non-constitutional appeal to natural law, no longer as a part of the British constitution, but as the rights of man in general; an appeal addressed no longer to Englishmen, but to the world." [35] I do not think that it is possible to distinguish in such a clear-cut way between constitutional matters on the one hand and the "political, non-constitutional appeal to natural law." Here I would like to refer to Erich Angermann's thesis on the significance of *"ständische"* traditions of law in the Declaration of Indepedence. [36] To these traditions with their interplay of allegiance and protection, forfeiting allegiance as a result of withholding protection, no clear-cut separation of positive constitutional law and natural law is known. The best example for an area in-between these two spheres that the modern mind has separated so sharply would seem to be Blackstone's law of redress against public oppression that I have described earlier in this paper.

In conclusion I would like to make two observations. First, what I have tried to analyze in this paper is perhaps apt to supplement, though by no means to supplant the recent findings of scholars like Bernard Bailyn who, being inspired by Caroline Robbins' research on the Commonwealthmen in England, have stressed the significance of the *radical* Whig tradition for American political thought. But if a student of Bernard Bailyn, Gordon Wood, says that "for all English Whigs, Trenchard and Gordon as well as Burgh, the fundamental law they believed in was one enforceable only by the people's right of revolution," we ought to add that a conservative Whig

35. Charles H. Mcllwain, *The American Revolution, a Constitutional Interpretation* (1923, reissued Ithaca, 1958), p. 152.

36. Erich Angermann, "Ständische Rechtstraditionen in der amerikanischen Unabhängigkeitserklärung," *Historische Zeitschrift*, no. 200 (1965), 61–91. Not being available in English, this significant paper seems to have evoked little response in the United States. I am in fundamental agreement with Prof. Angermann, though I would stress the significance of 1689 perhaps more than he does. Prof. Angermann has not dealt with Blackstone and his role in the revolutionary debate.

like Blackstone *shared* this belief.[37] It may well be that for the socially conservative Whigs, Southern planters or merchants like Drayton for example, the right of revolution was made more palatable, more easily acceptable by a man like Blackstone than by James Burgh.[38]

Second, this paper should serve as a challenge to study the significance of Blackstone's work for the American Revolutionaries much more closely than has been the case so far. It is strange indeed that Edmund Burke's well-known comment in March, 1775, about the Americans' assiduous reading of Blackstone has not produced more intensive research on Blackstone's impact on the reasoning of the colonists.[39] It is strange that the vast array of subscribers, mentioned in vol. IV of the first American edition of Blackstone's *Commentaries* in 1771/72—the alphabetical list is headed by John Adams Esq. of Braintree—has not supplied a motive for looking more

37. Gordon S. Wood, *The Creation of the American Republic 1776–1787* (Chapel Hill, NC, 1969), p. 292. In an interesting recent essay, John Dunn has discounted the direct influence of Locke's Second Treatise in the colonies in favor of the writings of the radical Whigs. Here, too, the void left by reducing the effect of Locke's influence might have been partially filled by taking Blackstone's role into account, even if it was limited to the last ten to fifteen years prior to independence. "The Politics of Locke in England and America," in John W. Yolton, ed., *John Locke: Problems and Perspectives* (Cambridge, 1969), pp. 45–80, esp. p. 79.

38. James Burgh did explicitly deal with Blackstone's law of redress against public oppression in the third volume of his *Political Disquisitions,* published in London in the summer of 1775 and reprinted in Philadelphia in September, 1775. Both Burgh's radicalism (in fact thinly veiled republicanism) and his utter incapacity for legal reasoning appear in his polemic against Blackstone: "The judge says, the prudence of future times must find new remedies upon new emergencies; and afterwards adds, that we have a precedent in the Revolution of 1688, to shew what may be done if a king runs away, as James II did. Insinuating, that, if we had not such a precedent, we should not know how to proceed in such a case, and says expressly, that 'so far as this precedent leads, and nor farther, we may *now* be allowed to lay down the *law* of redress against public oppression.' Yet he says, p. 245 that 'necessity and the safety of the whole, may require the exertion of those inherent (though latent) powers of society, which no climate, no time, no constitution, no contract, can ever destroy, or diminish.' *For my part, I cannot see the use of all this hesitating, and mincing the matter* [my italics]. Why may we not say at once, that without any urgency or distress, without any provocation by oppression of government, and though the safety of the whole should not appear to be in immediate danger, if the people of a country think they should be, in any respect, happier under republican government, than monarchical, or under monarchical than republican, and find, that they can bring about a change of government, without greater inconveniences than the future advantages are likely to balance; why may we not say, that they have a sovereign, absolute, and uncontrolable right to change or new-model their government as they please?" James Burgh, *Political Disquisitions* (London, 1775), III, pp. 276–77.

39. "I hear that they have sold nearly as many of Blackstone's Commentaries in America as in England"—Burke in his speech on Conciliation with the Colonies on March 22, 1775, quoted in David A. Lockmiller, *Sir William Blackstone* (Chapel Hill, NC, 1938), p. 172. His chapter on "Blackstone in America" is too brief and general on the period prior to 1776.

deeply into this question.[40] Indeed, it must be pointed out that the Americans' use of Blackstone antedates the publication of the *Commentaries*.[41] When James Otis in the spring of 1765 explained the rights of Englishmen with reference to Blackstone, he did not, as Bernard Bailyn has supposed, refer to the *Commentaries*, but to Blackstone's earlier *An Analysis of the Laws of England*.[42] Though this paper has been concerned merely with the significance of Blackstone's interpretation of the Glorious Revolution, his exposition of the rights of Englishmen was also used as weapon by the Americans and deserves detailed examination.[43] In other words, the cliche of Blackstone's "Toryism," of his "honeyed Mansfieldism," as Jefferson put it, his championship of parliamentary sovereignty has obscured too long the fact that the "Tory" Blackstone was no Jacobite. He stood on

40. Catherine Spicer Eller, "The William Blackstone Collection in the Yale Law Library," *Yale Law Library Publications*, No. 6 (June, 1938), 37, observes that the first American edition was printed with an advance subscription of 1,587 sets and that the list of subscribers lists 839 names of individuals, libraries, and booksellers.

41. More than three years prior to the publication of the Commentaries, on January 22, 1762, John Watts of New York introduced Peter DeLancey, Jr. to a business partner in England with the observation that the young DeLancey was to study law and added: "We have a high Character of a Professor at Oxford, who they say has brought that Mysterious Business to some System, besides the System of confounding other People & picking their Pockets . . . ," "Letter Book of John Watts," in *Collections of the New York Historical Society for the Year 1928*, LXI, 13.

42. Otis' *Vindication of the British Colonies* explicitly refers to Blackstone's *Analysis* (which first was published in 1756), but the word "analysis" is not italicized or in quotation marks, and thus its significance as book title has been missed, Bailyn, *Pamphlets*, pp. 558–59. The editor's conjecture on p. 738n. 6 and 7, on Otis' reading of the *Commentaries* does not seem to be justified, the observations on p. 546 consequently need to be revised. The reference to the *Commentaries* in Bailyn, *Pamphlets*, p. 107 (and in *Ideological Origins*, p. 186) ought to be to the *Analysis*. Though the preface of the first edition of vol. I of the *Commentaries* has no date, the American edition as well as the third English edition date the preface with November 2, 1765. Though exact research about the first arrival of the *Commentaries* in the colonies is lacking, this would seem to imply that in March 1765 Otis could not have used the *Commentaries*. In fact, Otis was quoting rather precisely from *An Analysis of the Laws of England* (I used the 2nd ed. 1757), pp. 7–8 and "Table of Contents."

43. Two prominent examples should be given: Sam Adams in 1769 asserted that at the revolution (of 1689) the British constitution was again "restor'd to its original principles, declared in the bill of rights; which was afterwards pass'd into a law, and stands as a bulwark to the natural rights of subjects." And then Adams extensively quotes Blackstone on the rights of Englishmen, including the right of having and using arms for self-preservation and defense as "a public allowance, under due restrictions, of the *natural right of resistance and self preservation*, when the sanctions of society and Laws are found insufficient to restrain the *violence of oppression*," Article from the *Boston Gazette*, Febr. 27, 1769, signed "E. A.," in H. A. Cushing, ed., *The Writings of Samuel Adams* (New York, 1904), I, pp. 317–18. The reference is to Blackstone, I, pp. 140, 136, 139; the italics are Adams.' John Dickinson in June 1774 extolled the right of trial by jury with the help of an extensive quotation from Blackstone, III, pp. 378–81, "To the Inhabitants of the British Colonies in America," Letter II, in *Political Works*, I, pp. 478–80.

"revolution principles"—and that means, that he had a Whig message to convey.

Some readers may have suspected that the title of this paper has been inspired by Caroline Robbins' article on Algernon Sidney's *Discourses* as "Textbook of Revolution."[44] With the bicentennial of 1776 only a few years ahead, students of the American Revolution should pay renewed attention to the author of another "Textbook of Revolution," to a man who justified "the exertion of those inherent (though latent) powers of society, which no climate, no time, no constitution, no contract, can ever destroy or diminish."[45]

44. In the *William and Mary Quarterly*, 3rd series, IV (July 1947), pp. 267–96.

45. A further illustration of the point made in this paper is provided by a report on a "Meeting of the Body" of Boston on November 30, 1773, where Dr. Thomas Young said that he had "read in judge Blackstone that when the Laws and Constitution do not give the Subject Redress in any Grievance, that then he is in a State of Nature . . . ," L. F. S Upton, ed., "Proceedings of Ye Body Respecting the Tea," in *William and Mary Quarterly*, 3rd ser., XXII (1965), p. 293; I owe this reference to Mr. Dirk Hoerder. That Blackstone accepted the people's (revolutionary) resumption of their original right has been rightly stressed, with reference to Blackstone's passage central to this paper, in Herbert Storing's essay on Blackstone in Leo Strauss and Joseph Cropsey, eds., *History of Political Philosophy* (Chicago, 1963), p. 541.

CHAPTER THREE

Constitution:
Changing Meanings of the Term from the Early Seventeenth to the Late Eighteenth Century *

The constitution of a state, Emmerich de Vattel wrote in 1758, is the fundamental settlement that determines the manner in which public authority shall be exercised: "Le règlement fondamental qui détermine la manière dont l'autorité publique doit être exercée, est ce qui forme la *constitution de l'État.*"[1] Vattel's work, which soon became widely known in the English-speaking world as well—among its early users was James Otis in Boston—is placed, as it were, at a turning point in the significance of the word "constitution."[2] With its emphasis on the fundamental settlement of public authority, Vattel's definition reflected traditional thinking in early modern Europe, which had been informed through generations by the categories and the vocabulary of Aristotelian political science and particularly by the meaning given to the term *politeia.*[3] Yet the meaning

---

* First published in Terence Ball and J.G.A. Pocock, eds., *Conceptual Change and the Constitution*, Lawrence, KS, 1988, pp. 35–54. The permission to reprint was gracefully granted by the University Press of Kansas.

1. Emmerich de Vattel, *Le Droit des gens; ou, Principes de la loi naturelle*, ed. M. P. Pradier-Fodéré, 3 vols. (Paris, 1863), vol. 3, chap. 3, sec. 27, p. 153.

2. An English translation of the above-named work appeared, without a translator's name, under the title *Law of Nations* in London in 1759.

3. This paper is based partly on my essay *Fundamental Laws and Individual Rights in the Eighteenth Century Constitution*, Bicentennial Essay no. 5 (Claremont, CA: Claremont Institute, 1984), and it draws also on my more detailed study, available only in German, "Staatsformenlehre und Fundamentalgesetze in England und Nordamerika im 17. und 18. Jahrhundert: Zur Genese des modernen Verfassungsbegriffs," in *Herrschaftsverträge, Wahlkapitulationen, Fundamentalgesetze*, Studies Presented to the International Commission for the History of Representative and Parliamentary Institutions no. 59, ed. R. Vierhaus (Göttingen: Vandenhoeck & Ruprecht, 1977), pp. 294–328. The latter essay is reprinted under the title "Vom aristotelischen zum liberalen Verfassungsbegriff" in Gerald Stourzh, *Wege zur Grundrechtsdemokratie. Studien zur Begriffs- und Institutionengeschichte des liberalen Verfassungsstaates* (Vienna: Böhlau Verlag, 1989), pp. 1–35.

of *politeia*—as given in the most frequently referred to passage in Politics 1278 b—was for a long time rendered in English in terms other than "constitution." The earliest English version of the *Politics*, published in 1598, reads as follows: "Policy therefore is the order and description, as of other offices in a city, so of that which hath the greatest and most soveraine authority: for the rule and administration of a Commonweale, hath evermore power and authority joined with it: which administration is called policie in Greek, and in English a Commonweale." The commentary to this passage sums it up thus: "Policy is the order & disposition of the city in regard of Magistrats & specially in regard of him that hath soveraine authority over all, in whose government the whole commonweale consisteth." That was a translation from the French version of and commentary to the *Politics* by Louis Le Roy.[4] The first direct translation from Greek into English appeared in 1776. The translator, William Ellis, translated politeia by "form of government" and rendered the Aristotelian definition of *politeia* as a *taxis*, as "the ordering and regulating of the city, and all offices in it, particularly those wherein the supreme power is lodged."[5] It was not until the nineteenth century, with Benjamin Jowett's translation, that *politeia* was rendered as "a constitution," being "the arrangement of magistracies in a state, especially the highest of all."[6]

There are other indications as well that in early modern times, Aristotle-inspired political science did without the word "constitution." Englishmen of the Tudor age, applying their Aristotelian learning to England, did not speak of an English constitution. One of the best known political scientists of the Elizabethan age, Sir Thomas Smith, consciously fashioned his survey of the *republica Anglorum*, of the "manner of government or policie of the realm of England," after Aristotle. In a letter, Smith indicated that he had written his book as he conceived Aristotle's lost works about the Greek *politeiai* to have been.[7] Yet he never spoke about the

4. *Aristotle's Politiques, or discourse of government, translated out of the Greek into French, with expositions taken out of the best authors specially out of Aristotle himselfe, and Plato . . . by Loys le Roy called Regius.* Translated out of French into English (London, 1598). The translator's preface is signed I. D.; I have not yet been able to identify the translator's name. On the popularity of Le Roy's edition of the *Politics* in England see J. H. M. Salmon, *The French Religious Wars in English Political Thought* (Oxford, Eng.: Clarendon Press, 1959), pp. 24, 167.

5. Aristotle, *A Treatise of Government*, ed. A. D. Lindsay (London: Everyman Library, n.d.), p. 76.

6. Aristotle, *Politics*, trans. B. Jowett, ed. M. Lerner (New York: Modern Library, 1943), p. 136.

7. Letter dated 6 Apr. 1565, cited in Sir Thomas Smith, *De republica Anglorum: A Discourse on the Commonwealth of England*, ed. L. Alston (Cambridge, Eng.: Cambridge University Press, 1906), pp. xiiif.

constitution of England; *politeia* was variously rendered as "Common-wealth," "polity," or "government"; different kinds of *politeiai* were referred to as "kinds" or "fashions" or "forms" of commonwealths or governments. The last term, in the combination "form of government," was to be the most durable one, to last far into the late eighteenth century and the time of American constitution building. One might add, to enlarge a list of "nega-tive evidence," that the *topos* of the *metabole politeion*, which was of such importance in early modern political thinking that was inspired by the Greek political tradition, seems to have been dealt with without the help of the word "constitution." One of the most important places in which the *topos* of the *metabole politeias* or *commutatio status rei publicae* was dis-cussed—chapter 1 of book iv of Jean Bodin's *Six livres de la République*—makes no use of "constitution" at all. The English translation, done by Richard Knolles and published in 1606, speaks about the "Conversion of a Commonweale."[8] Alternative seventeenth-century terms for a *metabole politeias* are "change of government" or "alteration of government"—as used, for example, in the Rump Parliament's declaration on the reasons for changing England from a monarchy into a Commonwealth in 1649.[9]

One of the most interesting items in such a list of "negative evidence" is a document often called England's first (and only) "written constitution," the so-called Instrument of Government of 1653. Samuel R. Gardiner once referred to it as a constitution entitled "Instrument of Government";[10] that is, however, not an exact description of the document. Its official title was "The government of the Commonwealth of England, Scotland, and Ireland, and the dominions thereto belonging." "Government" is the central term, and the word "instrument" (from the Latin *instrumentum*) merely indicated "document." "Instrument of Government," then, merely meant, in contemporary parlance, the document that settled the supreme

---

8. Jean Bodin, *The Six Bookes of a Commonweale* (1606), new print, with an introduction by K. D. McRae (Cambridge, MA: Harvard University Press, 1962), pp. 406ff.

9. "Declaration of the Parliament of England, expressing the Grounds of their late Proceed-ings, and of settling the present Government in the way of a free State," dated 21 Mar. 1649, in *Parliamentary History of England*, ed. W. Cobbett (London, 1806–1820), vol. 3, cols. 1292–1303. Of great interest as an illustration of "constitutional" discourse without (and before the general acceptance of) the term "constitution" is John Pym's speech at the impeachment of Manwaring (4 June 1628), which is extensively quoted by J. G. A. Pocock in *The Machiavellian Moment: Florentine Political Thought and the Atlantic Republican Tradition* (Princeton, NJ: Princeton University Press, 1975), p. 358. Pym speaks about forms of government and their "alterations," every "alteration" being a "step and degree towards a dissolution," very much in the tradition of the *metabole politeion*.

10. S. R. Gardiner, *History of the Commonwealth and Protectorate*, vol. 2 (London, 1897), p. 291n. 1.

authority of the nation. "Instrument of Government," translated into modern parlance, means nothing other than "document of constitution" or "written constitution" (the German expression *Verfassungsurkunde* renders perhaps most precisely what "Instrument of Government" conveyed to contemporaries).[11] Let it be added, because it is little known, that the fundamental document drawn up by the Scottish estates in 1689, the "Claim of Rights" (which is analogous to the English "Declaration of Rights") was designated as an "Instrument of Government" and was published as such in the Scottish statute book.[12]

I would like to consider the significance of the term "government" during the late sixteenth and seventeenth centuries, because it is an important precursor of what "constitution" was going to mean later, in the eighteenth century. Two brief observations: First, "government" at that time had a much more inclusive meaning than merely "executive"; that restriction or reduction was to be the consequence of the breakthrough of the doctrine of separation of powers, less fully or less strictly carried out in the English-speaking world than in the German-speaking countries (*Regierung* is a

11. Of great terminological interest are contemporary references to the parliamentary debates in 1654/55 on the subject of transforming the "Instrument of Government" into an act of Parliament, jointly agreed upon by Parliament and the Lord Protector. If anything the bill under debate was a "constitutional bill," and Gardiner uses this expression (*The Constitutional Documents of the Puritan Revolution, 1625–1660*, ed. S. R. Gardiner [Oxford, Eng.: Clarendon Press, 1906; reprinted in 1968], pp. iii, 427); yet this was emphatically not a contemporary expression, which Gardiner knew. Contemporaries often simply spoke about the "Government" being debated or about the "Articles of Government." Cf. the following significant examples: Bulstrode Whitelocke, one of the eminent jurists of the Interregnum, noted in Sept. 1654 that a certain vote in Parliament had not concerned "the whole Government, consisting of Forty two Articles" (!), but only certain parts of it (*Memorials of English Affairs* . . . [London, 1682], p. 588; also ibid., p. 591; the expression "Articles of Government" ibid., pp. 587, 590). A member of Parliament, Guibon Goddard, noted on one occasion that "the Government, or Instrument of Government, might be speedily taken into consideration," and on another that "the House was free to debate the Government" (for this see *The Diary of Thomas Burton*, ed. J. T. Rutt, vol. 1 [London, 1828], pp. xxi, xxiii). Edmund Ludlow also on one occasion spoke about "the whole Government contained in the forty two Articles of the Instrument" (*Memoirs*, vol. 2 [Vevey, 1698], pp. 501f.). The bill itself, which caused these comments, was entitled "An Act declaring *and settling* the government of the Commonwealth of England, Scotland, and Ireland, and the dominions thereto belonging" (emphasis supplied; *Constitutional Documents*, pp. 427–47); of interest is the term "settling" or (as in the Act of 1701) "settlement," meaning a basic "constitutional," as one would say later, regulation of public authority. It should be added—although this anticipates the question of the emergence and the earlier uses of the word "constitution," to be sketched in the pages to follow—that the bill of 1654 on one occasion referred to "the foundation and constitution of the government of this Commonwealth" (ibid., p. 428).

12. *The Acts of the Parliaments of Scotland*, vol. 9 (n.p., 1822), pp. 40–41; also *An Account of the Proceedings of the Estates in Scotland*, ed. E. W. M. Balfour-Melville, Publications of the Scottish History Society, 3d ser., vol. 46 (Edinburgh: Scottish History Society, 1954), pp. 38–39.

narrower term than "government"; therefore the usual German translations of Locke's Treatises "of Government" with *über die Regierung* are
faulty). Second, and more important, is the place of "government" within
the tradition of political thinking inspired by Aristotelian terminology.
Fundamentally, it is the most frequently used English equivalent to a *politeia* reduced to the *politeuma*—the ruling authority. The reduction of *politeia* to *politeuma* in *Politics*, 1278 b—which is rendered in Jowett's translation as "the constitution is in fact the government"—is of importance
for early modern Aristotelian political science. A German scholar, Horst
Dreitzel, some time ago quite aptly spoke about Aristotle's "original fall"
(*der Sündenfall des Aristoteles*) in having reduced the meaning of *politeia*,
in a definition so much commented upon by early modern scholars, to *politeuma*.[13] It is of great interest, I think, that the narrowing of *politeia* to
"rule" —or to "government"—caused uneasiness to one important writer
of the Elizabethan age, Richard Hooker. In his work *The Laws of Ecclesiastical Polity*, Hooker felt moved to justify his choice of the word "polity"
rather than "government": ". . . because the name of Government, as commonly men understand it in ordinary speech, doth not comprise the large-
ness of that whereunto in this question it is applied. For when we speak of
Government, what doth the greatest part conceive thereby, but only the
exercise of superiority peculiar unto Rulers and Guides of others?"[14]
    The evidence presented so far would tend to indicate that the term
"constitution" was apparently rather a latecomer in early modern political discourse. English-speaking people began to speak of "constitution" in
connection with bodies corporate and the body politic around the turn of
the sixteenth to the seventeenth century; yet it should be said at the outset that older forms of speech, particularly those connected with "forms"
and also "frames" of government, coexisted or survived a long time, even
as people with increasing frequency began to avail themselves of the newer
term "constitution." By beginning to speak of the "constitution" of bodies corporate, Englishmen in the early seventeenth century initiated a

    13. Horst Dreitzel, *Protestantischer Aristotelismus und absoluter Staat* (Wiesbaden:
Steiner, 1970), p. 344. This is a book about the German scholar Arnisaeus. Dreitzel correctly
points out that Otto von Gierke had already drawn attention to the fact that early modern
(Aristotelian) political science understood *res publica* primarily to mean the relation between
offices and competences (*Ordnungsverhältnisse*); thus the character of *politeia* as taxis, true
to the famous passage in *Politics* 1278 b, was one-sidedly stressed (ibid., pp. 338f. n. 10, refers
to Otto von Gierke, *Das deutsche Genossenschaftsrecht*, vol. 4: *Die Staats- und Korporations-
lehre der Neuzeit* [1913; reprint, Graz: Akademische Druck- und Verlagsanstalt, 1954], p. 286).
    14. Richard Hooker, *Of the Laws of Ecclesiastical Polity*, Everyman ed., vol. 1 (London,
1907; reprint, London, 1969), p. 297.

process of conceptual development that was essentially completed during the great period of constitutional reflection in North America toward the end of the eighteenth century. (By "period of constitutional reflection" I mean the period reaching from the Stamp Act crisis through the making of the state constitutions and the federal Constitution to *Marbury v. Madison*.)

There are, I submit, two quite distinct roots of applying the word "constitution" to the sphere of government (in the largest sense). The first, and by far the more important one, is to be found in the application of analogies from nature to politics, or, to be more precise, in the transfer to bodies corporate or political of a term that is usually applied to the physical body. The second root is to be found in the rise in importance, around the middle of the seventeenth century of the legal term "constitutions" (always used in the plural form), which ultimately can be traced back to the *constitutiones* of Roman and canon law.

Now, in greater detail to the first and, I would stress, more important area of origin of "constitution": In 1602 the jurist William Fulbecke observed, "Corporations in the whole course *and constitution of them* doe verie much resemble the naturall bodie of man." [15] The venerable topic of analogies between medicine and politics, between the medical healer and the statesman, found systematic treatment in Edward Forset's book *A comparative Discourse of the Bodies natural and politique*, in which he stated that as "the bodies constitution is thought perfect and at the height" at a certain time of life, similarly the state also "hath such a time, of his good estate." As in medicine, so it was important in politics "exactly to know the constitution and complexion of the bodie politique" before applying the appropriate remedies.[16] The question arises as to whether the doctrine of the "King's two Bodies" might have given occasion to formulate similar analogies, yet my inspection of Ernst H. Kantorowicz's book has yielded only one text, of 1561, that refers to the body politic as "a Body that cannot be seen or handled, consisting of Policy and Government, and constituted for the Direction of the People, and the Management of the public weal." [17]

The most interesting "discovery" tracing early uses of "constitution" in

15. William Fulbecke, *The Pandectes of the law of Nations: contayning severall discourses of the questions, points and matters of Law, wherein the Nations of the world doe consent and accord* (London, 1602), p. 52 (emphasis supplied).

16. Edward Forset, *A comparative Discourse of the Bodies natural and politique* (London, 1606), pp. 60, 78.

17. Ernst H. Kantorowicz, *The King's Two Bodies* (Princeton, NJ: Princeton University Press, 1957), p. 7, citing the case of the duchy of Lancaster from Edmund Plowden's *Commentaries or Reports* (London, 1816), p. 212a.

connection with bodies corporate, concerns the use of "constitution" with reference to the Church of England. First in 1592—and not earlier, as far as I can see, in spite of careful search—Henry Barrow, the separatist who was to be executed in 1593, summed up his critique of the Church of England with the statement that its "constitution" was faulty. One of his chief criticisms was aimed at the unchristian composition of the parishes of the Church of England, and thus he denounced the "antichristian constitution of your churches," the important question being that of "the true constituted church," a frequently recurring expression. Barrow raised the question of "the orderly gathering of those parishes at any time into true constitution." In his denunciation of falsely constituted churches, Barrow included *a fortiori* the Church of Rome, asking whether "the publike constitution of the church of Rome in the people, ministrie, ministration, worship, government, etc. be according to the ordinanse of Christ or of Antichrist." [18]

From then on, the notion of the true or false constitution of the Church of Christ played a considerable role in separatist writings and documents. "This false and Anti-christian constitution" of the Church of England was accused in a separatist document of 1596, "A True Confession of the Faith." Anglican writers, in polemical writings against the separatists, took up the issue of "constitution." In 1608 the Anglican writer Richard Bernard took the separatists to task for paying more attention to the church's constitution than to the word of God. Bernard rather ridiculed the word constitution, which was so important to the separatists. What was "lesse talked on any where," in the New Testament, "then [*sic*] a constitution?" "Christ never condemned such as spake the truth in his name, for want of

---

18. The references cited occur in Barrow's comments on an Anglican tract by H. Gifford, *A Short Reply unto the Last Printed Books of Henry Barrow and John Greenwood . . .* , published December 1591. One exemplar of this book, with Barrow's handwritten marginal notes containing most of his references to "constitution," is in the University Library, Cambridge, England, sign Bb.11.29, where I inspected it. These marginal notes have also been edited in *The Writings of John Greenwood and Henry Barrow, 1591–1593,* ed. Leland H. Carlson (London: Allen & Unwin, 1970), pp. 127ff.; for the passages quoted here see pp. 145, 162, 168, 172; see also pp. 129, 134, 137, 173, 176, 177, 182, 191, 192. Cf. also, apparently in time somewhat preceding these marginal notes, Barrow's "A Few Observations to the Reader of Mr. Giffard [*sic*] his last Replie," ibid., pp. 93ff., here p. 126. Barrow's use of "true constitution" aims at the rightly composed church; his new term "true constitution" is close to meaning true composition. It is of interest that in Barrow's voluminous main work, *A Brief Discoverie of the False Church* (1590), the term "constitution" is not yet applied; there is a long disquisition on the church as the body of Christ, yet no use of the term "constitution," although in another part of that book there is a reference to "cunning physicians" who "wil verie soone espie the constitution and inclination of their patientes" (see *The Writings of Henry Barrow, 1587–1590,* ed. Leland H. Carlson [London: Allen & Unwin, 1967], pp. 586–90: "his church compared to an humane body"; p. 492: "cunning physicians").

a constitution." Bernard reproached the separatists for not having defined "this constitution." He poured further scorn and ridicule on them: "Thus like nimble Squirrels, they skip from one tree to another, to save themselves from being taken: name corruptions, they skippe to constitution: tell them of constitution, they will tell you of corruption." Bernard, countering separatist criticism that the constitution of the Church of England was an idol, now charged the separatists with making "an idoll of their owne Constitution"; sarcastically Bernard reminds his readers of another idol, the goddess Diana at Ephesus; "great is the Goddess Constitution, great is *Diana* of the Brownists."[19]

Bernard was answered by several separatists; one of them was John Smyth, who had just split away in the direction of adult baptism.[20] Another one was John Robinson, the minister of the Leyden congregation and hence of the Pilgrims prior to their departure for America.[21] The most interesting separatist writer, however, was Henry Ainsworth, a minister in Amsterdam, who did indeed meet Bernard's challenge by giving a definition of "constitution," thus demonstrating, incidentally, that he knew his Aristotle well:

> But as the constitution of a commonwealth or of a citie is a gathering and uniting of people togither [*sic*] into a civill politie: so the Constitution of the commonwealth of Israel (as the church is called) and of the citie of God the new *Jerusalem*, is a gathering and uniting of people into a divine politie: the form of which politie is Order, as the hethens [sic] acknowledged, calling politie an order of a citie.

In the margin, Ainsworth carefully supplied the reference to book III of the *Politics*: τάξιν τῆς πόλεως[22] Replying in his turn to Ainsworth, the

---

19. *A True Confession of the Faith* . . . (facsimile reprint, Amsterdam: Da Capo Press, 1969), p. C 1 verso; Richard Bernard, *Christian advertisements and counsels of peace; also dissuasions from the Separatists schisme, commonly called Brownisme* . . . (London, 1608), exemplar inspected in the library of Emmanuel College, Cambridge, sign 9.5.92, passages quoted on pp. 54, 62, 69, 79–80.

20. *The Works of John Smyth*, ed. W. T. Whitley, 2 vols. (Cambridge, Eng.: Cambridge University Press, 1915), vol. 1, p. xcvii and esp. vol. 2, "Parallels, Censures, Observations" . . . pp. 338–53, 375, 376, 377, 464, 476f.; "The Character of the Beast, or The False Constitution of the Church" (also 1609), esp. pp. 565f.

21. *The Works of John Robinson*, ed. Robert Ashton, 3 vols. (London, 1851), esp. "Mr. Bernard's Reasons against Separation discussed," vol. 2, pp. 120, 355; also of interest p. 140: "the visible church being a polity ecclesiastical, and the perfection of all polities"; also vol. 3, p. 407: Robinson's "Answer to 'a Censorious Epistle,'" a letter by Joseph Hall.

22. H. A. [Henry Ainsworth], *Counterpoyson* (n.p., 1608), pp. 169–70.

Anglican writer Bishop Joseph Hall noted that the separatists used a new term: whether "Physicke, or Lawe, or Architecture" had lent it to the separatists, no one had used that term as "scrupulously" as the separatists. "It is no treason to coyne tearmes: What then is Constitution?"[23]

To his reference to the classic passage from the *Politics*, Ainsworth had added that this order (taxis) "is requisite in all actions and administrations of the church, as the Apostle sheweth, and specially in the constitution thereof." The matter of the constitution of a church was its people: the form was the people's "calling, gathering and uniting togither." It is apparent that Ainsworth had some difficulties with his attempt to fit the separatists' conception of constitution, which very much included the people as its central element, into a definition of polity that stressed the organizational aspect—the aspect of *taxis*, of offices and magistracies, of "government."

The separatists'—or, rather, Ainsworth's—attempt to integrate the word "constitution" with the discourse on *politeia* anticipated a development that in the realm of political and constitutional discourse occurred more slowly and haltingly. In political and constitutional discourse during the first half of the seventeenth century the notion of "constitution" as "disposition," as a "quality" of the body politic in analogy to the body physical, prevails; and it survives well into the eighteenth century. A few telling examples ought to be given.

In 1607 the legal dictionary of John Cowell refers to "the nature and constitution of an absolute monarchy," with "nature" and "constitution" meaning basically the same thing—namely, disposition or quality (the German word *Beschaffenheit* very precisely renders what was meant by constitution in that context).[24] An extraordinary piece of writing appeared in 1643, by an as-yet-unknown author: *Touching the Fundamental Laws, or Politique Constitution of this Kingdome.* About the author it has been said that he was "one of the half dozen clearest and most profound thinkers supporting the claims of parliament during the civil war."[25] The author ar-

23. J. H. [Joseph Hall], *A Common Apology of the Church of England against the unjust challenges of the over-just sect, commonly called Brownists* . . . (n.p., 1610), p. 21 (in sec. viii, entitled "Constitution of a Church," he comments that "Constitution is the very state of Brownisme"). It is in this work that the *Oxford English Dictionary* thinks it finds the earliest use of "constitution" as "mode in which state is constituted," citing the "constitution of the Commonwealth of Israel"; yet Hall was using this expression by merely quoting it from Ainsworth's preceding "Counterpoyson."

24. John Cowell, *The Interpreter: or Booke containing the Signification of Words* . . . (Cambridge, Eng., 1607; no pagination); the words cited occur in the entry on "Parliament."

25. Margaret A. Judson, *The Crisis of the Constitution* (New Brunswick, NJ: Rutgers University Press, 1949; reprint, New York: Octagon Press, 1964), p. 413. The pamphlet *Touching*

gued against contractual models of the fundamental Laws of the kingdom. "Fundamentall Laws then are not things of capitulation between King and people, as if they were Forrainers and Strangers one to another"; instead, fundamental Laws were *"things of constitution"* (emphasis supplied). Fundamental laws give both king and subjects "existence and being as Head and Members, which constitution in the very being of it is a Law held forth with more evidence, and written in the very heart of the Republique, far firmlier than can be by pen and paper."

An interesting text, for our purposes, is a book published in 1649 by Nathaniel Bacon, an antiroyalist writer, entitled *A Historical and Political Discourse of the Laws and Government of England from the first Times to the End of the Reign of Queen Elizabeth.* Bacon, applying the celebrated topic of return to first principles, quite directly points to the medical analogy of original health: "For as in all other cures, so in that of a distempered Government, the Original Constitution of the Body is not lightly to be regarded." Note that Bacon almost constantly uses the traditional term "government" for what we would today call "constitution," and he uses "constitution" in the sense of "disposition" or "quality." This emerges very clearly when Bacon, toward the end of his work, sets out to contemplate "the natural Constitution of the People of England": northern melancholy and the choleric temper of the southern peoples meet in England, "in their general Constitution," and make the English "ingenious and active." [26]

A marvelous instance of this kind of thinking is found in an essay from Virginia. In *An Essay upon the Government of the English Plantations on the Continent of America* (1701), the author, perhaps Robert Beverly, wrote that the air and the climate of these colonies were most agreeable for "Constitutions of Body"—the most important thing lacking to make the colonists happy was a "good Constitution of Government." [27] Even at a time when the meaning of constitution has arrived at our modern understanding—at the time of the debate on the federal Constitution in 1787/88—the old analogy crops up again, in Madison's Federalist

---

the Fundamental Lawes, or Politique Constitution of this Kingdome . . . (London, 1643; exemplar inspected in the British Library, London, E.90 [21]), passages cited are on pp. 3–4; anticipating Jowett's terminology: "The outward constitution or polity of a Republick," ibid., p. 5. The thinker that comes closest to the thoughts expressed in this piece seems to me to be Henry Parker, yet this would need further investigation.

26. I used the fourth edition, London, 1739; the passages cited are on pp. iii and 174.

27. *An Essay upon the Government of the English Plantations on the Continent of America,* ed. Louis B. Wright (San Marino, Calif.: Huntington Library, 1945), p. 16.

number 38, where the prescriptions to improve (or poison) a patient's constitution are compared with the advice on the proposed (political) constitution for the United States.[28]

The application of "constitution" to the body politic of the state without
explicit reference to "nature," with the original analogy to the constitution
of the body physical receding into the background and finally to be quite forgotten, sets in about 1610. The parliamentary debate on the "Impositions"
of James I provided the occasion. William Hakewill warned that impositions that were imposed upon the people without the consent of Parliament
would lead to the "utter dissolution and destruction of that politic frame
and constitution of this commonwealth." He was soon followed by the famous jurist James Whitelocke, who said that the royal decision on impositions was "against the natural frame and constitution of the policy of this
kingdom, which is ius publicum regni, and so subverteth the fundamental
law of the realm and induceth a new form of State and government." [29]

Many years ago, Charles Howard McIlwain referred to the just cited
passage by Whitelocke as the first "modern" use of the term "constitution" known to him. After 1610, McIlwain added, the use of the term had
become so frequent that additional references were not necessary.[30] Because I do not quite agree, I would like to make two comments.

First, keeping in mind the profoundly "constitutional" character of
the conflict between the monarchs and the Commons in the twenties and
thirties of the seventeenth century (think of the Shipmoney case), one is
rather surprised to see that the notion of "constitution" does not occur so
frequently. It does occur on important occasions, however, and in a context that was gaining in political significance—namely, the context of
original health and goodness. In 1626, John Pym pointed to "the ancient
and fundamental law, issuing from the first frame and constitution of the
kingdom." A few weeks later, the Remonstrance of the Commons against
tonnage and poundage referred to "the most ancient and original constitution of this kingdom." [31] It was not until the 1640s that the frequency

28. *The Federalist*, ed. Jacob E. Cooke (Middletown, CT: Wesleyan University Press, 1961),
no. 38, p. 243.

29. J. R. Tanner, *Constitutional Documents of the Reign of James I* (1930; reprint, Cambridge, Eng.: Cambridge University Press, 1961), pp. 253, 260.

30. Charles H. McIlwain, "Some Illustrations of the Influence of Unchanged Names for
Changing Institutions," in *Interpretations of Modern Legal Philosophies: Essays in Honor of
Roscoe Pound*, ed. P. Sayre (New York: Oxford University Press, 1947), pp. 484–97.

31. Pym's speech, which is referred to by J. G. A. Pocock (see above, n. 9), is in *The Stuart
Constitution*, ed. J. P. Kenyon (Cambridge, Eng.: Cambridge University Press, 1966), pp. 16–17.
The remonstrance is in Gardiner, *Constitutional Documents*, p. 71. The passage quoted from

in use increased noticeably, particularly after the publication of the well-known *His Majesties Answer to the XIX Propositions of . . . Parliament.* Here the "Ancient, Equall, Happy, Well-poysed and never enough Commended Constitution of the Government of this Kingdom" was praised; in another passage, more briefly, the "Constitution of this Kingdom."[32] This progress within the same writing to a kind of shorthand expression is of interest, because it indicates the way in which the common usage was to develop. One would speak of the "constitution of government," but time and again, and ultimately more or less regularly, "of government" would be dropped, because everybody knew that "constitution" referred to government.[33]

Second, commenting again on McIlwain, I would like to stress that it was a long time before the term "constitution" emerged in documents of a publicly binding character. We have previously seen how the debates on England's first and only "written constitution," the so-called Instrument of Government, took place in an older and more traditional sphere of speech. Among republican writers during the Interregnum, there was a search for a new "constitution" in the writings of Sir Henry Vane,[34] and James Harrington rather systematically distinguished between the "institution" and the "constitution" of government.[35] During the Restoration, the Tory writer Roger North noted that the word "constitution" was more

the remonstrance is an early example of referring to the ancient constitution, a term of rarer occurrence than might be supposed in view of J. G. A. Pocock's book on the ancient constitution and the feudal law. In the reissue of this work, Pocock concedes in his "Retrospect from 1986" that the term "constitution" as used in his book had not been systematically cleared of anachronism and that there was a time when it was more usual to speak of "the laws" as "ancient" (*The Ancient Constitution and the Feudal Law: A Study of English Historical Thought in the Seventeenth Century: A Reissue with a Retrospect* [Cambridge, Eng.: Cambridge University Press, 1987], p. 261).

32. *His Majesties Answer* is republished as an appendix in Corinne C. Weston, *English Constitutional Theory and the House of Lords, 1556–1832* (London: Routledge & Kegan Paul, 1965), pp. 263ff., here pp. 270, 272; see also Michael Mendle, *Mixed Government, the Estates of the Realm, and the "Answer to the XIX propositions"* (University: University of Alabama Press, 1985).

33. There are queries about "a new constitution" or "this constitution," quite "modern" sounding, in the Putney and Whitehall debates of 1647 and 1648/49 respectively (see *Puritanism and Liberty*, ed. A. S. P Woodhouse [Chicago: University of Chicago Press, 1951], esp. pp. 128, 136, and [chiefly Ireton in Putney] pp. 70f., 78f., 80, 88f., 91, 110f., 120f.).

34. On him and other writers see Michael Weinzierl, "Republikanische Politik und republikanische politische Theorie in England, 1658–1660" (Doctoral diss., University of Vienna, 1974), esp. pp. 43f.

35. *The Political Works of James Harrington*, ed. J. G. A. Pocock (Cambridge, Eng.: Cambridge University Press, 1977), p. 230; cf. also ibid., p. 179, when Harrington, comparing the monarchical and popular forms of government, adds, referring to the latter: "for which kind

frequently supplanting older expressions such as "the Laws of this Kingdom, his Majesty's Laws, the Laws of the Land"; North commented that
the word "constitution" was usually presented "with a republican face."[36]
It was not until the Glorious Revolution that the term "constitution" was
used in a fundamental act of state. In the resolution of the convention that
declared the "abdication" of James II and the vacancy of the throne, James
was charged with having attempted "to subvert the constitution of the
kingdom."[37] From then on—that is, from the time of the Glorious Revolution—the golden age of the "British Constitution" must be dated. *The British Constitution: or, the Fundamental Form of Government in Britain* is
the title of a book praising that constitution, which appeared in London in
1727. Soon, in 1733, Bolingbroke would explain:

> By constitution we mean, whenever we speak with propriety and ex-
> actness, that assemblage of laws, institutions and customs, derived
> from certain fixed principles of reason, directed to certain fixed ob-
> jects of public good, that compose the general system, according to
> which the community hath agreed to be governed. . . . We call this a
> good government, when . . . the whole administration of public affairs
> is wisely pursued, and with a strict conformity to the principles and
> objects of the constitution.[38]

Finally, in 1748, the publication of Montesquieu's *De l'Esprit des Lois*
spread the reputation of the constitution of a free state, that of England, to
the reading public of the civilized word.

Yet we must go back, once more, to some other beginning, to other
rather curious roots. Quite apart from the meaning of constitution as the
disposition of the body natural or politic, the legal term *constitutio* had
existed and survived from Roman times. That term, in the civil law, had
referred to imperial decrees. In canon law, too, it was used in the sense of
(fixed) law, or regulations.[39] In medieval and even early modern English

of constitution I have something more to say than Leviathan hath said or ever will be able to
say for monarchy."
   36. Quoted by Weston, *English Constitutional Theory,* pp 99–100.
   37. Quoted in William Blackstone, *Commentaries on the Laws of England*, vol. 1 (Oxford,
1765), p. 204.
   38. A Dissertation upon Parties, in *The Works of Lord Bolingbroke*, vol. 2 (1851), p. 88.
   39. E.g., William of Lyndwood's collection of the *constitutiones* of the ecclesiastical province of Canterbury: *Constitutiones provinciales, or Provinciale, seu Constitutiones Angliae*,
in many editions (I inspected the edition of Oxford, 1679); in 1604 there appeared the collec-

law, the term referred to specific written regulations, as opposed to custom or convention. In medieval and early modern times, the term was usually referred to in the plural form, designating a series or collection of regulations passed at a particular time or referring to a particular object. With the rise of the term "statute" to indicate a law that had duly been passed by the king in parliament, the term "constitution(s)" was reduced to refer to regulations of a lower, often local, rank.[40] Yet, during the crisis of the mid-seventeenth century in England, the plural term "constitutions" rose from its inferior position, to which it had sunk in the later Middle Ages, and was wedded to the word "fundamental"—taken from the expression "fundamental laws," which was first documented in England toward the end of the sixteenth century and rose to great significance during the indeed fundamental constitutional crises of the seventeenth century.[41]

The "upgrading" of "constitutions"—plural form—starts in the early seventeenth century. Forset spoke in 1606 about "original constitutions," and in 1625, Sir Robert Phelips said in the Commons: "Wee are the last monarchy in Christendome that retayne our originall rightes and constitutions." [42] In 1640 the expression "fundamental constitutions" emerged in a famous antiroyalist tract, Henry Parker's *The Case of Shipmoney briefly discoursed*. In what I think is a rather magnificent expression, it said that "by the true fundamental constitutions of England, the beame hangs even between the King and the Subject." [43] In the trial of King Charles I for high treason in 1649, Charles was accused of having subverted the "fundamen-

---

tion of post-Reformation English ecclesiastical law under the title "Constitutions and Canons Ecclesiastical."

40. Examples: a statute of the first years of Elizabeth I was entitled "An Acte towching certayne Politique Constitutions made for the maintenance of the Navye," in *Statutes of the Realm*, ed. A. Luders (London, 1810–1828), vol. 4, pt. 1, pp. 422–28. In 1601, Thomas Wilson wrote that in cities and boroughs it was the task of the mayor "to make a lawe and constitutions for the benefit of the Citty, which must be confirmed by Common Counsell" (*The State of England anno Domini 1600*, ed. F. J. Fisher, Camden Miscellany no. 16 [London: Camden Society, 1936], p. 21). In 1610 a member of Parliament said that the king, by his letters patent, may incorporate a town, city, or company of merchants, "*and give them Power to make constitutions and by-laws for the better order and government of the same*" (emphasis supplied; in *Proceedings in Parliament 1610*, ed. E. R. Foster, vol. 2 [New Haven, CT.: Yale University Press, 1966], p. 193).

41. The expression "fundamental laws," which apparently originated in France in the 1570s, is first documented in England in Francis Bacon's Epistle Dedicatory to his "Maxims of the Law" (8 Jan. 1596 old style; see J. W. Gough, *Fundamental Law in English Constitutional History* [Oxford, Eng.: Clarendon Press, 1955], p. 51).

42. Forset, *Comparative discourse*, p. 63. Phelips is quoted by G. A. Ritter in "Divine Right und Prärogative der englischen Könige 1603–1640," *Historische Zeitschrift* 196 (1963): 613.

43. Published in London in 1640, p. 7.

tal constitutions" of the kingdom, yet it was not specified what these fundamental constitutions, or any single one of them, actually were.[44]

In North American history, the plural term "constitutions" plays no negligible role during the early colonial period. "Constitutions"—in the generic sense of regulations or rules—are mentioned in several colonial documents and collections or compilations of laws.[45] On the higher level of the "fundamental constitutions," let us look at two well-known documents. John Locke drafted the "Fundamental Constitutions of Carolina," 120 of them. In the last of these constitutions, he said: "These Fundamental Constitutions, in number a hundred and twenty, and every part thereof, shall be and remain the sacred and unalterable form and rule of Carolina forever."[46] A few years later, William Penn drafted twenty-four "Fundamental Constitutions" for Pennsylvania. Penn's Preamble to them is of interest for the history of constitutional terminology, since he uses the term "constitution" in both the singular and the plural forms.[47] The form "fundamental constitutions" was, however, relatively short-lived: one encounters it during about four decades after 1640, yet it did not survive into the eighteenth century.

There is, however, in the eighteenth-century colonies a not-infrequent reference to the "constitution" of a colony—a long time before the constitutional disputes with the mother country of the 1760s and the early 1770s. The meaning on the whole is analogous to that used in Britain—namely, to the complex of government, but not yet to one specific document. There is a text from Virginia from 1736; there is an interesting essay by Cadwallader Colden from 1744/45, dealing with the constitution of the colony of New York; and there are various references in Massachusetts. Thomas Hutchinson says in his *History* that because every year from 1749 to 1766 he had been on the Council of the Province, he had had "sufficient opportunity to acquaint himself with the constitution and publick affairs of the province."[48] No doubt an additional and systematic search through

44. Gardiner, *Constitutional Documents*, p. 372.

45. These are only a few of several illustrations available: reference to "the framing of their Politique Constitutions" is in *Records of the Colony of New Plymouth in New England*, ed. D. Pulsifer, vol. 11 (Boston, 1861), p. 21; ". . . the said Laws, Constitutions and Punishments . . ." is in *Records of the Colony of Rhode Island and Providence Plantations, in New England*, vol. 1 (Providence, RI, 1856), p. 145.

46. *The Works of John Locke*, 8th ed. (London, 1777), vol. 4, pp. 519–37.

47. *The Papers of William Penn*, ed. Richard S. Dunn and Mary Maples Dunn, vol. 2 (Philadelphia: University of Pennsylvania Press, 1982), p. 142.

48. For Virginia see a speech by Sir John Randolph after his reelection as Speaker of the House of Burgesses in 1736, which already seems to include a reference to a written document

colonial records, notably of the eighteenth century, would reveal further pertinent materials.

What changed and what was new during the American Revolution and as a result of the Revolution? Documents of the "period of constitutional reflection" from the early sixties down to *Marbury v. Madison* abound and are well known. I shall only stress the following five points, which I believe to be of particular interest for a history of the changing meanings of our term.

1. A heightened awareness of the differences, or even cleavages, between laws and the underlying constitution developed because of conflicts such as the Writs of Assistance case in Boston and, above all, the Stamp Act crisis. The word "unconstitutional," which was apparently first used by Bolingbroke, yet was rarely and uncommonly used for about three decades, suddenly mushroomed as a result of the Stamp Act crisis. I have shown, in an earlier publication in German, how the use of the word "unconstitutional" suddenly spread in North America, once it had first been used in 1764/65 in Rhode Island.[49] Theoretical awareness that the legislators were inferior to the constitution and not, as traditional early modern political theory from Jean Bodin to Sir William Blackstone had it, "sovereign," was greatly helped by the clear expression of this relation of subordination by Emmerich de Vattel. Vattel was the first to clarify an ambiguity that had been left by Locke. Locke had variously used the concept of "supreme power"—he preferred these English words to the term "sovereignty"; "supreme power," as used by Locke, applied both to the legislative power and to that power that "remained in the people." Seventy years later, Vattel

---

with the meaning of "constitution," to what he calls the "charter" of 1621, officially entitled "An Ordinance and Constitution of the Treasurer, Council and Company" in England; Randolph also still used the older plural form "constitutions," meaning a plurality of rules (see *American Colonial Documents to 1776*, ed. Merrill Jensen [London: Oxford University Press, 1955], pp. 268–71); for New York see Cadwallader Colden's essay "Observations on the Balance of Power in Government" (1744/45), in which he argues that "Our Constitution of Government" was nearly the "same with that which the People of England value so much" and proceeds to give a description of the "proper Ballance" of that constitution (see Jack P. Greene, ed., *Great Britain and the American Colonies, 1606–1763* [New York: Harper & Row, 1970], pp. 252ff.). For Massachusetts see Thomas Hutchinson, *The History of the Colony and Province of Massachusetts Bay*, ed. L. S. Mayo, vol. 3 (Cambridge, MA: Harvard University Press, 1936; reprint, Kraus, 1970), p. 184 and passim.

49. For details see Gerald Stourzh, *Vom Widerstandsrecht zur Verfassungsgerichtsbarkeit: Das Problem der Verfassungswidrigkeit im 18. Jahrhundert*, Collection of the Institute for European and Comparative Legal History of the Law Faculty of the University of Graz, no. 6, ed. B. Sutter (Graz: Institut für Europäische und Vergleichende Rechtsgeschichte der Universität, 1974), p. 37. Reprinted in the author's volume *Wege zur Grundrechtsdemokratie* (Vienna: Böhlau Verlag, 1989), pp. 37–74.

clearly distinguished between the constitution and the legislative power, which depended on the former and was inferior to it. Vattel wrote—as quoted by James Otis in 1764: "For the constitution of the state ought to be fixed; and since that was first established by the nation, which afterwards trusted certain persons with the legislative power, the fundamental laws are excepted from their commission." Even clearer is the sentence that immediately follows, which I do not quote from Otis, but which I give in the original French: "Enfin, c'est de la constitution que ces législateurs tiennent leur pouvoir, comment pourraient-ils la changer, sans détruire le fondement de leur autorité."[50] Let it be added that there is an extraordinary similarity (which Edward Corwin noted many years ago) between Vattel and the Massachusetts Circular Letter of 1768, which said: "That in all free States the Constitution is fixed; & as the supreme Legislative derives its Power & Authority from the Constitution, it cannot overleap the Bounds of it, without destroying its own foundation."[51]

2. As a result of the feeling of oppression, the Americans, after independence, were keenly aware that they wanted protection against "encroachments" on the part of the rulers, be they legislative or executive. The most telling expression of this wish, which again is well known but essential to the story that I outline in this paper, is to be found in the resolves of the Concord, Massachusetts, town meeting of 21 October 1776: "[W]e Conceive that a Constitution in its Proper Idea intends a System of Principles Established to Secure the Subject in the Possession and enjoyment of their Rights and Priviliges, against any Encroachments of the Governing Part."[52] A result of this feeling has been the entrenchment of individual rights—themselves a heritage of the English tradition, of the rights of freeborn Englishmen!—in the Bills of Rights (first in Virginia), in state constitutions (both in the organizational parts of these constitutions and in their Bills of Rights), and finally in the Bill of Rights of the United States Constitution, as amended by Amendments I through X (and later, above all, XIV). In this chapter, I shall not dwell on this often-commented-upon development, yet it should be stressed that this process of *constitutionalizing* human rights, including what German scholars

50. Bernard Bailyn, ed., *Pamphlets of the American Revolution*, vol. I (Cambridge, MA: Harvard University Press, 1965), p. 476; Vattel, (supra n.1), vol. III, § 34, p. 168.

51. Henry Steele Commager, ed., *Documents of American History*, vol. I (New York: Appleton-Century-Crofts, 7th ed., 1963), p. 66; also, Edward Corwin, *The "Higher Law" Background of American Constitutional Law* (Ithaca, NY: Cornell University Press, 1955), p. 79.

52. Oscar Handlin and Mary F. Handlin, eds., *The Popular Sources of Political Authority* (Cambridge, MA: Belknap Press of Harvard University Press, 1966), p. 153.

have called *Positivierung des Naturrechts*, is one of the great innovations of North American constitutionalism; it has had world-wide consequences which have reached far down into the twentieth century and our own days (Canadian constitutional development is a case in point).[53]

3. Briefly I would like to point to the fact, yet to be systematically explored, that not merely the state constitutions, but the Articles of Confederation as well, were considered to be and were called a Constitution. Montesquieu, in his chapter on the federation of republics as a means to provide for external security, spoke about "une manière de constitution qui a tous les avantages interieurs du gouvernement républicain, et la force extérieure du monarchique . . . la république fédérative." In a chapter heading he also spoke about the "constitution fédérale."[54] Thus it may not be too surprising to encounter various references to the Articles of Confederation, such as Madison's letter to Monroe in August 1785 on trying to include the regulation of trade in the "foederal Constitution." George Washington also referred in the same year to "the Constitution."[55] The task of 1787, then, grew out of the efforts to strengthen a "constitution" that already existed, though that effort was very quickly to take on the form of drafting a new federal Constitution.

4. Well known and hardly in need of comment is the growth of "written constitutions" on the state level and subsequently on the federal level.

53. Cf. Stourzh, *Fundamental Laws*, pp. 11–12.

54. *De l'Esprit de Lois*, bk. 9, chaps. 1 and 2.

55. As early as 2 Jan. 1775, Silas Deane wrote that if one general Congress had caused the colonies to be associated with each other, "another one may effect a lasting Confederation which will need nothing, perhaps, but time, to mature it into a complete & perfect American Constitution, the only proper one for Us, whether connected with Great Britain or not" (emphasis supplied); cited by Jack N. Rakove in *The Beginnings of National Politics* (New York: Knopf, 1979), pp. 141ff. Madison to Monroe, 7 Aug. 1785, in *The Papers of James Madison*, ed. R. A. Rutland, vol. 8 (Charlottesville: University of Virginia Press, 1973), p. 333; Washington to McHenry, Aug. 1785, in *The Writings of George Washington*, ed. J. C. Fitzpatrick, vol. 28 (Washington, DC: U.S. Government Printing Office, 1938), pp. 228f. Of great conceptual interest in this context is Madison's usage of the term "constitution" both in his "Notes on Ancient and Modern Confederacies" and in his "Vices of the Political System of the United States." In the former piece, Madison noted explicitly the "Vices of the Constitution" of the Amphyctionic Confederacy, of the Achaean Confederacy, of the Helvetic Confederacy, of the Belgic Confederacy, and of the Germanic Confederacy. Cf. *The Papers of James Madison*, ed. W. T. Hutchinson, Robert A. Rutland, et al., vol. 9 (Chicago: University of Chicago Press, 1975), pp. 6, 8, 11, 16, 22. In the "Vices of the Political System of the United States" (Apr. 1787), point 7, Madison noted: "A sanction is essential to the idea of law, as coercion is to that of Government. The federal system being destitute of both, wants the great vital principles of a *Political Constitution. Under the form of such a constitution*, it is in fact nothing more than a treaty of amity of commerce and of alliance, between independent and Sovereign States" (emphasis added), ibid., p. 351.

The wish to assemble in one document the fundamental rules of government, assigning distinct powers and competences to the various organs or
"branches," was a result of the conflict with England as well as the tradition of written basic documents from colonial times. The latter is illustrated by the fact that both Rhode Island and Connecticut retained their
colonial Charters well into the nineteenth century. It might be advisable
to refer to constitutions that assemble all important provisions of the powers of government, separation of the branches, and the protection of individual rights in one document as *documentary* constitutions, as James
Bryce suggested more than one hundred years ago.[56] That clarification
in terminology would be helpful, perhaps, to do away with a confusion
that continues to bedevil contemporary discourse on constitutionalism,
particularly in the United States but elsewhere as well—a confusion that
ascribes to "written constitutions" per se *paramount* validity. This confusion has been magnified and perpetuated by one of the most famous dicta
of American constitutional law, John Marshall's pronouncement in *Marbury v. Madison:* "Certainly all those who have framed written constitutions contemplate them as forming the fundamental and paramount law
of the nation, and consequently the theory of every such government must
be that an act of the legislative repugnant to the Constitution is void."[57]

5. This brings me to my fifth and last point. The rise of the Constitution as the *paramount law,* reigning supreme and therefore invalidat-
ing, if procedurally possible, any law of a lower level in the hierarchy of
legal norms, including "ordinary" legislator-made law, is *the* great innovation and achievement of American eighteenth-century constitutionalism. Awareness of *this* innovation, not of constitutions reduced
to written documents, was what evoked the proud commentary of
eighteenth-century Americans such as Tom Paine, James Iredell, and
James Madison. All three of them compared the new American system
with that of Great Britain. All three of them—an interesting illustration
of historical awareness and its political use—pointed to the same example of legislative omnipotence in Britain: the Septennial Act of 1716,
by which a Parliament in session not merely had provided a longer
duration for subsequent Parliaments, from three to seven years, but had *prolonged its own duration* from three by another four years. The opposition
of the day had considered that measure an infraction of the British Consti-

56. James Bryce, *Studies in History and Jurisprudence,* vol. 1 (Oxford, Eng.: Clarendon
Press, 1901), p. 205.
57. 1 Cranch, 137.

tution, but indeed there was no device that could have arrested the sovereign, constitutional, and legislative power of Parliament from doing what it did. The advancement of American constitutionalism was measured in comparison to Britain's Septennial Act. For Tom Paine, this act was proof that "there is no Constitution in England." In 1786, James Iredell of North Carolina denounced the "principle of unbounded legislative power" in Britain, which "our constitution [meaning the North Carolina State constitution] reprobates." Iredell also pointed to the Septennial Act as proof that "in England, therefore, they are less free than we are." James Madison, in *The Federalist* number 53, also denounced with the same example "dangerous practices," the possibility of changing "by legislative acts, some of the most fundamental articles of the government." In contrast, James Madison extolled a "constitution paramount to the government." [58] And this, indeed, is the most significant innovation of constitutionalism in America.

58. Paine, in *The Rights of Man*, as quoted by Charles H. McIlwain, *Constitutionalism, Ancient and Modern* (Ithaca, N.Y.: Cornell University Press, 1947; paperback, 1958), p. 2; *Life and Correspondence of James Iredell*, ed. G. J. McRee (New York, 1858), vol. 2, p. 148; *The Federalist* no. 53, p. 361. On the "paramount" character of a constitution vis-à-vis the legislative, cf. the interesting texts by Noah Webster (1790) and by Thomas Tudor Tucker (1786) referred to by Gordon S. Wood, *The Creation of the American Republic* (Chapel Hill: University of North Carolina Press, 1969), pp. 278, 280–81. To Wood's contention that no other piece of writing prior to 1787 revealed as clearly and cogently as Tucker's pamphlet *Conciliatory Hints . . .* (published on 21 Sept. 1786 in Charleston, SC) how far Americans had departed from the English conception of politics, I would submit that James Iredell's article, to which reference has been made in this note, published in Newbern, N.C., on 17 Aug. 1786, is at least as important a document on the "newness" of the Americans' concept of a constitution as is Tucker's; Iredell's text is referred to by Wood, *Creation of the American Republic*, pp. 461–62. On an earlier statement by Iredell in 1783 that the Constitution was "superior even to the Legislature" see *The Papers of James Iredell*, ed. Don Higginbotham, vol. 2 (Raleigh: North Carolina Division of Archives and History, 1976), p. 449.—The idea of a constitution as fundamental and paramount law beyond the reach of normal legislative enactment and alteration was central to Thomas Jefferson's criticism of the political system of Virginia. For this see, first, Query XIII "Constitution" of his *Notes on the State of Virginia*, which shows that Jefferson was aware of older legal usages of the term "constitution" as well as of "the magic supposed to be in the word constitution" (see point 5 of his list of the defects of the constitution); second, his "Draught of a Fundamental Constitution for the Commonwealth of Virginia" of 1783; and third, the last paragraph of Jefferson's bill (and act) for establishing Religious Freedom (1786). These three pertinent texts are conveniently found in Thomas Jefferson, *Notes on the State of Virginia*, ed. William Peden (New York: W. W. Norton & Co. for the Institute of Early American History and Culture, 1972), pp. 121–25 (especially 123–24), 209–22, 224–25. For details on the bill on Religious Freedom and its enactment see *The Papers of Thomas Jefferson*, ed. Julian P. Boyd et al., vol. 2 (Princeton, NJ: Princeton University Press, 1950), pp. 547–53; on its last paragraph see most recently the reflections in Ralph Lerner's essay "Jefferson's Pulse of Republican Reformation," in *The Thinking Revolutionary: Principle and Practice in the New Republic* (Ithaca, NY: Cornell University Press, 1987), pp. 87–88.

⚜

CHAPTER FOUR

Charles A. Beard's Interpretations
of American Foreign Policy *

Few future historians of the American mind are likely to deny the great
significance of the stimulus which Charles Beard injected into the intellectual life of America in the first half of the twentieth century, of the
challenge which he presented to traditional ways of thought in the social
disciplines, above all in history and political science. But beyond the undoubted fact of his significance, disagreement about its nature may not so
easily be resolved. After a few years of relative silence, imposed by respect
for Beard's human and moral stature as well as by embarrassment about
the erratic and antagonizing polemics of his last years, friends and critics
alike have of late taken up the task of appraising important features of his
work. Two main subjects of Beard's lifework, the politics of the Founding
Fathers—the core of his earlier work—and his concern with the theory
and methodology of history—a main interest of his later years—have come
under recent scrutiny.[1]

---

* First published in *World Affairs Quarterly*, vol. 28 (1957), 111–48. This paper originated
in a seminar on American Historiography in the History Department of the University of Chicago in 1952, given by Professor William T. Hutchinson, to whose inspired teaching I remain
very much indebted.

1. Most recently see Robert E. Brown, *Charles Beard and the Constitution* (Princeton:
Princeton University Press, 1956); also Eric F. Goldman, "The Origins of Beard's Economic Interpretation of the Constitution," in *Journal of the History of Ideas*, XIII (1952), 234–49; Harry J.
Marks, "Ground Under Our Feet: Beard's Relativism," ibid., XIV (1953), 628–33; and the excellent article by Lloyd R. Sorensen, "Charles A. Beard and German Historiographical Thought,"
in *Mississippi Valley Historical Review*, XLII (1955–1956), 274–87. The best discussion of both
aspects remains Morton G. White, *Social Thought in America: The Revolt Against Formalism*
(New York: Viking Press, 1949), chs. viii and xiv. The most comprehensive survey is offered in
the essays edited by Howard K. Beale, *Charles A. Beard: An Appraisal* (Lexington: University
of Kentucky Press, 1954), where admiration and friendly criticism prevail.

The present paper sets out to analyse what may well be called the third great concern of Beard's work: the place of the United States in the world, its foreign affairs. A detailed examination of Beard's writing devoted to foreign policy—small and insignificant at first, steadily increasing in bulk and significance as the years went by—might well warrant a monographic study. This paper, necessarily selective, will examine the process which led Beard from internationalism to isolationism, the various factors or events contributing to it, and more particularly the varying and often puzzling connection between the assumptions underlying Beard's general conceptions of history or the social process and his analysis of some specific problems of American foreign policy.[2]

I

No more striking contrast can be imagined than the one between the utter gloom and bitterness of Beard's last books on Franklin D. Roosevelt's foreign policy, and the perhaps vague and careless, but glorious optimism of a young Adjunct Professor of Politics at Columbia University, who in the academic year 1907–1908 assumed the task of defining and describing the subject matter of "Politics" in Columbia's series of "Lectures on Science, Philosophy, and Art." "Society," Beard exuberantly exclaimed, "has come from crude and formless associations beginning in a dim and dateless past and moves outward into an illimitable future, which many of us believe will not be hideous and mean, but beautiful and magnificent. In this dynamic society, the citizen becomes the co-worker in that great and indivisible natural process which draws down granite hills and upbuilds great nations."[3] So much have we taken on the habit of measuring Beard's theories of politics against the professed influence of his acknowledged master Madison, or criticizing them in view of the unavowed influence, sometimes exaggerated, of Marx,[4] that we have tended to overlook the

2. Thus far there have been two retrospective articles, published after Beard's death, devoted to his views on foreign policy: George R. Leighton, "Beard and Foreign Policy" in Howard K. Beale's volume *Charles A. Beard: An Appraisal* (see n. 1); and Fred H. Harrington, "Beard's Idea of National Interest and New Interpretations," in *American Perspective*, IV (1950), 335–45; this article is not included in the comprehensive bibliography of *Charles A. Beard: An Appraisal*.

3. Charles A. Beard, *Politics* (New York: Columbia University Press, 1908), pp. 9–10.

4. E.g., Bernard C. Borning, "The Political Philosophy of Young Charles A. Beard," *American Political Science Review*, XLIII (1949), 1177, remarks that young Beard owed more to Marx than he later cared to admit, but omits any mention of Darwinism. The best discussion of Marxian and Madisonian elements in Beard is M. G. White, *op. cit.*, pp. 119 ff.

Darwinian background of Beard's thought, so pervasive for conservatives and reformers alike in the climate of opinion of his formative years.[5]

In this same lecture on "Politics," Beard, several decades before the flourishing of curricula on international relations and textbooks on international politics, stated that an "almost new division of political research may be denominated world politics."[6] Setting this new division apart from traditional fields like diplomatic history or international law, Beard exultantly told his audience that "the marvelous expansion of trade and commerce which have refashioned the map of Africa in our own day, awakened the slumbering nations of the East and the islands of the seas, has brought new problems of universal interest which we have scarcely begun to analyse." There was indeed little attempt at analysis: less than one page in this lecture of thirty-five pages was devoted to that "new division of political research." Quite incongruous statements and allusions were united by no other denominator than the faith, as vague as it was noble, that somehow the ever denser network of worldwide economic activity was furthering the progress of mankind. The picturesque statement that "so far as our political economy is concerned Japan is as much a part of the United States as Oregon; Matabeleland is the next door neighbor to Saskatchewan" might indicate a preference for or belief in free trade uninhibited by protectionist or imperialist obstacles. But the placid enumeration of "the meaning and tendency of race conflicts, the control of the tropics, the attitude of imperial nations toward subject races, the best forms of colonial administration" as elements of the new branch of political science, if viewed together with Beard's ardent faith in "that great and indivisible natural process . . . , which upbuilds great nations," suggests that his attitude towards imperialism was by no means one of violent disapproval, though far removed from the fervent advocacy of the Theodore Roosevelt–A. T. Mahan school. This stood out more clearly two years later, in 1910, when Beard, in the first edition of his text on American Government and Politics, calmly placed the "new" American imperialism into the mainstream of the American political tradition:

> We have been a world power, as far as has been necessary, from the beginning of our history. In a word, the protection of our government

5. Beard himself observed in this lecture that "the influence of the historical school on correct thinking in politics has been splendidly supplemented by that of the Darwinians." *Politics*, p. 9.

6. For this and the following quotations, *Politics*, p. 30.

has steadily advanced with the extension of our material interests, and
the foreign policy of the last ten years is no breach in our historical
development. . . . The protection of those very commercial interests,
however, has drawn us into intimate connections with other foreign
powers and may at any time lead us to the necessity of co-operating
with them in military expeditions.[7]

But then there was also a more radical doctrine or expectation to be found
in Beard's lecture of 1908:

> The shuttle of trade and intercourse flies ever faster and faster and it
> may be weaving the web for a world state. It may be that steam and
> electricity are to achieve what neither the armies, nor the law, nor the
> faith of Rome could accomplish—that unity of mankind which rests
> on the expansion of a common consciousness of rights and wrongs
> through the expansion of identical modes of economic activity.[8]

If there might be a tinge of Marxian thought in the concluding words,
the somber rigidity of persistent Marxist analysis ill accorded with young
Beard's enthusiasm—and lack of discrimination—concerning the "marvelous expansion of trade and commerce."

In the pre–World War I days, then, Beard's few allusions to foreign affairs were distinguished by their lack of precision as well as by their tendency to stress "those material and moral forces which are linking our
destinies to the world at large" and which could not possibly be overcome
by "any political doctrines with regard to our independence from the rest
of the world."[9] Beard's rejoicing about the world's attainment of economic
unity[10] reflected the general climate of opinion of the 19th century, the
triumphant pride of a Benjamin Constant, an Auguste Comte, or a Herbert Spencer, on the victory of commerce over war, of industrialism over
militarism, much more than any specific Marxist influence which might
make itself felt more strongly in the domain that had captured the minds
and hearts of progressively-minded intellectuals like Beard to the virtual
exclusion of foreign affairs. Progress was thought to meet its decisive test

7. Charles A. Beard, *American Government and Politics*, first ed., (New York: Macmillan,
1910), p. 331.

8. *Politics*, p. 30.

9. *American Government and Politics*, p. 333.

10. In a book review of several European periodical publications in the *Political Science
Quarterly*, XXIV (1909), 165.

on the battlefields of industrial democracy; conflicts across the horizontal cleavage of class lines were thought to be infinitely more significant than conflicts across the vertical cleavage of national boundaries, the latter being rare, limited, and remote; thus the analysis of international relations was either absent or no more than an afterthought.

This neglect was even greater in America than in Europe, owing both to the prolonged absence of sustained international conflict and to the lack of neatly packed "ideologies" on the European model, encompassing theories on domestic and international affairs alike. All this became strikingly obvious in the uncertainties, hesitations, and splits of American progressives at the advent of World War I.[11]

Beard, in these years more exclusively devoted to scholarship and less given to publicistic activity than later in the thirties and forties, took no conspicuous part in the anguished public soul-searching of American progressives. His chief contribution to that great debate, a communication to the *New Republic* on "The Perils of Diplomacy" in June 1917, showed him at his very best. Realism and high moral purpose, not yet disjointed by grave disappointments, produced an eminently sober as well as moving appeal to avoid the pitfalls of muddleheadedness and self-righteousness. Steering clear of the isolationist pacifism of the George Norris-Bob La Follette school as much as of the aggressive interventionism of Theodore Roosevelt, Beard warned his countrymen that "the war is to be won by diplomacy as well as by soldiers and high explosives."[12] Diplomacy called for "poise, coldbloodedness, and a Machiavellian disposition to see things as they are and to deal with them as they are—whether we like them or not." This diplomacy, however, was to be employed for a peace policy essentially amounting to the Wilsonian "peace without victory." Beard at that time was more of a Wilsonian than anything else, although, if he shared Wilson's idealism in terms of justice and of moral purpose, he then as always lacked the peculiarly legalistic optimism concerning international politics which became the outstanding feature of Wilsonianism. Beard warned then that "the pat little phrase 'liberty against autocracy' is more likely to deceive ourselves than the Germans." More particularly, Beard now talked about Anglo-American imperialism in a sardonic vein quite absent seven or eight years before. German publicists had "long been dwelling upon our 'world politics,' our ambitions in the Orient, our Philippine

11. See the excellent chapter "Internationalists in War" of Eric F. Goldman's *Rendezvous with Destiny* (New York: A. A. Knopf, 1952; pocket edition 1956).

12. This and the following quotes from the *New Republic*, XI (May–July, 1917), 136–37.

policies, and our enterprises in the Caribbean. They suspect that we have not been purified by fire. . . ." Beard wanted the Germans, and particularly German radicals, to know that "the people of the United States will not shed one drop of blood to enlarge the British empire. . . ." Only a few months later, early in October 1917, Beard resigned from Columbia University in protest against the dismissal of a professor who had opposed America's entrance into the war; and yet in his very letter of resignation, Beard expressed his support of "the just war on the German empire." [13]

The psychological effects of the war in terms of its restrictions on freedom of expression had only a slow and by no means exclusive impact on Beard's changing views on America's place in the world. In addition to the repressive atmosphere at home during the war, there came after its end the long process of debunking. It was initiated by the Soviet government's publication of secret treaties in the allied camp, and soon brilliantly supported by the magic prose of John Maynard Keynes—the *New Republic* serialized the *Economic Consequences of the Peace* almost immediately after its appearance. It was continued by a partial opening of the archives and publication of documents in many countries; to debunk the good cause became the main occupation of many disillusioned liberals in this country, and it provided never-ending material for the volumes of the Revisionists. In view of Beard's front rank position among the Revisionists of World War II, it is important to note that Beard cannot by any means be counted among the leading Revisionists of the twenties. Even if he assigned to France and Russia "a Titan's share of guilt," Beard never went so far as Harry Elmer Barnes in exonerating Germany.[14] The terrible complexity of assigning moral responsibility for war guilt, however, impressed itself heavily on Beard's mind; and in due course, in the threatening international constellation of the thirties, this thought was to assert itself with overwhelming force in Beard's stand against Franklin D. Roosevelt's foreign policy.

Beard's first major statement on America's place in world politics after the great process of debunking had set in, was a series of lectures at Dartmouth College in 1922. They presented by no means a violent departure from older ideals; rather, they reflected an uncertain balance of long held convictions about the world's economic unity, of a more recent, faint hope

13. See Goldman, *op. cit.*, pocket edition, pp. 199–200.

14. In a review article, "Viscount Grey on War Guilt," *New Republic,* XLIV (Oct. 7, 1925), 172–75, quoted by S. Adler, "The War–Guilt Question and American Disillusionment, 1918–1928," *Journal of Modern History,* XXIII, (1951), p. 14.

in international organization, but also of a growing belief in the United
States keeping apart from it all. "The East and West have met and they are
one. The world is an economic unit and the United States is being woven
into the very fabric of that unity."[15] Beard also thought that

> A new constitution of nations, a grand European league, appears to be
> the only alternative to new combinations, new wars more ghastly and
> deadly than ever. It is, however, another thing to say that the United
> States, enjoying the comparative security of this hemisphere, should
> attempt to take part in the conduct of a co-operative system for all na-
> tions of the earth.[16]

Some Wilsonian hopes for organized internationalism thus were connected with what by 1940 was to become the isolationist theory of "continentalism": According to what Beard then baptized "Little Americanism,"
the American government would cease to lend support to investment
bankers placing loans abroad, it would not seize any more territory, nor
would it annex spheres in the Caribbean. It would instead invite Latin
American nations to participate in a cooperative system for settling disputes. Entering a league of nations should only be considered if all other
countries were prepared to accept a similarly anti-expansionist policy.[17]
How tentative this first approach to isolationism had been became apparent seven years later in *The American Leviathan*, written on the eve
of economic disaster in America and all over the world. Here Beard expounded a message of enlightened internationalism more explicitly than
ever since his lecture of 1908, and certainly more realistically than on
that earlier occasion:

> If the ancient objections to 'entangling alliances' are still valid, the
> theory that the United States can, in its own interest, refuse to take
> part in world adjustments becomes more doubtful every day. . . . It can
> formulate no important policy without affecting the European balance
> of power. It cannot safely curtail its expenditures for national defense
> without reaching an agreement with competing countries. No shift

15. Charles A. Beard, *Cross Currents in Europe To-day.* (Boston: Marshall Jones Company,
1922), p. 2. In spite of all "revelations of archives," Beard in these lectures placed heavy blame
on Wilhelm II for having encouraged Austria to light the European fire. Ibid., p. 76.
    16. Ibid., p. 139.
    17. Ibid., p. 269.

can be made in European affairs without affecting its destiny. Hence the creed of isolation which once seemed convincing, unless wisely interpreted, may be employed to defeat its own purposes, namely, the maintenance of national security.[18]

The chapter on foreign policy in *The American Leviathan* may well be termed the most reasonable, detached, and balanced of Beard's papers on foreign policy. An intelligent critique of Wilsonian "open diplomacy," all too likely to become prey of chauvinistic sentiments and destined for home consumption rather than the dispatch of business,[19] was thus combined—at least in theory—with a clear-sighted grasp of the power relationships linking America with the rest of the world. In view of Beard's foreign policy writings in the thirties and forties, it seems ironic that the paper having the greatest relevance for our contemporary situation should have been written just before the Great Depression set in.

II

The great crash and America's involvement in the world's economic crisis profoundly shook Beard; its direct impact accounts more than does World War I for his shift toward isolationism. This is illustrated by the radical break with doctrines espoused as recently as in *The American Leviathan*. From then on, and for the first time in Beard's career as a writer and scholar, foreign affairs assumed primary importance. Two volumes were the first result of this concern, the historical and "fact-finding" *The Idea of National Interest* and its programmatic companion, *The Open Door at Home*. Both were published in 1934; they were the outcome of a suggestion made by Beard in 1931 to Frederick P. Keppel of the Carnegie Corporation, recommending an inquiry into the mending of that much used slogan "national interests."[20] These two volumes present the most substantial part of Beard's writings on foreign policy.

Before we follow Beard on his road toward isolationism and before we examine his policy conclusion regarding America's foreign relations, we must take a closer look at the underlying assumptions of his conception of American foreign policy past and present. What were his views of the

18. Charles A. Beard, *The American Leviathan* (New York: Macmillan, 1930), p. 733.
19. Ibid., p. 729–31.
20. George R. Leighton, *loc. cit.*, p. 169.

historical process and of human nature as far as they colored his outlook
on what international relations were all about? Back in 1929, Beard had
given a description of what went into the making of foreign policy:

> Foreign policy—upon what does that depend? Upon the state of inter-
> nal affairs. Upon frontiers, political and economic. Upon historic griev-
> ances cherished by and against neighboring powers. Upon rivalry of
> trade, territory and resources. Upon a concept of values accepted by the
> peoples. Upon ambitions and economic strivings of the masses. Above
> all, upon calculations of enduring national interests.[21]

While at first sight one might be struck by the comprehensiveness of
this definition, the flavor of its economic and rationalist interpretation is
undeniable. Both volumes under discussion were even more biased in this
direction. More particularly, the historical volume, *The Idea of National
Interest*, essentially presented little more than what remains to this day
one of the most elaborate studies of American commercial and financial
expansion abroad and of its domestic background. It thus illustrates a
striking shortcoming of Beard's scholarship: the very comprehensiveness
and theoretical articulateness of his conceptual framework all too often
remained on the level of abstraction, of intention, without ever seeping
through to the level of specific historical investigation. Nevertheless,
little insight would be gained if we contented ourselves with putting the
correct, but insufficient label of "economic interpretation" on these two
books. We must ascertain the complexity of different layers of analysis
which actually went into the making of that "economic interpretation."

As the first layer of this interpretation, there emerges Beard's conviction of the peculiarly "economic" character of the modern era of Western
history, to which reference has already been made. In the context of the
idea of "National Interest," this means that the very formula of national
interest is associated with the rise of the "national commercial state," and
the evolution of "republican control over national affairs."[22] It arose under
the impact of "the great expansion of economic relations," replacing older
formulas like reason of state, the will of the prince, dynastic interest,
or national honor. Monarchical rule had gone into eclipse. Reason of state
and the "feudalistic conceptions of national honor"—did it really sound

21. Charles A. Beard and G. Radin, *The Balkan Pivot: Yugoslavia* (New York: Macmillan 1929), p. 303.

22. *The Idea of National Interest* (New York: Macmillan, 1934), p. 22.

right to Beard thus to unite these historically incongruous terms?—broke down under the "impact of economic relations and popular control of government." The rationalist in Beard revealed himself in proclaiming the superiority of modernity over these obsolete formulas:

> In the light of modern demands for a foreign policy truly expressive of realities, stable, consistent, and capable of being handled by logical and analytical methods, these old formulas, with their personal associations, their emotional content, their uncertainties and needless hazards, are recognized as deficient.[23]

On this level then, Beard's economic interpretation of American foreign policy is but an application of his general scheme of Western history, Marxist in a vague sense, but held by many non-Marxist believers in progress both in the 19th and in the early 20th century, propounding the replacement of the feudal stage of civilization, with its hazards and uncertainties, by the superior, more rational era of commercial, industrial, financial expansion. This kind of interpretation assumes peculiar significance when applied to America, a nation whose growth virtually coincided in time with the rise and preponderance of "economic" relationships in Western history. In Europe the vestiges of older ways of life or thought still linger on; America is more exclusively "modern" than Europe:

> The American nation is republican, secular, and *essentially economic* in character. It is not feudal, clerical, monarchical, or "spiritual" in the European sense of that term; that is, it does not sustain an aristocratic or clerical elite engaged in the enjoyment of its own social and intellectual virtues and standards.[24]

Let us sum up. The international relations of the modern era are more clearly "economic" in a double sense The modern era is distinguished by the rise of a class or classes more directly or exclusively devoted to the pursuit of material, acquisitive, "economic" activities; also, modern foreign policy is more distinctly "economic" in the sense that this term is generally used to designate those commercial, industrial and financial activities which have unquestionably played a greater part in the last two

---

23. Ibid., p. 21.
24. Charles A. Beard, *The Open Door at Home* (New York: Macmillan, 1934), p. 208. (My italics.)

or three centuries than they did before when contests for territory dominated. And, we must add, territorial contests inevitably involved questions of sovereignty and military occupation; that is, they were "political"
or "military" in a more obvious sense than the subtler and more hidden
rivalries for markets or financial control, even if those might also issue in
military conflagrations.

There is, however, a deeper layer of economic interpretation which pervades Beard's work: It is the assumption that action or interpretation based
on the grasp of economic factors is more "truly expressive of realities." In
1913 Beard had explicitly based his most famous work on a "theory of economic determinism."[25] Two decades later, Beard as explicitly disavowed
theories of economic determinism. Under the influence of European
thinkers he had come to repudiate theoretically any schools of thought
trying to force history or politics into the straightjacket of scientific laws.[26]
The great new departure in Beard's reflections on the nature of history and
politics was his discovery of the problem of statesmanship—and histori-
anship as well—as a problem of moral choice irreducible and unamenable
to scientific laws. Beard was aware of the magnitude of that shift:

> This introduction of good, better, and best—ethics and esthetics—into
> economics and politics calls for more than the mere insertion of moral
> maxims into the interstices of private and class interests. It means noth-
> ing short of a revolution in attitude, procedure, and emphasis, a frank
> recognition of the fact that ethics and esthetics underlie and are es-
> sential to the operation of any great society—a reversal of the approach
> to policy made by the so-called empirical or practical sciences. . . . The

25. Beard first said that his study was "based upon the political science of James Madison," then quoted extensively, but with significant omissions, from Federalist No. X, which he
called "a masterly statement of the theory of economic determinism in politics." *An Economic
Interpretation of the Constitution of the United States* (New York: Macmillan, 1913 with new
introduction, 1935), pp. 14, 15. For Beard's misinterpretation of Madison, see Douglass Adair,
"Federalist No. X Revisited," *William and Mary Quarterly*, 3rd series, VIII (1951), 48–67.

26. The chief influences were Benedetto Croce and Kurt Riezler. These two historicist
thinkers emphasized the uniqueness and spontaneity of the creative act of the historian as
well as the statesman. Whereas Beard took from Croce chiefly the idea of the historian as creator of history, Riezler contributed the idea that "ideas" in political history—the element of
moral preference—are irreducible to, in no way derivative from "interests." See his "Idee und
Interesse in der politischen Geschichte," *Die Dioskuren*, I (1924), pp. 1 ff. The historiographical implications of these influences were worked out by Beard in his famous Address "Written
History as an Act of Faith," *American Historical Review*, XXXIX (1933–1934), 219 ff.; the implications for political action and statesmanship were discussed in *The Open Door at Home*,
chs. I, II, VII.

three great schemes of thought which have been evolved as solutions to
the problem of the periodical crisis and have gained ascendancy in foreign policies—laissez faire, imperialism, and communism—are alike
in resting their structures on material interests and in either rejecting
or minimizing ethical and esthetic considerations. . . .[27]

Yet Beard's new construction rested on a precarious basis. He admitted
that the choice of an ethical frame of reference was irrational, "at bottom
assertions of values, not demonstration of mathematics." Even more dangerous, beneath the choice of "an idealized conception of American society to which are to be referred choices of policy and action as they arise
and are made," there was no fundamentally revised notion of human nature; there lurked the same *homo economicus* whom Beard had debunked
twenty years before in his study of the framers of the Constitution. "That
the difficulties of this procedure"—the choice of "the best" policy for
America—"are great is not to be denied, but no other course is open, save
perhaps *the blind following of acquisitive impulses expressed by private
parties with pecuniary interest at stake*—a procedure that has eventuated
in the present crisis."[28]

Beard's conception of human nature—and his factual analysis of
American foreign policy—remained under the spell of an economic interpretation in spite of his formal repudiation of economic determinism and
his acceptance of a voluntaristic set of ideas.[29] Beard failed to bridge the
gulf between his new conceptual framework and his concrete researches.
On the level of concrete analysis, little had changed since 1913:

Public policies, as Secretary Hughes pointedly remarked, are not ab-
stractions. They are not manufactured in the Department of State by
phantoms. They are the products of concrete experience with concrete
economic phenomena, such as the production and exchange of American commodities, the acquisition of material sources and markets
abroad, the performance of services, the barriers (governmental and

27. *The Open Door at Home*, pp. 138–39. The mention of esthetics is an ill-digested part of
Croce's influence on Beard.

28. Ibid., p. 144. (My italics.)

29. In his 1935 introduction to *An Economic Interpretation of the Constitution*, Beard
contrived to acknowledge his new Machiavellian-Crocean-Riezlerian faith in the free play of
virtù, fortuna, and *necessità* in history; to deny that even in 1913 he had believed in "determinism" (p. xvi; cf. the contrast to pp. 14–16, see note 25 above); but also to say that he still
believed that in the great transformations of society, "economic 'forces' are primordial or fundamental and come nearer 'explaining' events than any other 'forces'" (p. xii).

private) to trade, the action of external forces upon opportunities for enterprise, the pursuit, gain or loss of profits, and the infinite variety of domestic and foreign influences, upon the occupations, the interests, and the welfare of the American people.[30]

The outstanding feature of Beard's brand of economic interpretation of politics, whether in 1913 or in 1934, was its un-Marxian stress, implicit or explicit, on the economic motives of individuals or groups.[31] This insinuation of the acquisitive instinct as the most crucial attribute of human nature lies at the very bottom of Beard's incapacity to take into account the genuinely political aspects of foreign policy. It was one of the reasons which led him to see in American foreign policy little else but the continuation beyond the water's edge of the economic quests of individuals and groups making up American society. From this conception derived his steady warning that "the foreign policies of nations are aspects of domestic policies and configurations,"[32] a point which could not "be too strongly emphasized or too often repeated."[33]

Beard's economic interpretation of human nature proved incapable of grasping adequately the phenomenon of power relationships, the very stuff of politics, whether domestic or international. Thus the fact that the exercise of power may work considerable transformations in people's outlook for good or for bad, that power may corrupt some people as it may sober others, never really entered the inner core of Beard's historical analysis. "Private citizens entering the service of the government," he argued, on the contrary

do not pass through a personal metamorphosis. A banker, called to serve in the Treasury Department from his post in a private banking

30. *The Idea of National Interest*, p. 112.

31. See the brilliant discussion by M. G. White (*op. cit.*, pp. 121–23) of this point. Beard himself was quite unable to distinguish clearly between an economic interpretation resting on the fundamental importance of means of production for historical development, and the altogether different problem of the predominance of acquisitive, rather "low" motivations in human nature.

32. *The Open Door at Home*, p. 130; cf. *The Idea of National Interest*, p. 311

33. *A Foreign Policy for America* (New York: Alfred A. Knopf, 1940), p. 9. Also ibid., p. 3. Characteristic in this context was Beard's angry exclamation that Mahan, T. Roosevelt, A. Beveridge, and H. C. Lodge, the arch-imperialists, were all of them "primarily phrasemakers, not men of hard economic experience." *Giddy Minds and Foreign Quarrels* (New York: Macmillan, 1939), p. 16 (my italics).

house engaged in the flotation of foreign loans, cannot be expected to divest himself of the customs and policies, the conceptions of interests and tactics of the banking fraternity in which he has been trained.[34]

This interpretation, in spite of his great care for comprehensiveness and objectivity of analysis, involved Beard in considerable contradictions. For instance, examining arguments advanced in Congressional hearings on independence for the Philippines, he observed that "no process of research or logical analysis" could indicate whether "the sense of moral obligation or estimates of substantial advantages weighed heavier in the minds of those who freely employed the terms" of moral concern over that question. But soon Beard concluded that the major part of this testimony was "occupied by the declarations and arguments of witnesses who frankly admitted that they spoke for particular economic interests. . . . Yet no one of them would admit that he was actuated *solely or even principally by economic considerations*"[35]—The American Navy presented a troublesome problem to Beard's psychology of *homo economicus*. At one point he took Admiral Mahan to task for having treated "naval power as if it were an independent force operating under its own momentum and at another as a mere agency of economic interests. Obviously it could not be both." But then Beard himself was constrained to admit precisely that—and here his "first layer" of economic interpretation was operating—that

> it would not be in strict accordance with the facts in the case to say that the Navy is a mere interest in the pecuniary or commercial sense of the term, even if in practice it is intimately associated with such interests. Unlike the State Department and the Department of Commerce, the Navy represents fighting traditions and standards of 'honor' older than commerce and purely civil institutions. It inherited a code of prestige, right, and property which sublimated the ancient motive of fighting, namely, desire for territory and loot.[36]

On the level of governmental action, as on the level of individual or group motivation, Beard failed to tackle the problem of political power. Most significant was his inability to provide a satisfactory explanation for

34. *The Idea of National Interest*, pp. 116–17.
35. Ibid., pp. 399 and 514. (My italics.)
36. Ibid., pp. 433 and 442.

the many instances of American foreign policy when "the Government, on its part, has not blindly followed a course plotted by the private pecuniary quest. In fact," Beard continued,

> the Government has often foreshadowed and searched out paths for private enterprise to follow. . . . With much justification, it has been said that there was more diplomacy than dollars in dollar diplomacy. The Government is, therefore, an interpreter of national interest on its own account as well as the promoter and executor of interpretations provided by private parties.[37]

Beard's handling of the idea of "power politics"—he used the German term *Machtpolitik*—throws revealing light on this inadequacy. At first, in *The Idea of National Interest,* Beard simply identified *Machtpolitik* with what he then called the Hamiltonian tradition of commercial expansionism:

> In its genuine form, the doctrine of Machtpolitik contains certain inevitable elements. It includes the pursuit of economic interests abroad with full preparation for the utmost consequences, the maintenance of a navy, not second to none, but clearly superior to the nearest competitor, and willingness to employ the ultimate arbiter, force, to break down resistance to the march of economic conquest.[38]

In *The Open Door at Home,* Machtpolitik—"pure Machtpolitik" it was now called—meant something entirely different. While writing this volume, Beard had become acquainted with the works of two European scholars, Joseph Schumpeter and Walter Sulzbach, who both explained imperialism or national aggressiveness by non-economic motives. These were either an atavistic urge to expansion for expansion's sake, or the will to power, national honor and prestige, etc.[39] There were, Beard summed up, four systems of thought concerning foreign affairs:

37. Ibid., pp. 415–16. For instance, discussing the memoirs of Paul S. Reinsch, former U. S. minister to China, Beard concluded: "The outstanding feature of the whole situation was not the aggressiveness of the private interests involved in the struggle, but the insistent and unremitting efforts of diplomatic representatives to consolidate their respective nationals . . ." (Ibid., p. 192). An explanation is conspicuously lacking.

38. Ibid., p. 142.

39. Joseph Schumpeter, *Zur Soziologie der Imperialismen,* now available in English "The Sociology of Imperialisms" in *Imperialism. Social Classes. Two Essays* by Joseph Schumpeter (New York: Meridian Books, 1955). Walter Sulzbach, *Nationales Gemeinschaftsgefuehl und*

Three of them—*laissez faire*, imperialism, and communism—are frankly founded on interests conceived in material terms. In the fourth system—pure *Machtpolitik*—the State is treated in theory as sheer power in itself, not governed by or devoted to the pursuit of interest conceived as material advantages.[40]

Beard's refutation of this kind of concept could not but express his economic interpretation:

> Neglect of economic interest may be charged up against the emotional conception of nationality. . . . If national feeling, will to power, joy in battle, love of courage, and national honor are the prime motive forces of policy, they are not separated in action from motives of acquisition and from the total situation of economic interests which condition their operation. . . . Emotions are a part of the historical process; so are interest and rationality.[41]

The striking fact remains that in the overall picture of Beard's historical analysis, those "emotions were singularly neglected in favor of motives of acquisition."

However, if we want to penetrate to the root of Beard's failure to understand the problem of power, we must proceed one step further. It seems to us that neither the stress of "emotions," like the will to power, nor the concept of interest conceived in terms of "motives of acquisition," do justice to the central problem of international politics, the security dilemma.[42] The competition for power for the sake of self-preservation generates the vicious circle of what has been so aptly called the "Hobbesian fear" which produces the never-ending striving of "power after power."[43] The deadly dynamics of power politics may come into play without any "lust for power" for its own sake. The dilemma of security is sufficient to account for the mechanics of the international balance of power. Beard's failure, in spite of verbal acknowledgments, to come to grips with the problem of

---

wirtschaftliches Interesse (1929); see now the author's English-language writings: *National Consciousness* (Washington: American Council on Public Affairs, 1943), and *Capitalist Warmongers—A Modern Superstition* (Chicago: University of Chicago Press, 1942).

40. *The Open Door at Home*, p. 154.

41. Ibid., pp. 172, 175.

42. See especially John H. Herz, *Political Realism and Political Idealism* (Chicago: University of Chicago Press, 1951), pp. 2–5.

43. Herbert Butterfield, *Christianity and History* (London: G. Bell, 1949), pp. 89–90.

the balance of power may be due, then, to a minimizing of the factor of security. Naturally there was the theoretical realization that security was at the core of any solid conception of the national interest. But the very extent of Americans security prevented Beard from ever thinking through, or applying to his historical analysis of American foreign policy, the political and psychological implications of the security dilemma.[44] Beard's analysis stopped at a combination of economic and strategic considerations, the latter being based on and limited by the conclusions reached by an evaluation of tendencies of economic expansion.[45] The seemingly unchallenged fact of America's security actually became a third, and perhaps the deepest, because not wholly conscious, assumption—a *third layer* of Beard's economic interpretation of American history and foreign policy.

To this general tendency there had to be added the particular impact of the world's economic crisis. At this particular juncture, when long-standing assumptions of Beard's thought were re-enforced by the immediate crisis, he formulated a "tentative law of American foreign policy":

> The degree of the probability that the United States will become involved in any war arising anywhere in Europe or Asia bears a direct relation to the extent of the economic interests possessed by American nationals in the affected area, and in the fortunes of the respective belligerents.[46]

Beard's fundamental programmatic conclusion, presented with passionate insistence, was that stability in economy "is a good in itself and conducive to those individual and social virtues necessary to the continuance of society." This stability inevitably

> involves the utmost emancipation from dependence upon the economies, rivalries, revolutions, and wars of other nations. It involves as a corollary the utmost emancipation from dependence upon the course

44. A chapter on "America and the Balance of Power" in *Cross Currents in Europe Today*, as well as eh. XXVIII of *The Rise of American Civilization* (New York: Macmillan, vol. II, 1927), called "America in the Balance of Power" (cf. pp. 618 and 631) may illustrate this assertion. Even the wise and just remarks in *The American Leviathan* (see above, pp. 106–7) go to show that on the level of general observations Beard took account of phenomena which he minimized or neglected on the level of concrete analysis.

45. See the chapter on "The Problem of National Defense" in *The Open Door at Home*.

46. Ibid., p. 269.

of international exchange, which is, in brutal fact . . . spreading havoc over great regions of the earth.[47]

For this conclusion, Beard was heavily indebted to the theories of John A. Hobson, the British economist who has been called the most influential writer on the subject of imperialism in the English-speaking world.[48] Hobson's classic on *Imperialism* had been published in 1902, and it may reasonably be conjectured that Beard was familiar with Hobson's theory of under-consumption when in 1922 he first sketched his philosophy of "Little Americanism." Strangely enough, Hobson's name was not mentioned in *The Open Door at Home.*[49] Beard acknowledged his influence only in 1939 when he revealed that the "central economic thesis" of what by then he called "the continentalist school" "probably came from the writings of the British economist, John A. Hobson." Their central tenet was described accurately enough, even if in simplified terms by Beard:

> The primary force in the rivalry of nations for market outlets . . . is the inefficient distribution of wealth at home—in other words, the enormous accumulations of capital that cannot find high profits in domestic expansion and must go abroad or burst. . . . The solution for the problem of attaining well-being or 'prosperity' . . . lies not in the 'world-market' but in domestic economy—in the wider distribution of wealth to sustain continuous and expanding buying power among the people.[50]

III

From 1934 on, then, this theory was the very pivot of Beard's conception of what American foreign policy ought to be, and in due course it also came to modify his view of what Americans foreign policy had been in the past. At the point of departure of his new foreign policy outlook, in the

---

47. Ibid., pp. 211–12.

48. Cf. the excellent chapter on Hobson in E. M. Winslow, *The Pattern of Imperialism* (New York: Columbia University Press, 1948), pp. 92–110.

49. This is a parallel to the no less amazing omission of Karl Marx's name in the first edition of Beard's *The Economic Basis of Politics* (New York: A. A. Knopf, 1922). Only a chapter added in 1945 mentioned Marx!

50. Charles A. and Mary Beard, *America in Midpassage* (New York: Macmillan, 1939), p. 453.

1934 volume *The Idea of National Interest,* Beard emphatically upheld the
accepted dualism of the American tradition in foreign affairs: Jeffersonians
vs. Hamiltonians. We may disregard in this context the agrarian, continental, territorial, anti-Navy expansionism of Jefferson. Hamiltonianism
in foreign affairs meant to Beard "the promotion of trade in all parts of the
world by the engines of diplomacy, the defense of that trade by a powerful
navy, the supremacy of the United States in the Western Hemisphere, and
the use of military and naval strength in the rivalry of nations to secure
economic advantages for the citizens of the United States."[51]

In fact Beard went so far as to state that A. T. Mahan restored the "pattern of *Machtpolitik* outlined in the *Federalist*"[52] and to criticize James
Bryce for having thought that something unforeseen had happened, when
through the acquisition of the Philippines "the Americans drifted into
dominion. . . ."[53] Beard called the post–1897 period of American diplomacy an intensification of earlier conceptions, but no radical departure.[54]
Contrary to the popular belief that the closing years of the 19th century
marked a "new era," Beard insisted, "the facts in the case warrant no such
arbitrary break in the history of the country."[55] Dollar diplomacy actually
"resembled in many respects the philosophy of policy expounded by leaders in the establishment of the American Republic," even if it was lacking
in their precision of thought and realism.[56] Commercial expansion accompanied by appropriate diplomatic and naval policies was one of the prime
considerations of national interest as conceived by the Founding Fathers.[57]
The commercial relations which Washington "favored and advocated led
to powerful obligations abroad and to actual entanglements more binding
than the prescriptions of formal treaties."[58]

We have for good reason adduced such a large number of passages, because Beard's violent departure from this point of view is probably the
most striking example of the profundity of the change which occurred in
his interpretation of American foreign policy after 1934. The reversal was
complete by 1939, when Beard, discussing the closing years of the 19th
century, spoke of a "departure from accepted traditions," of a "new Spirit"

51. *The Idea of National Interest*, pp. 48–49.
52. Ibid., p. 101.
53. Ibid., p. 52n. 1.
54. Ibid., p. 116.
55. Ibid., p. 166.
56. Ibid., p. 111.
57. Ibid., p. 166.
58. Ibid., p. 313.

that appeared in various quarters.[59] This reversal was glaringly apparent in the following statement of September, 1939:

> On what should the foreign policy of the United States be based? . . . It is the doctrine formulated by George Washington, supplemented by James Monroe, and followed by the Government of the United States until near the end of the nineteenth century, when the frenzy for foreign adventurism burst upon the country. This doctrine is simple. Europe has a set of "primary interests" which have little or no relation to us, and is constantly vexed by "ambition, rivalship, interest, humor, or caprice." The United States is a continental power separated from Europe by a wide ocean which, despite all changes in warfare, is still a powerful asset of defense. . . . Washington's doctrine has remained a tenacious heritage, despite the hectic interludes of the past fifty years. . . .[60]

The long way which Beard traveled in the brief five years from *The Idea of National Interest* to the fully developed "continentalist" doctrine of 1939 or 1940 is most strikingly shown by the following reversal: In 1934 he spoke of A. T. Mahan's "restoration of the pattern of *Machtpolitik* outlined in the *Federalist*," while in 1940 he charged that the imperialism of Mahan, T. Roosevelt, Beveridge and H. C. Lodge constituted "an uproarious departure from the staid tradition of George Washington, John Adams, Thomas Jefferson, and James Monroe."[61] The most thorough exposition of Beard's new position appeared in the chapter on "Shadows and Shapes of Foreign Policy" of *America in Midpassage* (1939), and, with several modifications indicating the rapid flux of Beard's ideas at that time, in the concise little book *A Foreign Policy for America* (1940). The old dualism of Jeffersonian continental expansion and Hamiltonian maritime expansion was abandoned in favor of a new, at first five-fold, then three-fold pattern.

59. Charles A. Beard, *American Government and Politics*, 8th completely revised edition (New York: Macmillan, 1939), pp. 275 and 271. It is highly instructive, though it goes beyond the scope of this paper, to follow the modifications of Beard's foreign policy views through the different editions of his textbook. Significantly, the pro-imperialist Statements of the 1910 edition (above, p. 103) were absent from the revised 4th edition in 1924, and were replaced by a strong statement in favor of hemispheric cooperation (p. 347). Considerable revisions also occur in the 7th (1935), 8th (1939), and 9th (1945) editions. The space devoted to foreign affairs grew from revision to revision.

60. *Giddy Minds and Foreign Quarrels*, pp. 64–65, 67–68. This was also printed in *Harper's Magazine* for September, 1939 (CLXXIX). Cf. also *A Foreign Policy for America*, p. 15.

61. *A Foreign Policy for America*, p. 52.

In *America in Midpassage* Beard juxtaposed one traditional school of American foreign policy, called "isolationism pure and simple" (!), with four schools of more recent vintage. "The isolationist creed of the early republic was abandoned and the United States government set out on a course of imperialist conquest in the Far East and trade expansion everywhere under naval pressures."[62] This new departure was called by Beard— with a fine and rare sense for nuances—"Imperial Isolationism." With this qualification Beard wanted to convey the distinction between the more open and thoroughgoing imperialism of England, France, or Germany and its American counterpart, which was more concerned with hemispheric security and operated through the channels of mere trade expansion to a greater extent than through outright colonialism or territorial conquest.[63] Yet with a lack of consistency explicable by the very magnitude of the shift in interpretation, Beard still refused to count American imperialism as a distinct school of thought, contemptuously calling it a "bastard conception," even though he charged this policy with having "destroyed" the policy inaugurated by Washington. The second school, then, was the "collective internationalism" of Woodrow Wilson, for which Beard had little but sarcasm born of disappointment and of the anxiety over the repetition of Wilsonian blunders by the Roosevelt administration.[64] The third school, understandably not given more than passing attention, was international communism. Finally, there was a fourth, newly emerging school, going back to what Beard in 1922 had tentatively called "Little Americanism," and which in 1934 he had worked out under the motto of "The Open Door

62. *America in Midpassage,* pp. 442–43.

63. Ibid., pp. 443–46.

64. Ibid., pp. 446–51. Beard was at his critical best in a concise critique of the assumptions of Wilsonianism in his *The Republic* (New York: Viking Press, 1944), pp. 307–308. This has lost nothing of its pertinence in view of more recent critiques of what is now referred to as the "moralistic-legalistic" approach. The "four huge assumptions" of Wilsonianism were: "First, that the supreme object of our national life is to bring permanent peace to all nations. . . . Second, that world peace is desirable or good for mankind or a majority of mankind. Third, that the constitution of our universe makes it possible to effect and maintain permanent world peace for all mankind. Fourth, that it is possible for the Government of the United States to secure at home adequate and continuous support for making and keeping this world at peace, a support that will provide all the military, economic, and other sacrifices which it would entail upon our people." By way of contrast, see Beard at his polemical worst in his definition of the "Wilsonian creed of world interventionism and adventurism" in *Giddy Minds and Foreign Quarrels,* pp. 23–25: "Imperialism is bad (well, partly); every nation must have a nice constitutional government, more or less like ours, . . . that old history, full of troubles, is to be closed; brethren, and presumably sisters, are to dwell together in unity; everything in the world is to be managed as decorously as a Baptist convention presided over by the Honorable Cordell Hull; if not, we propose to fight disturbers everywhere (well, nearly everywhere)."

at Home." He refused (with one exception)[65] to apply to this school the name of isolationism. It is in *America in Midpassage* that the most balanced and persuasive, polemically undistorted statement of Beard's theory occurs:

> At the center of its philosophy was the idea that through domestic measures, adopted by the democratic process, vast improvements could be and should be effected in American civilization, . . . moreover, that this civilization could be defended in its continental home under prudent policies by small but appropriate military and naval establishments. Associated with this vision was the conviction that American democracy should not attempt to carry the Atlas load of the White Man's Burden in the form of imperialism all over the earth, or assume that it had the capacity, even with the best of good will, to settle the difficult problems of European nations encrusted in the heritage of their long and sanguinary history. . . . Perhaps, in a world beset by clamant ideologies, the name "continental," or "American civilization," was most appropriate, if still inadequate, to characterize the thought of the fourth school of foreign policy.[66]

Little more than a year later Beard presented in *A Foreign Policy for America*, an admittedly more programmatic work, a new, more simplified pattern. The "isolationism" of the Fathers and the new continental school were fused under the title of "Continental Americanism" or "continentalism." The two other schools were imperialism and internationalism. Previously avowed links between the early tradition of American foreign policy and imperialism were negated; on the other hand, the resemblances between imperialism and internationalism, their longing for worldwide entanglements, were stressed.

The outstanding characteristic of the development of Beard's thought during the thirties was the increasing rigidity of his views. This tendency manifested itself not only in the amount of programmatic writings which in itself presented a departure from the professedly analytical works of his earlier life; more disturbing was the transformation of his historical interpretation of the period of the Fathers and of post-1897 imperialism, as it fitted only too well Beard's new creed of continentalism.

65. This exception was *American Foreign Policy in the Making 1932–1940* (New Haven: Yale University Press, 1946), p. 17n. 2.
66. *America in Midpassage,* pp. 452–53.

This transformation postdated the definitive adoption of the as yet unla-
beled continentalist program in 1934 as a consequence of the world's economic crisis. It was intimately linked up, then, with the perseverance and
mounting bitterness with which Beard continued to fight for this program
against what he considered the increasingly dangerous foreign policy of
Franklin D. Roosevelt. After the disappointments caused by World War
I and the economic crisis, Beard's fight against Roosevelt emerges as the
third great factor responsible for the far-reaching change from his early
enthusiasm for world unity to his latter-day exhortations to America to
cultivate its own garden.

IV

The concluding pages of *The Idea of National Interest* mirrored the ambivalent expectations of fear and hope with which Beard viewed the prospects of F.D.R.'s foreign policy. On the one hand, there was satisfaction
and relief about Roosevelt's stand at the London Economic Conference of
1933:

> It furnished the occasion on which President Roosevelt disclosed his
> conception of American national interest. . . . After the collapse of the
> economic structure in 1929, a new conception of national interest in
> foreign commerce appeared—a conception that a high standard of na-
> tional well-being is possible with a minimum reliance on foreign trade
> and is desirable besides. . . .[67]

On the other hand, Beard's rejoicing over Roosevelt's economic foreign
policy was dampened by grave doubts regarding his naval policy. "In em-
barking on naval construction, the Roosevelt administration was running
in the course of *Machtpolitik*,"[68] Beard gloomily remarked. Even a couple of years earlier, Beard had devoted an independent little volume to
an attack on the Navy's "vested interests" to defend Americans interests
everywhere on the globe.[69] By the first half of 1935, Beard's apprehensions
concerning Roosevelt's naval policies definitely had superseded his initial
satisfaction concerning tendencies of economic policy. Beard now issued a
solemn warning against Roosevelt's policy:

67. *The Idea of National Interest*, pp. 543 and 545.
68. Ibid., p. 546.
69. *The Navy: Defense or Portent* (New York: Harper, 1932).

President Roosevelt . . . has, to be sure, spoken of peace with his wonted geniality, but Herr Hitler has done as much. . . . Deeds speak louder than words. President Roosevelt has adopted the biggest navy program in the history of the country in peace time. . . . President Roosevelt has not given any indication whatever that he intends to relax the competition of the United States with Great Britain and Japan for prestige and "sea power." Judging by the past and by his actions, war will be his choice—and it will be a "war for Christianity against Paganism" this time. . . . This is not saying that President Roosevelt will deliberately plunge the country into a Pacific war in his efforts to escape the economic crisis. There will be an "incident," a "provocation." Incidents and provocations are of almost daily occurrence. Any government can quickly magnify one of them into a "just cause for war." [70]

It is in the light of this very warning, issued as early as 1935, that Beard's later crusade against F. D. R. must be understood. Doubtless incidents unconnected with foreign affairs, like the Supreme Court Crisis of 1937, heightened his opposition to the President. But the tenor of self-righteousness, bitter, sometimes heavy-handed sarcasm, and deep moral indignation, characteristic of numerous writings of the pre-World War II years and of his last two books on foreign affairs—*American Foreign Policy in the Making 1932–1940* and *President Roosevelt and the Coming of the War 1941* [71] flowed from what Beard held to be the vindication of his early Cassandra calls which had been unable to prevent disaster.

The guiding theme of Roosevelt's foreign policy was, according to Beard, the idea of the "Holy War" to right the world's wrongs. As the thirties progressed towards their ominous end, the impact of World War I loomed larger and larger in Beard's writing. This impact, unlike the impact of the economic crisis which had led Beard to adopt a certain economic-political theory, was above all moral in its nature. Two elements can be distinguished in Beard's war trauma. One was the threat to liberty, to the ideals of American civilization wrought by the war. As Beard dramatically told an interlocutor in 1939, "I slowly awoke to my abysmal ignorance"; he had seen Columbia University use the war to suppress men, freedom of the press trampled upon, leaders of liberal movements silenced. [72] Second,

70. "National Politics and War," *Scribner's Magazine*, XCVII (Jan.–June, 1935), 70.

71. (New Haven: Yale University Press, 1948).

72. Hubert Herring, "Charles A. Beard. Free Lance Among the Historians," *Harper's Magazine*, (CLXXVIII) (Dec. 1938–May 1939), 652.

there were the complexities of the war guilt question, the disappointment of his hopes of 1917 in a diplomacy both realistic and righteous, neither utopian nor self-righteous. These apprehensions, having led a somewhat subterranean existence in the twenties, broke forth with unremitting vigor in the middle and late thirties. Unless Americans were convinced they knew enough to right Europe's wrongs, it would be the better part of wisdom to be cautious. "We nearly burnt our house down with one experiment."[73]

Moral indignation rather than cool analysis was also the undertone of a small but famous book, *The Devil Theory of War*, occasioned by the investigations of the Nye Committee. In his most sarcastic vein, Beard denounced the myth that wicked bankers, wicked politicians, "or if the source of the trouble is not some wicked person, . . . a wicked 'force,'" might be the single cause of wars. In theory, Beard's emphatic warning against the fallacy of the single cause was sound; but his very recognition of the intractable complexity of the war guilt resulted in a moralistic, despairing judgment: "My trouble lies in the fact that greed, lust and ambition in Europe and Asia do not seem to be confined to Italy, Germany and Japan; nor does good seem to be monopolized by Great Britain, France and Russia."[74]

Thus the stage was set for the increasing vigor of Beard's crusade against Roosevelt, culminating in the two volumes on American foreign policy up to Pearl Harbour.[75] In a twofold sense, *American Foreign Policy in the Making 1932–1940* and *President Roosevelt and the Coming of the War 1941* reflect characteristic elements of Beard's outlook. First, there was the assumption that American security was not threatened from the outside world, but could only be jeopardized through unwise actions emanating individually or collectively from America herself. Second, there followed, as a corollary, the idea that war for America, since her basic security was not threatened, could only have the utopian purpose of setting right the world's wrongs. Even though clad in the tone of grave scholarship,

---

73. Charles A. Beard, "Heat and Light on Neutrality," *New Republic*, LXXXVI (Feb.–May 1936), 9.

74. Charles A. Beard, *The Devil Theory of War*, (New York: Vanguard Press, 1936), p. 118

75. For details of Beard's anti-Roosevelt campaign, see the article by G. Leighton quoted in n. 2 above. Roosevelt's quarantine speech of October 5, 1937 and his Navy Bill of January 1938 were milestones for Beard's increasing hostility. See also the frequent articles in the magazine *Events* from 1937 to 1940, and particularly *Giddy Minds and Foreign Quarrels* of September, 1939.

Beard's indictment of Roosevelt in 1946 had lost nothing of the moral fervor of his pre-war Cassandra calls:

> If studies of diplomatic history and international law under Professor John Bassett Moore and on my own account had taught me anything, it was that the high officials of great States could not continue indefinitely to lay down moral rules for other governments to follow without being called upon to retract or to employ the historic instrument for enforcing them—war.[76]

These assumptions led Beard into the trap of a double set of false alternatives. First, there was the erroneous alternative making national defense and collective security or alliances mutually exclusive instead of complementary. For instance, discussing the Navy Bill of 1938, Beard implied deception when he said that

> supporters of the Administration program had doubly assured the country that in adopting the recommendations for increase in naval constructions they had in mind *only defense, not collective security,* quarantine, or intervention in foreign political controversies.[77]

The possibility of collective security actually becoming a necessity of national defense never entered Beard's mind. He thus became the prisoner of rigid formulas like collective security, entangling alliances, foreign wars, concepts without any concrete meaning unless viewed in the context of specific and ever changing political realities and objectives. An apologist for Roosevelt's policy, prone to some conceptions opposite to, but as deceptive as Beard's, nevertheless was right in his assertion—specifically concerned with Lend Lease—that Beard ignored what the administration and its supporters had made amply clear: that the decision as to whether a certain nation should receive aid would be determined not by the nature of its internal, social, economic, or governmental structure but by its foreign policy in relation to American defense.[78]

76. *American Foreign Policy in the Making 1932–1940*, p. 162n. 13.

77. Ibid., p. 219. (My italics)

78. Basil Rauch, *Roosevelt from Munich to Pearl Harbour* (New York: Creative Age Press, 1950), p. 309. Rauch remarked correctly that "in Beard's vocabulary discussion of war is synonymous with a desire for war." (Ibid., p. 472). On the other hand, Rauch's attempts to minimize Roosevelt's inconsistencies and ambiguities are tortuous, e.g., his assertion that the states-

The second deceptive alternative—perhaps more astounding than the
first—was a strange juxtaposition of freedom and necessity in burdening
President Roosevelt with gigantic responsibilities. From the assumption
that any American involvement in world affairs, and particularly in war,
was an active effort emanating from America—, from this exaggeration of
America's freedom of choice there arose a rather crude and one-sided theory of total freedom of action—on the part of President Roosevelt. Beard's
failure in both volumes to give even remotely adequate consideration to
the international setting in which Roosevelt's foreign policy evolved lent
additional power to his indictment of Roosevelt:

> If the President was driven into war by the overt acts of aggression and
> in no manner contributed to bringing on the war, he was a victim, and
> not a maker, of history; he did not lead the nation into war for rea-
> sons of world morality but was forced into it or drawn into it or com-
> pelled to take up arms against his will, by circumstances beyond his
> control. . . .
> . . . How elusive are such phrases as 'war was inevitable,' 'drawn into
> war,' 'compelled to take up arms,' 'forced into war,' and 'America has
> been wantonly attacked.' They connote a determinism of events for the
> United States, as if President Roosevelt was a mere agent of forces be-
> yond his initiation or control, not an active agent in a conjecture of cir-
> cumstances which he has helped to create by deliberate actions on his
> own part. Of course, it may be assumed that the whole world drama
> has been determined from the beginning of human time and that all
> the men and women who have taken any part in it have been mere ac-
> tors, mere puppets speaking lines and acting roles assigned to them by
> fate or 'the nature of things.'[79]

I have tried to show how this unbalanced condemnation grew out of
some elements deeply rooted in the background of Beard's thought. On
the other hand, it must be added that the conceptual framework of the
two books on Roosevelt's foreign policy is a distorted offshoot of the main
body of Beard's thought as it evolved over several decades. In a three-fold
respect, it conflicts with some important tenets of Beard's thought, some
of long standing, some of more recent or even very recent origin. First, it

---

manship of Roosevelt, Stimson and Hull consisted in devising techniques permitting the U. S.
to take part in the collective security without forming entangling alliances (Ibid., p. 3).
    79. *President Roosevelt and the Coming of the War 1941*, p. 407 and 407n. 1.

was obviously a total departure from the economic and at least implicitly deterministic tendencies of his previous works. "Time was," as Professor Morison observed in his famous critique of Beard's last book, "when history through a Beard moved with the sweep of relentless, dynamic forces."[80] Second, it fell sadly short of those insights—theoretically asserted more often than observed in the practice of historical writing—on the insoluble complexity of human relationships, the Machiavellian interplay of virtue, fortune, and necessity, which Beard first developed in the middle thirties and which he emphatically restated toward the end of his life.[81] Third, Beard's books on Roosevelt failed to do justice to what was perhaps the most fruitful, if, alas, unexploited new development in the thought of his later years, a fundamental revision of his thought on politics in general and international politics in particular. One of Beard's most insistently held convictions had been his belief in the primacy of domestic over foreign policy; this means that the sources of foreign policy have to be sought in the domestic configurations of a country rather than in its geographical or power constellation with respect to other countries. This conception had two distinct, though not unrelated, sources. One was Beard's "economic interpretation," implying that the economic, or more precisely the acquisitive pursuits of a country's citizens, once they transcend its borders, are at the bottom of its foreign policy. The second, more basic because never totally realized assumption was the fact of America's unchallenged security—which itself was also one premise of Beard's economic interpretation. In practice then, the primacy of domestic policy meant to convey the primacy of economic, acquisitive pursuits over military, power- or security-centered activities. Perhaps Henry Adams had grasped the fundamental issue involved more clearly than anyone else including Beard, when he wrote in the conclusion to his majestic *History*:

> Should history ever become a true science, it must expect to establish its laws, not from the complicated story of rival European nationalities, but from the economical evolution of a great democracy. North America was the most favorable field on the globe for the spread of a society so large, uniform, and isolated as to answer the purposes of science. . . . In the fierce struggle characteristic of European society,

80. S. E. Morison, "Did Roosevelt Start the War?" *Atlantic Monthly*, CLXXXII (August 1948), 94.

81. See above p. 111n29, and Beard's Presidential Address to the American Political Science Association, "Neglected Aspects of Political Science," *American Political Science Review*, XLII (1948), 213 f.

systems were permanent in nothing except the general law, that, whatever other character they might possess, they must always be chiefly
military.[82]

These were, more clearly expressed than Beard ever contrived to state
them, the premises of Beard's younger years. History could be reduced to
science; its true laws were economic; the economic, then, was a more fundamental layer of reality than the military; finally—and this thought was
unexpressed in Beard—the fact of American isolation made it possible in
actuality as well as in observation to penetrate to this deepest layer of
reality.

In 1945 Beard added a new chapter to an older statement of his early
views, *The Economic Basis of Politics*. This new chapter lowered the cur-
tain on a whole epoch of social and historical thinking and writing, an
epoch of which Beard himself was the latest and perhaps most articulate
representative. Unlike Henry Adams, unlike the mainstream of his own
lifework, Beard now admitted that the primacy of economics over politics,
of well-being and gain over power and security, did not, after all, express
the deepest layer of reality:

"The political man" has been gaining in independence from, and in
power over, "the economic man" and is now often in a position to order
him about rather than to take dictation from him.
. . . .
From Aristotle's time down through the centuries that theory had been
limited by the condition that economic forces operate freely only in the
absence of military force; but during the long period between the close
of the Napoleonic wars in 1815 and the opening of the first World War
in 1914, the conditional clause, which severely limited the theory, had
been regarded as largely academic, particularly in the United States.[83]

Toward the close of his long career then, Beard's intellectual outlook,
which never had lacked contradictions, was enriched by a new paradox: at
the very time when his unrestrained condemnation of President Roosevelt

82. Henry Adams, *History of the United States of America during the Administration of Thomas Jefferson and James Madison*, 9 vols. (New York: Scribner's, 1921), IX, 222.
83. Charles A. Beard, *The Economic Basis of Politics* (new ed.; New York: A. A. Knopf, 1945), pp. 72 and 75. The resurrection of the *homo politicus* was accounted for, or recognized, by Beard under the impact of the growing bureaucracy of the New Deal without any clearcut "economic interests," as well as under the impact of totalitarian movements in Europe.

subjected some of his work to the extremes of the "fallacy of the single cause," he nevertheless began to enter new realms of political inquiry, to discover new perspectives, and to draw new conclusions. After all, if today the analysis of foreign policy in terms of the impact of military configurations on domestic and foreign policy alike is spreading fast, if indeed it has not become commonplace, it is only fitting to point out that, at least in theory, Beard indicated the way which now is walked upon by many.

In conclusion, we may ask ourselves what the salient features of Beard's lifework were, so far as we were able to discuss them in this paper. Is there a common denominator among so many contrasts, is there steady progress amidst changing views? It seems that we may discern two different lines of development in Beard, leading to different and in the end quite disjointed goals. First, there is the development from simplicity to complexity in Beard's theory of history and the social process. From a rather crude and unexamined, if straightforward, economic determinism, Beard moved steadily on to discover new layers of reality. In the early thirties, there was his discovery of the realm of "ethics and esthetics," as he called it, the discovery of freedom and moral choice in history. The reading of authors like Machiavelli, Croce, Riezler and Meinecke, but also the unfolding of terrible new forces like Fascism and Nazism, exploding in the holocaust of World War II, led Beard to a restatement of his faith in terms of the unpredictable interplay of virtue, necessity and fortune on the stage of history; it led to an increased awareness of military and political forces, of forces irreducible to the level of acquisitiveness which was his point of departure and, alas, only too often his point of return as well. In the second place, in the field of foreign affairs, Beard's progress was altogether different: it led from the exuberant optimism and internationalism of his youth to the bitter and distorted isolationism of his old age; it was a development from comprehensiveness to simplification quite opposite to the advancement of his theoretical insight.

Three factors, we have said, can be singled out to account for the cumulative force of Beard's changing views on foreign affairs. There were first the disappointments of World War I—the threat to liberty at home and the defeat of a just international order abroad. There was, second, the lightning-like impact of the Great Depression and its connection with the world's economic crisis. There was, finally, Beard's increasing hostility to Franklin D. Roosevelt, compounded of elements of earlier fears—the threat to liberty and prosperity at home through involvements abroad that finally led to a distorted perspective of great magnitude.

The very breadth of Beard's mind and of his interests, his openness not only to the influence of books, but to the impact of deep moral conviction and of the fast moving world around him as well, were bound to produce conflicts and inconsistencies. The most painful one, in terms of Beard's scholarship, would seem to be the contrast between the complexity of Beard's theoretical insights, particularly in later years, and the one-sidedness of his historical researches on specific problems—whether it was the Constitution, the "Idea of National Interest," or F.D.R.'s foreign policy. In spite of Beard's efforts in the field of theory, the fallacy of the single cause crept twice into his work: first under the guise of the *homo economicus,* and later in his single-minded attack on President Roosevelt. And yet, there are unity and a touch of greatness amidst diversity and failings. There is a greatness running through the whole of Beard's life and work which he may not have claimed for himself, because his pride was set on the detached realism of the scholar. But there is little doubt that Beard's enduring fame will rest on the conviction that he was one of America's great moralists. Without the salt of his nonconformist conscience, America would have been much duller; and as the dangers of conformity increase, there may be more need to remind ourselves of his example.

PART II

Austrian History—Imperial and Republican

CHAPTER FIVE

The Multinational Empire Revisited: Reflections on Late Imperial Austria
Robert A. Kann Memorial Lecture 1989*

I

R obert Kann's first book, *The Multinational Empire*, published in two large volumes in 1950, has become a classic in its field. As Stanley Winters has well said: "It is rare when a scholar's first book establishes its author in the front rank of his field, and it is rarer still when the book remains a standard work for the balance of his lifetime."[1] In 1964, a considerably enlarged German edition was published.[2]

As an introduction to the growth of national self-awareness of the Habsburg Monarchy's nationalities, and as a guide to the unfolding of the multiple attempts to reform the Monarchy's structure and to improve the relations among its peoples, Kann's work has been mined by generations of scholars and students.

Kann's influence on historical scholarship both in America and Austria (and beyond) is evidenced by the fact (as I have written before) that more of his books were published both in English and in German than those of any other Scholar in the field.[3] In addition to *The Multinational*

---

* The Robert A. Kann Memorial Lecture, given at the Center for Austrian Studies of the University of Minnesota on 5 April, 1989. This Memorial Lecture is annually given in memory of the Austro–American historian Robert A. Kann (1909–1981). First published in: *Austrian History Yearbook*, XXIII (1992), 1–22. The permission to reprint was gracefully granted by the Center for Austrian Studies, University of Minnesota. The lecture was slightly revised and expanded for publication.

1. Stanley B. Winters, "The Forging of a Historian: Robert A. Kann in America, 1939–1976," *Austrian History Yearbook* XVII–XVIII (1981–82), 7.

2. Robert A. Kann, *Das Nationalitätenproblem der Habsburgermonarchie*, 2nd ed., 2 vols. (Graz and Cologne: Böhlau, 1964).

3. Gerald Stourzh, "Robert A. Kann—A Memoir from Austria," *Austrian History Yearbook* XVII–XVIII (1981–82), 25.

Empire, let me mention four more books: *The Habsburg Empire: A Study in Integration and Disintegration* (1957); *A Study in Austrian Intellectual History from Late Baroque to Romanticism* (1960); *The Problem of Restoration: A Study in Comparative History* (1968); and *A History of the Habsburg Empire, 1526–1918* (1974).

Kann was indeed a man of two countries; for three decades, his work spanned America and Austria. Being Austrian, I am particularly grateful to Robert Kann for his many reflections, admonitions, and advice to Austria and Austrians in his later years. Kann had been a liberal democrat as a young man in Austria, and yet his belief in liberal democracy became strengthened and enriched through his life in America and as an American citizen. His credo as a liberal democrat has been expressed on a number of memorable occasions in Austria.[4] Liberal democracy—or "Western" democracy, as he also put it—enshrined the unlimited recognition of the principle of the equality of all citizens on the basis of individual freedom in a legal as well as moral sense.[5] Kann elaborated this principle by stressing that equality was to be understood both in the legal sense of equality before the law as well as in the social sense of the equality of chances ("Gleichheit der Aussichten") for every citizen.[6] Kann—trained as a lawyer before he became a historian, and deeply committed to the rule of law—also provided important insights into the function of law. The legal and constitutional order provides a framework for the predictability of the consequences of human action. Such predictability, Kann said, was a precious treasure, not merely for the system of legal protection, but for human culture in general.[7]

Kann's profound commitment to the values of liberal democracy, for equal rights and social justice, emerges time and again in his scholarly work. Speaking, for instance, of the Magyar oligarchy in the pre-1914 days and its approach to the other national groups, Kann has perceptively observed that the oligarchy lacked "the understanding that national discrimination, added to social discrimination, aggravated the lot of the socially underprivileged non-Magyar peasant and worker still further."[8] In

4. References are given in Stourzh, ibid., 25–26.
5. Robert A. Kann, "Das geschichtliche Erbe—Gemeinsamer Nenner und rechtes Maß," in *Österreich—Die Zweite Republik,* ed. Erika Weinzierl and Kurt Skalnik, 2 vols. (Graz: Styria, 1972), 1:19.
6. Ibid., 25.
7. Ibid., 48–49.
8. Robert A. Kann, *A History of the Habsburg Empire, 1526–1918* (Berkeley: University of California Press, 1974), 461.

more general terms, Kann has developed the same idea in a piece written for the Austrian Academy and available only in German: "National equality without the social basis of equal rights is a mere travesty that reduces supranational compromise to an empty formula."[9] I shall have occasion, in this lecture, to return on various occasions to the work of Robert Kann, to his judgments and his interpretations.

II

The point of departure for my reflections on the late Habsburg Empire is a railway station in fin-de-siecle Vienna. From railway stations people depart for travel, and I would like to draw your attention to two travelers who went to Vienna's Western Railway Station, the Westbahnhof, on August 11, 1898, their destination being the Austrian Salzkammergut.

One of these travelers was Sigmund Freud. To his *Interpretation of Dreams,* and to the magnificent commentary by Carl Schorske, we owe the account of the following episode.[10] Freud was about to go on holiday to Bad Aussee. Arriving at the Western Railway Station a bit early, Freud pacing back and forth on the platform suddenly saw Count Franz Thun, Austria's prime minister (1898–1899), approach the platform, wave aside the ticket taker in an imperious manner, and board the train bound for Bad Ischl; his train left earlier than the one that was to take Freud to Bad Aussee. Something should be explained that may be known only to connoisseurs of Austria's railway geography: Bad Ischl was usually reached from the north via Linz and the junction of Attnang-Puchheim; Bad Aussee, which also could be reached from the north, could be reached from the south as well via the Gesäuse and the junction of Stainach-Irdning. So on that August night of 1898, these two gentlemen departed from Vienna to reach the Salzkammergut. Freud—how could it be otherwise?—took the low road, as it were, and Count Thun took the high road.

9. "Nationale Gleichheit ohne die soziale Unterlage der Gleichberechtigung ist eine bloße Travestie, die den übernationalen Ausgleich zu einer leeren Formel reduziert." Robert A. Kann, "Die Habsburgermonarchie und das Problem des übernationalen Staates," in *Die Habsburgermonarchie 1848–1918,* ed. Adam Wandruszka and Peter Urbanitsch, vol. 2: *Verwaltung und Rechtswesen* (Vienna: Verlag der Österreichischen Akademie der Wissenschaften, 1975), 22.

10. For the following see Sigmund Freud, *Die Traumdeutung* (1900), in Sigmund Freud, *Studienausgabe,* ed. Alexander Mitscherlich, Angela Richards, and James Strachey (Frankfurt: Fischer, 1972), 218–26, 418–20. English translation in *The Standard Edition of the Complete Psychological Works of Sigmund Freud,* trans. and ed. James Strachey et al. (London: Hogarth Press, 1953–1964), 4:208–19; also 5:431–35. Carl Schorske, *Fin-de-siècle Vienna: Politics and Culture* (New York: Knopf, 1980), 193–99 and 206.

Thousands of readers of Carl Schorske's book are by now familiar with Freud's impressions at the Western Railway Station and the dream he had while on the train to Bad Aussee. Count Thun's imperious gesture stimulated rebellious feelings in Freud and led him to hum the tune of Figaro's aria in *The Marriage of Figaro:*

> *Will der Herr Graf ein Tänzelein wagen, Tänzelein wagen,*
> *Soll er's nur sagen, ich spiel' ihm eins auf.*

Freud's rebellious mood while watching newcomers to the platform is enhanced when a bureaucrat known to Freud asks some favor from the train attendant—the bureaucrat paying only half fare for his first-class ticket, while Freud is obligated to pay full fare. During the train ride to Bad Aussee, these impressions gathered at Vienna's Western Railway Station triggered Freud's "Revolutionary Dream." In it Count Taaffe, a predecessor of Thun's, appears, a symbol of conservative, antiliberal rule. Freud responds angrily to the prime minister and identifies with Adolf Fischhof, a Jewish-German liberal doctor of medicine, hero of the 1848 revolution, and, incidentally, one of the great theorists of a multinational empire based on the equality of nationalities.[11] Victor Adler, another physician and leader of Austria's Social Democrats, appears in the dream as well. From Thun to Taaffe to Fischhof to Adler—an encounter with the episode of Freud's and Thun's departure from the Westbahnhof on August 11, 1898 and Freud's "Revolutionary Dream" is bound to send the student off on a double journey: the first journey taking "the low road" through the subconscious life of the mind, its psychological roots as well as its social setting in late imperial Austria, and the second taking "the high road" through the life of the body politic. We thus are set to reflect briefly on

---

11. On Fischhof's approach to the nationality conflict (he greatly influenced Karl Renner) and his ideas of transforming the multinational empire into a monarchical Switzerland, see Kann, *Nationalitätenproblem der Habsburgermonarchie,* 2:149–55, and more recently Gerald Stourzh, *Die Gleichberechtigung der Nationalitäten in der Verfassung und Verwaltung Österreichs 1848–1918* (Vienna: Verlag der Österreichischen Akademie der Wissenschaften, 1985) 200–202, and idem, "Wandlungen des Österreichbewußtseins im 20. Jahrhundert und das Modell der Schweiz," in *Schweiz-Österreich. Ähnlichkeiten und Kontraste,* ed. Friedrich Koja and Gerald Stourzh (Vienna: Böhlau, 1986), 12–14. Ludwig von Mises has admiringly referred to "den fähigsten und reinsten aller österreichischen Patrioten, Adolf Fischhof" (the "most capable and purest of all Austrian patriots"). Ludwig von Mises, *Erinnerungen* (Stuttgart and New York: Fischer), 20.

two dimensions of life in late imperial Austria that have been—though perhaps on unequal terms—of interest to recent historical scholarship.

III

The life of the mind and its sociocultural or sociopolitical setting in late imperial Austria, and more precisely in fin-de-siècle Vienna, has of course been one of the most fashionable, I would even say the most "trendy" research object of recent years. Vienna 1900 "has become big business," as it has been rightly said.[12] The claim that Vienna was the birthplace of the modern world[13] has recently been reduced to a more balanced view.[14] Yet the question of the concentration of genius, of the proliferation of originality, of the pursuit of excellence in a particular place at a particular time remains a continuing challenge to scholarship and to reflection. I fully agree with Robert Kann, who has spoken of "basically unexplainable causes for the great achievements of the human spirit,"[15] yet it is permitted to look for more favorable or less favorable supporting or surrounding conditions. A multinational setting may not be an essential precondition of cultural development, but presumably, as Kann has said, it is a favorable one.[16] Kann had in mind not cultural development in general, but indeed the creative "high culture" of late imperial Austria, of which Freud has become the most towering and most influential figure. It might be mentioned in passing that Freud's early collaborator Joseph Breuer, the originator of the first observations leading to the development of the new method of attacking psychic disturbances, was the paternal grandfather of Robert Kann's wife, Dr. Mariedl Kann.

Let me mention two examples in support of Kann's suggestion that a multinational setting may favor—or has favored—creative excellence. Fritz Mauthner, the well-known theorist of language, has written in his autobiography on the conditions that stimulated interest in the psychology of language "to a passion." He reports how, as a Jewish boy in bilingual

12. Steven Beller, "Modern Owls Fly by Night: Recent Literature on Fin-de-siècle Vienna" (review article), *Historical Journal* 31 (1988),665.

13. Norman Stone, *Europe Transformed, 1878–1919* (Cambridge, MA: Harvard University Press, 1984): "But it was in Vienna that most of the twentieth century intellectual world was invented. Practically in every field, from music to nuclear physics, Austro-Hungarian subjects were leaders" (407).

14. See the excellent discussion by Beller, "Modern Owls," particularly 667 and 669–71.

15. Kann, *History of the Habsburg Empire,* 564.

16. Ibid., 562–63.

Bohemia in the 1850s, he was exposed to German, Czech, Hebrew, and to the mixed idioms of "Kuchelböhmisch" [a simplified version of Czech spoken to and by kitchen personel] and "Mauscheldeutsch" [Yiddish].[17]

A second example is Hans Kelsen, the celebrated legal theorist and co-author of the Federal Constitution of the Republic of Austria, and the creator of the Pure Theory of Law (Reine Rechtslehre). In an autobiographical note, Kelsen has reflected on the sociopolitical conditions of the emergence of his theory:

> In view of the Austrian state that was composed of so many different groups according to race, language, religion, and history, theories that based the unity of the state on some sociopsychological or sociobiological connection of the people that juridically were part of the state were proved to be fictions. Insofar as this theory of the state [i.e., Kelsen's theory of the state as a purely juridical construct, the state as a system of norms] is an essential component of the Pure Theory of Law, the Pure Theory of Law may claim to be a specifically Austrian theory.[18]

The extraordinary pursuit of intellectual excellence in fin-de-siècle Austria to which I have just referred may have had additional preconditions that favored the emergence and proliferation of originality and creativity. I would like to single out two such preconditions; one of these seems to have elicited less comment, as far as I see it, the other one rather more.

One precondition may best be described as the survival of rules or rather patterns of conduct and expectations of partly premodern origin, best summed up in the imperative: Strive for something higher, take your cue from something above you; strive for excellence—morally, socially, and intellectually. A great variety of seemingly diverse standards of

---

17. Fritz Mauthner, Erinnerungen, 1: Prager Jugendjahre (Munich: Georg Müller, 1918), 32–33, 50. Mauthner's autobiography is a mine of information on mentality in a multinational and multilingual land. Of great interest is his account of the last event that united Czechs and Germans in Prague in a common demonstration—the centennial of Friedrich Schiller's birth in 1859. Ibid., 127.

18. "Angesichts des österreichischen Staates, der sich aus so vielen nach Rasse, Sprache, Religion und Geschichte verschiedenen Gruppen zusammensetzte, erwiesen sich Theorien, die die Einheit des Staates auf irgendeinen sozial-psychologischen oder sozial-biologischen Zusammenhang der juristisch zum Staat gehörigen Menschen zu gründen versuchten, ganz offenbar als Fiktionen. Insofern diese Staatstheorie ein wesentlicher Bestandteil der Reinen Rechtslehre ist, kann die Reine Rechtslehre als eine spezifisch österreichische Theorie gelten." Quoted in Rudolf Aladár Métall, Hans Kelsen. Leben und Werk (Vienna: Franz Deuticke, 1969), 42 (My translation). Kelsen's autobiographical sketch has not been found. The passages in Métall's book are thus our only access to this most interesting document.

conduct—Christian (both Catholic and Protestant), *bildungsbürgerlich*, and, of course, Jewish as well, had one common denominator: they were antipermissive. A variety of life-styles and backgrounds thus shared one requirement: the application of a discipline that included forgoing immediate benefits for the sake of ulterior rewards. This meant: no premature contentment; one could not afford self-indulgence. Such an attitude might apply to the bureaucrats emulating the discipline and diligence of the Emperor as well as to the military wearing *des Kaisers Rock* (the Emperor's uniform), to individuals who from humble beginnings (or, if they were Jewish, from beginnings burdened by discrimination) were determined to climb the ladder of social mobility, of which there was a great deal in nineteenth-century Austria—whether that ladder led to material reward in business or, characteristically for the Habsburg Empire, to rewards of a nonpecuniary nature.

These rewards of a nonpecuniary nature were numerous: degree and rank in the military or bureaucratic hierarchy, distinctions conferred by the Emperor (*Orden*), titles in the (normally lower) nobility. But of course, and in many ways more importantly, there were also the nonpecuniary status rewards of *Bildung*, the great goddess of the nineteenth century.[19] The deprivations incurred in order to get through Gymnasium and university and finally to reap the doctorate degree were great, particularly among those social strata where sending children to the Gymnasium and to the university was a first-generation experience.[20]

Standards and patterns of denial of permissiveness and self-indulgence, while originally set within a quite rigid social context, underwent a pro-

19. The greatest symbol of the passion for *Bildung*, uniting intellectual, moral, and political commitment, was the enthusiasm for Friedrich Schiller. This has been rightly stressed in the brilliant book by Steven Beller, *Vienna and the Jews, 1867–1938: A Cultural History* (Cambridge: Cambridge University Press, 1989), 150–51. One might add to the examples given by Beller the magnificent novel by the Austrian-Jewish writer Karl Emil Franzos (1848–1904), *Schiller in Barnow*, which impressively shows the redeeming promise of Schiller in a most miserable Jewish settlement in Eastern Galicia ("Barnow" of Franzos's novels is the town of Czortków, where Franzos spent his early youth). Beller discounts too much, however, the non-Jewish part of the *bildungsbürgerliche* developments in nineteenth-century Austria. Beller also exaggerates, perhaps, the difference between the "Puritan-like" life-style of the German (including Jewish-German) middle class in the Bohemian lands and the "hedonism"of Vienna (ibid., 169f.), given the vast influx of German, Jewish, and an also diligent Czech population from the Bohemian lands into Vienna in the nineteenth century. Of great general interest for the history of the central place of *Bildung* in the nineteenth century is the recent book by Ulrich Engelhardt, *"Bildungsbürgertum." Begriffs-und Dogmengeschichte eines Etiketts* (Stuttgart: Klett-Cotta, 1986).

20. The recruitment of the student body of the philosophical faculties of the Austrian universities as distinguished from the faculties of medicine and law, as well as the social structure of the Gymnasialprofessoren of late nineteenth-century Austria, would deserve close analysis.

cess of individualization in late nineteenth-and early twentieth-century
society: the pursuit of excellence became individualized and opened the
way for the proliferation of originality. "The ladder of the spirit was a social ladder, too," as Carl Schorske has inimitably put it,[21] yet it was a ladder that was prepared, perhaps, in earlier times than those of the generation driven to climb it after the demise of political liberalism.

The second precondition, much in the forefront of recent scholarly discussion, is Jewish emancipation and assimilation. Vienna, with a Jewish
population in 1910 of 175,318, had the third largest Jewish population in
Europe after Warsaw and Budapest. By 1910 the Jewish population of Vienna, as Robert Wistrich has recently pointed out, had increased twenty-
eight times over what it had been in 1857. He adds that this extraordinary
rate of growth was unparalleled after 1860 anywhere in the Habsburg Empire or on the European continent. The percentage of the Jewish population in Vienna in 1910 was 8.6, much lower than in Budapest (23 percent)
but noticeably higher than in Berlin (3.7 percent).[22] These statistics do not,
of course, include persons who had left the Jewish community and converted to Catholicism or Protestantism; these converts, while statistically
less significant than one might suppose (from 1868 to 1903, 9,085 persons
left the Vienna Jewish community),[23] came overwhelmingly from the upper social strata of the Jewish population.[24] It is, therefore, no accident that
recent studies of the Jewish element in Austrian high culture are bound to
pay great attention to the sociocultural problems of conversion.[25] It is also
worth repeating Marsha Rozenblit's observation that "Vienna's Jewish
conversion rate far outranked that of any other city in the Dual Monarchy
or elsewhere in Europe."[26] Finally, it should be added that a considerable

21. Schorske, Fin-de-siècle Vienna, 148.

22. Robert S. Wistrich, The Jews of Vienna in the Age of Franz Joseph (London: Oxford
University Press, 1989), 41–42.

23. Marsha L. Rozenblit, The Jews of Vienna, 1867–1914: Assimilation and Identity (Albany: State University of New York Press, 1983), 132.

24. For this, see the remarkable observations by Franz Borkenau, Austria and After (London: Faber & Faber, 1938), 110–14. Addition 2006: Recent research suggests that conversions
concerned much wider social strata than I thought in 1989; this has to do with the fact that
probably the most important motive of conversion was a planned marriage with a Christian,
since Austrian law prohibited marriages between Christians and non-Christians. See Anna L.
Staudacher, Jüdisch-protestantische Konvertiten in Wien 1782–1914, 2 vols. (Frankfurt/Main:
Peter Lang, 2004), notably vol 1, 90–96, 240–47.

25. See Beller, Vienna and the Jews, particularly 35–36 and 189–90. Also most recently
Michael P. Steinberg, The Meaning of the Salzburg Festival: Austria as Theater and Ideology,
1890–1938 (Ithaca, NY: Cornell University Press, 1990), particularly 170–75.

26. Rozenblit, Jews of Vienna, 132.

amount of intermarriage took place between persons who had converted from Judaism and persons of non-Jewish descent. This sociocultural phenomenon is again pertinent chiefly in the social strata of the lower nobility, upper bureaucracy, industrial *Großbürgertum*, and *Bildungsbürgertum*.[27] The observation may be permitted that although the destruction of Austrian Jewry by Hitler (with the willing help of Austrian Nazis) is a terrible fact, a relatively large number of descendants of mixed marriages have survived and are part of the Austrian people of today—a sociocultural phenomenon that ought not to be forgotten.

Many assimilated Jews, whether extending their assimilation to conversion or not, were seeking, in Steven Beller's words, "a realm beyond the power of social, religious or racial prejudice, where the individual, and not his background, counted."[28] This individualism à outrance of assimilated Jews was increasingly confronted or even jeopardized by the rise of the "new" anti-Semitism from the 1880s onward.[29] This individualism was

27. An interesting comment on the frequency of mixed marriages in Vienna is in Toni Stolper, *Ein Leben in Brennpunkten unserer Zeit: Wien-Berlin-New York. Gustav Stolper, 1888–1947* (Tübingen: Rainer Wunderlich Verlag, 1960), 160. Ivar Oxaal has convincingly critized Marsha Rozenblit for underestimating the presumable frequency of mixed marriages in Vienna. Ivar Oxaal, "The Jews of Young Hitler's Vienna: Historical and Sociological Aspects," in *Jews, Antisemitism and Culture in Vienna*, ed. Ivar Oxaal, Michael Pollak, and Gerhard Botz (London: Routledge & Kegan Paul, 1987), 32.

28. Beller, "Modern Owls," 682. On the centrality of the individualism theme in fin-de-siècle Vienna, both Jewish and non-Jewish, and the ensuing identity crises, see the suggestive book by Jacques Le Rider, *Modernité viennoise et crises de l'identé* (Paris: Presses Universitaires de France, 1990), and its German translation, *Das Ende der Illusion. Die Wiener Moderne und die Krisen der Identität* (Vienna: Österreichischer Bundesverlag, 1990).

29. On anti-Semitism in the last decades of imperial Austria, I would single out four outstanding contributions: Robert Kann, "German-speaking Jewry during Austria–Hungary's Constitutional Era (1867–1918)," *Jewish Social Studies*, 10 (1948): 239–56; John Boyer, *Political Radicalism in Late Imperial Vienna: Origins of the Christian Social Movement, 1848–1897* (Chicago: University of Chicago Press, 1981); Peter Pulzer, *The Rise of Political Anti-Semitism in Germany and Austria*, rev. ed. (Cambridge, Mass.: Harvard University Press, 1988); and Franz Borkenau, *Austria and After*. Borkenau's book has an original chapter entitled "Liberalism and the Jewish Question" (92–117). Without in any way minimizing the precariousness of the Jews' position in Austria, he has pointed to the contrast between countries like Romania and Russia, where the Jews were barred from all participation in public life and from many economic activities, and Austria, where such legal discrimination did not exist, but where "in actual fact the Austrian Jews had won an important place in public and in intellectual life" (ibid., 112–13). Julius Braunthal, a Socialist and assimilated Jew, could write in his autobiography: "In the invigorating air of this remarkable cosmopolis, . . . Jewish talent blossomed as vigorously as it did in Granada under Moslem rule." Quoted in Pulzer, *Political Antisemitism*, 13, from Julius Braunthal, *In Search of the Millennium* (London, V. Gallancz Ltd., 1945), 17. On the legal and constitutional rights of the Jews of Austria in relation to assimilationist tendencies on the one hand and the new surge of diaspora nationalism around 1909 an the other, see Gerald Stourzh, "Galten die Juden als Nationalität Altösterreichs?" in *Studia Judaica*

apt to provide a stimulating milieu for the pursuit of innovative excellence on account of the very insecurity of the quest for assimilation. Oskar Kokoschka has recorded that most of his sitters were Jews. "They felt less secure than the rest of the Viennese Establishment, and were consequently more open to the new and more sensitive to the tensions and pressures that accompanied the decay of the old order."[30] And even towering genius, ultimately inexplicable and irreducible, might have been enticed to more daring and more searching questions, as has indeed been said of Freud: "The prevalence of antisemitism creates in the minds of the Jews a passionate 'Why?' In favorable circumstances, this urgent questioning may have results of considerable scientific importance."[31] Steven Beller has drawn the conclusion that "the cultural effluorescence in Vienna . . . received its central impetus from the crisis faced by assimilating Jewish individuals in a society which no longer recognized that assimilation as totally legitimate."[32]

Although very suggestive, and in many respects convincing,[33] this may not be all. Returning to Sigmund Freud, one of our travelers on that summer night of 1898, I would like to draw attention to a thoughtful reflection by Robert Kann. The resistance, the harassments that blocked Freud's academic career on Austrian soil, Kann has written, presumably derived from an even more powerful motivation than racial prejudice: fear. Freud's contemporaries everywhere—not only in Austria—so Kann continues, shrank from the consequences, which his exploration of the subconscious and unconscious in the human psyche might have on their lives.[34]

Approaching the end of these reflections on some of the sociocultural and sociopolitical preconditions for the astounding flowering of the life of the mind in fin-de-siècle Austria, it is important to remind ourselves

---

Austriaca 10 (1984), 73–117, reprinted in Gerald Stourzh, *Wege zur Grundrechtsdemokratie. Studien zur Begriffs-und Institutionengeschichte des liberalen Verfassungsstaates* (Vienna: Böhlau, 1989), 259–307. See also chapters 7 and 8 in this volume.

30. Quoted in Edward Timms, *Karl Kraus, Apocalyptic Satirist: Culture and Catastrophe in Habsburg Vienna* (New Haven and London: Yale University Press, 1986), 6, from Oskar Kokoschka, *My Life*, trans. D. Britt (London, Thames & Hudson, 1974), 35.

31. Quoted in Beller, *Vienna and the Jews*, 217, from Fritz Wittels, *Sigmund Freud* (London, 1924), 247.

32. Beller, "Modern Owls," 681.

33. I think, however, that Beller overextends his argument by speaking of Vienna's fin-de-siècle "cultural creativity, in which, to put it bluntly, Jews led and the rest followed" (ibid., 681). A more differentiated view emerges from a most suggestive "diagram of creative interaction in Vienna" in Edward Timms's *Karl Kraus*, 8. See also Steinberg, *The Meaning of the Salzburg Festival*, 172.

34. Kann, *History of the Habsburg Empire*, 560.

again that the intellectual and artistic take-off of the turn of the century carried on beyond the breakup of imperial Austria in 1918. The greater break came in 1938.

Thus, almost forty years after his departure from Vienna's Westbahnhof for Bad Aussee on August 11, 1898, Sigmund Freud, on June 3, 1938, departed from the same station for London. Three days later he wrote to an old friend: "The feeling of triumph at being freed is too strongly mingled with grief, since one always greatly loved the prison from which one has been released."[35] So there was ambivalence at the end.

IV

I now propose to follow the other traveler speeding toward the Salzkammergut on that summer night of 1898—Count Franz Thun. I do not know, of course, whether Count Thun—called Count "Nichtsthun" by his critics, as Freud had observed—had a dream during his journey to Bad Ischl, a trip presumably more comfortable than Freud's. Yet Count Thun might well have had nightmares as he traveled to Bad Ischl. His voyage to the summer residence of the Emperor Franz Joseph was connected with a grave crisis in Austro-Hungarian relations, the renewal of the *Ausgleich* or Compromise of 1867—more precisely the renewal of the economic and financial parts of the *Ausgleich*, which took place every ten years.

Everybody is aware, of course, that the Habsburg Monarchy, during the last half century of its existence was a dual monarchy, but there seem to me to be reasons to call special attention to that phenomenon. Yet let me first return to the preoccupations of Count Thun as he approached Bad Ischl. The periodicity of the Ausgleich, more precisely the need to renegotiate its financial and economic clauses every ten years, presented the Dual Monarchy with a built-in crisis every decade, one that is often compared to a cancer besetting the Habsburg Empire.[36]

---

35. "Das Triumphgefühl der Befreiung vermengt sich zu stark mit der Trauer, denn man hat das Gefängnis, aus dem man entlassen wurde, immer noch sehr geliebt . . ." To Max Eitingon, June 6, 1938. Sigmund Freud, *Briefe 1873–1939*, ed. Ernst L. Freud (Frankfurt: S. Fischer Verlag, 1960), 439.

36. Thus Ignaz von Plener in the Austrian Herrenhaus (chamber of peers) on May 18, 1878. See Gerald Stourzh, "Die dualistische Reichsstruktur, Österreichbegriff und Österreichbewußtsein 1867–1918," in *Innere Staatsbildung und gesellschaftliche Modernisierung in Österreich und Deutschland 1867/71 bis 1914*, ed. Helmut Rumpler (Vienna: Verlag für Geschichte und Politik, 1991), 53–68, here 62. Attention to this speech was first called by Berthold Sutter, "Die Ausgleichsverhandlungen zwischen Österreich und Ungarn 1867–1918," in *Der österreichisch-ungarische Ausgleich von 1867. Seine Grundlagen und Auswirkungen.*

In 1898, the renewal was overdue. Conferences in Ischl and in Vienna in August 1898 finally led to a temporizing compromise, wrongly known as the "Ischl agreement," because the final agreement was reached in Vienna. It amounted to a provisional continuation of existing conditions, as long as one of the partners (Hungary more likely than Austria) did not put the other partner on notice of terminating the existing regulations. This was called, in Austro-Hungarian bureaucratese, a *Perennierungsklausel*— a clause perpetuating the conditions of the existing *Ausgleich*. It was, incidentally, a clear violation of the basic legislation of 1867 that had stipulated that the renewal of the compromise must be passed by the parliaments of Budapest and Vienna every ten years.

Why do I mention these details that Count Thun and his Hungarian counterpart, Baron Bánffy, worked out in the summer of 1898? Because they throw into relief a phenomenon to which Peter Hanák, my distinguished Hungarian colleague, has drawn attention in a brilliant piece published a few years ago.[37] Psychoanalysis, *Sezession*, atonality, Hanák observes, have become household words in the vocabulary of educated people; yet virtually no one, he adds, knows the significance of words of everyday use in the press of fin-de-siècle Austria and Hungary like *Ausgleichsprovisorium, ex lex* condition, or "perpetuity clause."

We must rediscover the institutional structure of the late Habsburg Empire. Much has been virtually forgotten, and I believe this is particularly true of the dualistic structure of the empire. Symbolically, of the two travelers speeding toward the Salzkammergut on that August night of 1898, we know much more about Freud and his concerns; we know too little of Thun and his preoccupations. From my experience as a university teacher, I would like to put it this way: The Habsburg Monarchy in the last half century of its existence affords the only example of a territorial unit where, for practical purposes of instruction, there is a glaring—and what is worse, often unreflected—incongruity between the unit covered by diplomatic history and the unit covered by the history of domestic developments; the former is twice as big as the latter. Diplomatic history focuses on the history of the entire Austro-Hungarian Empire; domestic history more often than not is taught as the history of one half of the Dual Monarchy, Austria, whereas

Buchreihe der Südostdeutschen Historischen Kommission, vol. 20 (Munich, 1968), 87, though there ascribed to Ignaz Plener's son Ernst von Plener. Sutter's study remains to this day the most useful survey of the *Ausgleich* issue from 1867 to 1918.

37. Peter Hanák, "Die Parallelaktion von 1898. Fünfzig Jahre ungarische Revolution von 1848 und fünfzigjähriges Regierungsjubiläum Franz Josephs," *Österreichische Osthefte* 27 (1985), 366–80.

what was going on in the other, Hungarian, half of the Dual Monarchy is typically ignored. From rather nebulous perceptions of what was going on in the Hungarian half of the Dual Monarchy, occasional glimpses of isolated events—Franz Joseph's 1903 army order of Chlopy intended to maintain the army's unity, or the Hungarian government and suffrage crisis of 1905, emerge and find their way into textbooks and teaching aids otherwise chiefly concerned with Cisleithanian history. It is easy, for example, for students to glide imperceptibly from the introduction of universal manhood suffrage in 1906–1907 in Austria to the annexation crisis of 1908–1909, without being too clearly aware that "Austria" and the (Dual) "Monarchy" or "Empire" were two units of very different size and structure.

These difficulties of perception date back to the 1867–1918 era. After 1867, data for most sectors of social, demographic, and economic developments were compiled separately by the different statistical offices of Hungary and of Cisleithania/Austria. There exist maps with statistical data that, while outlining the boundaries of the whole Dual Monarchy, contain information only for the Austrian half, leaving a void for the other half of the Empire. Another example: the historical exhibition devoted to the age of Franz Joseph (the Lower Austrian *Landesausstellung* held in Grafenegg in 1987) presented statistical data on the origins of the population of Vienna. Not only were the strong ties to the Bohemian lands demonstrated; in addition, there was a display on "foreign citizens." There was, however, nothing to inform visitors that the vast majority of "foreign citizens" came from Hungary—Hungary and Austria granting, under the regime of the Dual Monarchy, separate kinds of citizenship. Thus domestic servants from Slovakia, migrant workers from Western Hungary (now the Burgenland), or Jews from Budapest, all residing or working in Vienna or surrounding parts of Lower Austria while maintaining their Hungarian citizenship, were statistically treated as "foreign citizens." Awareness of these peculiarities of "Kakania," it may be presumed, is scant; yet the phenomenon of separate citizenship was of considerable practical significance in the late Habsburg Monarchy, given that the more liberal divorce legislation in Hungary after 1894 might make it advisable for Austrian citizens seeking divorce to change over to Hungarian citizenship. Thus the recovery of half-forgotten details of institutional and legal history may help one to grasp the realities of social history in the fin-de-siècle Habsburg Empire!

There is, however, another and perhaps even more important reason why I think it is imperative to rediscover the institutional history of the Dual Monarchy. Apart from the debates in the field of cultural and intellectual history from Carl Schorske onward, addressed in the first part of this essay, the most rapidly advancing field of Habsburg history has been economic history. Since much of the recent research and writing in this field—involving among others the work of Alexander Gerschenkron, John Komlos, and Richard Rudolph—has been recounted and carried on in the work of David Good, notably in his book on the economic rise of the Habsburg Empire,[38] I shall not rush into a field where I depend wholly on the findings of my colleagues. Certain results, like the insight that on balance the Hungarian half of the Monarchy benefited more from the union than it lost, first pointedly formulated by Peter Hanák in 1967 and basically confirmed both by Komlos and Good, deserve mentioning;[39] so does the finding that in the last half century of the Monarchy, unevenness of development and regional disparities may have been less pronounced than depicted by conventional wisdom;[40] likewise the confirmation and corroboration of the longer known fact that fiscal policy largely responded to contending forces in the national struggle, economic development merely being accidentally served as a by-product.[41] The strong bias toward the "visible hand" mode of resource allocation, of which David Good has spoken,[42] can be illustrated, for example, by the unfortunate ways of the Austrian government in financing, for political reasons, the wrong schools in the wrong province for the wrong people, as happened in Bukovina.[43]

Yet there remains an unresolved problem. It results from one of the most interesting findings of recent research into the economic development of the Habsburg Monarchy. I refer to the view that it was not economic failure that induced political failure in the Habsburg Monarchy, but that instead one may detect successful modern economic growth,

38. David F. Good, *The Economic Rise of the Habsburg Empire, 1750–1914* (Berkeley: University of California Press, 1984).

39. Peter Hanák, "Hungary in the Austro-Hungarian Monarchy: Preponderancy or Dependency," *Austrian History Yearbook*, III, pt. 1 (1967), 260–302; this article was republished in Hungarian and in German, the latter appearing in the collection of many of Hanák's papers published under the title *Ungarn in der Donaumonarchie* (Vienna, Munich, and Budapest: Verlag für Geschichte und Politik, Oldenbourg Verlag, Akademiai Kiadó, 1984), 240–80. John Komlos, *The Habsburg Monarchy as a Customs Union: Economic Development in Austria-Hungary in the Nineteenth Century* (Princeton: Princeton University Press, 1983), particularly 7ff.; and see Good, *Economic Rise of the Habsburg Empire*, particularly 135–46, 156–61.

40. Good, *Economic Rise of the Habsburg Empire*, 125ff.

41. Ibid., 249.

42. Good, ibid., particularly 232, 236, 238, 249, 251.

43. This phenomenon was violently criticized by the noted legal scholar, sociologist, and sometime rector of the University of Czernowitz, Eugen Ehrlich, in his booklet *Die Aufgaben der Sozialpolitik im österreichischen Osten, insbesondere in der Bukowina mit besonderer Beleuchtung der Juden-und Bauernfrage* (Czernowitz, 1909).

clashing, however, with badly adjusting institutions. David Good has concluded that apparently "the political institutions of the empire had tremendous difficulties adapting to the pressures imposed by modern economic growth. Why this was so, remains a puzzle for future research to
untangle."[44] So the ball has been returned by the economic historians, but
to whom? Has it been thrown back to the historians with the "traditional,
narrative-descriptive approach" grounded in the humanities?[45]

My reply—tentative and preliminary—is that historians with a grasp
of the functioning of institutions are likely to have a share in untangling
that puzzle. Elsewhere I have put forward my view that the history of institutions is at the crossroads where social, political, economic, and indeed
legal history meet or ought to meet.[46]

Even in the past, historical research and reflection on the late Habsburg
Empire have yielded a number of distinguished works whose outstanding
feature is their analytical rather than their narrative quality. I have in
mind, first, Joseph Redlich's Österreichisches Staats-und Reichsproblem
of 1920–1926, as well as the same author's magnificent book on Austria's
government and administration during World War I (part of the Carnegie
Endowment's multivolume enterprise on the social history of World War I)
published in 1925. Second, I think of Oscar Jászi's Dissolution of the
Habsburg Empire of 1929. And third, I think of Robert Kann's The Multinational Empire of 1950 as well as several of his other works, notably his
1957 volume on the Habsburg Empire and his highly analytical reflections—
at times perhaps too abstract—on the supranational state, in the Austrian
Academy's multivolume work on the Habsburg Monarchy from 1848 to
1918.[47] My own work on the process of national conflict resolution in

44. Good, Economic Rise of the Habsburg Empire, 256. Though slightly overdrawn, there
is a point in Alan Milward's comment: "The ironic conclusion to be drawn from Good's work
is that successful integration within the framework of a common market will do nothing to
stop catastrophic political disintegration." Alan S. Milward, Review of David F. Good, The
Economic Rise of the Habsburg Empire, Economic History Review 38 (1985), 471.

45. Good, Economic Rise of the Habsburg Empire, 7.

46. See Gerald Stourzh, "Zur Institutionengeschichte der Arbeitsbeziehungen und der
sozialen Sicherung," first published as introduction to Historische Wurzeln der Sozialpartnerschaft, ed. Gerald Stourzh and Margarete Grandner, Wiener Beiträge zur Geschichte der
Neuzeit 12–13 (1986), 13–37, particularly 35–37; republished with slight modifications in Gerald Stourzh, Wege zur Grundrechtsdemokratie, 335–61, particularly 358–61. See also James G.
March and Johan P. Olson, Rediscovering Institutions: The Organizational Basis of Politics
(New York: Free Press, 1989).

47. Robert A. Kann, The Habsburg Empire: A Study in Integration and Disintegration
(New York: Praeger, 1957); idem, "Die Habsburgermonarchie und das Problem des übernationalen Staates," in Die Habsburgermonarchie 1848–1918, vol. 2; idem, "Zur Problematik der

Austria's administrative and judicial institutions and, more recently, on the problems of the changing dimensions of the concept of Austria and of Austrian consciousness,[48] has led me to appreciate the enduring value of the analyses of Redlich, Jászi, and Kann.[49]

An institutional analysis of the late Habsburg Empire is likely to confirm the view—by no means new, yet thrown into relief more acutely than ever by the contemporary history of East-Central Europe, Southeastern Europe, and Eastern Europe—that ethnicity, ethnic rivalry, and the striving for institutional arrangements expressing the increasing importance of ethnic relations within the Empire were the great issues dominating other social and power constellations. I shall single out two areas in which an institutional approach to the history of the late Habsburg Empire has discovered, and is about to appreciate more acutely than before, important facets of the multinational empire.

First, I shall return briefly to the dualist structure, and second, I shall venture some comments on the issue of national autonomy so-called, in the Austrian part of the Empire. The multinational empire of the Habsburgs consisted, in the last half century of its existence, of two states with radically different structures. The kingdom of Hungary conceived of itself as a Magyar national state, with national and linguistic minorities to be sure, yet nevertheless a state embodying a political nation *une et indivisible*, as was expressly proclaimed in the "nationality law" of 1868. In the preamble to that law, sketched by Ferenc Deák, all citizens of Hungary, whatever their language, were declared members of the one and indivisible political Hungarian nation. Accordingly, the Magyar language was proclaimed as the official state language. While this view was at first moderated by the fairly liberal language regulations for minorities in the "nationality law" of 1868, later generations pushed the primacy of the Magyar language and the Magyar people to the level of national chauvinism. "We have only one

Nationalitätenfrage in der Habsburgermonarchie, 1848–1918," in *Die Habsburgermonarchie* vol. 3: *Die Völker des Reiches* (1980), 1304–38.

48. See Gerald Stourzh, *Die Gleichberechtigung der Nationalitäten;* this is a revised reprint of my contribution to vol. 3 of Die Habsburgermonarchie 1848–1918, 975–1206, enlarged by a new introduction, a selection of annotated sources, and a bibliography. See also my *Vom Reich zur Republik. Studien zum Österreichbewußtsein im 20. Jahrhundert* (Vienna: Edition Atelier, 1990); and "Der Umfang der österreichischen Geschichte," in *Probleme der Geschichte Österreichs und ihrer Darstellung*, ed. Herwig Wolfram and Walter Pohl (Vienna: Verlag der Österreichischen Akademie der Wissenschaften, 1991), 3–27.

49. It is perhaps worth recalling that both Redlich and Kann—the latter having dedicated his *Multinational Empire* to Redlich's memory—originally underwent the broad legal curriculum of Austrian universities in the late nineteenth and early twentieth centuries, while Jászi was a sociologist by training rather than a historian.

single categorical imperative, the Magyar state idea," said Prime Minister Koloman Széll in 1908, "and we must demand that every citizen should acknowledge it and subject himself unconditionally to it." Two years later, Count Stephen Tisza added: "Our citizens of non-Magyar tongue must, in the first place, become accustomed to the fact that they belong to the community of a nation state, of a state which is not a conglomerate of various races."[50]

"Kakania," to use Robert Musil's immortalized expression, as it manifested itself in Budapest around the turn of the century, was a very different thing from "Kakania" as seen and felt in Vienna at the same time. It is instructive to recall that as urbane and progressive a thinker as Otto Bauer, a Social Democrat, felt impelled to recommend the use of "k.u.k." violence to change things in Hungary. The Crown, Otto Bauer wrote in 1907,

> cannot remain the organ of two distinct wills and still rule both Austria and Hungary. Therefore, it must take care that Hungary and Austria should have one will, and should constitute one empire. The tattered conditions of Hungary give a possibility to this unity. The Crown will not hesitate to send its army to Hungary in order to re-conquer it for the Empire, but it will write on its flags: Unadulterated, universal suffrage and secret ballot! Right of coalition for the agricultural proletariat! National autonomy! It will oppose to the idea of the independent Hungarian national state the idea of the United States of Greater Austria, the idea of a confederative state in which each nation will administer independently its national affairs and all the nations will unite in one state for the protection of their common interests.[51]

There is in Austria today, in my judgment, an insufficient perception of what the "Hungarian" dimension of the late Habsburg Empire implied. Kakania, Musil has written, referred to itself "on paper" as the Austro-Hungarian Monarchy; yet

> in speaking . . . one referred to it as Austria, that is to say, it was known by a name that it had, as a State, solemnly renounced by oath, while preserving it in all matters of sentiment, as a sign that feelings are just

---

50. Both quotes taken from Oscar Jászi, *The Dissolution of the Habsburg Monarchy* (Chicago: University of Chicago Press, 1929; paperback ed. 1961), 321.

51. Quoted in English translation ibid., 181, from Otto Bauer, *Die Nationalitätenfrage und die Sozialdemokratie* (Vienna: Deuticke, 1908), 373.

as important as constitutional law and that regulations are not the really serious thing in life.[52]

At the risk of provoking criticism because of my iconoclasm with
regard to Musil's definition of "Kakania," I daresay that around 1900 or
1910, it was not understood in Budapest in that way. There were feelings
and sentiments, not merely constitutional law, that impelled Magyars to
feel themselves part of the Empire, but not of Austria.

Just in the year of Freud's and Count Thun's journey to the Salzkammergut, a double jubilee brought this conflict to the foreground, as Peter
Hanák has impressively shown.[53]

The year 1898 saw Franz Joseph's golden jubilee as Emperor—
December 2, 1848, having been the date of his accession to the throne.
This jubilee was celebrated in Vienna most impressively, the murder of the
Empress Elisabeth in September of that year notwithstanding. Yet 1898
was also a memorial year for the Hungarian revolution of 1848 against
Habsburg absolutism, and the clash between Hungarian patriotism and
dynastic loyalties broke out with great bitterness. The Hungarian authorities trod gingerly on the narrow path between Hungarian patriotism fed
by the anti-Franz Joseph memories of 1848–49 and the loyalty due to the
constitutional monarch crowned in 1867. Hanák shows this in his masterful essay, where, alluding with fine irony to Musil, he speaks of the "Parallelaktion" of the two jubilees with such divergent objects. After having
read it, one is bound to revise any exaggerated estimates of the strength of
"kakanian" sentiment in the kingdom of Hungary.

Let me add a second iconoclastic attack against Musil's kakanian pan-
orama. Musil writes that "there was a parliament, which made such vigorous use of its liberty that it was usually kept shut; but there was also an
emergency powers act by means of which it was possible to manage without Parliament."[54] Musil is referring to the famous/infamous section 14
of the Fundamental Law on Imperial Representation (*Grundgesetz über
die Reichsvertretung*). But the emergency powers clause was, of course, applied only in one half of what Musil had said was just "Austria." In Hungary, there was no such provision; Franz Joseph ruled differently, and had
to rule differently, in the two halves of his empire.

52. Robert Musil, *Der Mann ohne Eigenschaften*, in English translation as *The Man without Qualities*, trans. Eithne Wilkins and Ernst Kaiser, vol. 1 (New York: Coward-McCann,
1953; Capricorn Books, 1965), 33.

53. See note 37 above.

54. Musil, *The Man without Qualities*, 33.

Of course reform thinkers thought and dreamed of the "United States of Greater Austria." Not merely the Romanian, strongly anti-Magyar author Aurel Popovici, who wrote a book about it,[55] but even such a sober and critical thinker as Otto Bauer evoked the vision, as I have shown above, of the transformation of the Dual Monarchy into a "United States of Greater Austria."[56] Yet I fully agree with the skeptical judgment of Robert Kann: "The transformation of the whole empire into a federal order on an ethnic basis without regard to the state borders between Austria and Hungary probably would have led in war as in peace to the splitting of the Empire."[57]

In Cisleithanian Austria, as opposed to Hungary, the principle of the equality of nations had been proclaimed and embodied in the Constitution of 1867, and it must be said that in spite of the growing bitterness of ethnic conflict in Austria, culminating in the 1897 language crisis in which Germans and Czechs opposed each other, the institutional framework at the disposal of conflict resolution was remarkable and grew more refined in the decades between 1867 and 1918. The case law developed during these decades by the two highest courts of public law, the Reichsgericht (Imperial Court, a kind of constitutional Court), and the Verwaltungsgerichtshof (Supreme Administrative Tribunal) is impressive. The minority protection afforded by these institutions finds no parallel in the Transleithanian part of the Monarchy or elsewhere in Europe during that period (or, with few exceptions, in the interwar period).[58]

This leads me to the second issue mentioned above, and the concluding one to be raised in this lecture—that is, the issue of national, or as

55. Aurel von Popovici, *Die Vereinigten Staaten von Groß-Österreich* (Leipzig, 1906).

56. See note 51.

57. Robert A. Kann, "Die Habsburgermonarchie und das Problem des übernationalen Staates," *Die Habsburgermonarchie 1848–1918*, 2:38–39. The sentence is important enough to be rendered fully in the German original: "Die einzige logisch folgerichtige Lösung der nationalen Frage, die Umwandlung des Gesamtreiches in eine bundesstaatliche Ordnung auf ethnischer Grundlage ohne Rücksicht auf die Staatsgrenzen zwischen Österreich und Ungarn, mußte voraussichtlich im Kriege wie im Frieden zur Reichsspaltung führen." It should be added that Robert Kann, in the same essay, is skeptical regarding hopes (sometimes even retrospectively expressed) that the heir to the throne, Francis Ferdinand, might have been in a position to carry through a reform of the empire; Kann stresses the fact that Francis Ferdinand did not give priority to federalism per se but rather to the idea of a decentralized unitary state "in which the weight of power should reside in a significantly increased position of the crown." Kann adds that it is unlikely that such goals could have been reached in the second decade of the twentieth century, even if the world war had not broken out. Ibid., 37.

58. I must refer the reader to the evidence presented in my monograph *Die Gleichberechtigung der Nationalitäten*. Of particular interest as a case study is the way in which public elementary schools for minority populations were created by the case law of the *Verwaltungsgerichtshof*; cf. ibid., 166–76.

one might say more precisely today, ethnic autonomy. It is, of course, perfectly true that institutional resources for ethnic conflict resolution in Cisleithanian Austria were not equal to the task of satisfying the growing demand of the ethnic groups for autonomy and, finally, self-determination as nations in the full political sense of the word.

The great political question that emerged from the disaster of Austrian parliamentarism in 1897 on the occasion of the "Badeni" crisis was the double problem of how to assure the protection of permanent minorities in a constitutional system fundamentally predicated on the principle of majority rule, and to satisfy the growing demand for national autonomy—national autonomy understood as autonomy for the *Volksstämme* (peoples in an ethnic sense) of imperial Austria. The outburst of creative writing on these questions in the period from 1897 to about 1910 (e.g., Georg Jellinek's thought-provoking lecture on the right of minorities of 1898, many of Karl Renner's most original writings, Otto Bauer's work on the nationality question and social democracy of 1907, and Edmund Bernatzik's magisterial lecture-essay on ethnic registers of 1910) is unique in Europe at that time.[59] These pathbreaking works on the political theory of national autonomy are not the least significant contributions to "fin-de-siècle" Austria, though they are often disregarded in the current debates on "Vienna 1900." It is one of the great qualities of Robert Kann's book on the multinational empire that it has established a lasting monument to this innovative series of writings on minority protection and ethnic autonomy.

"National autonomy" became the great battle cry in Austria in the decade prior to the outbreak of World War I. The "national compromises" in Moravia in 1905–1906 and in Bukovina in 1909–1910 are the most important and best documented attempts to put into practice some of the original ideas generated since 1897.[60] The organization of ethnic groups for purposes of provincial and imperial elections, including the construction of double or (in Bukovina) multiple networks of constituencies along ethnic lines and the drawing up of ethnically or linguistically separate voters' registers (the celebrated *nationale Kataster*), and in Moravia furthermore the organization of elementary education on a strictly ethnically and linguistically separate basis—all this was part of a tendency I would

59. There is no need for references to the writings of Renner and Bauer. I would like to draw attention, though, to Georg Jellinek, *Das Recht der Minoritäten* (Vienna, 1898), and Edmund Bernatzik, *Über nationale Matriken* (Vienna, 1910).

60. For the following, see the detailed discussion in Stourzh, *Die Gleichberechtigung der Nationalitäten*, 189–240.

like to call "the ethnicizing of Austrian politics"—*die Ethnisierung der österreichischen Politik.*

More and more, in the last two decades of imperial Austria's existence, did the *Volksstämme* (the official German term for nationalities or ethnic groups) emerge as the truly constituent factors of political decision.[61] The *Volksstämme*, wrote Prime Minister Ernest von Koerber to Franz Joseph in 1900, "subordinate everything, even their most important interests, to the language conflict."[62] More and more the Crown—the Emperor's government—desisted from acting, if a consensus of the nationalities was not attained. The new emphasis on *Volksstämme* tended to deemphasize the position of the state and even of the historic provinces, the Länder. Karl Renner put this characteristically in a speech in Parliament in 1917: "The nation [in an ethnic sense] today has assumed the position of the 'Land.'" Austria needed a constitution, Renner added, that would invest the nations with the position of the bearers, the pillars of the Empire.[63]

The new and increasing primacy of the ethnic groups tended not merely to deemphasize the traditional role of the provinces and of the imperial government; this primacy also tended to reduce the position of the individual as citizen of the state, stressing, instead, the individual's role as a member of an ethnic group. In the pattern of organization along ethnic lines one may roughly discern three types. First, there were the numerous associations organized along national (i.e., ethnic) lines that had sprung up in the second half of the nineteenth century, particularly those promoting the cause of schooling.[64] A second type were the ethnic umbrella organizations springing up around the turn of the century, like the Národni rada ceská, or the Deutsche Volksrat für Böhmen and its equivalent for

61. Cf. the evidenc submitted in Stourzh, *Die Gleichberechtigung der Nationalitäten,* 14, 156, 221, 231, 244–45. Brilliant contemporaries recognized the expanding dynamics of the process of ethnicizing institutions—whose functions might not be connected with "national" questions—by adding rules concerning compulsory linguistic/ethnic attribution; like Joseph Lukas, a Professor of public law in Czernowitz, did in 1908 (quoted ibid., 208–209). The compulsory ethnic separation of colleges of physicians, of engineers, and so forth, particularly in the Bohemian lands, are cases in point (ibid., 210, 229).

62. Alfred Ableitinger, *Ernest von Koerber und das Verfassungsproblem im Jahre 1900* (Vienna, Cologne and Graz: Böhlau, 1973), 198.

63. Speech on June 15, 1917, Haus der Abgeordneten, *Stenographische Protokolle,* 7. Sitzung der XXII. Session, 338.

64. A magnificent case study that has become a classic is Monika Glettler's *Die Wiener Tschechen um 1900. Strukturanalyse einer nationalen Minderheit in der Großstadt* (Munich and Vienna: Oldenbourg, 1972).

Moravia.[65] The third type consisted of organizations of public law, fulfill-
ing functions of public authority. Characteristically, the first organizations of this type emerged in connection with the administration and supervision of public schools. The ethnically separate local school boards in
Bohemia created in 1873 were the first examples of this new type of public authority structured along ethnic/linguistic lines; they were followed
by the ethnic restructuring of the provincial school board for Bohemia in
1890, and of the school boards on all levels in Moravia in 1905.

The creation of public bodies structured along ethnic lines produced
a new need: the attribution of ethnic membership (*Volkszugehörigkeit*)
to individuals. Individuals tended to be treated, in late imperial Austria,
more and more as members of a new collectivity: the *Volksstamm*, the
nationality, the people, the nation, the ethnic group, whichever of these
varying denominations one chose or chooses to use. This trend had several consequences. First, it tended to put a premium on persons who not
merely "belonged" clearly to one or the other nationality, but who were
"nationally minded" (*nationalgesinnt*).[66] Second, and even more sinister,
was a trend toward attribution of ethnic membership by imperial authorities, as, for example, in Moravia as a result of the 1905 settlement. The
very notion of an "objective" way of attributing ethnic membership on the
basis of evidence gathered through official investigation—even specially
designed questionnaires were used for this purpose![67]—was strongly criticized at the time.[68] The authoritative attribution of ethnic membership on
the basis of "objective" criteria was to have terrible effects after the end of
the Habsburg Empire, when persons of Jewish origin from Galicia, citizens
of the defunct imperial Austria, were denied the possibility of declaring

65. The translation into English of the terms Volksrat and národní rada is not easy: "ethnic council,"; "people's council," "national council" all are possible. With the increasing po-
liticization and self-articulation of the nationalities as "nations," the term "national council"
becomes the most appropriate rendering, and indeed there emerge in the fall of 1918 "national
councils" as engines of national self-determination in various parts of the disintegrating multinational empire.

66. Such persons were qualified as particularly suited to serve on the provincial school
board in Moravia—a qualification approved by German and Czech representatives alike. See
the evidence cited in Stourzh, *Die Gleichberechtigung der Nationalitäten*, 15 and 218.

67. Such questionnaires, designed by the imperial authorities in Moravia (Statthalterei)
in 1911, have been found by the author in archival materials and will be published in a study
devoted to the effectiveness of the Moravian compromise. For this, see the immediately following essay (Ch. 6).

68. Bernatzik, *Über nationale Matriken*, 84–86. See also the study by Stourzh, "Ethnic
Attribution in Late Imperial Austria. Good Intentions, Evil Consequences" in this volume
(immediately following essay).

themselves ethnically German and gaining the citizenship of republican Austria.[69] The authoritative attribution of ethnic membership had, of course, much more horrible effects when legal and social discrimination, persecution, and destruction broke loose under Nazi rule.

Finally, returning to late imperial Austria, it should be kept in mind that the division of people into groups according to ethnic attribution was of course part and parcel of the program of "national autonomy." National autonomy, the last panacea of imperial Austria, was intended to reduce national strife, to bring about national peace. Yet it was, as pointed out by contemporaries, a policy of pacification by the means of separation and isolation, not by true conciliation and integration.

A soberer, less enthusiastic interpretation of national autonomy and its implications is presented here than corresponds to general opinion of national autonomy legislation in late imperial Austria. Yet a comparative view of the "multinational empire" of late imperial Austria within the context of other multiethnic states and empires still leads me to concur with the judgment rendered by Oscar Jászi in 1929: There can be no doubt, Jászi wrote, "that the Austrian half of the dual monarchy made gigantic efforts toward the solution of the national problems," and he concluded that as "a matter of fact, the first foundations of a state based on national equality were laid down in these tempestuous decades."[70]

V

On April 1, 1989,[71] there took place in Vienna an event apt to evoke the most variegated reflections on the Habsburg Empire: the funeral of the last Empress of Austria and Queen of Hungary, Zita, the widow of Charles I/IV.

The Viennese—and untold numbers of television viewers—were treated to a ceremony known to the readers of Josef Roth. To the question of the Capucin guardian behind the closed door of the Capucin convent on Vienna's Neuer Markt, "Who is requesting admittance?" the answer given was the full title of the last Habsburg ruler: "Zita, Empress of Austria, Apostolic Queen of Hungary, Queen of Bohemia, Queen of Galicia and Lodomeria, Queen of Croatia, Slavonia, and Dalmatia, Queen of Jerusalem, Archduchess of Austria below the Enns . . . Duchess of Salz-

69. This problem is treated in more detail in the immediately following essay.
70. Jászi, *The Dissolution of the Habsburg Monarchy,* 296.
71. This was four days before this Robert Kann Lecture was delivered at the Center for Austrian Studies at the University of Minnesota.

burg, Styria, Carinthia, Carniola, and of Bukovina, Great Princess of Transylvania, Duchess of Upper and Lower Silesia, of Modena, Parma, Piacenza, and Guastalla, of Auschwitz and Zator, of Teschen, Friaul, Princely Countess of Habsburg and Tyrol, of Kyburg, Görz, and Gradisca . . . Countess of Hohenems, Feldkirch, Bregenz, and Sonnenberg, Mistress of Trieste, of Cattaro," etc.

As is widely known, the guardian's reply to this request for the dead body's admittance to the *Kapuzinergruft* is negative: "We do not know her." After a second request for admittance, a second knock on the door of the convent, and a second question as to who requests entry, the reply is briefer: "Zita, the Empress of Austria and Queen of Hungary." Again, the request is turned down, the father guardian saying: "We do not know her." A third knock on the door, a third question as to who requests admittance, and now the answer: "Zita, ein sterblicher, sündiger Mensch"—"Zita, a mortal and a sinner." Only then the guardian says: "We know her." The doors are opened, and the dead body is admitted.

The imperial funeral rites of April 1, 1989, were a most impressive presentation of "death and transfiguration." As nonconservative a writer as the great Austrian essayist Hilde Spiel, after having watched the funeral rites, wrote a thoughtful essay inspired by them.[72] There is no question that in this grand spectacle of death and transfiguration, transfiguration prevailed.

It is the transfiguration of the late Habsburg Empire that is one of the most interesting mental and psychological phenomena in present-day East Central Europe. This transfiguration does not—one should make no mistake about it—imply any serious or widespread wishes for a restoration. Yet this transfiguration implies more, I think, than pure nostalgia, though that plays its role, too. The amazing intensity of the rapprochement between Austria and Hungary, the intensity of the nationality conflict in Yugoslavia, the resurgence of national feelings within the Soviet orbit, and the partly exhilarating, partly disturbing developments that have occurred since this lecture was presented, invite memories of and comparisons with the final decades of the Habsburg Empire. All the more is it the scholar's task to weigh with caution and detachment the evidence of the historical record, a task Robert Kann fulfilled in a masterful way.

---

72. Hilde Spiel, "Abschied. Vom Sinn der Monarchie," *Frankfurter Allgemeine Zeitung,* April 3, 1989, 27.

CHAPTER SIX

Ethnic Attribution in Late Imperial Austria: Good Intentions, Evil Consequences*

A n important dimension of the conflict of nationalities in late Imperial Austria—I shall limit myself to the non-Hungarian, Austrian parts of the Habsburg Empire in its post-1867 period—concerns the language question. To what extent could the native speakers of the many languages spoken use their native language when in contact with public authorities on the local, provincial or central level; to what extent could representatives of various nationalities use their own language in various representative bodies, again on the local, provincial or central level, or in official correspondence with other public authorities; was the native language available in public schools, or was it not?[1] The disputes on the 'language question' fill volumes; there is general agreement that in the "Badeni crisis" of 1897 a climax of bitterness, recrimination and hostility was reached. Yet I shall not deal with this dimension of the nationality conflict on this occasion.

Neither shall I deal with an issue that has been extensively covered in the brilliant and informative dissertation and book of a student of mine, Emil Brix, on the language census in Austria from 1880 to 1910.[2] Brix has shown how the language census—since no additional ethnic census was taken—was used as evidence for the ethnic distribution of the Austrian population, for the distribution of the nationalities or "Volksstämme," as

---

* First published in *The Habsburg Legacy. National Identity in Historical Perspective*, ed. by Ritchie Robertson and Edward Timms (*Austrian Studies*, vol. 5), Edinburgh 1994, pp. 67–83. The permission to reprint was gracefully granted by Edinburgh University Press.

1. See Gerald Stourzh, *Die Gleichberechtigung der Nationalitäten in der Verfassung und Verwaltung Österreichs 1848–1918* (Vienna, 1985), esp. pp. 83–189: "Gleichberechtigung und Sprachenrecht."

2. Emil Brix, *Die Umgangssprachen in Altösterreich zwischen Agitation und Assimilation*, Veröffentlichungen der Kommission für Neuere Geschichte Österreichs, 72 (Vienna, Graz, Cologne, 1982).

the *verbum legale* went, of the Empire. Brix has also discussed the reasons for the pro-majority, anti-minority bias of the language census in ethnically mixed places, and he has produced ample evidence for the way in which political agitation and campaigning quite analogous to an electoral campaign accompanied the preparation of the language census every ten years.

Yet there is another dimension of the nationality problem, concerned not with the language question as sketched above, but asking a quite different question: to which ethnic group or "Volksstamm" or nationality or—as the postulate of self-determination gained ground and terminology changed—to which people, to which nation (in the ethnic sense) did a citizen of Austria belong? The question of Austrian citizens *belonging* to a certain nationality, and the problem of finding out, when in doubt, to which nationality a person belonged, was to loom larger and larger in some ethnically mixed provinces of Austria-Cisleithania in the last decades of its existence. In addressing this question, I do not find it easy to render in English the terms used in the official German of the period—"Zugehörigkeit" or "Nichtzugehörigkeit" to a particular "Volksstamm" or nationality; words like "belonging" to a certain nationality, or "membership" of a certain nationality come of course to mind. I shall prefer to speak of "ethnic attribution," hoping that this expression clarifies what is at issue: that individual citizens by legislative enactment were supposed to be attributed, in certain cases or for certain functions, to one or another of the nationalities living within a province, and that, when in doubt, one had to devise a method of finding out who was to be attributed to one nationality or another, and according to which criteria. One also frequently encounters the term "Angehörige" of a particular nationality; translating it as "dependent" would be misleading, however. I employ the word "member," though with some hesitation because it suggests a membership of a kind of voluntary association, to be entered into or left at one's discretion at any time. The attribution of "membership" ("Angehörigkeit") was, however, as I shall try to show, a more serious, because less easily changeable, matter than membership in some kind of association.[3]

Why and how did the question of ethnic attribution arise at all? It arose out of the legal recognition of the existence of "Volksstämme"—nationalities, in Austrian constitutional texts beginning in 1848. Once the "equal

---

3. This question was first addressed several decades ago, without access to archival sources, by an Austrian jurist: Wolfgang Steinacker, *Der Begriff der Volkszugehörigkeit und die Praxis der Volkszugehörigkeitsbestimmung im altösterreichischen Nationalitätenrecht* (Innsbruck, 1932). Since then, archival finds in both Vienna and Prague have yielded interesting results: See Stourzh, *Gleichberechtigung*, pp. 200–40, 311–16.

rights" ("Gleichberechtigung") of the "Volksstämme" were recognised, the question of who belonged to them, or who was to be attributed to them, was bound to be raised sooner or later. Normally, the question was easy to answer: all those who considered themselves and were considered by others (including the authorities) to be Czechs, Germans, Poles etc., were such. The question became more urgent when public institutions in Austria began to be shaped that were designed to express explicitly the will of nationalities in specific matters. Discussions of national "curias," as they were called, took place as early as 1848–1849, on Czech initiative, but came to nothing; however, the idea of a kind of court of arbitration in national matters to be established by the provincial constitutions was indeed embodied in the Kremsier (Kroměříž) constitutional draft, though no details were worked out.[4]

An interesting proposal was put forward by Adolf Fischhof—the Jewish liberal reformer of 1848 fame—in 1867 and in slightly revised form a couple of years later. Fischhof suggested that in provinces with national minorities forming not less than a fifth of the population, the deputies elected to the diet would form national "curias" in the diet for the purpose of voting on certain matters of national (in the ethnic sense) concern. Deputies from districts with a mixed language population would join their curia depending on the national sentiments of their electors and according to their own acknowledgement of the nationality to which they belonged ("nationales Bekenntnis") at the time of putting forward their candidacy.[5]

Under the influence of Fischhofs ideas, in 1871 a bill for Bohemia was drafted on equal rights for the Czech and German nationalities. This provided for instituting national "curias." Deputies from ethnically mixed districts were free to choose which curia they wished to join. The presumption was, of course, that Czech deputies would undoubtedly join the Czech curia, and German deputies the German curia. Fischhof, however, was critical, and feared—these now are my words—a kind of "Trojan Horse" development.

A deputy not limited in his choice might join, as Fischhof wrote to Ladislav Rieger, the curia of the opposite side in the interest of his own national party. The national curia, Fischhof wrote in ringing words, "is the fortress within which the national minority may defend itself successfully against the attacks of the national majority, as long as the garrison is an unmixed national one, a reliable one. If there are joined to this national

4. Ibid., pp. 190, 200.
5. Ibid., pp. 200–201.

garrison strange, doubtful or even hostile elements, then the fortress becomes a trap." ("Mengt man aber dieser nationalen Besatzung fremde, zweifelhafte oder gar feindliche Elemente bei, so wird aus der Festung eine Falle.") Rarely has the language of war been applied as tersely to ethnic conflict in imperial Austria as on this occasion; and, comparatively speaking, as early as 1871![6]

That draft bill never became law, yet two years later, in 1873, the diet of the kingdom of Bohemia did indeed pass a bill that became law, concerning the school boards in Bohemia. There, it was provided that, in communities with Czech as well as German schools, separate school boards would be set up for each of these schools. The purpose was to avoid majority decisions overruling an ethnically different minority. Pacification by separation was the idea, or, to put it more precisely: pacification not by territorial separation—which might end in ethnic cleansing—but by institutional separation.

The school law therefore provided that the representatives of the municipality for each school board had to be taken from among the members of that nationality for which the school in question was destined. The chairman of the school board was also to be taken from the members of that nationality. The German text says that the representatives of the municipality and the board chairman "müssen [. . .] den Angehörigen jener Nationalität entnommen werden, für welche die Schule, die der Ortsschulrat vertritt, bestimmt ist." So, *for the first time*, the question of the ethnic attribution of persons charged with a certain office entered the statute book, rather than the mere regulation of the official use of languages. In the moment in which persons to be attributed to a certain nationality were charged with specific duties by law, the idea of national autonomy in its pure form entered the legislative and constitutional make-up of Austria. Obviously territorial autonomy in its various forms, from municipal autonomy to provincial autonomy, had served as a substitute, or rather as a disguised form of national autonomy for those nationalities that commanded a majority in municipal councils or provincial diets—for instance, for the Czechs in Prague or the Poles in Galicia. Yet, in the moment in which members of a certain nationality as such were charged with certain decision-making duties, the idea of national autonomy emerged in its pure form, though for the time being only on the local level, concerning a limited sphere of competence, and not really noticed in its fundamental

6. Ibid., p. 201, quoted from Richard Charmatz, *Adolf Fischhof. Das Lebensbild eines österreichischen Politikers* (Stuttgart and Berlin, 1910), pp. 270–71.

significance at the time. The great days of national autonomy were only to come in the 1890s, and chiefly between the turn of the century and the outbreak of the First World War.

But let us return to the lowly sphere of the local school boards as set up in Bohemia in 1873. What happened when doubts arose as to the national attribution of members of such a school board? Such a problem arose in 1879, when the municipal council of Pilsen (Plzeň), with a Czech majority, elected one Alois Formanek to serve on the German school board of Pilsen. A group of German representatives doubted that Mr Formanek was correctly attributed to the German nationality; they thought him to be Czech, having been nominated for the German school board for "Trojan Horse" reasons. The Germans brought the case to the High Administrative Court in Vienna, always writing the name with a Czech accent on the "a"—"Formánek"; they argued that Formanek was notoriously a Czech and that he had admitted sympathies towards the Czech party in Pilsen. Formanek, in the course of the administrative proceedings, indicated that he spoke both German and Czech, that he had lived in German communities and that he sent his child to the German school. The court, weighing contradictory assertions, came to a remarkable conclusion, formulated, incidentally, in beautiful language, and therefore I quote the original German prior to giving the English translation:

Sowie nun zum Wesen einer Nation, einer Nationalität gehört, daß sie andern gegenüber sich als Einheit und als abgeschlossenes Ganzes erkennt und bethätigt, so wird auch für den Einzelnen die Zugehörigkeit zu einer bestimmten Nationalität wesentlich Sache des Bewußtseins und des Gefühls sein.

Sicherlich wird der einzelne Angehörige einer Nationalität die Sprache der Nation sprechen, wohl auch ihre Sitten theilen, allein ebenso gewiß ist, daß die Kenntniß der Sprache, die Bethätigung der Sitten einer Nation auch bei Dritten, Fremden zutreffen kann, weshalb diese Merkmale für sich allein zur Bestimmung der Nationalität nicht ausreichen. Eben darum wird, wenn im concreten Fall die Nationalität eines Einzelnen in Frage steht und es an äußeren Bethätigungen nationaler Gesinnung mangelt, sicherlich nichts anderes erübrigen, als ihn um seine Nationalität zu befragen und als Angehörigen jener Nationalität zu behandeln, zu welcher er selbst sich bekennt.[7]

7. German text quoted in Stourzh, *Gleichberechtigung*, pp. 204–205, as well as in Robert A. Kann, *Das Nationalitätenproblem der Habsburgermonarchie* (Graz and Cologne, 1964),

[As it is in the nature of a nation, a nationality, to regard itself and to act vis-à-vis others as a unit and as a complete entity, thus to the single individual adherence (belonging) to a definite nationality will be essentially a matter of consciousness and feeling.

To be sure, the individual member of a nationality will speak its language, presumably share its customs, yet it is equally certain that command of the language and practising the customs of a nation may apply to strangers as well; thus these features in themselves are not sufficient to determine (a person's) nationality.

Therefore, if in a concrete case the nationality of an individual is in doubt and if external manifestations of national consciousness are lacking, it will be necessary to question him concerning his nationality and to treat him as a member of that nationality to which he belongs according to his own declaration.]

Thus the individual's declaration, his (or her) "Bekenntnis," was in the last resort considered to be decisive.

Other doubtful cases followed.[8] A rather comical sequence of events took place around 1887 in Schüttenhofen (Sušice) in Bohemia. The Czech-oriented municipal council had elected persons to the German school board, concerning whose German nationality the appointing council seemed to have some doubts; the Council informed the imperial authorities (k.k. Bezirkshauptmannschaft) that in case the persons nominated should not declare themselves as belonging to the German nationality ("sich zur deutschen Nationalität nicht bekennen sollten"), it would not matter, because the German school was meant for children of both nationalities anyway, and the persons elected knew both languages of the province perfectly well. The persons elected informed the authorities repeatedly that they "belonged to both nationalities" ("daß sie beiden Nationalitäten angehörten"); the imperial authorities suspended the election of these persons to the school board, and the Administrative Court in Vienna upheld that decision. This case is interesting because it shows that persons who for whatever reasons did not wish to attribute themselves either to the German or to the Czech nationality were not eligible for the school board as established by the law of 1873. In 1900, nationally-minded

---

vol. 2, pp. 396–97. The English translation follows, with modifications supplied by myself to render it more precise, the English version of Kann's book: *The Multinational Empire* (New York, 1950), vol. 2, p. 311.

8. For the following, cf. Stourzh, *Gleichberechtigung*, pp. 205ff.

Czechs in Prachatice (Prachatitz) in Bohemia challenged the membership of three persons elected to the Czech school board there; it was argued that the declaration of these three people was not sufficient, so that one would have to look into their family relations and would have to take into account their behavior, conduct and their views in all national questions ("Verhalten, Auftreten und ihre Gesinnung in allen nationalen Fragen"). So here, in an administrative proceeding, we hit on that terrible phenomenon to be found in all illiberal and chauvinistic movements: inquiring into one's "Gesinnung," one's views—"Gesinnungsschnüffelei" ("snooping on one's views"), as the really untranslatable word goes.

In this specific case, two of the persons were recognised as bona fide Czechs by the Administrative Court, but the third one was not: it turned out that in June 1898 he had declared himself to be a Czech, yet in December 1898 he declared that he had German parents and sent his children to the German school; thus his election to the Czech school board was revoked. Bad times for a trimmer.

As late as 1907, the Administrative Court in a case concerning four people from Karlín (Karolinenthal) near Prague found that notwithstanding various inquiries by the authorities, a person's declaration as to his national adherence was to be considered decisive. The so-called "Bekenntnisprinzip"—ethnic attribution on the grounds of personal declaration—had reached its apogee.

By that time, the ethnic or national splitting of institutions—within a common territory—was reaching an ever-increasing range of institutions in state and society, particularly in the Bohemian lands, thus giving increasing impetus to the idea of national autonomy. In 1890, the provincial school board for Bohemia was split into a Czech and a German section, with mandatory provisions on the national attribution of several members. Another Bohemian board (on agricultural matters) followed in 1891, and the analogous institution in Moravia followed suit in 1897. The University of Prague had already been divided into two universities, one Czech, one German, in 1882.[9] In 1894, the College of Physicians for Bohemia was split into two sections; it was left to the individual physicians to indicate whether they were willing to vote for the Czech or the German section. Omitting for the moment the vast innovations occurring in Moravia in 1905–1906, to which I shall return, let me sketch the further spread of the partitioning of institutions along national, or should one say ethnic, lines.

9. Cf. the volume *Die Teilung der Prager Universität 1882 und die intellektuelle Desintegration in den böhmischen Ländern* (Munich, 1984).

In Silesia in 1910, the provincial council of agricultural matters was split into three national sections—German, Czech and Polish. The association of apothecary assistants ("Apothekergehilfen") was split along national lines in Bohemia in 1912. When, for the whole of Austria, Colleges of Engineers ("Ingenieurskammern") were created by law in 1913, ethnically separate sections were created in Bohemia, Moravia and Silesia, in the Tyrol, and in Trieste (the latter covering Carniola, Gorizia, Gradisca, the City of Trieste itself, Istria and Dalmatia); there, three sections, an Italian one, a "Slavic" one and a German section, were established.[10] The very triviality of some of the examples mentioned indicates a significant trend: the range of matters to fall within the regulation of "nationality law"—"Nationalitätenrecht"—extended enormously once the ethnic attribution of persons spread among a great number of institutions, meaning that more and more domains of social life fell prey to the omnivorous demand for "national [i.e. ethnic] separation."[11] The enumeration is far from complete, since reference is only made to the ethnic splitting of institutions provided for by imperial or provincial legislation, and not to the innumerable ethnically separate voluntary associations, such as fire brigades or more importantly the national/ethnic umbrella organisations like the Národni rada česka (Czech People's Council) or the Deutsche Volksrat für Böhmen (German People's Council for Bohemia), with equivalents in other provinces, that had sprung up since the turn of the century.[12]

The principle of "pacification by separation" found its most notable expression in the Moravian Compromise of 1905–1906. Without listing all elements of that great package deal, suffice it to indicate three parts of it.[13]

First, in the field of school boards, already quite familiar to us, nationally/ethnically separate boards were set up on the local level, also for the city of Brünn/Brno, and separate national sections were established in the provincial school board; again, the law required "members"—"Angehörige"—of the respective nationalities to be nominated for these boards.

Second, in order that children of school age should not be alienated from their nationality, it was required that children "as a rule" were to attend only those schools whose language of instruction they were speak-

10. See Stourzh, Gleichberechtigung, pp. 229–33, for additional cases.

11. This trend was brilliantly grasped and analysed by the legal scholar Josef Lukas, "Territorialitäts- und Personalitätsprinzip im österreichischen Nationalitätenrecht," Jahrbuch des öffentlichen Rechts der Gegenwart, 2 (1908), 333–401.

12. See also Gerald Stourzh, "The Multinational Empire Revisited: Reflections on Late Imperial Austria," in this volume, pp. 133–56.

13. For more detail, see Stourzh, Gleichberechtigung, pp. 213–28.

ing. This new provision was going to cause interminable contention, particularly the somewhat ambiguous clause "as a rule"—"in der Regel," to which I shall return.

Third, and very importantly, in order to avoid national strife dominating electoral contests, the whole province of Moravia was divided into two separate nets of constituencies, a Czech one and a German one, each one covering the whole province. To deal with this point first: voters (with the exception of certain privileged groups like the owners of great estates) were to be registered in two nationally separate voting registers ("Wahlkataster"), one Czech and one German. The new system of ethnically split voting registers and constituencies was to be applied both to provincial elections and to elections to the Parliament in Vienna. The local authorities were supposed first to enter people in either of the two registers according to their knowledge; the individuals concerned had the right to claim a transfer to the other national list; and, more peculiarly, individuals entered in one list had the right to claim that other persons on the same list whom the claimants considered erroneously to be on that list should be transferred to the other register. The head of the municipality decided on all these claims; individuals thinking that they were registered on the wrong list were entitled to appeal to the next higher government agency. The government agency, eventually the governor's office or "Statthalterei" in Brünn/Brno, decided definitively.

Before discussing some developments following from the Moravian settlement of 1905–1906, suffice it to add briefly that the last-mentioned aspect of the Moravian Compromise, electoral reform, was also negotiated for the Bukovina a few years later, in 1909–1910—the situation being more complicated by the existence of five groups claiming recognition as "national" components of the Bukovina—Romanians, Ukrainians ("Ruthenes"), Poles, Germans, and Jews. This will be the theme of the two immediately following essays.

In 1914, a national compromise was also struck among the Poles and Ukrainians of Galicia, which differed from the models of Moravia and the Bukovina insofar as the linguistic/ethnic attribution of the electorate was indicated through the language entries of the census rather than in special electoral registers. The Moravian system of double constituencies was adopted only for a part of the province. The more prosperous segments of the Jewish electorate were also assured of special representation.[14]

---

14. Cf. Stourzh, *Gleichberechtigung*, pp. 238–39.

We see that public authorities had a considerable say in the matter of whom to attribute to which national/ethnic register. On the whole, the system worked; yet on the occasion of the parliamentary elections of 1907, there were, in Moravia, more than 3,000 complaints concerning allegedly mistaken ethnic attribution to be dealt with by the Statthalterei in Brno.[15] Three members of the German electoral register even filed a suit with the Austrian Imperial Court ("Reichsgericht") in Vienna, which was competent to judge on citizens' complaints as to the violation of constitutionally guaranteed personal rights. These three persons complained to the High Court in Vienna that their claims concerning *other* persons considered by them wrongly to be on the German voters list had not been accepted by the imperial authorities in Brno.

These three German voters, strangely enough, were represented by a Czech lawyer, Dr. Pluhař, known to be an exponent of the Czech National Council for Moravia, the Národni rada česka. It turned out that an at least partly successful "Trojan Horse" operation had been taking place. Three persons with presumably Czech sympathies had uncontestedly placed themselves on the German register and had proceeded to demand that a large number of persons should be struck off the German list; the idea was that in a German-dominated city, the Czech voters were under-represented and the German voters over-represented.

In the proceedings of the Imperial Court, it appeared that the governor's office in Brno had not had time to examine thoroughly the merits of more than 3,000 cases of contested national attribution. Thus the three complainants—though obviously engaged in a "Trojan Horse operation"—actually won their case; the Imperial Court held that their constitutionally guaranteed right to claim that someone else be struck off the national voters' register—"das Recht des 'Hinausreklamierens'"!—had been violated by the inaction or insufficient action of the authorities in Brno. It may be puzzling that this claim that someone else should be struck off the national voters' register and transferred to the other ethnic register should be a constitutionally guaranteed right. The explanation is as follows: the unimpaired right to vote was a constitutionally guaranteed right (for those entitled to vote only!), and the right to claim that someone be transferred to the other ethnic voters' register was an offshoot of the right to vote. The right to have someone else struck off the ethically determined electoral list was perhaps the most peculiar of all the citizens' rights guaranteed by the Austrian constitution.

15. For the following, see ibid., pp. 226–28.

The important consequence of the judgement of the Imperial Court in October 1907 was that, according to the Moravian Compromise law, the state's authorities were indeed both competent and obliged to settle, in doubtful cases, on the basis of objective indications, the national/ethnic attribution of a person. This meant that the role of the personal declaration, the "Bekenntnis" ("confession") of a person as to his or her national attribution, was not any longer, as it had been since 1881, the criterion of last resort. In its place, the findings of the public authorities became the criterion of last resort for settling a person's national attribution.

Spurred into action by the Imperial Court's judgment of 1907 and by the actions of the Administrative Court as well, the imperial authorities in Brno drew up an elaborate questionnaire in preparation for the parliamentary elections of 1911. This questionnaire, found in archives in Vienna,[16] was to be used for the purpose of settling the national attribution of Moravian voters in doubtful cases. The questionnaire, drawn up in both German and Czech, consisted of nine questions, as follows:

1. In favor of which nationality do you declare yourself? ("Zu welcher Nationalität bekennen Sie sich?")

2. Your parents' names, place of present (or, in case of death, last) residence, and nationality ("Welcher Nationalität gehörten Ihre Eltern an?")

3. Did you attend German or Czech schools, and which ones?

4. Which language do you use in the family, and which in your social life ("im geselligen Leben")?

5. Where did you give your information for the census of 1910? Which language of communication ("Umgangssprache") did you indicate then?

6. Do you belong to German or to Czech associations ("Vereine")? (In the Czech version, the sequence was reversed: "Do you belong to Czech or to German associations?")

7. Are you otherwise active in public life as far as national matters are concerned ("in nationaler Beziehung")?

8. Do your children attend German or Czech schools?

9. Which other factors relevant to your national attribution could you indicate? ("Welche sonstigen für die Beurteilung Ihrer nationalen Zugehörigkeit in Betracht kommenden Umstände können Sie anführen?")

16. Allgemeines Verwaltungsarchiv Wien, Bestand Unterricht, Mähren in genere, with no. 33.621 (1911). The questionnaire exists in both German and Czech, the only difference being that in questions mentioning the words "German" and "Czech," for reasons of "Gleichberechtigung" the word "Czech" takes precedence in the Czech questionnaire and the word "German" takes precedence in the German questionnaire.

Returning now to the "school theme" of the Moravian compromise already sketched above, a virtually identical questionnaire was drawn up a few months later to clarify the national attribution of parents who wished to send their child or children to German schools, but whose decision to do so was contested—as was legally possible—by the local Czech school boards, who were entitled to claim children whom they considered to be Czech children for the Czech schools. To the nine questions given above, the new questionnaire, prepared for the beginning of the school year in the autumn of 1911, added only two more questions. In which national voters' register were the parents registered for the parliamentary elections of the same year? Had the parents' national attribution been challenged ("Ist Ihre nationale Zugehörigkeit bei diesen Reichsratswahlen reklamiert worden?"); and if so, by which authority, and what had been the final decision? [17]

The importance of mandatory national/ethnic attribution was stressed within the context of certain provisions of the school legislation of the Moravian Compromise of 1905, to which reference has been made above. In 1910, occasioned by a conflict over the ethnic attribution of the members of the German school board in the municipality of Třebič (Trebitsch), the Administrative Court in Vienna reversed, in fact, the criteria for the determination of such an attribution formulated in 1881.[18] In the conflict in question, the municipality of Třebič, with a Czech majority, had nominated four members for the German school board whose German ethnic attribution was contested by various German citizens of Třebič; the controlling district school board had indeed found, on the strength of its own investigations, that these four persons belonged to the Czech nationality, and had therefore suspended their nomination to the local German school board. The Administrative Court in Vienna upheld that decision, holding that in cases of doubt as to the national attribution ("Zugehörigkeit") of a person, "this attribution has to be determined by tangible evidence ("fassbare Merkmale"), and it is admissible for this purpose to include in the evidence activities in the private, social and public life (of the person in question) which are credible and serious manifestations of national attribution" ("glaubwürdige und ernste Kundgebungen der nationalen Zugehörigkeit"). Thus the objective determination of national attribution had won priority over the subjective declaration of the persons themselves as to where they belonged.

17. Ibid., with no. 41.680 (1913).
18. Cf. Stourzh, *Gleichberechtigung*, pp. 217–18.

The Court also said that Moravian school legislation included the means for a "sufficient guarantee for the election of nationally-feeling members of the local school boards" ("national empfindenden Ortsschulratsmitgliedern"). It is interesting to see that both Czech and German jurists, members of the Administrative Court, stressed the importance of national sentiment. Jaroslav Srb, a member of a well-known Prague family advocating the case of the Czech nation, held that whoever entered the local school board as national representative should—I translate somewhat freely—be firmly committed to the nation that he represented ("von dem müsse feststehen, daß er Sinn und Herz für die von ihm vertretene Nation besitze"). And a German national jurist, Johann von Hiller-Schönaich, was fully of the opinion that "nationally indifferent persons were not suited to enter the school board as national representatives." The idea of the Moravian law on school boards was, he thought, that the local school board should only include persons who gave a guarantee that they were "nationally minded" ("die eine Gewähr dafür geben, national gesinnt zu sein"). Here one detects, in 1910, and in the judgement of one of the highest courts of the realm, overtones or undertones that were to have a terrible history two to three decades later, when they escalated into the notion of "gesundes Volksempfinden" ("the people's healthy sentiment").

This case is of quite exceptional interest for two reasons. First, the notion of "tangible evidence"—"fassbare Merkmale"—was to find its way, after the breakdown of the Monarchy, into the public law of the Republic of Austria in connection with the issue of (chiefly Jewish) citizens of the former Austria-Cisleithania wishing to opt for the citizenship of the small Republic. This issue will be dealt with later in this chapter. In order to stress continuities too often neglected in legal/ethnical thinking in pre-1918 and post-1918 Austrian history, I would like to observe at this point that an Executive Order of the Austrian republican government of August 1920 determined that, in cases of option applications in view of race and language according to Article 80 of the Treaty of Saint-Germain, "that tangible evidence" ("jene fassbaren Merkmale") had to be shown from which the attribution of the claimant to the majority of the population of Austria was to be concluded.[19] I shall return to the grave consequences of those views.

Second, I would like to stress at this point that one of the "nationally-minded" jurists just referred to, Dr. Hiller-Schönaich, was to play an important role in post-1918 judgements of the Administrative Court of

---

19. For this, see the doctoral dissertation by Oskar Besenböck, "Die Frage der jüdischen Option in Österreich 1918–1921" (University of Vienna, 1992), pp. 77–78.

republican Austria stressing the ethnically/racially different nature of Jews from the majority of the population of the Austrian Republic. In a notorious judgement of June 1921 written by Hiller-Schönaich, the Administrative Court forbade a Jewish person from Galicia (and therefore a citizen of the defunct Austrian Empire) to opt for the citizenship of the Republic of Austria, because he had not produced "tangible evidence" ("fassbare Merkmale") for his belonging ("Zugehörigkeit") to the German race.[20] Thus the legal criterion of "tangible evidence" ("fassbare Merkmale") of ethnic attribution applied to Czechs and Germans in Moravia in Habsburg times was to survive the great divide of 1918 in order to be applied to Jews in the early 1920s. We shall come back to this.

The central place of mandatory ethnic attribution in Moravia after the compromise settlement is also demonstrated by another conflict in the field of schooling. In 1910, the Administrative Court held, in a case involving a conflict over schoolchildren in Ungarisch-Hradisch (Uherské Hradiště), that the local school boards were not merely school authorities in a technical sense, but organs of the nationality (in the ethnic sense), competent to see that the children should not be taken away from the schools of that nationality.[21] The Court recognised a right of the nationalities of the province to keep those belonging to them; therefore there was to be recognised the "legal claim" of a nationality that the children enrolled in the (public) schools of this nationality should not be taken away from it—"dass die nach dem Gesetz den Schulen dieses Volksstammes zugehörigen Kinder diesem nicht entzogen werden." The Court held that the liberty of parents to choose a school for the education of their children, guaranteed by the Austrian Civil Code of 1811, had now been considerably limited in favor of the national group by the Moravian law of 1905. The Court also held that the truthfulness and credibility of the declaration of the parents as to their nationality would have to be disproved, in cases of doubt, by objectively tangible evidence ("durch objektiv fassbare Merkmale der Nationalität"). In cases of ethnically mixed marriage, the ethnic attribution of the father was to be decisive.

One consequence of this ruling was the Lehar case of 1912.[22] Johann Lehar (or Léhar), of Hohenstadt/Zábřeh in northern Moravia, was a grocer who wished to send his six-year-old daughter Anna to the German school.

20. Ibid., pp. 173–74.

21. Stourzh, *Gleichberechtigung*, pp. 220–21.

22. Archival sources on this case from the Prague Státni ústřední archiv are published in Stourzh, *Gleichberechtigung*, pp. 311–16.

On being questioned as to his national/ethnic attribution, he said that he felt himself to be a German, and that he even belonged to the German fire brigade of his town and to another German association; yet he admitted that in the past he had inscribed himself in the Czech voting register, though he had taken steps to be transferred to the German voting register. He argued that, having Czech clients in his grocery store, he had been intimidated by the fear of losing Czech clients. Mr. Lehar argued like a trimmer, yet his arguments have, through the ages, great plausibility. He—or his lawyer—argued that indications given in the (ethnically separate) electoral register, or on the occasion of the census, were often determined by economic considerations and were motivated not by national feeling but out of fear of the results of a possible boycott. He had experienced this as a grocer on repeated occasions, he added, and he insisted on his right to select for his young daughter a school with German as the language of instruction, since a knowledge of German was important for his daughter's professional future. Yet though Mr. Lehar, the grocer, went all the way to the highest appeal authority, the Administrative Court in Vienna, he did not win. The authorities concluded that Mr. Lehar was a Czech and he was forced against his will to send his daughter to the Czech school.

In Moravia, then, as a result of the compromise legislation of 1905 and its judicial interpretation, the task of national attribution fell more and more on the authorities; the questionnaires of 1911 are striking evidence. Yet, even before they had been drawn up, a critic of the "objective" method of national attribution, Edmund Bernatzik, a great constitutional lawyer, had warned of the kind of inquiries that the authorities might make in trying to decide on a person's ethnic attribution: "From various indications, perhaps from talks in a pub, visits to the theatre, from the reading of suspect books, proofs for or against a nationality would be sought." Bernatzik foresaw the menace of trials that might remind us, he said, of the trials of heretics in the time of the Inquisition.[23]

There is no question that both ways of approaching ethnic attribution had their drawbacks. The subjective approach, advocated by Bernatzik, laying chief or exclusive emphasis on the personal declaration, the "Bekenntnis," was open to abuses, the least objectionable of which was opportunism, shifting one's "national declaration" according to social and economic advantage; a rather worse abuse was the mounting of "Trojan Horse" operations. The objective approach, so called, led easily to prying into one's private life, as the questionnaires cited have shown.

23. Edmund Bernatzik, *Über nationale Matriken* (Vienna, 1910), pp. 28–30.

The question of "subjective" versus "objective" methods of ethnic attribution opened up an additional dilemma. Advocates of the "subjective" approach were often adherents of that nationality or language group commanding, or believed to be commanding, the better social and economic position; the "objective" approach was usually advocated by representatives of peoples believed to suffer disadvantage from the attraction of a nationality offering better social and economic advancement through assimilation. In the Bohemian lands, for a long time and well into the twentieth century, Czechs believed that they needed the "objective" way of ethnic attribution in order to keep their people within their own fold. There was more fear of Czechs crossing to the German side than the other way round, and this asymmetrical situation colored, even if it did not determine, the debate on ethnic attribution.

After the dissolution of the Habsburg Empire, mandatory ethnic attribution acquired a new—and, as will become apparent, more sinister—significance. In view of the emergence of the "succession states," the peace settlements in Central Europe had to provide, among other and better-known things, for the reattribution of citizenship in the vast territories of the Habsburg Empire where up to 1918 only two citizenships had existed: Austrian citizenship and (separate from it—a little-known fact) Hungarian citizenship. Limiting myself to the Austrian/Cisleithanian case, holders of (imperial) Austrian citizenship ("holders of Austrian passports") were now becoming citizens of Romania, Poland, Czechoslovakia, Italy, the Kingdom of Serbs, Croats and Slovenes (SHS), or the Republic of Austria. In view of the freedom of movement and freedom of settlement that had existed within the confines of the monarchy, the problem of "opting" for one of the new citizenships was an acute one. Therefore, the Treaty of Saint-Germain provided various procedures for "opting" under specific circumstances. One of these procedures provided that persons who differed "by race and language" from the majority of the population of that territory where they possessed rights of citizenship,[24] and who wished to possess the citizenship of that country where the majority of the population consisted "of persons speaking the same language and having the same race" as themselves, could opt, within a certain time limit, for the citizenship of Austria, Italy, Poland, Romania, the SHS-state or the Czechoslovak state.[25]

---

24. This is the awkward English rendering of the legal term "Heimatrecht," also awkwardly rendered in the French text by "indigénat." The Italian term "pertinenza" is added variously in English and French texts to make the meaning clearer.

25. Article 80 of the Treaty of Saint-Germain.

Though the treaty contained certain general rules for the conditions of opting for one of these citizenships, it gave no hints as to how evidence of "speaking the same language and having the same race" as the majority population of one of the states mentioned was to be produced or evaluated.

How did provisions on "race" enter the Paris Treaties? References to "race" are not limited to the Treaty of Saint-Germain; they occur notably in the Minority Protection Treaties concluded in 1919. It appears that "race" and "racial" were terms applied in Anglo-American parlance to entities that were referred to as "nationalities" ("Nationalitäten") in Central European, notably Habsburg Austrian, parlance, and that now tend to be qualified as "ethnic" groups.[26] Woodrow Wilson had once observed that "nation for us [i.e. the Anglo-Americans] connoted 'community of organization, of life, and of tradition,' not origin and blood." Wilson added that "nationality did not mean to Germans what it meant to Englishmen or Americans. The Germans regarded it as meaning race."[27] It has been shown that Wilson, as well as his chief legal adviser and architect of the minority protection clauses in the Paris peace settlement, David Hunter Miller, frequently employed the words "race" and "racial" also in connection with the Jewish population groups of East-Central and South-Eastern Europe.[28] Following the Minority Treaty concluded with Poland on 28 June 1919, in which "racial, religious or linguistic minorities" were mentioned, similar terms referring to the rights of persons or inhabitants of "different race, language or religion" entered other Paris agreements, including the Treaty of Saint-Germain.[29]

26. For the following, cf. the careful and excellent research presented in the book by Erwin Viefhaus, *Die Minderheitenfrage und die Entstehung der Minderheitenschutzverträge auf der Pariser Friedenskonferenz 1919* (Würzburg, 1960). The term "ethnic" appears in 1919 sometimes in French-language texts, but not, as far as I can see, in English or American texts.

27. Quoted ibid., p. 110, from Harley Notter, *The Origins of the Foreign Policy of Woodrow Wilson* (Baltimore, 1937), p. 104.

28. Ibid., pp. 54–55, 104–18 and elsewhere. The "Committee on New States" in charge of drafting the Minority Treaty with Poland wrote in a report for the Council of Four of the Paris Peace Conference, dated 13 May 1919, that the Jews were "both a religious and a racial minority": David Hunter Miller, *My Diary at the Conference of Paris, With Documents*, vol. 13 (New York, 1925), p. 55. Texts influenced by Jewish spokesmen, including those from East-Central Europe, tended to refer to the Jews as a "national minority"; compare, for example, ibid., pp. 17–18.

29. Compare, for example, Articles 7, 8, 9 and 12 of the Minority Treaty with Poland; Article 86 of the Treaty of Versailles; Articles 7, 8 and 9 of the Minority Treaty with Czechoslovakia; Articles 51, 57, 60, 63, 66–69 and 80 of the Treaty of Saint-Germain. The following peculiarity should be noted: the English text uses the words "race" or "racial" in all articles indicated; the French text in most of the articles mentioned uses "race" or "de race." However, in Articles 8 and 9 of the Polish Minority Treaty, as well as in Articles 67 and 68 of the Treaty

In Austria, the government proceeded to make the "option" provisions of the Treaty of Saint-Germain operational. It did so in an Executive Order ("Vollzugsanweisung") on 20 August 1920 where, as has already been pointed out above, "tangible evidence"—"fassbare Merkmale"—was required to show that the person wishing to opt for the Republic of Austria belonged to the majority of the population of Austria. The Executive Order further indicated that, as proof of "linguistic attribution," information was admissible pertaining to school attendance, census data, past attribution to national (ethnic) electoral registers (a reference to the pre-1918 settlements in Moravia and Bukovina), etc. It was absolutely silent on proofs of "racial" attribution.[30] In February 1921, the Minister of the Interior, Dr Glanz, a Christian Social, admitted that there were difficulties in defining the meaning of "race"; in practice, he added, the authorities were chiefly relying on the criterion of language?[31]

Yet, on 9 June 1921, disaster struck, in the unaccustomed form of a judgement of the Administrative Court in Vienna. The option claim of one Moses Dym, of Lisko in Galicia, formerly a citizen of the Austrian Empire, was refused on appeal. The Court (by majority) concluded that Moses Dym—though evidence on his linguistic attribution to German had been produced—"had not even tried to produce tangible evidence ["fassbare Merkmale"] for his attribution to the German race," and therefore, the Court concluded, Dym's option for Austria was not founded in law. The Court, though no instructions as to how to produce tangible evidence of belonging to the German race had been provided by the authorities, reproached Dym for not having produced such evidence.[32] The Court now

---

of Saint-Germain (structured according to the corresponding articles of the Polish Treaty), the English text speaks of "racial, religious or linguistic minorities", while the French text speaks of "minorites ethniques, de religion ou de langue." On the other hand, in Article 12 of the Polish Minority Treaty as well as the corresponding Article 69 of the Saint-Germain Treaty, the "racial" minorities of the English text are rendered as "minorites de race." The German translation always speaks of a "Minderheit nach Rasse, Religion oder Sprache," thus following the English rather than the French text. Compare among others, the following publications: Nina Almond and Ralph H. Lutz (eds.), *The Treaty of St Germain* (Stanford, 1935); Emil Hofmannsthal (ed.), *Der deutsche und österreichische Friedensvertrag* (Vienna, 1920); *Nouveau Recueil Général de Traités*, ed. H. Triepel, 3rd series, vol. 13 (1924), pp. 504–507 (French text of Minority Treaty with Poland).

30. Besenböck, "Die Frage der jüdischen Option," p. 78; also Lukas Langhoff, *Staatsbürgerschaft und Heimatrecht in Österreich* (Vienna, 1920), p. 19, and a later edition entitled *Bundesbürgerschaft, Landesbürgerschaft und Heimatrecht in Österreich* (Vienna, 1928), p. 15.

31. Besenböck, "Die Frage der jüdischen Option," p. 80.

32. Dissenting views are not made public, yet Dr. Besenböck's discovery in the archives of the Court's confidential deliberations on this case reveals that one prominent member of the Court, Baron Paul Hock, a distinguished progressive liberal known as "the Red Baron,"

argued that the language used by a man did not prove his belonging to a certain race. Race, the Court reasoned, was a permanent quality inherent in a particular person, characterized by physical and psychic elements, a state of being that could not be taken off at discretion and could not be changed at will.[33]

This appalling judgement provided the legal basis—one should rather say screen—for the strongly anti-Jewish policies pursued by a new Minister of the Interior, Leopold Waber, from the "Großdeutsche Volkspartei," who took office twelve days after this judgement had been rendered. Waber issued instructions that the claims of Jewish claimants wishing to opt for Austrian citizenship should be uniformly rejected on the basis of the legal views of the Administrative Court. As Waber—whose tenure of office lasted seven months—once wrote, the Court's opinion to the effect that a claimant ought to belong to the same race as the majority of the Austrian population was binding for the Ministry of the Interior.[34]

Though in some cases Jewish claimants did procure a procedural respite from the Administrative Court, the Court did not, contrary to views expressed in earlier scholarly writings, change its basic views.[35] As late as 8 June 1923, the Court affirmed its rejection of Jewish claims, and it now combined its interpretation of "race," taken from Article 80 of the Treaty of Saint-Germain, with the "objective" interpretation of the "Volksstamm" or nationality as it had developed just prior to the First World War in Habsburg Austria. The Court now argued that "race" according to the Treaty was to be interpreted as "Volksstamm." This term meant, the Court held in an interpretation going beyond anything that had been said on "objective attribution" in Imperial Austria, that one belonged to a people through descent.[36] Thus, in addition to linguistic attribution to a

---

expressed his disagreement with the majority arguments prepared by Dr Johann Hiller-Schönaich. The archival materials on this case (from the Allgemeines Verwaltungsarchiv in Vienna) are published in Besenböck, pp. 153–93. A brilliant public critique of the Administrative Court's judgement is the article by Julius Ofner, a distinguished left-liberal lawyer and politician, "Das Optionsrecht der Juden," *Neue Freie Presse*, Morgenausgabe, 12 August 1921, p. 2, republished in Besenböck, pp. 194–201.

33. Ibid., p. 190: "Sie ist eine ihm angestammte, ihm inhärente, durch physische und psychische Momente bestimmte und charakterisierte Eigenart dauernden Charakters, ein ihm anhaftender Zustand, der nicht willkürlich abgelegt und nicht nach Belieben verändert werden kann."

34. Quoted ibid., p. 124.

35. See ibid., p. 111, for findings which refute such earlier views as those expressed by J. Moser, "Die Katastrophe der Juden in Österreich," *Studia Judaica Austriaca*, 5 (1977), p. 92.

36. Besenböck, p. 115: "Es ergibt sich sonach, daß Rasse nach dem Staatsvertrag als Volksstamm aufzufassen ist. Dieses Wort bedeutet aber mehr als Volks- oder Kulturgemeinschaft,

people, the Court requested evidence of a claimant belonging to a people according to descent—"dem Stamme nach."

In conclusion: The ethnic splitting of institutions, as it began to develop in Bohemia in the 1870s, reaching its fullest development in Moravia after 1905, as well as the mandatory ethnic attribution of persons grew out of good intentions. Pacification through separation was the guiding idea. Yet I believe that evil consequences were the outcome. The individual person increasingly became absorbed by the group—the "Volksstamm," the nationality or nation. The notion of "citizen" paled, while the notion of "member" of an ethnic group grew stronger. The "Staatsbürger" was about to give way to the "Volksbürger."[37] This could perhaps be borne, as long as there existed guarantees for the equal rights of various ethnic groups; if and when the idea of equality of rights broke down and discrimination set in, things became more sinister.

The growing tendency to stress the sense of belonging to the ethnic group at the expense of the sense of citizenship turned even more sinister when ethnic attribution was taken away from the will and choice of individual persons and transferred to the decision of public authorities on the basis of so-called "objective evidence." Thus ethnic attribution could become a trap for many, for example the Moravian grocer Johann or Jan Lehar/Léhar, who was prevented from sending his daughter to the school of his choice. For the Jews of Central Europe, once the National Socialists took over, this trap was to become deadly.

es schließt in sich, daß jemand zu einem Volke der Abstammung nach gehöre." On this judgement, also the result of a divided Court, see ibid., pp. 112–16.

37. Cf. Brigitte Fenz, "Zur Ideologie der 'Volksbürgerschaft.' Die Studentenordnung der Universität Wien vom 8. April 1930," *Zeitgeschichte*, 5 (1977/78), pp. 125–45.

CHAPTER SEVEN

The National Compromise
in the Bukovina 1909/1910*

First a personal remark: when, in 1978, I gave a lecture on the Franz Joseph University in Czernowitz (now Chernivtsy) from 1875 to 1918, on the occasion of a conference at the Austrian Institute of East and South-East European Studies in Vienna, I never thought that I ever would give a lecture at the University of Chernivtsy itself. One can therefore understand how gratified and thankful I was to have the opportunity in September 1994 to do so.

What was the National Compromise ("Ausgleich") in the Bukovina in the years 1909/1910? The compromise meant that the politics of the province, the voting public, the provincial parliament and the autonomous provincial administration were based on a balanced representation among the ethnic groups living in the Bukovina.

What were the preconditions that must be considered in order to understand the Compromise of 1909? I would like to examine three such preconditions.

1. It is important to recall that the Habsburg Monarchy during the last half century of its existence was made up of two constituent states with radically different structures. The Monarchy had one army, but two militia systems (Landwehr, Honvéd), one joint foreign policy and customs

* This essay goes back to a lecture given at the University of Chernivtsy/Czernowitz, in September, 1994 (in German). First published in English in *Viribus Unitis. Österreichs Wissenschaft und Kultur im Ausland. . . . Festschrift für Bernhard Stillfried aus Anlass seines 70. Geburtstags.* Ed. by Ilona Slawinski and Joseph P. Strelka, Bern et al., 1996, pp. 371–84. I am grateful to Dr. Bernhard Stillfried for having enabled me to lecture at the University of erstwhile Czernowitz, now Chernivtsy. In this paper, the name "Czernowitz" will be used when speaking of pre-1918 history, the name "Chernivtsy" when referring to the present.

area, but different juridical systems as well as two citizenships. The greatest difference, however, lay in the different structures concerning ethno-linguistic groups (or simplified ethnic groups), referred to by contemporaries as "Nationalitäten"—"nationalities," or—as the old Austrian *verbum legale* put it—"Volksstämme."

Hungary was a nation state with numerous minorities. In 1868 Hungary proclaimed the Magyar language as the official state language: other languages became minority languages. Only Croatian enjoyed a particular Status in the (semi-autonomous) kingdom of Croatia-Slavonia. In the Nationality law of 1868 Hungary proclaimed that all Hungarian citizens, regardless of their native tongue, were members of one, indivisible Hungarian political nation. This phrase clearly was derived from the expression of the French Revolution—*nation une et indivisible.* Austria, i.e. the kingdoms and lands represented in the Imperial Parliament (Reichsrat) in Vienna, was not a national state with minorities, but rather a state comprising many nationalities (Nationalitätenstaat) in the true sense of the word. Naturally in the various towns, cities and provinces there were minority factions which suffered time and again as the result of decisions taken by the majority in local councils or provincial diets. Nevertheless, the basic principle that all ethnic groups (nationalities) and recognized languages were equal was of practical significance. After 1867, Austria did not have an official state language, although German was the primary language for both historical and practical reasons.

Austria—and here I mean the non-Hungarian, so-called "Cisleithanian" part of the Monarchy to which seventeen crown lands, including Bukovina, belonged—passed several basic laws in December 1867 which became known as the "December constitution." The Fundamental Law on the General Rights of Citizens ("Staatsgrundgesetz über die allgemeinen Rechte der Staatsbürger"), which was also in force in Bukovina, contained the famous Article 19, which may be called the "Magna Charta" of the peoples of Imperial Austria. It states:

(Paragraph 1) All peoples [Volksstämme] of the State have equal rights, and every people has an inviolable right to maintain and cultivate its nationality and language.
(Paragraph 2) The equal rights [Gleichberechtigung] of all languages used in a crown land [landesübliche Sprachen] in schools, government institutions as well as in public life is recognized by the State.
(Paragraph 3) In crown lands [Länder] in which several nationalities live, public schools should enable each nationality to receive the means

for education in its own language without any obligation to learn a second language of the crown land [Landessprache].

A plethora of regulations concerning the use of various languages in governmental agencies, public life as well as in the schools was to conform to these laws. Two superior courts in Vienna, the Imperial Court and the Administrative Court, often heard cases concerning ethnic and language conflicts. The interpretation often varied and yielded sometimes disappointing results. In addition, social and political factors often worked at cross purposes to the principle of equality. I would like to pay special attention to two such factors:

a) Differences in the social standing among language groups. In a multilingual society, easy (or easier) access to a de facto dominant language was an advantage. Certainly German, Italian, Hungarian and Polish facilitated social and economic advancement, albeit with strong temporal and local variations. Consequently, the tendency was strong to assimilate with an ethnic or language group which offered better chances of social and economic improvement.

b) The Emperor and his government often switched alliances among various nationalities and their leaders, as in 1867 with Hungary to the detriment of the Romanians, or with the Germans to the detriment of the Czechs (although the latter alliance did not last long), and with the Poles in Galicia to the detriment of the Ukrainians or "Ruthenians" as they were known. These shifting alliances naturally influenced the standing of individual groups in the various crown lands.

2. The second of the preconditions mentioned initially is the idea of "national autonomy." National and linguistic conflicts grew to include not only questions of language rights, but also the principle of self-rule and self-administration. Correspondingly in the last years of the Monarchy the terms "Volksstamm" or "nationality" were increasingly replaced by "peoples" or "nations."

National autonomy was tantamount to a magic word which many, in the final two decades of imperial Austria, hoped would save the Habsburg Monarchy. National autonomy was to be implemented in two different ways: first, as territorial autonomy; this, however, promised to be successful only in areas in which individual nationalities lived on their own territory. Second, the idea of individual or personal autonomy arose. This second type of autonomy was to be applied principally in areas in which two or more nationalities lived together in one territory, i.e., national groups which could not be separated or, if so, only by force.

From 1873 onwards, as was shown in the preceding paper, this second type of autonomy came to be used increasingly, first in Bohemia, as a way to solve national conflicts and establish national peace. The theoretical promoters of this concept, notably Karl Renner, took as an example the diversity of religions which existed: each religion was organized independently and yet peacefully co-existed with others on the same territory.

The Social Democraty Karl Renner was the most original theoretician of the idea of personal autonomy; beginning in 1898, he published numerous writings on the subject. The idea of personal autonomy, cut loose from territorial autonomy as a way of obtaining equal rights for two (or more) peoples living on the same territory, was first fully achieved (after earlier beginnings in Bohemia described in the preceding essay) in Moravia. The Moravian Compromise of 1905 was the most important—actually the only—precedent for the compromise in Bukovina four years later.

What happened in Moravia? As has been described in the preceding chapter, in order to avoid national, ethno-linguistic conflicts in the election campaigns, the voters were divided into two groups, Czechs and Germans. Henceforth, Czech voters would elect Czech representatives and Germans would elect German representatives. The number of Czech and German deputies was fixed, with slightly more Czech deputies, based on population.

Eligible voters were registered in two separate lists based on nationality. If a voter believed that he was registered in the wrong list, he could ask to be placed in the other. Even more significant and certainly more controversial was the fact that members of one ethnic group could apply to have third persons switched if they believed these persons to be in the wrong list. Although the analogous system in the Bukovina will be treated later, it may be noted right away that the elections of 1911 in Czernowitz were accompanied by 2,000 complaints regarding registration in the wrong list: it is not known how the situation was resolved.[1]

A final point regarding the Moravian Compromise and its significance as a model for the Compromise in the Bukovina: Moravia was covered by two distinct nets of constituencies, one Czech and one German. These districts, however, were in no way congruent with one another. These regulations were complicated by the fact that certain groups of privileged voters as well as deputies were not subject to this system, namely the group of

---

1. John Leslie, Der Ausgleich in der Bukowina 1910: Zur österreichischen Nationalitäten-politik vor dem Ersten Weltkrieg. In *Geschichte zwischen Freiheit und Ordnung. Gerald Stourzh zum 60. Geburtstag.* Ed. by Emil Brix, Thomas Fröschl, Josef Leidenfrost. Graz 1991, pp. 113–44, here p. 136.

the great landowners and of the Chambers of Commerce. Further details would go beyond the scope of this paper.

3. The third precondition for understanding the Compromise in the Bukovina is the ethno-linguistic and political situation in the Bukovina around 1905–1910. In 1848 the administrative union between Bukovina and Galicia was dissolved, and Bukovina was elevated to the status of a crown land. Subsequently an important development occured: population growth was rapid, in particular in the capital, Czernowitz/Chernivtsy, where the population increased from 22,000 in 1857 to 87,000 in 1910. In 1875 the Imperial Franz Joseph University was founded.[2] In the sixty years between 1850 and 1910, the population of Bukovina doubled. Growth was particularly strong among the Jewish population: in 1857 they numbered about 29,000 (i.e., 6.9%) of the total population of 457,000, and in 1910 about 103,000 (i.e., 12.8%) of the total population of 800,000.[3]

The last census before the National Compromise, that of 1900, resulted in the following numbers which are important for our topic. In this context it should be noted that the census did not include any data on nationality or ethnic origin, but only on language (and —important for the Jewish population—on religion). These data, which often tended to favour dominant ethnic groups in areas of ethnic conflict,[4] show the following results (for the resident population):

Ruthenian[5]	297,798	(=41.16%)
Romanian	229,018	(=31.65%)
German	159,486	(=22.04%)
Polish	26,857	(=3.71%)
Hungarian	9,516	(=1.32%)
Other languages	829	(=0.12%)

Those professing Judaism numbered 93,015, or 12.8% of the local population: of these 91,907 declared themselves to be German speaking, 491 Ru-

---

2. Cf. Gerald Stourzh, Die Franz-Josephs-Universität in Czernowitz, 1875–1918. In *Wegenetz europäischen Geistes, Wissenschaftszentren und geistige Wechselbeziehungen zwischen Mittel- und Südosteuropa vom Ende des 18. Jahrhunderts bis zum Ersten Weltkrieg.* Ed. by Richard G. Plaschka, Karlheinz Mack. Vienna 1983, pp. 54–59.

3. Cf. the informative study by Martin Broszat, Von der Kulturnation zur Volksgruppe. Die nationale Stellung der Juden in der Bukowina im 19. und 20. Jahrhundert. In *Historische Zeitschrift* 200 (1965), pp. 572–603.

4. Cf. the excellent and exhaustive book by Emil Brix, *Die Umgangssprachen in Altösterreich zwischen Agitation und Assimilation.* Vienna/Cologne/Graz 1982.

5. This is the official designation for Ukrainian.

thenian, 263 Romanian, 171 Polish, and 165 Hungarian. From these figures it can be seen that a clear majority of all German speaking persons professed Judaism.[6]

What is the result of such ethnic diversity? Many observers have emphasized the relative balance in the plurality of the ethno-linguistic groups in the Bukovina, in contrast to the conflicting dualism between Germans and Czechs in Bohemia or, to a lesser extent, in Moravia. The Bukovina is sometimes even referred to as the "Austrian Switzerland" or as "Little Austria," and Czernowitz as "Little Vienna." Perhaps the political climate in the Bukovina was idealized from the perspective of far-off Vienna or under the influence of the descriptions of Karl Emil Franzos.[7] In particular, the tension between Romanians and Ruthenians should probably be more emphasized than is normally the case from an Austrian perspective.

What was the political situation at the turn of the century and in the years following? A brilliant description comes to us from the English historian John Leslie, who died prematurely in 1994. His study of the Bukovina Compromise, published in 1991, is the best that I know.[8]

About 1890, a new generation of politicians came to the forefront, with more grass-root appeal but also with more demagoguery than their predecessors. A Ruthenian national movement, the Ruthenian National Democratic Party, took root under the leadership of Nikolaj Wassilko—the "Young Ruthenians" so-called, as opposed to the conservative and often Russophile "Old Ruthenians." The first elections held for the Vienna Imperial Parliament (1907) following the introduction of universal equal male suffrage (1905) resulted in five of the fourteen Bukovina mandates going to the "Young Ruthenians." In 1900 a Romanian Democratic Party was formed which distanced itself from the older and more conservative Romanian National Party which represented the interests of large landholders and the clerical (orthodox) hierarchy: the most important politician in this new Romanian party was Aurel von Onciul. There was a small German national group led by Professor Arthur Skedl. The Jewish population was also represented at the turn of the century by a new generation of leaders; here we must go into greater detail.

The Jewish population of the Bukovina in the second half of the 19th century spoke chiefly Yiddish among themselves, but the path to higher

---

6. Figures in Brix, *Umgangssprchen*, p. 392 as well as Broszat, *Kulturnation*, p. 581.

7. Karl Emil Franzos, "Von Wien nach Czernowitz" and "Ein Culturfest" in his book *Aus Halb-Asien. Culturbilder aus Galizien, der Bukowina, Südrußland und Rumänien*, Vol. 1. Leipzig 1876.

8. Cf. Leslie, *Ausgleich*, pp. 116–17.

education and social betterment was assimilation to German language and culture, as can be seen in the overwhelming choice of German as a *lingua franca*. There were three reasons for the movement towards assimilation to German language and culture.

First, Yiddish as spoken in domestic or local usage had much greater affinity to German than to Polish, Russian, Ukrainian or Romanian.

Second, the German language signified and functioned as a type of "emancipation language" for the Jewish population.[9]

Third, the strong position of the German language in public administration as well as in education in the Bukovina made the choice of German even more plausible. During the 1870s both universities in Galicia, i.e., Krakau/Kraków and in particular Lemberg/Lvov/Lviv, switched from German as language of instruction to Polish: the founding of the University of Czernowitz in 1875 with instruction in German was the immediate response to this change. No other language in the Bukovina, neither Romanian nor Ukrainian, enjoyed the strong position that the Polish language had in Galicia after 1868—which incidentally led to increasing Polish assimilation of numerous Jews in Galicia, especially among the upper and middle classes.

The years before and after the turn of the century saw the first renunciation of the ideal of assimilation: the Zionist movement was born. At the first Zionist congress in Basel in the year 1897, a young Zionist from Czernowitz, Dr. Mayer Ebner, rejected assimilation to German culture. In the same year the most prominent politician among the Jewish population in the Bukovina, Dr. Benno Straucher, was elected to the Vienna Parliament as a national Jewish deputy. Straucher became president of the Jewish (religious) Community in Czernowitz in 1903, and in 1906 he founded the National Jewish Party in the Bukovina. Indeed, the Zionist movement should be distinguished from the national Jewish movement, although concurrent allegiance to both groups did occur. The latter, also known as Diaspora nationalism, which became widespread in eastern Galicia and in particular in the Bukovina in the first decade of the 20th century, tried to force the development of Yiddish as a written and literary language. Czernowitz was the center of this movement in 1908 and 1909. This will be discussed at greater length in the ensuing chapter, as will the fight for the recognition of the Yiddish language on an equal basis with other recognized languages of the Austrian Empire, fought with great vigor by a Jewish lawyer, Dr. Max Diamant.

9. Broszat, *Kulturnation*, p. 582.

The National Compromise in the Bukovina as agreed to in 1909 was actually the work of three politicians already mentioned: the Young Ruthenian Baron Nikolaj Wassilko (supported by the scholar and Professor Stefan Smal-Stocki); the founder of the Romanian Democratic Party Aurel von Onciul; and the founder of the National Jewish Party Benno Straucher. Baron Alexander Hormuzaki, a high public servant in Czernowitz and Romanian democratic deputy, did the detailed legal drafting work. Based on files of the Vienna Ministry of the Interior which were found by John Leslie in the Central Historical Archives in Bucharest/Bucuresti[10] and on files which I found in the State Archives of the Chernivtsy Region in Chernivtsy, it is possible to reconstruct both the details of negotiations held in the framework of a Permanent Committee ("Permanenz-Ausschuss") of the diet of the Bukovina starting in 1909, and the correspondence concerning the continuation of these negotiations between the chief of the state administration ("Landespräsident") of the Bukovina, Baron Bleyleben, and the Ministry of the Interior in Vienna.[11]

Draft bills were mostly modeled on, and sometimes even literally taken from the Moravian Compromise, previously mentioned. There were, however, not two but, counting the Jewish population as an ethnic group, five national (in the ethnic sense) electorates and correspondingly not two, but five national (again in the ethnic sense) elected bodies in the diet: Ruthenians, Romanians, Germans, Poles and Jews. The fact that the Jewish population was considered a separate national (ethnic) electorate was the actual sensation of the compromise negotiations in Czernowitz. There was a consensus among all other national groups concerning the recognition of the Jews as a separate national group. The planned incorporation of the Jewish population as a separate national group in the system of political and ethnic representation of a crown land was unique in all of Austria.

However, the consensus agreed to in Czernowitz was rejected by the government in Vienna, which vetoed the introduction of a separate Jewish national electorate and a separate Jewish electoral body in the diet. John Leslie has found source material in the Central Historical Archives in Bucharest which throws light on the motivation behind this decision. Previously it had been known that Jewish organizations which favored assimilation and which were much stronger than Zionist or national Jewish

10. Leslie, *Ausgleich*, pp. 124–32 and pp. 140–41, footnotes 33, 41, and 42.

11. I examined the corresponding files in September 1994. Deržavnyj Archiv Černivec′koï Oblasti (State Archives in Chernivtsy), Collection Provincial Government Bukovina, Fond 3, opis 1.

organizations in western Austria, notably the *Österreichisch-israelitische Union*, had expressed their reservations and concern about the Bukovina model. They feared that the recognition of a separate Jewish ethnic group could harm the equality of all citizens achieved in 1867 and open the door to antisemitic attempts to annul the assimilation which had been accomplished in, for example, the school system.[12]

A detailed file protocol of the Austrian Ministry of the Interior found by Leslie in Bucharest includes the statement that the Zionist movement "promotes the treatment of the Jews as a separate nation and thus parallels antisemitic efforts"; the actual difference between Zionism and "Diaspora nationalism" was not perceived by the Interior Ministry (nor by eminent persons belonging to assimilated Jewry like Theodor Gomperz, a scholar and member of the Upper House of the Austrian Parliament).[13] The Ministry of the Interior was of the (legally correct) opinion that Austrian law recognized the Jews only as a separate religious community. Yet the Ministry had additional misgivings: the recognition of the Jews as a separate ethnic group would have weakened the position of the German population in the Bohemian lands (vis-à-vis the Czechs), especially in Moravia, where the Jews supported the cause of the Germans. The promotion of the idea of granting the Jews a separate status would "be counterproductive to assimilation which is in the interest of the State as a whole" and would also appear "politically unwise in light of the consequences it would have for the situation in Galicia."[14] This meant that the government did not wish to create difficulties for the Poles in Galicia, who traditionally supported the governments in parliament and promoted Polish assimilation among the Jews in Galicia: the recognition of national Jewish movements in the Bukovina certainly would have favored the same trend in Galicia. The legal, if not the political, argumentation of the government was conveyed in an order ("Erlass") dated 4 October 1909 by Interior Minister Baron Haerdtl to the provincial President Bleyleben in Czernowitz. This order stated that "the treatment of the Jewish population as a separate nation" would be "incompatible with fundamental Austrian law" because "the Jewish population as such" [i.e., both those favoring as well as those

12. Cf. Stourzh, Galten die Juden als Nationalität Altösterreichs? In *Studia Judaica Austriaca?* 10 (1984), pp. 92–93.

13. Theodor Gomperz, Das Wahl-Ghetto. In *Neue Freie Presse*, 26 September 1909 (Morgenblatt), p. 2; also Stourzh, Galten die Juden . . . ?, p. 92–93.

14. This document is published in its entirety in Leslie, *Ausgleich*, pp. 137–39.

opposing assimilation—the author] is "recognized by the state as a religious community." [15]

The results of the Interior Ministry's decision can be seen in an extract from the minutes of a session of the Permanent Committee of the
Bukovina diet from 8 to 9 October, 1909 found in the archives of Chernivtsy. The most important change (as opposed to the compromise which
had been negotiated the previous summer) was the following (it incidentally had already been discussed on the occasion of Baron Hormuzaki's
presence in Vienna). As stated in the minutes, in view of the "unfortunate
resistance of the government" to a separate Jewish mandate, which had to
be respected, the Permanent Committee has "united the German and the
Jewish ethnic groups ("Volksstamm") in a single national curia; however,
in the interest of peace between these two groups it has also searched for
a way to secure, on the one hand, Jewish, and on the other hand, German,
mandates." [16]

The Jewish population, which was overwhelmingly German-speaking,
was thus added to the (non-Jewish) German electorate. In order to secure
representation both to the (Jewish) majority and the (non-Jewish) German
minority, constituencies were formed in the cities with two mandates,
though every voter was given only one vote, in order to assure both to the
majority and the minority one mandate. In the countryside an exact territorial separation was the goal. Other less important changes would go
beyond the scope of this paper.

The national Jewish deputy Benno Straucher protested passionately
against the fact that a separate Jewish electorate had not been recognized.
The Permanent Committee drafted a resolution, subsequently approved by
the diet, according to which the diet, given the situation in the Bukovina,
was of the opinion that "the Jews have their own national identity and
form a separate ethnic group ("Volksstamm"), which entitles them to a
separate national curia." [17] Documents in the Chernivtsy archive attest
to the voluminous correspondence between the authorities in the Bukovina and the Ministry of the Interior in Vienna concerning the naming
of the electoral groups, groups of deputies etc., which had been formed by

15. Erlass Zl. 10.925 M. I., 4. October 1909. The text as preserved in the Files of the Ministry of the Interior was discovered by Leslie in the Central Historical Archives in Bucharest (cf.
Leslie, *Ausgleich*, p. 142, footnote 52). I found the original (with Haerdtl's signature) which had
been sent to Chernivtsy in the State Archives in Chernivtsy in September 1994 (Collection
Provincial Government Bukovina, Fond 3, opis 1, Nr. 10504, fol. 49).

16. Ibid., fol. 95–99.

17. Ibid., fol. 99.

the union of the German and Jewish electorates and their deputies. The Permanent Committee asked Vienna whether the designation "German respectively Jewish" was allowed, or "German, respectively German-Jewish"—the last word in brackets—or "German-Jewish"—last two words in brackets—or at least whether such designations were allowed to characterize the population, because, as the provincial president had put it in a telegram on this subject to the Interior Ministry, the "Jews were complaining that otherwise mandates for them would be nameless." The reply of the Minister of the Interior to the provincial president was categorical: any designation of the electorate, etc. as "Jewish" or "German-Jewish" was absolutely prohibited. In addition any characterization of the population as "Jewish" or "German-Jewish" in draft laws or other documents was "not acceptable."[18]

In general the electoral system of the National Compromise in the Bukovina must have been the most complicated—or one of the most complicated—in all of Europe.[19] In its final form, the electoral reform was basically as follows: electoral classes with voting privileges—large landholders, chambers of commerce, urban and rural communities (with census voting rights)—continued as before; in addition, however, a general electoral class was introduced (universal male suffrage) in which the privileged groups could also vote. As many as six different electoral bodies were created within the electoral class of the large landholders—in order to secure representation for the different groups within this class: three were awarded to the Greek Oriental (Greek Orthodox) clergy with a distinction made between the Romanian and Ruthenian clergy; the three secular electoral bodies of the large landholders were composed of one Romanian, one Polish (including Armenopolish) and—finally—one electoral body for "other nationalities"—this referred to Jewish large landholders. Both deputies representing the Chamber of Commerce of Chernivtsy were given de facto to Jewish representatives. In the electoral class of the communities (electoral census) and in the general electorate (no census), the entire Bukovina was covered by a fourfold network of voting districts: for both electoral classes there were separate Ruthenian, Romanian, German and Polish districts, although, since the Polish population was small, only one Polish electoral district covered the entire crown land. Within the

18. Telegram provincial president (Landespräsident) to the Ministry of the Interior, 8 October 1909. Telegram Interior Minister to the provincial president, 9 October 1909. Ibid. fol. 55 and 105.

19. For further details cf. Gerald Stourzh, *Die Gleichberechtigung der Nationalitäten in der Verfassung und Verwaltung Österreichs 1848–1918*. Wien 1985, pp. 235–38.

German electorate there was, as already described, a modus vivendi for the inofficial Jewish electorate. In the countryside, gerrymandering assured that a given constituency contained either a safe German or a safe Jewish (German-speaking) majority. In the cities, especially in Czernowitz, a system for majority and minority representation was set up in each district, by which two deputies were to be elected for the urban districts, but each eligible voter could vote for only one deputy. In this way it was hoped that both Germans and Jews would be satisfied. However, in the elections of 1911 the Jewish groups split and put forward two candidates in one district: both Jewish candidates won and the non-Jewish candidate (Arthur Skedl) lost.[20]

Unique was also the fact that the government ascribed different colors to the ballots for each nationality: Ruthenians–light blue, Romanians–bright red, Poles–orange/yellow and Germans–white. Violet was for the first electoral body of the large landholders, which consisted of the members of the Orthodox Archbishop's Consistorium and heads of the monasteries in Dragomirna, Putna and Suczawitza (Suceviţa) as well as for the Chamber of Commerce in Czernowitz. We do not know the reasons for this riot of color.[21]

The Bukovina diet grew considerably as a result of the reform, i.e., from 31 to 63 members. It included ex officio the Greek Oriental Archbishop in Czernowitz and the Rector of the University of Czernowitz, 13 deputies of the large landholders, two from the Chamber of Commerce, 28 representatives of the district communities and 18 for the universal suffrage class. Running through this division were six national curias which also took religious and property aspects into consideration. The first curia consisted of representatives of the Orthodox clergy (both Romanian and Ruthenian) and the Romanian large landholders; the second curia was overwhelmingly Polish; the third included all other Romanian deputies; the fourth all other Ruthenians; the fifth or de facto German curia comprised seven non-Jewish representatives from the German electorate as well as the Rector of the University of Czernowitz. The sixth curia was de facto the Jewish one and included deputies of the Chamber of Commerce as well as five representatives elected by Jewish voters in the German districts.[22] The first (and due to the outbreak of World War I only) elections following the new system were held in the Bukovina in April and May of 1911. The results

20. For details see Leslie, *Ausgleich*, pp. 134–35.
21. Stourzh, *Gleichberechtigung*, p. 237.
22. Ibid., pp. 237–38.

were deemed positive, namely the elimination of inflammatory national agitation. Elections to the Imperial Parliament in June of 1911, however, as Leslie established, had to be conducted according to the old electoral system (without an ethnically separate registry—"nationale Kataster"), because the legal framework for elections to the Imperial Parliament did not yet exist.[23] I would like to give the final word to the late John Leslie:

"In the final years of peace [prior to World War I], the Bukovina serves as a model, albeit a rather utopian one, for peaceful coexistence among various peoples in a limited area of settlement and shows us, who live in the last years of the twentieth century, possible solutions for the—by no means less pressing—national and ethnic problems of today."[24]

23. Leslie, *Ausgleich*, p. 134.
24. Ibid., p. 136.

CHAPTER EIGHT

Max Diamant and Jewish Diaspora Nationalism in the Bukovina *

A round 1908 to 1910, Czernowitz (now Chernivtsy in the Ukraine) became a significant center of Jewish diaspora nationalism.[1] The usual
dichotomy between assimilation and Zionism is so widely accepted that
a third tendency, albeit shorter-lived, tends to be neglected: diaspora or
galut nationalism. Yet *galut* nationalism played a considerable role in the
Bukovina and its capital city Czernowitz in 1909/1910 and even later. An
eminent personality in the movement for anti-assimilationist Jewish renewal, Nathan Birnbaum, who had coined the term Zionism, relocated
from Vienna to Czernowitz several years after a bitter conflict with Theodore Herzl. Having broken with Zionism, Birnbaum espoused the cause
of *galut* nationalism.[2] As early as 1905 on the occasion of a lecture in
Czernowitz, Birnbaum extolled the richness and importance of the Yiddish language, a truly popular language spoken by eight million people, as
he noted.[3] Birnbaum resided in Czernowitz between 1908 and 1911, cham-
pioning the cause of (Eastern) Jewish nationalism in the diaspora and the

* First published in *Simon Dubnow Institute Yearbook*, vol. I (2002), 153–67. The permission to reprint was gracefully granted by Simon-Dubnow-Institut, Leipzig.

1. This paper was presented in November 1999 to a conference on Jewish culture in
Czernowitz at Tel Aviv University, jointly sponsored by the Institute of German History of
this University and the Internationales Forschungszentrum Kulturwissenschaften in Vienna,
and organized by Prof. Dan Diner. I am grateful to Professor Diner for the opportunity to publish this essay in the *Simon Dubnow Institute Yearbook* in English, thus making the results
of research and the editing of German language sources available to a wider public. All translations of German sources into English are mine.

2. On this conflict, see Robert S. Wistrich, *The Jews of Vienna in the Age of Franz Joseph*,
Oxford 1989, 407–12.

3. Birnbaum's lecture of July 8, 1905, quoted in Adolf Gaisbauer, *Davidstern und Doppeladler. Zionismus und jüdischer Nationalismus in Österreich 1882–1918*, Vienna/Cologne, 364.

conjoint cause of Yiddish.[4] The role of the Yiddish language in the eastern provinces of the Habsburg Empire went beyond its significance for the promoters of *galut* nationalism as distinguished from, or opposed to, Zionism. In the Habsburg Empire, as distinguished from the Russian Empire, census data (or personal documents) contained no reference to a person's nationality in the ethnic sense (*narodnost*). Questions for the census aimed only at language—and from the language indicated, conclusions were drawn as to a person's ethnic allegiance. Thus even the Zionists were compelled, in order prevent assimilationist tendencies and to mobilize the Jews' sense of belonging to their own people, to urge them to indicate "Jewish" (and not German, Polish or another language) in reply to the census' question about the language spoken. And they did so, in full cooperation with *galut* nationalists and Jewish socialists, on the occasion of the Austrian census of 1910.[5] However, this effort was impeded by the fact that the answer "Yiddish" or "Jewish" to the census questionnaire was against the law, since Yiddish (unlike Polish, German, Ukrainian ["Ruthenian"] or Italian etc.) was not recognized as one of the Empire's languages protected by the constitution.[6]

Birnbaum was the principal organizer of the first Yiddish Language Conference in Czernowitz. He had various helpers, particularly the Zionist Löbl Taubes, who was nonetheless a strong advocate of strengthening Yiddish and editor of the newspaper *Jüdisches Volksblatt*. The conference opened on August 30, 1908, attended by more than fifty participants from both Europe and North America, including Sholem Asch, J. L. Perez, Abraham Reisen or Chaim Zhitlovsky. After controversial discussions,

4. Cf. the excellent chapter on "The Metamorphoses of Nathan Birnbaum" in Wistrich, *Jews of Vienna*, 381–420, particularly 412–18.

5. The census, taking place every ten years, asked for the "language of common communication" (Umgangssprache) in the non-Hungarian parts of the Habsburg Monarchy (which included the Bukovina), and for the "maternal language" (Muttersprache) in the Hungarian lands. Only one language could be indicated, thus favoring the individual's decision, even if he or she was fluent in several languages, to indicate the language closest to his or her personal identity. On the fascinating topic of the language census, with full treatment of the Yiddish language problem, see the excellent monograph by Emil Brix, *Die Umgangssprachen in Altösterreich zwischen Agitation und Assimilation*, Vienna/Cologne 1982. On the cooperation of Zionists with *galut* nationalists and Jewish socialists on the occasion of the census of 1910, see Gaisbauer, *Davidstern und Doppeladler*, 497.

6. For interesting law cases arising out of the Austrian census of 1910, see Gerald Stourzh, Galten die Juden als Nationalität Altösterreichs?, in Anna M. Drabek, Mordechai Eliav, Gerald Stourzh (eds.), *Prag–Czernowitz–Jerusalem* (Studia Judaica Austriaca 10), Eisenstadt 1984, 88–91. This essay, including the source texts, was reprinted in Gerald Stourzh, *Wege zur Grundrechtsdemokratie. Studien zur Begriffs- und Institutionengeschichte des liberalen Verfassungsstaates*, Vienna/Cologne 1989, 259–307.

where some participants demanded that Yiddish be recognized as the national language of the Jewish people, the conference resolved that Yiddish was "one national language of the Jewish people," demanding that Yiddish be accorded political, social and cultural equality (*Gleichberechtigung*).[7]

Jewish diaspora nationalism in imperial Austria was influenced by the broader movement for national autonomy that sprang up around the turn of the twentieth century, gaining ground in the next decade. The central idea of "national autonomy"—to which reference has been made in the two preceding essays—was to move away from the purely territorial administration of public affairs in areas with mixed ethnic groups; in these territories, the majority population normally dominated, while minority populations were left disempowered, underprivileged or even worse, discriminated. Ethnic groups or "nationalities" (*Volksstämme* in Austrian legislative and administrative discourse of the time), which increasingly referred to themselves or were referred to as "peoples" or "nations," strove for a system based on autonomous administration, a kind of self-government within imperial Austria, not dissimilar to the self-government granted to the official religious groups (*Konfessionen*) recognized by the state. However, the political relevance and political ambitions of the "nationalities" far exceeded that of the recognized religious communities.[8]

1905 was a key year in the struggle for "national autonomy" in imperial Austria, because of a national compromise negotiated in Moravia. Political theorists and activists in Austria were impressed by the national settlement in Moravia, and in Vienna an association named National Autonomy was established; present at its founding meeting were such notable personalities as Thomas Masaryk, Karl Renner and Nathan Birnbaum. There is evidence as to how Birnbaum envisaged applying the Moravian settlement to the compact Jewish population living in the eastern territories of the Austro–Hungarian Empire.[9] That same year, the 1905 Revolution in tsarist Russia encouraged hopes for greater autonomy in Austria-Hungary. The year also saw the publication in Berlin of Simon Dubnow's *Die Grundlagen des Nationaljudentums*. Robert Wistrich has rightly stressed that Birnbaum's "espousal of Diaspora nationalism and adoption of autono-

---

7. Gaisbauer, *Davidstern und Doppeladler*, 364.

8. Ort the relevance of "national autonomy" in late imperial Austria, see Gerald Stourzh, The Multinational Empire Revisited. "Reflections on Late Imperial Austria," in this volume, pp. 133–56.; *idem*, "Ethnic Attribution in Late Imperial Austria: Good Intentions, Evil Consequences," in this volume, pp. 157–76.

9. Solomon A. Birnbaum, Nathan Birnbaum and National Autonomy, in Josef Fraenkel (ed.), *The Jews of Austria: Essays on their Life, History and Destruction*, London 1967, 131–46.

mism as a realistic political program for the mass of Austrian Jewry was thus part of a wider trend in both the Jewish and non-Jewish worlds."[10]

In 1909, a national compromise was worked out in the Bukovina, including the Jewish population as well, its principles modeled on the Moravian settlement of 1905/1906. How the 1909/1910 national compromise in the Bukovina was achieved has been described in the immediately preceding chapter.[11] One of the salient features of the political situation in the Bukovina was the remarkable equilibrium among the most important ethnic groups of the province, including the Jews. According to the language census of 1910, there were in the Bukovina 305,101 (38.38 percent) Ukrainian-speaking, 273,254 (34.37 percent) Romanian-speaking, 168,851 (21.24 percent) German-speaking and 36,210 (4.56 percent) Polish-speaking inhabitants.[12] The percentage of the Jewish population can be derived from another section of the census statistics, on religion: 102,919 inhabitants, or 12.86 percent of the population of the Bukovina, were counted as Jewish.[13] Be it also recalled that the Bukovina Jews, unlike the Jews of Galicia, continued to be oriented towards the German language. This meant that the majority of the population counted as "German-speaking" was Jewish.[14]

The fact that not a single one of the Bukovina's ethnic groups was in the majority, or at least in a clearly dominant position, facilitated political compromise. By 1909, all the political/ethnic groups in the Bukovina favored a compromise on the Moravian model.

This is the background against which the activities of Max Diamant, a Czernowitz lawyer, are best viewed. Diamant, born in 1878, graduated from the *Gymnasium* in 1897[15] and enrolled that same year as a law student at the University of Czernowitz. There he was a founding member in 1897 of the Jewish student society Zephirah. When an eminent Czernowitz Jewish

10. Wistrich, *Jews of Vienna*, 413. See also Robert S. Wistrich, *Socialism and the Jews. The Dilemmas of Assimilation in Germany and Austria-Hungary*, London 1982, 208.

11. See, with additional bibliographical references, *supra* pp. 177–89.

12. Brix, *Umgangssprachen*, 400.

13. This was the highest percentage in any of the Austrian provinces; in Galicia the percentage of the Jewish Population in the 1910 census was 10.86 percent. Cf. the excellent survey by Wolfdieter Bihl, Die Juden, in Adam Wandruszka, Peter Urbanitsch (eds.), *Die Habsburgermonarchie 1848–1918*, vol. 3, *Die Völker des Reiches*, Vienna 1980, 880–948, here 882.

14. For the strata of the Jewish population striving to advance socially and economically, German was particularly important as the language of instruction in many (though not all) of the Gymnasien in the Bukovina, and particularly as language of instruction of the University of Czernowitz (with some exceptions in the Faculty of Christian-Orthodox Theology)—while the language of instruction of the University of Lemberg/Lwov/Lviv in Galicia was Polish.

15. He received his Matura leaving certificate in 1897 at the age of 19; I am grateful for this information to Dr. Adolf Gaisbauer, Librarian of the Austrian State Archives, Vienna.

politician, Dr. Benno Straucher, deputy in the Austrian Parliament in Vienna, founded the Jewish National Party in 1906, Diamant was elected vice-
chairman of the party. Diamant, originally a Zionist, became increasingly
attracted by *galut* nationalism and the cause of the Yiddish language.[16] It
must be said that in the Bukovina, distinctions between Zionism and *galut*
nationalism were less sharply drawn than elsewhere; *Landespolitik* (politics centered on addressing the situation in the presently settled territory
or "land" as opposed to the future-orientation of the Zionist program) was
important in the Bukovina, chiefly due to the considerable weight of Jewish
political participation in the political balance of the Bukovina.[17] In 1908,
Diamant was active together with Birnbaum as one of the organizers of the
Yiddish language conference in Czernowitz. A friend of his, Dr. Markus
(Mordechai) Kraemer, has reported that Diamant had great enthusiasm for
the Yiddish language, though his fluency in the tongue left something to
be desired.[18] In 1910, Diamant was engaged in calling for Yiddish to be included among the official languages to be counted in the Austrian census
of that year, though without success. Diamant authored a legal treatise on
municipal law and municipal electoral regulations in the Bukovina (1913).
After the break-up of the Habsburg Monarchy, he was a member of the Jewish National Council for the Bukovina and together with Markus Kraemer
was sent to Paris to participate, as delegates of the Jewish National Council
in Czernowitz, in the work for the minority protection articles to be incorporated in the peace treaties or special minority protection treaties of the
Versailles peace system. He also served briefly in the Rumanian Parliament
from 1931 to 1932 as deputy of the Jewish Party (Jüdische Reichspartei,
as it was called in the Jewish German-language press of the Bukovina).[19]
Diamant had a strong interest in Jewish folk art and Jewish gravestones in

16. I owe this information to Dr. David Schaary, Jerusalem.

17. The most successful Jewish politician in Czernowitz and, as a member of the central
Parliament in Vienna, for many years also in cisleithanian Austria, has been rightly characterized "in the first place a national politician, and besides also a Zionist"; Gaisbauer, *Davidstern und Doppeladler*, 487. Personal differences between Jewish politicians in the Bukovina,
which were frequent and acrimonious, were perhaps more significant than purely "ideological" differences.

18. Dr. Kraemer published his recollections about Max Diamant in *Die Stimme des Oleh*
(later *Die Stimme*). *Mitteilungsblatt der Vereinigung der Juden der Bukowina in Israel*, June/
July 1949. I wish to thank again Dr. David Schaary, Jerusalem, for having drawn my attention
to Kraemer's article. Addendum 2006: A book in Hebrew by David Schaary on the Jews of the
Bukovina between the two World Wars was published in 2004 (Publications of the Diaspora
Research Institute of Tel Aviv University, vol. 127).

19. In 1931, five deputies were elected on the ticket of the Jewish Party, three of whom
were elected in the Bukovina. Information kindly supplied by Dr. David Schaary, Jerusalem.

the Bukovina, and together with Arthur Preis wrote a book on Jewish folk art (*Jüdische Volkskunst*), published in Vienna and Jerusalem (in German) in 1937. Max Diamant was among the approximately 3,000 Czernowitz notables and intellectuals and their families, some 80 percent of whom were Jewish, who were suddenly arrested and deported by the occupying Soviet authorities on June 13, 1941, a year of horror for Czernowitz Jewry. The deportation by the Soviets to Siberia and other remote parts of the Soviet Union took place a mere nine days prior to the German attack on the country. Diamant was sixty-three years old at the time and apparently did not survive for long. He died, as has become known only very recently, in the Gulag camp Ust'Vym, in the northeastern part of European Russia (autonomous Republic Komi).[20]

Let us return to 1909. Early that year, Max Diamant took the necessary legal steps to help establish an association for a Yiddish theater in Czernowitz (Verein Jüdisches Theater). At this conjuncture, cultural history, namely the attempt to create a Yiddish theater, took on dimensions of legal and even constitutional history. Austrian legislation on voluntary associations was, unless they were deemed "political," very liberal. The by-laws of any proposed association had to be submitted to the public authorities, which in due course issued an order that either rejected or approved its establishment. Diamant did something unheard of at the time: he decided to submit the by-laws of the proposed Jewish theater association not in German or another of the languages officially recognized in the Bukovina—Romanian, Ukrainian (Ruthenian), even Polish—but in Yiddish and in Yiddish orthography. The provincial authorities in Czernowitz

20. The place of Diamant's death was published in *Die Stimme* (Tel Aviv), vol. 57 (July 2001), in the second part of a list entitled "Vor dem Vergessen bewahren." This list contains the names of persons deported from Czernowitz to the Soviet Union, chiefly Siberia, in June, 1941, and having died there. It was initiated and mainly compiled by Margit Bartfeld-Feller, Tel Aviv; the first part appeared in *Die Stimme*, vol. 56 (November 2000). The information on Diamant was supplied by Dr. Karl Klinger, Tel Aviv, to Mrs. Bartfeld-Feller. I am most grateful to Mrs. Bartfeld-Feller for conveying this information to me. Margit Bartfeld-Feller was deported with her family from Czernowitz at the same time as Max Diamant. She has reported on her Siberian deportation in several books, notably Margit Bartfeld-Feller, *Dennoch Mensch geblieben. Von Czernowitz durch Sibirien nach Israel 1923–1996*, edited by Erhard Roy Wiehn, Konstanz 1996. On the eve of World War II, Czernowitz (Cernăuţi) had a Jewish population of nearly 43,000, even larger than the Jewish community in Kishinev in Bessarabia, see Martin Gilbert, *Atlas of the Holocaust*, London 1982, 70, 72. On the camp Ust'Vym, a part of the large Gulag system stretching from Kotlas to Vorkuta, see now, Ralf Stettner, *"Archipel Gulag." Stalins Zwangslager—Terrorinstrument und Wirtschaftsgigant. Entstehung, Organisation und Funktion des sowjetischen Lagersystems 1928–1956*, Paderborn 1996, 223–25 (with additional references).

refused to deal with Dr. Diamant's submission and the matter was sent
on to the Ministry of the Interior in Vienna. This ministry informed Diamant in April 1909 that his submission concerning the creation of a Jewish theater association could not be granted official consideration, because
it was not written in any of the languages used (and recognized) in the
"realms and lands" represented in parliament.

Two explanations of terminology are called for: The realms and lands
represented in the Imperial Council (*die im Reichsrate vertretenen Köni-
greiche und Länder*) was the official term for the non-Hungarian lands of
the Austro-Hungarian Monarchy, more often referred to as Cisleithania
(i. e. the Lands on "this side" of the Leitha River) or simply Austria.[21] The
languages used in a "Land" or more precisely a *Kronland* (Crown Land,
province) were called "languages customary in the province" (*landesübliche Sprachen*), a term used in a prime constitutional document, the Fundamental Law on the General Rights of Citizens of 1867, which contained
stipulations on the equal rights of the nationalities and of the use of such
landesübliche Sprachen in the non-Hungarian ("cisleithanian") lands of
the Dual Monarchy.

His submission having been turned down, Diamant followed through
with what he had doubtless intended from the outset. He initiated a test
trial before the highest court of public law in the Land, the Imperial Court
(*Reichsgericht*) in Vienna. This Imperial Court was a kind of constitutional court, or more precisely, the forerunner of a constitutional court. It
was not competent to invalidate legislation deemed to be unconstitutional,
a power conferred only upon its successor court in the First Austrian
Republic, the republican Constitutional Court (*Verfassungsgerichtshof*).
However, it was empowered to render judgment on Law suits brought by
citizens claiming that their constitutional rights had been violated by an
act of the administrative authorities.

In his formal complaint to the Imperial Court,[22] Diamant claimed that
his constitutional right "to maintain and cultivate his Jewish nationality"
had been violated by the Ministry of the Interior, because it had refused

21. *Reichsrat* (literally "Imperial Council") was the name of the bicameral parliament created in 1861 with the reemergence of constitutional government in the Habsburg Monarchy.
The *Reichsrat* was boycotted from the beginning by the Hungarians. With the transformation into the "Dual Monarchy" (*Doppelmonarchie*) in 1867 the Reichsrat in Vienna remained
the parliament for those "Realms and Lands" which did not belong to the Hungarian Crown
until 1918.
22. The legal term in German is "Beschwerde vor dem Reichsgericht."

to deal with his Yiddish submission on the creation of the Jewish theatre association.

What was the legal or rather constitutional point on which Max Diamant based his complaint to the Imperial Court? The relevant paragraphs of Article 19 of the Fundamental Law on the General Rights of Citizens (*Staatsgrundgesetz über die allgemeinen Rechte der Staatsbürger*) of 1867 read as follows:

> "(1) All peoples [*Volksstämme*] of the State have equal rights, and every people has an inviolable right to maintain and cultivate its nationality and language.
>
> (2) The equal rights of all languages used in a land in schools, offices and in public life is recognized by the State."[23]

Diamant's claims were two: first, that the Jewish *Volksstamm* was as much an entity recognized by this constitutional law as the Czech or Polish or German or Ukrainian *Volksstamm* and second, that Yiddish was as much a *landesübliche Sprache* in the Bukovina as German, Rumanian or Ukrainian, etc.

On October 26, 1909, the Imperial Court convened in Vienna to hear Dr. Diamant, who had traveled there for the occasion. Diamant's quite lengthy plea before the Imperial Court is a remarkable document in the history of Jewish self-awareness and Jewish national revival in the early twentieth century, even though it is a document of *galut* nationalism, not Zionism. I have published the handwritten records of the Imperial Court proceedings, housed in the Austrian State Archives, in its original German,[24] and the following is drawn from this source.[25]

Max Diamant was aware that his case addressed the fundamental issues. He stressed that this was the first case where the problem of

---

23. Art. 19, § 1: "Alle Volksstämme des Staates sind gleichberechtigt, und jeder Volksstamm hat ein unverletzliches Recht auf Wahrung und Pflege seiner Nationalität und Sprache." Art. 19, § 2: "Die Gleichberechtigung aller landesüblichen Sprachen in Schule, Amt und öffentlichem Leben wird vom Staate anerkannt."

24. Österreichisches Staatsarchiv Wien, Abteilung Allgemeines Verwaltungsarchiv, Bestand Reichsgericht. Extant materials document the public session of October 26, 1909, including Diamant's lengthy speech, arguments presented by the representative of the Ministry of the Interior, Diamant's reply, some texts submitted by Diamant and the confidential sessions of October 26 and 27, 1909, where the judgment to be rendered was deliberated.

25. "Quellenanhang: Dr. Max Diamant vor dem Reichsgericht in Wien, Oktober 1909," appendix to Gerald Stourzh, *Galten die Juden als Nationalität Altösterreichs?*, 99–117; also reprinted in *idem, Wege zur Grundrechtsdemokratie*, 288–307.

nationality itself had been brought before the Imperial Court. This was
perhaps a bit of an exaggeration,[26] yet Diamant indeed forced the Imperial
Court to consider what the essence of a nationality was. He argued that
this was something spiritual, subjective, "a creative source of culture."
He referred to several scholars sharing this view—Julius Stahl, Robert von
Mohl, Friedrich J. Neumann and the renowned jurist Georg Jellinek, son
of Adolf Jellinek, noted Chief Rabbi of the Viennese Jewish Community.[27]

Diamant emphasized that he was specifically referring to "the Jews of
the East." Like Birnbaum when advocating *galut* nationalism, Diamant
distinguished clearly between Jews of the West and Jews of the East (*Juden
des Westens* and *Juden des Ostens*). Only for the latter did Diamant claim
the character of a *Volksstamm* in the sense of Austrian constitutional law,
in view of their compact settlement, their cultural traditions, and their
language. Diamant emphasized religion as the central unifying cultural
characteristic of the Jews of the East. What the law was for the ancient
Romans, art for the ancient Greeks, that was religion for the Jews. For his
people, religion was more than the work of a founder, it was not merely

26. On earlier cases, where the problem of nationality appeared indeed mostly in the form
of conflicts on the use of languages, sec Gerald Stourzh, *Gleichberechtigung der Nationalitäten*, 83–189.

27. Among the cited texts submitted in writing to the Imperial Court as an appendix to
his own submission, only texts by Neumann and Jellinek are extant. Diamant quoted from
the book by Friedrich J. Neumann, *Volk und Nation*, Leipzig 1888, 132, who stressed "high distinctive cultural achievements" as essential ingredient of a nation. Diamant also submitted
a passage from the famous *Allgemeine Staatslehre*, first published in 1900, by Georg Jellinek.
This passage also stressed that the "subjective unity of a nation" was "the product of higher
culture." The passage submitted by Diamant can most easily be found in a 1966 reprint of the
third edition of 1913; Georg Jellinek, *Allgemeine Staatslehre*, Berlin 1914 (reprint Bad Hom-
burg, Zürich 1966), 119: "Nation ist vielmehr etwas wesentlich Subjektives, d. h. das Merkmal
eines bestimmten Bewußtseinsinhaltes. Eine Vielheit von Menschen, die durch eine Vielheit
gemeinsamer, eigentümlicher Kulturelemente und eine gemeinsame geschichtliche Vergangenheit sich geeinigt und dadurch von anderen unterschieden weiß, bildet eine Nation. Die
objektive, durch gemeinsame Abstammung begründete Gemeinsamkeit einer Vielheit, die
Rassen- oder Stammeseinheit ist so alt, wie die historische Erinnerung zurückreicht, und weit
darüber hinaus. Die subjektive Einheit der Nation hingegen ist ihrer Natur nach ein Produkt
höherer Kultur und tritt daher, obwohl schon längst im Keime vorhanden, in voller Stärke erst
in neuester Zeit auf." Diamant also submitted passages from Michael Stöger, *Darstellung der
gesetzlichen Verfassung der galizischen Judenschaft*, Lemberg 1833, 144, stressing the continuities between the autonomy of Polish Jewry under the kingdom of Poland and under the
early Austrian administration. He also referred to a brochure by the famous Czernowitz law
Professor Eugen Ehrlich, *Die Aufgaben der Sozialpolitik im österreichischen Osten, insbesondere der Bukowina mit besonderer Beleuchtung der Juden- und Bauernfrage*, Czernowitz
1909, 19–20, stressing the ignorance in the West about the problems of the Jewish question in
Eastern Europe—and by implication, the differences between *Ost-* and *Westjuden*, which was
the point important to Diamant.

the sum of various dogmas, religion was the entirety of their historical development down to the present day. Diamant went on to describe in great detail the autonomous position of the Jewish communities in the old Kingdom of Poland. He noted that Jewish cultural life had flourished in what formerly had been the Polish kingdom. Diamant referred to important personalities, such as Ahad-Ha'am[28] (pseudonym for Ascher Hirsch Ginsberg) and Micha Josef Berdyczewski among Eastern Jewry.[29] He also drew the Imperial Court's attention to contemporary political movements or parties like the Yiddish-speaking Jewish Social Democrats in Galicia and the Bundists in Russia.

Diamant then turned to the phenomenon of assimilation. He criticized Austrian policies, and particularly the Austrian school system, for favoring and promoting assimilation. In the higher social classes, Diamant said, one entire generation had been lost through assimilation; yet this had not sufficed to destroy the Jewish nation, and today's generation was different—in other words, Diamant suggested that the new generation was turning against assimilation.

In the last major part of his presentation, Diamant dealt with the Yiddish language. Was it in fact a genuine language? Diamant affirmed this emphatically in the case of Eastern Jewry, pointing out that Western Jews spoke a German spoilt in the prison of the ghetto. Diamant then addressed one of the more difficult parts of his argument, the fact of assimilation: many Jews, particularly in the West, had gone down this path. He stressed that his legal brief was a plea solely for the position of *Ostjudentum* and its language. He argued that for the recognition of a nationality—Diamant used the *verbum legale* of Austrian constitutional law, *Volksstamm*—and its language (within the framework of the constitutional provisions referred to earlier), it was not necessary for all elements of the people to remain faithful to the language. Though members may break away from the nation, it still continues to exist. In Galicia, too, Diamant observed, a portion of the Jewish population was going over to the Poles, yet that segment which asserted itself "in its own peculiar character" (*in seiner Eigenart*) nonetheless possessed Jewish nationality.

Diamant rejected the argument put forward by his opponent, the representative of the government, to the effect that Yiddish was not a full-fledged language but merely a "jargon" or "dialect." The jargon of certain

28. The Viennese stenographer apparently misunderstood Diamant and wrote down "Achaba."

29. The stenographer recorded "Berczewski."

social groups, the jargon of students, or of sailors, was based on one particular language, Diamant noted. But the language of the Jews was not based in this same way on another. Quite to the contrary, the language of the Jews in the "ghettos of London or New York" (as he put it) was derived from the language of the Jews in Warsaw or Lemberg. He also pointed to the use of Yiddish in various legal documents (contracts, commercial registers). One of Diamant's major arguments was the fact that Yiddish was indeed represented as a language of modern literature. He referred to the poetry of Morris Rosenfeld (1862–1923) and David Einhorn (1886–1920), and to the Czech Scholar Jaroslav Vrchlický, who had praised these examples of literature. In the field of drama, Diamant mentioned the playwright Sholem Asch (1880–1957). He underlined the fact that works by Spinoza, Herbert Spencer, Oscar Wilde and others had been translated into Yiddish. Diamant drew attention to the existence of a Yiddish press in Russia and the United States. A Yiddish daily and an illustrated weekly newspaper were being published in Lemberg.

Commenting on the existing legal situation in the Bukovina, Diamant admitted that the official published Statutes of the Bukovina contained no Yiddish version. Nonetheless, he pointed out, certain public notifications in the municipality of Wisnitz had been made in Yiddish. The nonexistence of a Yiddish version of the statutes was no argument against the existence of the Yiddish language. He stated that the central concern of his suit was the denial of Jewish collective rights. The Jews had to struggle for their rights, because at the beginning of the movement of the nationalities, they had lacked leadership and thus had come late to the field of struggle. The Jews possessed their own "non-German" intellectuals and it was inadmissible to ignore them as mere "illiterates." Diamant referred to the contemporary negotiations for a national compromise in the Bukovina, where the Diet of the Bukovina had envisaged a special representation for the Jewish *Volksstamm*. The government in Vienna had rejected this, and a solution had been found where the Jewish population was organized de jure for electoral purposes as part of the German nationality; de facto, Diamant added, this measure had reduced the non-Jewish Germans to the status of a minority.

Here a comment on Diamant's argument is called for. As has been mentioned above, the unanimous agreement among all ethnic groups in the Bukovina to give the Jewish group their own electoral register, their own constituencies and their own representation in the provincial parliament had foundered on the opposition of three opponents: first, the Poles of Galicia, who feared a slowdown in the ongoing pro-Polish process of assimilation and the rise of a competing ethnic and political group; second, the representatives of assimilated Jewish organizations in the western part of the Habsburg Monarchy, who strongly urged the government not to give in to the demands of *galut* nationalism; and third and most importantly, the government in Vienna itself, which heeded these voices and also was apprehensive that a legal recognition of the Jews as a nationality might endanger the success of assimilation—or even integration—where it existed.

Concluding, Diamant argued that Eastern Jewry, this "highly intelligent people," would, if impediments were set aside, be "a force in the service of the commonwealth." Now, because hindered in its full development, it was only ballast. He hoped the Imperial Court would hand down a decision that would open up possibilities of new cultural development for his people. Diamant finally thanked the Imperial Court for its attention and expressed his conviction that he had fought for the rights of his people.

The confidential deliberations of the Imperial Court make interesting reading. There was a good deal of uncertainty. One of its members, Edmund Bernatzik, a distinguished constitutional lawyer, suggested that expert advice be called in on the question of what constituted a "people" (in the event, no such expert was consulted). Bernatzik felt it could not be denied there was indeed a Jewish *Volksstamm* in the sense of Art. 19 of the Austrian Fundamental Law on the General Rights of Citizens. Bernatzik was less sure about the character of the "Jewish idiom" (as he termed it) as a genuine language.

In the end, two arguments prevailed rejecting Diamant's plea. The first concerned the question of the Jewish population; the second the question of Yiddish as a language. In regard to the first problem, the Imperial Court agreed with a line of reasoning put forward by its President, the noted legal scholar and liberal politician Joseph Unger, himself of Jewish origin, assimilated and baptized many decades before. He argued that the Jews of Austria enjoyed the protection of the laws as a religious community. Another member of the Imperial Court contended that though perhaps in future Austrian legislation might recognize a Jewish *Volksstamm*, it was not the Imperial Court's task to create (by judicial means) such a new *Volksstamm*, but to protect the *Volksstämme* recognized as such under Austrian law. Yet another member of the Imperial Court maintained quite plausibly that the existence of the Jews as a religious community did not preclude the possibility that they were a people (i.e. *Volksstamm*) as well.

In its final decision, the Imperial Court handed down a ruling that rested on two major points. First, the Imperial Court ruled that the Jews in the "Kingdoms and Lands represented in the Reichsrat" (i.e. Cisleithanian Austria) did not constitute a bona fide *Volksstamm*, the views of the plaintiff Diamant notwithstanding.[30] This was a legal finding, yet the Imperial Court remained deliberately vague about the actual situation. Whatever might be the views and efforts of the Jews in Galicia and the Bukovina regarding their legal status in the state, the Imperial Court asserted that the entire historical development of Austrian legislation concerning the legal status of the Jews tended to regard them as a religious community, a *Konfession* and not a *Volksstamm*.[31]

In responding to the second question on the status of Yiddish, the Imperial Court followed the arguments advanced by its Polish member, count Leo Piniński. Piniński put his finger on one of the weaker points in Diamant's line of argument, contending Yiddish was not the "common language" of a "people." The Polish, the German and Czech *Volksstämme* all had their own distinctive language, but the Jews, depending on where they lived, spoke a variety of tongues. Yiddish, though undoubtedly widely spoken in Galicia and the Bukovina, was not generally recognized by Jews in other countries. In a shrewd rejoinder, Piniński observed that "the Zionists of the West either use Hebrew" or are a people without a special language of their own, like the Swiss. "The idiom of the Eastern Jews" was not a genuine language, even though it might be used in print; it was a vernacular, spoken by the lower strata of the population, even in America. If one were to accept Diamant's law suit, Piniński maintained, one would create "a privilege for the Jews of East Galicia." Here he did not even mention the Bukovina, and it is clear that count Piniński was very much pleading pro domo—for Polish interests in Galicia. Piniński concluded by maintaining that Yiddish could be characterized "as a dialect of local character," not a proper language.[32]

30. The judgment and the Imperial Court's reasons (*Begründung*)—dissenting opinions were and are not known in Austrian judicial procedure—is published in Anton Hye Freiherr von Glunek, Karl Hugelmann (eds.), *Sammlung der nach gepflogener öffentlicher Verhandlung geschöpften Erkenntnisse des k. k. österreichischen Reichsgerichtes*, Vienna 1912, vol. 14, 766–73, no. 1722. A brief notice on this case can be found in: Max Weinreich, *History of the Yiddish Language*, vol. 3, New York 1973 [in Yiddish], 317 (note to vol. l, chap. IV, sec. 78).

31. The German original in full is as follows: "Mögen die Anschauungen und Bestrebungen der Juden in Galizien und der Bukowina über ihre rechtliche Stellung im Staatswesen welche immer sein, die ganze historische Entwicklung der österreichischen Gesetzgebung in Ansehung dieser rechtlichen Stellung geht dahin, die Juden nicht als einen Volksstamm (eine Nationalität), sondern—als Bekenner der mosaischen Religion—als eine Religionsgesellschaft anzusehen und als solche zu behandeln." Hye, Hugelmann, *Sammlung*, 772; also quoted in Stourzh, Juden, in Drabek, Eliav, Stourzh, *Prag—Czernowitz—Jerusalem*, 87 (cf. supra n. 6).

32. Stourzh, Juden, in Drabek, Eliav, Stourzh, *Prag—Czernowitz—Jerusalem*, 110–11.

With slight linguistic emendations, the Imperial Court followed Piniń-ski's line of argument, holding that one could speak of the language of a *Volksstamm* only if it were spoken by all its members, especially in Austria. Yet it was a generally known fact, the Imperial Court asserted (and this had been "admitted by the plaintiff himself"), that the "Jewish language spoken in Galicia and the Bukovina was not spoken in the western Crown lands of the monarchy." Consequently, the Jewish language could not be classified under Austrian law as a "national language" but merely as a "local language (a dialect of local character)," and thus "the legal protection accorded by Art. 19 of the Fundamental Law on the General Rights of Citizens does not extend to it."[33]

Dr. Max Diamant thus lost his case. Yet the proceedings constituted a major test case in the final years of the Habsburg Empire and should be grouped together with other litigation that aimed to achieve fundamental legal or constitutional rulings, like various key civil rights suits in American constitutional history or the Oswald Rufeisen ("father Daniel") case about the question "Who is Jewish?" in Israel (1962).[*] In addition, the arguments put forward by Diamant, particularly his speech before the Imperial Court in Vienna, deserve wider recognition as an outstanding document of *galut* nationalism and a resounding defense of the Yiddish language.

33. Hye, Hugelmann, *Sammlung,* 772; also quoted in Stourzh, Juden, in Drabek, Eliav, Stourzh, *Prag—Czernowitz—Jerusalem,* 87–88.

[*] Explanatory note (addition 2006): Oswald Rufeisen (1922–1998) was a Jew from Poland who during World War II was able to save about 200 Jews threatened by extermination and supported partisans in their struggle against Nazi units. In 1942, hiding in a convent of Carmelite nuns, he converted to Christianity and in 1945 became a Carmelite monk (taking the name of "father Daniel"), striving to settle on the Carmel in Haifa. In 1958 he came to Haifa and, considering himself to be a Jew in spite of his conversion to Christianity, requested Israeli citizenship under the Law of Return of 1950, which granted any Jewish immigrant the right of citizenship. However, in 1962 the Israeli Supreme Court in a 4:1 judgment denied his request in view of his Christian faith. Subsequently, father Daniel was naturalized by the administrative authorities and continued to live in Haifa. Legal information supplied by a document of the Pedagogic Center, Jerusalem "The Oswald Rufeisen/Brother Daniel Case Court Summations" is on the Internet at www.jajz-ed.org.il+Rufeisen&hl=en, dated 30 March 2001.

CHAPTER NINE

The Age of Emancipation and Assimilation: Liberalism and Its Heritage*

On December 21, 1867, the emperor Francis Joseph signed a bill entitled "Fundamental Law on the General Rights of the Citizens." Through the emperor's signature, the bill became a law, one of best known and most important laws of the last half century of imperial Austria and even beyond, because it remained in force from 1918 until 1934, and it has again been in force since 1945 up to the present day. It is also the most celebrated law in the history of Jewish emancipation in the Austrian part of the Dual Habsburg Monarchy. Actually, it merely completed a process that had been in the making for a while, starting with the measures of Joseph II, making a huge leap toward legal equality in 1848/49 at least on paper, suffering grave setbacks in the 1850s, gaining momentum again after 1860, and culminating in the *Staatsgrundgesetz*, the Fundamental Law of 1867.

Be it added right away that exactly seven days later, on December 28, 1867, Francis Joseph as king of Hungary signed the law article XVII of 1867 which completed the process of legal emancipation in Hungary, stipulating that "the Israelite inhabitants of the country are declared to have equal rights with the Christian inhabitants for the exercise of every civil and political right." In Hungary, Jewish emancipation had been a publicly discussed issue since the 1830s, and the most distinguished champion of Jewish emancipation, Baron Joseph Eötvös, published his booklet "The Emancipation of the Jews," written in German, in 1841.[1] Be it said that Eötvös

---

* First published in *Österreich-Konzeptionen und jüdisches Selbstverständnis. Identitäts-Transfigurationen im 19. Und 20. Jahrhundert*, ed. by Hanni Mittelmann and Armin A. Wallas, Tübingen 2001, pp. 11–28 (Conditio Judaica 35). This text was first given as a lecture at the Hebrew University of Jerusalem on 29 March, 2000.

1. On law no. XVII/1867 see Wolfdieter Bihl, Die Juden Ungarns 1780–1914. In *Studien zum ungarischen Judentum*. Eisenstadt: Roetzer 1976 (*Studia Judaica Austriaca* vol. III),

has been the most original and important political thinker of the Habsburg Empire in the 19th century—a Hungarian Tocqueville, as I once have said.[2] Jewish emancipation having been declared belatedly by the Republican anti-Habsburg Government in July of 1849, the cause of emancipation fell victim to the war between the Habsburg dynasty and the Hungarian republic and ensuing repression. So finally for Hungary too, the great year of fully completed legal equality was 1867. I shall briefly return to questions of Jewish assimilation in the Hungarian half of the Dual Monarchy a little later.

Now why was the Austrian Fundamental Law on the General Rights of the Citizens so important to the Jews of Austria? (I shall call "Austria" the non-Hungarian or "cisleithanian" part of the Habsburg monarchy—a usage which became increasingly common in the last decades of the 19th century.) I would like to mention some of the most important provisions.

Article 2 stipulated that all citizens were equal before the law and thus eliminated any legal discrimination of Jewish citizens. Article 3 stipulated that all public offices were equally accessible to all citizens—a rule that looked better on paper than in reality, it should be said at once. Article 6 stipulated the freedom of movement to and residence in every place of the national territory (*Staatsgebiet*), and the unimpaired right to acquire real property, as well as the right to exercise any trade under the conditions laid down by the laws. In practical terms this was the most important part of the law for the Jewish population, though symbolically of course Article 2 on the equality of all citizens before the law was central to its emancipatory character. Article 14 guaranteed to everybody full liberty of faith and conscience—"volle Glaubens- und Gewissensfreiheit." Article 15 stipulated that every legally recognized denomination or "Religionsgesellschaft" (an old-fashioned term not well translated into English by "religious association," which included the Jewish communities) enjoyed the right of public worship as well as the autonomous administration of its own affairs.

I would like to add two clarifications on this law which, as we shall see in a moment, was praised by Jewish spokesmen above and beyond any other law affecting the Jews of Austria.

---

pp. 17–31, here p. 21 (my translation of the German text). On Eötvös, see Catharine Horrel, *Juifs de Hongrie 1825–1849. Problèmes d'assimilation et d'émancipation.* Strasbourg: *Revue d'Europe Centrale* 1995, pp. 87–90.

2. Gerald Stourzh, Die politischen Ideen Joseph von Eötvös' und das österreichische Staatsproblem. In *idem, Wege zur Grundrechtsdemokratie. Studien zur Begriffs- und Institutionengeschichte des liberalen Verfassungsstaates.*Vienna/Cologne: Böhlau 1989 (Studien zu Politik und Verwaltung, 29), p. 237.

First, a misunderstanding ought to be done away with, which crops up time and again particularly in writings dealing with Jewish emancipation. The Fundamental Law on the General Rights of the Citizens was not the only *Staatsgrundgesetz* or Fundamental Law of 1867. Rather, there was a bundle of several fundamental laws that jointly made up the so-called Austrian December Constitution of 1867. Other fundamental laws concerned parliamentary representation, the executive powers, the judicial powers, and the institution of an imperial court, a kind of forerunner of a constitutional court. The rule of law, which indeed was institutionalized to a remarkable degree by the December Constitution, rested on the combined effect of several of these fundamental laws.

Second, it is worth noting that the Fundamental Law on the General Rights of the Citizens originated in an initiative by the Parliament in Vienna. It has been held, in an interesting recent volume on Jewish life in late imperial Austria by a young Austrian scholar that—with the exception of 1848—the granting of equal rights to the Jews was the result of orders decreed from above.

"Equal rights were decreed!"[3] Yet this was not so in 1867. The Fundamental Law on the equal rights of citizens had not been submitted to Parliament by the imperial government. It was the initiative of the liberal majority of the Parliament, where the memories of the constitutional ideas of 1848/49 were quite strong. The German liberals and their allies created this fundamental law, thereby exercising a kind of constituent power, and the crown accepted it. The government needed the support of the liberal majority in Parliament badly for the approval of the compromise settlement with the Hungarians, whereby the dualist structure of what now became to be known as the Austro-Hungarian monarchy had been created.[4]

Yet one must note that at the time one very important ethnic component of the Habsburg state was absent from Parliament in Vienna. The Czechs, of whatever political persuasion, boycotted the Parliament in Vienna in view of the German-Magyar dominance in the monarchy, and

---

3. *Als hätten wir dazugehört. Österreichisch–jüdische Lebensgeschichten aus der Habsburgermonarchie.* Edited by Albert Lichtblau. Vienna/Cologne: Böhlau 1999, pp. 41–42.

4. On the creation of the "December Constitution" in general and the Fundamental Law on the General Rights of the Citizens in particular, see Gerald Stourzh, Die österreichische Dezemberverfassung von 1867. In *idem, Wege zur Grundrechtsdemokratie* (note 2), pp. 239–58, and, with an extensive edition of the sources. Barbara Haider, *Die Protokolle des Verfassungsausschusses des Reichsrates vom Jahre 1867.* Vienna: Verlag der Österreichischen Akademie der Wissenschaften 1997 (Fontes rerum austriacarum, 2/88).

because they felt that the Hungarian lands had obtained a privileged treatment denied to the Bohemian lands. The Czech deputies were to lift their boycott only 12 years later.

The Jews of Austria, having achieved emancipation, the essence of which was legal equality—*Gleichberechtigung*, as the magic word went—, expressed gratitude in often superabundant terms in two directions: to the Emperor, on the one hand, and to the liberals, on the other.

> The Jews of Austria . . . know and remember in boundless gratitude what the emperor of Austria has granted them . . . From father to son and in Jewish prayer-houses it is loudly proclaimed that Francis Joseph the First made his Jewish subjects into real human beings and free citizens (*zu wahrhaften Menschen und zu freien Bürgern*).[5]

Thus wrote the preacher and eventually Chief Rabbi Adolf Jellinek, one of the great personalities of Vienna's Jews and exponent of the reform wing of Vienna's Jewish community, sixteen years later, in 1883.

The attachment to, or even the adulation of the Habsburg emperor has been strikingly illustrated in the memoirs of my immediate predecessor at the University of Vienna, Friedrich Engel-Janosi. Professor Engel-Janosi descended from a family of Hungarian-Jewish industrialists who had moved to Vienna. Writing of the pre-1914-years—Friedrich Engel-Janosi was born in 1893—, he recalled that his father had no interest in politics at all. "Loyalty had stepped into the place of politics." Engel-Janosi also recalled his father saying repeatedly, "If a decree were to enjoin on every Austrian to wear black-yellow stockings, I would walk that very day in the streets with black-yellow stockings." Black-yellow were the imperial colors.[6]

There had, of course, been a second source of emancipatory legislation—the liberals. Adolf Jellinek, in the article just quoted written for the *Neuzeit*, the periodical which most faithfully expressed the affinity

5. Adolf Jellinek, [Article] Jüdisch-österreichisch. In *Die Neuzeit* 23 (1883), Issue of 15 June, 1883, pp. 225–26. The English translation is taken from Robert S. Wistrich, *The Jews of Vienna in the Age of Franz Joseph*. Oxford: Oxford University Press 1989, p. 164. The German original is quoted in Klaus Kempter, *Die Jellineks 1820–1955. Eine familienbiographische Studie zum deutschjüdischen Bildungsbürgertum*. Düsseldorf: Droste 1998 (*Schriften des Bundesarchivs*, vol. 52), pp. 227 and 228.

6. Friedrich Engel-Janosi, . . . *aber ein stolzer Bettler. Erinnerungen aus einer verlorenen Generation*. Graz: Styria 1974, p. 22. The Engel-Janosi family tomb on the Döblinger Friedhof in Vienna is very close to Theodor Herzl's original grave.

between the Jewish "generation of 1867" and political liberalism, did not forget it. "The Jews of Austria also cannot forget," so Jellinek continued,

> that it was the central Parliament, representing the whole of Austria, which voted for the Bill of Rights, thanks to which all earlier laws of exception were abolished and Jews attained the precious possession of civil equality.[7]

Jellinek in his numerous writings represents the compatibility of Judaism, liberalism, acculturation to the German "Bildungswelt," and of deep loyalty to the Austrian dynasty and state. It is not quite wrong to speak of "Juden-Liberalismus," Jellinek wrote in his necrology for the Austrian liberal politician Eduard Herbst, one of the makers of the December Constitution of 1867: "Judaism is liberal, on its banner there shine the words Liberty, Equality, fraternity [Brudersinn], equal rights and equal duties."[8]

I should add that the great significance of Adolf Jellinek—whom Peter Landesmann has called a tragic figure in view of the ultimate failure of his high hopes[9]—has been more fully than before thrown into relief by the work of Wolfgang Häusler, Robert Wistrich, Peter Landesmann and most recently Klaus Kempter.[10] May I also say in passing that though I am aware of changing interpretations given to the term "assimilation," and though I am also aware that political correctness is asking its dues, which I am not willing to pay, I do not think that assimilation is identical with "absorption." "Assimilation"—"as a process of adaptation and adjustment on a continuum," to quote the brilliant and moving book by Leo Spitzer on assimilation and marginality in Austria, Brazil and West Africa, remains an employable term.[11]

7. Jellinek, *Jüdisch-österreichisch* in Wistrich, *The Jews of Vienna* (note 5), p. 164.

8. Quoted Kempter, *Die Jellineks* (note 5), p. 225, note 82, from *Die Neuzeit* 32 (1892), pp. 263–64 (my translation).

9. Peter Landesmann, *Rabbiner aus Wien. Ihre Ausbildung, ihre religiösen und nationalen Konflikte.* Vienna/Cologne: Böhlau 1997, p. 266.

10. Wolfgang Häusler, "Orthodoxie" und "Reform" im Wiener Judentum in der Epoche des Hochliberalismus. In *Der Wiener Stadttempel 1826–1976.* Edited by Kurt Schubert (Studia Judaica Austriaca, VI, 1978), pp. 29–56, particularly pp. 41–45; Wistrich, *Jews of Vienna* (note 5), chap. 8 on "Adolf Jellinek and the Liberal Response," pp. 238–69; Landesmann, *Rabbiner aus Wien* (last note), pp. 106–10, pp. 264–71; Kempter, *Die Jellineks* (note 5), passim, yet particularly pp. 137–54.

11. Leo Spitzer, *Lives in Between. Assimilation and Marginality in Austria, Brazil, West Africa 1780–1945.* Cambridge: Cambridge University Press 1989, p. 28. I would also like to

The affinity to political liberalism, the admiration and gratitude for those liberal politicians who had established civil equality for the Jews, is illustrated in that magnificent source book on Vienna in the last third of the 19th century, Sigmund Freud's *Interpretation of Dreams*—with acknowledgments to Robert Wistrich's work on the Jews of Vienna, where I got the cue, though I will elaborate on it a bit.[12]

Freud tells us that as a boy of 11 or 12, around 1868, he was taken along by his parents to a restaurant in the Prater; someone told him that one day he might become a government minister—it was a versifier going from table to table to produce little rhymes and getting small tips for it. Freud remembers having been impressed by that expectation, and he adds: "It was the time of the *Bürgerministerium*"—the liberal government appointed by the emperor at the end of 1867. *Bürger* must be understood in the double sense of this German word, as *citoyen* as well as *bourgeois!* But the most interesting detail supplied by Freud is yet to come. Freud—writing at the end of century—recalls that before this trip to the Prater his father had briefly brought home portraits of these "bürgerliche Doktoren"—of these bourgeois doctors of law, we have to add, who were now government ministers, and the Freuds' apartment had been illuminated in honor of these men. Freud adds: "There were even Jews among them; every diligent Jewish boy, then, carried in his school-bag the portfolio of a government minister." Freud, looking back in 1899, recalls the names, though he makes one mistake—if I may add a footnote for a future critical edition of the *Interpretations of Dreams*. He recalls the names of Herbst (Minister of Justice), Giskra (Minister of Interior), Berger (Minister without portfolio) and Joseph Unger, eminent jurist and Jewish convert. Yet Unger was not a member of the *Bürgerministerium*, he was member of a subsequent liberal government appointed in 1871, which incidentally included a second Jewish convert, Julius Glaser, as well. So Freud's memory blended recollections of the first *Bürgerministerium* of 1868 with a second liberal government after 1871, and his recollection that Jews could become government ministers suppressed the fact (here the Freudian term

refer to the following works: *Assimilation and Community: The Jews in Nineteenth-Century Europe*. Edited by Jonathan Frankel and Steven Zipperstein. Cambridge: Cambridge University Press 1992, including the essay by Marsha L. Rozenblit, Jewish Assimilation in Habsburg Vienna, pp. 225–45, and to *Paths of Emancipation: Jews, States, and Citizenship*. Edited by Pierre Birnbaum and Ira Katznelson. Princeton: Princeton University Press 1995, particularly to the introductory essay by the editors: "Emancipation and the Liberal Offer," pp. 3–36 (see especially pp. 18–19).

12. Wistrich, *The Jews of Vienna* (note 5), p. 546.

"verdrängen" may be applied to the inventor himself) that Unger (and Glaser) were converts.[13]

Be it said that in later governments as well, in Austria and even more
frequently in Hungary, Jewish converts were appointed ministers; yet only
one person of Jewish faith, Vilmos Vázsonyi, was appointed to the Hungarian government as Finance Minister by King Charles in 1917.[14]

Freud, writing his "Interpretation of Dreams" toward the close of the
century, felt himself "taken back to the times of the *Bürgerministerium*,
full of hope"—"die hoffnungsfrohe Zeit des Bürgerministeriums."[15] It
must have been connected with the impressions of that era, says Freud,
that he planned to study law up to the very moment of enrolling in the
University. The study of law was of course in Austria, as elsewhere, the
royal road for the politically ambitious, those striving to devote themselves to the *res publica*.

To conclude on the Freud episode and its significance. Freud's father
bringing the portraits of the "bürgerliche Doktoren" home and illuminating the apartment in their honor, his son remembering this scene more
than thirty years later with nostalgic pleasure: there is a double pride in
this scene.

First, pride that "bürgerliche Doktoren" had conquered the imperial government, as it were. I need to add here that there is a strong anti-aristocratic
slant in this expression, visible to contemporaries, lost to us: most aristocrats planning to enter government service completed their law studies with a state certificate ("Staatsprüfungen"), without the doctorate
bestowed by the university; for the free profession of a lawyer, a classic
bourgeois occupation, on the other hand, the doctorate was required.

But there was also, second, the pride of a Jewish family assimilated or
rather acculturated to an environment that seemed to promise new avenues
of equal access even to public office via the liberal profession of the law.[16]

13. Sigmund Freud, *Studienausgabe*. Edited by Alexander Mitscherlich, Angela Richards
and James Strachey. Vol. 2: *Die Traumdeutung*. Frankfurt/Main: S. Fischer 1972, p. 204.

14. Wolfdieter Bihl, Die Juden. In *Die Völker des Reiches*. Edited by Adam Wandruszka
and Peter Urbanitsch. Vienna: Verlag der Österreichischen Akademie der Wissenschaften 1980
(*Die Habsburgermonarchie 1848–1918*, vol. III), pp. 880–948, here p. 941. May it be said that
this very comprehensive work by Professor Bihl—with whom I shared my first visit to Israeli
universities in 1982—remains a first rate reference work and a mine of information which deserves careful attention by non-Austrian scholars.

15. Freud, *Die Traumdeutung* (note 13), p. 204.

16. The particular slant of Freud's reference to the "bürgerliche Doktoren" is rather lost
by the English rendering "middle-class professional men" in Wistrich, *The Jews of Vienna*
(note 5), p. 546.

There were, in the liberal era, sufficient examples of the effectiveness of the new doctrine of equal rights or "Gleichberechtigung." In 1869, the President of the Vienna Chamber of Commerce, Simon von Winterstein, was nominated by the government for a seat in the Chamber of Pairs, the upper House of Parliament ("Herrenhaus"). While a Polish member of the government, Count Potocki, raised objections in view of Winterstein's Jewish faith, the majority of the government proposed Winterstein's name to the Emperor, stressing the argument of equal rights on the basis of the fundamental law on the general rights of the citizens ("vom Standpunkte der staatsgrundgesetzlichen Gleichberechtigung"), as is said in the minutes of the Council of Ministers. Winterstein was indeed appointed by the Emperor a member of the Chamber of Pairs.[17]

How long did the "golden years" of Austro-Jewish history last? Some authors speak of a "golden decade," more or less identical with the era of liberal political predominance, which actually lasted a dozen years after 1867, with a brief Interruption in 1871. One might also say that there was an even briefer "golden" period, from 1867 to the great crash of 1873. But from a different point of view one may argue that the whole period from 1867 down to World War I, was a "liberal period," indeed protected by the continuing framework of the 1867 Staatsgrundgesetz, in spite of increasing antisemitism, and one of an astonishing "épanouissement" of Jewish creativity. Peter Pulzer has observed that "the economic and political influence of the Jews during these decades paled beside their complete domination of Viennese cultural life in the generation before 1914."[18] And the social democrat Julius Braunthal has written that in "the invigorating air of this remarkable cosmopolis, Jewish talent blossomed as vigorously as it did in Granada under Moslem rule."[19]

I will single out two issues that were products of emancipation and assimilation, yet which in their beginnings antedated the liberal era and certainly outlasted it in their effects.

The first issue is that of higher education. I will bypass the role of the Austrian *Gymnasien* for Jewish acculturation, on which excellent work has been published by Gary Cohen and Hannelore Burger, with the exception

17. Gerald Stourzh, Die Mitgliedschaft auf Lebensdauer im österreichischen Herrenhause, 1861–1918. In *Mitteilungen des Instituts für österreichische Geschichtsforschung* 73 (1965), p. 83, note 77.
18. Peter Pulzer, *The Rise of Political Anti-Semitism in Germany and Austria* (revised edition). Cambridge, MA: Harvard University Press 1988, p. 13.
19. Cited ibid. from Julius Braunthal, *In Search of the Millenium*, with an Introduction by H. N. Brailsford. London: Gollancz 1945, p. 17.

of one point.[20] I would like to stress that there was a truly remarkable growth of *Gymnasien* in Galicia and Bukovina in the last two decades of imperial Austria; thus the chances of the Jewish population in the east to advance on the ladder of "Bildung" were vastly enhanced—two universities, that of Lemberg/Lviv, with Polish language of instruction, and that of Czernowitz/Chernivtsy, established as "Kaiser Franz Josephs-Universität" in 1875 and with German as the main language of instruction, were ready to receive the increasing numbers of "Maturanten," of the graduates of the *Gymnasien*.[21]

Now to university education. The phenomenal progress of Jewish students through the Austrian universities from the 1860s down to the eve of World War I has been shown by Albert Lichtblau in his book *Als hätten wir dazugehört*—"As if we had belonged"—published in 1999. There was a massive increase in the percentage of Jewish students studying at the Austrian universities during the seventies and early eighties, from 12.4% in the academic year 1873/74 to 19.9% in 1883/84, the most considerable increase during this decade taking place at the University of Vienna, from 22.5% in 1873/74 to about 33% in 1883/84. The breakdown for individual universities is most interesting. Virtually shunned by Jewish students were the universities of Innsbruck, Graz and the Czech University of Prague. Apart from Vienna, the universities most frequently attended by Jewish students were the German University of Prague and the universities of Lemberg and Czernowitz, much less that of Cracow. In Lemberg the percentage of Jewish students increased steadily, reaching about 27% in 1912/13; in Czernowitz the percentage was 33% in 1893/94 and reached an all time high with 40.5% in 1902/03, slightly declining to 37% in 1912/13. The developments in Lemberg and Czernowitz reflect of course, as pointed out already, the growing infrastructure of *Gymnasien* in the east of cisleithanian Austria.[22]

20. Gary B. Cohen, *Education and Middle Class Society in Imperial Austria 1848–1918.* West Lafayette, Ind.: Purdue University Press 1996, and Hannelore Burger, *Sprachenrecht und Sprachgerechtigkeit im österreichischen Unterrichtswesen 1867–1918.* Vienna: Verlag der Österreichischen Akademie der Wissenschaften 1995.

21. On the Bukovina, see also Hannelore Burger, Mehrsprachigkeit und Unterrichtswesen in der Bukowina 1869–1918. In *Die Bukowina. Vergangenheit und Gegenwart.* Edited by Ilona Slawinski and Joseph P. Strelka. Bern et al.: Peter Lang 1995, pp. 93–127, particularly diagrams showing the (very high) proportion of Jewish pupils in the Gymnasien of the Bukovina, ibid., pp. 122 and 123.

22. Lichtblau, *Als hätten wir dazugehört* (note 3), pp. 71–76, particularly p. 74. Very valuable also Cohen, *Education and Middle Class Society* (note 20), pp. 165–68.

The second issue I have singled out is a much more difficult, a more delicate one, since it reaches very deeply into the realm of emotions. It is the issue of conversion, or at least of leaving the Jewish community, the *Kultusgemeinde*, for the status of "konfessionslos"—being free of any religious denomination or affiliation, as "konfessionslos" is rendered a bit awkwardly in English. Connected with this was the issue of mixed marriages, if not in a legal, then in a cultural sense, of *connubium* between persons of Jewish and of non-Jewish origin.

These problems have been subject so far to more thorough scholarly treatment in Germany than in Austria, as in Kerstin Meiring's book on Christian-Jewish mixed marriages in Germany from 1840 to 1933.[23]

From 1868 up to and including 1917 approximately 18,000 persons left the Vienna Kultusgemeinde, many of whom converting to either Protestantism or Catholicism, some remaining konfessionslos—the latter group going to increase after 1918.[24] On motives—love and marriage, career advancement, spiritual conversion, much has been written, and I shall not add to it except one revealing illustration pertaining to the career aspect.

Hans Kelsen, the famous jurist, was born in 1881 and in 1905 decided in favor of (catholic) baptism, quite frankly in hopes of better chances for an academic career. In 1908 he was offered a post in the administration of the University of Vienna. Visiting his future office, he was told by the highly embarrassed director of the university administration, Karl Brockhausen, that in view of the constant contacts with German-nationalist and anti-Semitic student groups which of the position which Kelsen was supposed to fill, he could not assume the post in view of his Jewish origins. The director, a noted legal scholar himself, expressed his regrets that he originally had raised false hopes with Kelsen—who eventually was to obtain a full professorship at this University.[25]

Now permit me to make the following points on the problem of converts and mixed marriages.

---

23. Kerstin Meiring, *Die christlich-jüdische Mischehe in Deutschland 1840–1933*. Hamburg: Dölling und Galitz 1998 (*Studien zur Jüdischen Geschichte*, 4).

24. I am very grateful to my doctoral student, Ms. Philomena Leiter, for this as well as a number of additional informations. The following chapter will develop the theme of mixed marriages in greater detail and will present additional bibliographical references, including the important doctoral dissertation by Dr. Leiter.

25. Rudolf Aladár Métall, *Hans Kelsen. Leben und Werk*. Vienna: Franz Deuticke 1969, p. 13.

First, these phenomena had a much larger significance in Vienna than elsewhere in the Habsburg monarchy, and larger also than in the rest of Europe, only to be compared perhaps to Berlin.

Second, as far as mixed marriages are concerned, Ivar Oxaal has convincingly argued that Marsha Rozenblit has underestimated "the other type of mixed marriage—where the Jewish partner departs from Judaism altogether prior to marriage."[26] Yet this type of mixed marriage was important in Vienna, and this has to do, more than scholars so far seem to have investigated it, with the intricacies of Austrian marriage law, which down to 1938 was very much centered on marriage to be contracted before religious authorities. There existed no "obligatory civil marriage" (obligatorische Zivilehe) as in Germany since 1876 or in Hungary since 1894, only an "emergeny civil marriage" ("Notzivilehe") involving persons with no denominational affiliation. The Austrian Civil Code of 1811 provided that marriage contracts between Christians and persons who did not confess the Christian religion had no legal validity. The pecularities of Austrian marriage legislation[27] seem to be closely related to the fact that Vienna's conversion rate was the highest in late nineteenth-century Europe.[28]

The marriage of Adolf Jellinek's son Georg—the famous jurist—is a most interesting case story. Georg fell in love with Camilla Wertheim, Catholic daughter of the physician Gustav Wertheim, who himself descended from the Jewish family of Samson Wertheimer, and had converted to Catholicism (in 1859) only in view of his marriage with his non-Jewish fiancée, because of the non-admissibility of Christian-non-Christian marriages just mentioned. In the case of the marriage of Georg Jellinek with Camilla Wertheim—who must have been an absolutely wonderful person, she later got deeply involved in the legal protection movement for exploited women and girls in Germany—, Camilla Wertheim quit the Catholic church and became "konfessionslos" ("without religious affili-

26. Ivar Oxaal, The Jews of young Hitler's Vienna. In *Jews, Antisemitism and Culture in Vienna*. Edited by Ivar Oxaal, Michael Pollak, and Gerhard Botz. London: Routledge & Kegan Paul 1987, pp. 11–38, here p. 32, with reference to Marsha L. Rozenblit, *The Jews of Vienna 1867–1918: Assimilation and Identity*. Albany, NY: State University of New York Press 1983, p. 129.

27. The excellent monograph by Ulrike Harmat, *Ehe auf Widerruf? Der Konflikt um das Eherecht in Österreich 1918–1938*. Frankfurt/Main: Klostermann 1999 (Ius Commune—Veröffentlichungen des Max-Planck-Instituts für Europäische Rechtsgeschichte Frankfurt am Main, Sonderhefte: *Studien zur Europäischen Rechtsgeschichte*, vol. 121), has an extensive introduction dealing with pre-1918 developments in the Habsburg monarchy.

28. Addendum 2006: Current research by Anna L. Staudacher (Vienna) on conversions shows that the motive "love and planned marriage" seems to have been far more frequent than career considerations.

ation"), before Adolf Jellinek in 1883 accomplished the marriage rites for Georg and Camilla—not in the Stadttempel, but in the apartment of an uncle of Camilla's. In the marriage notice in the *Neuzeit* nothing was said about the religious (non-) affiliation of Camilla Jellinek, but only that she was a descendant of Rabbi Samson Wertheimer.[29]

A brief word on the socio-cultural relevance of mixed marriages. We know very little, because little research has been done so far for Austria about the non-Jewish partners in mixed marriages and their family background. If mixed marriages were an important phenomenon, as I believe they were, and if anti-Jewish prejudices were as important in Austrian society as unfortunately I think they were, we should know more about the social, intellectual and spiritual background of those who committed themselves to mixed marriages. In 1939 there were about 15,000 persons in Vienna, one of whose parents was Jewish or of Jewish origin, and one who was not.[30] Ilse Aichinger, the well-known writer, was one of them, and her novel *Die größere Hoffnung* is a most poignant testimony to the existence, and to the torments, of this group of persons.—Most of these persons did survive, many of them and their children and grandchildren live in Austria. Why do I say this? Because in Vienna there is a not so small group of persons mindful of this history, thoughtful about their own history. They form a socio-cultural ingredient of Austrian post-1945 society, too seldom thought of, yet quite resistant to those anti-Semitic tendencies whose continuing existence is so rightly and frequently deplored.

Third, the phenomenon of the converted Jews and their families was by no means exclusively, yet importantly, an upper middle class or upper class phenomenon—, of industrialists, of the upper bureaucracy, of the free professions, medical doctors and lawyers, of the "Bildungsbürgertum." As such it was a socio-cultural phenomenon of considerable importance in late 19th and early 20th century Vienna. Its scholarly analysis is not easy, and opposite tendencies have been apparent. On the one hand, the Jewish converts have been considered as apostates,[31] which of course they were when seen from within the Jewish community; and the "Konfession-

29. On Georg Jellinek's courtship and wedding and the problems attached to it see the discerning and detailed account in Kempter, *Die Jellineks* (note 5), pp. 204–206, pp. 239–40.

30. In the Nazi terminology of the period so-called "Mischlinge ersten Grades"; the figure is taken from reports of the statistical department of the municipal administration of Vienna for the year 1940 and quoted in the unpublished report by Dr. Georg Weis "Bericht über das jüdische erblose Vermögen in Österreich" (December 1952); copy in the possession of the author. The corresponding figure for all of Austria is slightly under 17,000, as will be shown in greater detail in the ensuing chapter (*infra*, pp. 245–46).

31. As in Marsha Rozenblit's book referred to supra note 26.

slose," too, have been receiving bitter comments, couched in the words of a dialogue in Arthur Schnitzler's *Weg ins Freie* between the Jewish patriarch Ehrenberg and the "konfessionslose" Nürnberger who says that he never felt like a Jew. Schnitzler lets Ehrenberg say rather rudely to Nürnberger: "When they will beat on your top hat on the Ringstraße because you have, with respect, a slightly Jewish nose, you will feel being attacked as a Jew, depend on it."[32] On the other hand, famous converts like Gustav Mahler or other renowned personalities of even partly Jewish descent like Hofmannsthal have been claimed, with pride, for the significance of Jewish culture in late 19th and early 20th century Vienna.[33]

History, and historians, are often said to be on the side of the stronger battalions. May I say that in today's historiography and in today's memory culture, the converts or the assimilated "Konfessionslosen" are not with the stronger battalions—unless they are very famous.

Let me return, in the concluding part of this paper, to my point of departure, the *Staatsgrundgesetz* on the General Rights of Citizens of 1867. The fundamental laws of the 1867 constitution, with the *Staatsgrundgesetz* on the General Rights of Citizens in the center, remained for the Jews of Austria the most precious piece of Austria's legislation protecting the rights of the Jewish Citizens. One Jewish voice put the fundamental laws into the very definition of what it meant to be an Austrian: "To be an Austrian means to hold high the fundamental laws"—"Österreicher sein heißt, die Staatsgrundgesetze hochhalten."[34]

The Austrian Jews' constant praise of the *Gleichberechtigung* guaranteed by the fundamental laws of 1867, almost an incantation sometimes, actually ought to be seen as a text within a double context.

One context was the fact that the Habsburg Empire bordered, along hundreds and hundreds of miles, on those two states which continued to maintain discriminatory, non-emancipatory legislation directed against the Jewish populations: the kingdom of Rumania, and the Tsarist Empire.

In Rumania, the constitution of 1866 had limited citizenship to Christians. Great pressure was brought on Rumania during the Berlin Congress

32. Ruth Klüger, Der Weg ins Freie—Juden in Wien. In *Theodor Herzl Symposion, Wien. 100 Jahre "Der Judenstaat," 17.– 21. März 1996, Wiener Rathaus. Der Bericht.* Vienna: Ideenagentur Austria 1996, pp. 15–22, here pp. 21–22. I am discussing Ruth Klüger's epochal autobiography *weiter leben. Eine Autobiographie* as one of the most important accounts of the Shoa in Gerald Stourzh, *Begründung und Bedrohung der Menschenrechte in der europäischen Geschichte.* Vienna: Österreichische Akademie der Wissenschaften 2000, pp. 14–15.

33. Steven Beller, *Vienna and the Jews 1867–1938: A Cultural History.* Cambridge: Cambridge University Press 1989.

34. Quoted by Steven Beller, *Vienna and the Jews* (note 33), p. 181, note 122.

of 1878 by the powers with the exception of Russia to drop this exclusionary discrimination. Rumania finally consented to modify the constitution and accept in principle the naturalization of Jews, yet every single naturalization required the approval of both chambers of Parliament! Within the following 38 years merely 2,000 Jewish persons were naturalized. The rest of the Jewish population (between about 267,000 and 240,000, the decrease due to emigration), was submitted to the arbitrary discrimination of foreigners until the end of World War I.[35] The Jewish press in the neighboring Dual Monarchy reported about developments in Rumania, and even more closely on what went on in Russia.[36]

The pogroms in the Tsarist Empire in 1881 had a very large echo in the Habsburg Monarchy, also beyond the Jewish communities and the Jewish press. Brody on the Austro-Russian frontier became the center of aid to refugees from Russia, non-Jewish committees of aid were established in Vienna, Brünn/Brno and in Budapest.[37] The emperor Francis Joseph received the Lemberg Rabbi Dr. Löwenstein and expressed his sympathy with the plight of the refugees and with the aid initiatives that had come under way.[38] There was, in other words, a contemporary and comparing awareness of what went on beyond the borders of the Habsburg monarchy that quite often, I think, is not shared anymore by some historians whose fields of specialization often are quite narrow. By referring to Russia or Rumania I do not deflect from developments within the Habsburg monarchy.

I have spoken of a text within a double context. The text—the incantation, as it were, of the *Staatsgrundgesetz* of 1867 and its guarantee of equal rights—has, of course, also to be seen, and above all to be seen in the second context: developments within the dual monarchy and more particularly within the cisleithanian half of it.

There is an uncanny symbolism in the fact that even before the beginnings of the "golden years" or the "golden decade" or the "golden period" of Jewish history in the Habsburg lands, the first signals of sinister things

35. Victor Karady, *Gewalterfahrung und Utopie. Juden in der europäischen Moderne*. Frankfurt/Main: Fischer Taschenbuch Verlag 1999 , pp. 108–12.

36. Helene Feuchter, Die Reaktion in der altösterreichischen jüdischen Öffentlichkeit auf die Pogromwellen in Rußland vor dem 1. Weltkrieg. Master's Thesis, University of Vienna, 1992. An excellent general survey is given by Manfred Hildermeier, Die jüdische Frage im Zarenreich. Zum Problem der unterbliebenen Emanzipation. In *Jahrbücher für Geschichte Osteuropas* 32 (1984), pp. 321–57.

37. Feuchter, *Die Reaktion* (last note), pp. 49–55.

38. Adolf Kessler, *Die Juden in Österreich unter Kaiser Franz Joseph I.* Doctoral Dissertation, University of Vienna 1932, p. 143.

to come were detected. As early as 1865—two years before the *Staatsgrund-gesetz!*—no one else but Adolf Jellinek expressed his fear that "a new Jewish question" was beginning to develop, which would touch the Jews much more deeply than the old Jewish question of legal and political equaliza- tion. A new scientific discourse, Jellinek observed with bitterness, had been introduced, and he referred particularly to Ernest Renan, who in his work on the life of Jesus had employed the term "race"; Jellinek noted that a sharp, quasi-biological contrast had been established—one had created "einen scharfen, gleichsam naturgeschichtlichen Gegensatz"—between Aryans or Indo-Europeans on the one hand and Semites on the other. This new biological way of thinking was, so Jellinek, "a much more important Jewish question" than the older anti-Jewish prejudices of Christian origin, because,—and I quote Jellinek first in the original German, and then will render the text in English:

> Es wird der Jude wieder in ein Ghetto verwiesen, wo er im Namen der unerbittlichen und unabänderlichen schaffenden Natur bleiben muß [. . .]. Hier, in dieser neuen Judenfrage handelt es sich nicht für die Juden um ein größeres oder geringeres Maß an politischen Rechten, sondern um den ganzen Menschen, um sein innerstes Wesen.[39]
> The Jew will be anew expelled into the Ghetto, where he is to remain in the name of an implacable and unchanging creative nature [. . .]. Here, in this new Jewish question, it is not the question of a greater or smaller measure of political rights for the Jews, but of the whole hu- man being, his innermost being.

This was written in 1865! It certainly is not possible to sketch the devel- opment of the rising "new" anti-Semitism, so-called. This has been done many times, and very convincingly. I would like to refer briefly to certain characteristics of that development in the Habsburg lands.

First, there is the problem or phenomenon of a "two-track" form of Anti-Semitism, of which Michael John has spoken in a paper on identity and ethnicity in Austria. The German acculturation of very many central European Jews during the 19th century brought the Jews into a double pre- dicament. Michael John has argued by taking his cue from Joseph Samuel Bloch, who rightly feared that the Jews were being caught between the fronts of the national quarrels (in his brochure *Der nationale Zwist und die*

39. Adolf Jellinek, Eine neue Judenfrage. In *Kalender für Israeliten 1865/66.* Edited by Simon Szanto. Quoted in Kempter, *Die Jellineks* (note 5), p. 134.

Juden in Österreich of 1886). On the one hand, Jews came under criticism or attack from opponents of German dominance, notably from the Czech; on the other hand, they suffered from anti-Semitic attitudes developing among the Austrian Germans themselves.[40] An analogous situation, incidentally, can be observed in Hungary. The pro-Magyar option of the overwhelming majority of Jews in Hungary particularly after 1867, many of whom thus passing through a second acculturation—from Yiddish to German, from German to Magyar—, was apt to fuse the anti-Magyar posture of Hungary's ethnic minorities with antisemitic sentiments.

This is the moment, though, to briefly reflect on differences between developments in the two halves of the Dual Monarchy. I am much obliged to the brilliant analysis of Jewish assimilation in Austria-Hungary by the late Peter Hanák.[41] In Hungary, acculturation and assimilation did occur and endure to a higher degree than in the cisleithanian half of the Monarchy. One critical period in the early eighties, connected with the name of the anti-Jewish polemics of Győző Istóczy and the Tiszaeszlár trial, was resolutely met by the Hungarian Prime Minister Kálmán Tisza, defending and affirming the equal rights of Hungarian citizens of Jewish faith. From the sixties onward, there developed an unwritten alliance, as it were, between the ruling elites of nobility and gentry and the Jewish, particularly the urban Jewish population willing to assimilate with the Magyars. The ruling stratum could not dispense, Hanák has written, with assimilation in its effort quantitatively to strengthen the Hungarian nation both in respect of material wealth and of intellectual capacity. Political anti-Semitism in Hungary was subordinated to the *lex suprema*, which was to preserve the Magyar hegemony and the integrity of Greater Hungary; Jewish assimilation fitted into this political program which was maintained until the disintegration of the Habsburg monarchy.

In the Austrian half of the Dual Monarchy, things developed differently. The increase of anti-Semitism, both of the Christian and the ethnic variety—to be precise, one ought to use the untranslatable word *völkisch* variety—set in later than in Hungary, but it proved more permanent. When the recipient societies, Hanák has written, arrived at the point of refusal of assimilation, the assimilated part of Jewry had a number of options. Some,

40. Michael John, "We Do Not Even Possess Our Selves." On Identity and Ethnicity in Austria, 1880–1937. In *Austrian History Yearbook* XXX (1999), pp. 17–64, here p. 32.

41. For the following cf. Peter Hanák, Problems of Jewish Assimilation in Austria-Hungary in the Nineteenth and Twentieth Centuries. In *Power of the Past: Essays for Eric Hobsbawm*. Edited by Pat Thane, Geoffrey Crossick, and Roderick Floud. Cambridge: Cambridge University Press, and Paris: Editions de la Maison de l'homme 1984, pp. 235–49.

particularly numerous in the free professions, transferred the older liberal assimilationist attitudes to a commitment to Social Democracy. Victor Adler obviously is the shining example for this shift. Robert Wistrich has analyzed this process masterfully and in great length in his work on Socialism and the Jews, but he has also pointed out that the commitment to the goal of the classless society was the secularization of the faith of the fathers and grandfathers.[42]

Those strata of the Jewish populations whose embourgeoisement had been most advanced—apart from those who had left the Jewish community—shrank away from de-assimilation. Yet a strengthening or re-assertion of Jewish interests definitely took place from the 1880s onwards, symbolized in the creation of the Österreichisch-Israelitische Union in 1886. The stronger assertion of Jewish identity and the fight against anti-Semitism was represented by Joseph Samuel Bloch and his Österreichische Wochenschrift.[43] Soon, some intellectuals and politicians raised in the atmosphere of acculturation and assimilation were to reassert the identity of the Jews as a people in a new and infinitely stronger way, with the rise of Zionism—stronger in the cisleithanian than in the transleithanian part of the Habsburg monarchy—and also, around 1905 and the years following, with the movement of Jewish diaspora nationalism in the Bukovina and Eastern Galicia.[44]

The attitude of those upper echelons of Jewish society who stuck to German acculturation and Austrian dynastic and state patriotism is shown in an exemplary way by Theodor Gomperz, Professor of classical philology at the University of Vienna, Member of the Chamber of Pairs ("Herrenhaus"), etc. etc. When in 1909 the champions of *galut* nationalism in Czernowitz tried to get the Jews of the Bukovina recognized as an ethnic group, to be represented as such in elections and in the Diet, Gomperz wrote an article entitled "The electoral Ghetto." He warned of possible dire effects of de-assimilation. Interestingly enough, he was not even aware of the difference between *galut* nationalism and Zionism. Also, he does not seem to have been aware that lower strata of the Jewish population in Galicia or the Bukovina were perhaps only in the beginning stages of Polish or

42. Robert S. Wistrich, *Socialism and the Jews: The Dilemmas of Assimilation in Germany and Austria-Hungary*. Rutherford, London: Fairleigh Dickinson University Press, Associated University Presses 1982 (The Littman Library of Jewish Civilization), pp. 333–34.

43. For the story of increasing Jewish self-assertion, see Wistrich, *The Jews of Vienna* (note 5), chap. IX–XIV.

44. On diaspora nationalism see chapter eight in this volume.

German acculturation or not even in the beginnings. Gomperz warned of giving the "Zionists"—but actually it was the *galut* nationalists— the privilege of a Jewish "nationality" in the Bukovina with special electoral lists, constituencies, deputies and group representation; such a *privilegium favorabile*, a positive privilege, might turn into a *privilegium odiosum*, an odious special legislation, "Sondergesetzgebung"—Gomperz actually used the word that would assume such horrible connotations a few decades later! Gomperz warned that one might end where the Jews had been, before the powerful voices of Lord Macaulay and Joseph von Eötvös had been raised in favor of the legal equality of all citizens—"die Rechtsgleichheit sämtlicher Staatsbürger."[45] So here we hear the authentic voice of assimilated Jewish liberalism, 42 years after the Staatsgrundgesetz of 1867.—There were also more progressive voices among the acculturated Vienna Jews (apart from the Social Democrats) like the distinguished jurist Julius Ofner, often a helper to the poor and downtrodden.[46]

If we ask for the heritage of liberalism, the most precious one for the Austrian Jews was no doubt the rule of law and the guarantee of equal rights. From the 1880s onwards, the legal aid bureau of the Österreichisch-Israelitische Union tried to mobilize the rule of law against discriminating practices, because, as Marsha Rozenblit has rightly described a paradoxical situation, "in the late 19th century all anti-Semites operated within the context of a society ruled by law."[47] This holds also true for the first decades of the 20th century until 1938, though the tightening of anti-Semitic pressures was on the increase, even in the first Austrian Republic, as shown in the racist overtones of the judicature of the Austrian Supreme Administrative Tribunal (Verwaltungsgerichtshof) in cases dealing with petitions of Jews from Galicia, former citizens of the Austrian Empire, in favor of the citizenship of the Austrian Republic,[48] or on the occasion

45. Theodor Gomperz, Das Wahl-Ghetto. In *Neue Freie Presse,* 26 September 1909, reprinted in Theodor Gomperz. *Ein Gelehrtenleben im Bürgertum der Franz-Josefs Zeit. Auswahl seiner Briefe und Aufzeichnungen, 1869–1912. Erläutert und zu einer Darstellung seines Lebens verknüpft von Heinrich Gomperz.* Edited by Robert A. Kann. Vienna: Verlag der Österreichischen Akademie der Wissenschaften 1974 (Österreichische Akademie der Wissenschaften, Philosophisch-Historische Klasse, Sitzungsberichte; 295), pp. 445–48.

46. Emil Lehmann, Julius Ofner. *Ein Kämpfer für Recht und Gerechtigkeit.* Doctoral Dissertation. University of Vienna, 1932.

47. Marsha Rozenblit, The Jews of the Dual Monarchy [Review article]. In *Austrian History Yearbook* XXIII (1992), pp. 160–80, here p. 176.

48. For this, see Ch. 6 of this volume, "Ethnic Attribution in Late Imperial Austria: Good Intentions, Evil Consequences."

of the introduction of a racist student government at the University of
Vienna in 1930, fortunately declared unconstitutional by the Constitutional Court one year later.[49]

Even during the authoritarian Schuschnigg-regime, the principle of the
equal rights of all citizens was invoked by a newspaper close to Chancellor Schuschnigg (and presumably on orders by Schuschnigg), criticising an
antisemitic initiative by the Vice-Mayor of Vienna Kresse under the Slogan "Christians, purchase only in Christian stores," as has been shown
in an informative paper on Catholic Antisemitism during the Dollfuß-
Schuschnigg dictatorship.[50]

On January 14, 1938 there appeared in the pro-Zionist weekly Der
Jude—Organ für das arbeitende Palästina, published in Vienna, two interesting articles.

An article by the well known statistician Dr. Leo Goldhammer on
the professional structure of the Viennese Jews showed on the one hand
the very small percentage of Jewish public employees (in the Service of the
federal government, the Länder and the municipalities, including teachers); there were about 682 Jewish public employees among a total of about
160,700. On the other hand, the continuing importance of Jews in the free
professions was apparent: In Vienna there were at the end of the year 1936
1,341 Jewish lawyers (62%) and 1,542 medical doctors (47.18%), the latter
not including the dentists (in Austria Zahnärzte with a full M. D.), namely
446 (62.72%). For the very rich information supplied on other professions I
must refer the reader to Goldhammer's excellent article.[51]

In the same issue, the editorial invoked once more the hallowed principle of Gleichberechtigung against an anti-Semitic threat by the governor
of Lower Austria, Josef Reither. The Austrian constitution of 1934, the editorialist wrote, contained the guarantee that the Jewry of Austria would
be saved from those persecutions and discriminations that had become
the fate of the German and the Rumanian Jews. The present Austrian
constitution had taken over the principles of the Constitution of the
Monarchy of 1867, inspired by a liberal-democratic spirit; in the present

49. Brigitte Fenz, Zur Ideologie der "Volksbürgerschaft." Die Studentenordnung der Universität Wien vom 8. April 1930 vor dem Verfassungsgerichtshof. In Zeitgeschichte 5 (1977/78),
pp. 125–45.

50. Helmut Wohnout, Die Janusköpfigkeit des autoritären Österreich. Katholischer Antisemitismus in den Jahren vor 1938. In Geschichte und Gegenwart 13 (1994), pp. 3–16, see esp.
pp. 5–6 and 15.

51. Leo Goldhammer, Über die Berufsgliederung der Wiener Juden. In Der Jude. Organ für
das arbeitende Palästina 5 (1938), No. 2, 14 January, 1938, pp. 2–3.

constitution, so the editorial, the principle of the equal rights of all citizens was entrenched.[52] Though surely the editorialist of *Der Jude* presented an overly generous interpretation of the constitution, obviously entreating the powers of the day to abide by the principles they had proclaimed, it was true that the magic *Gleichberechtigung* of all citizens was spelled out in the constitution.

These two articles were published, as already observed, on January 14, 1938. Two months later, everything had changed. No more Gleichberechtigung, not even on paper. The last vestiges of liberalism and its heritage had vanished overnight. Instead, utter meanness and venom, greed for the Jewish neighbors' properties, sheer sadism, reigned supreme. Carl Zuckmayer has given in his autobiography the most authentic and horrifying account of what happened:

> What was let loose here was the tumult of envy, of jealousy [. . .] of blind and malicious vindictiveness. It was a witches' Sabbath of the rabble and a funeral of all human dignity.[53]

Zuckmayer expresses his own reaction of anger, abhorrence, desperation and contempt. Among the dreadful scenes by now often described, Herbert Rosenkranz has on reliable testimony reported the words of the Chief Rabbi of Vienna Dr. Israel Taglicht, brushing the streets and trying to impart courage to his fellow victims: "I am cleaning God's earth. If it pleases God, then it pleases me."[54]

In view of what happened then, and worse things to come, may I say this: I stand in shame, inerasable. I stand in awe, reflecting on Dr. Taglicht's words. And I stand committed to pass on to younger men and women my conviction: This must not be allowed to happen ever, ever again.

---

52. Unsigned editorial, *Eine neue Phase des Wirtschaftsantisemitismus*, ibid., p. 1.

53. Carl Zuckmayer, *Als wär's ein Stück von mir. Horen der Freundschaft.* Frankfurt/ Main: S. Fischer 1966, p. 61 (my translation).

54. Herbert Rosenkranz, *Verfolgung und Selbstbehauptung. Die Juden in Österreich 1938–1945.* Vienna/Munich: Herold 1978, p. 23.

CHAPTER TEN

An Apogee of Conversions:
Gustav Mahler, Karl Kraus,
and *fin de siècle* Vienna[*]

Around the very end of 1892 or beginning of 1893, Theodore Herzl wrote to Moriz Benedikt, editor of *Die Neue Freie Presse*, that he would have no objection to convert pro forma—*formaliter*—to Christianity. Herzl added that he approved the baptism of every single Jew who had children. He had a son, Herzl continued. Because of his son, he would be willing to be baptized today rather than tomorrow, so that his son's time to become a recognised Christian ("his probation period," "seine Ersitzungszeit") would start as soon as possible.[1] His son would not experience the hurt and the humiliation which he himself had experiencd by reason of his being a Jew.

Sometime in the second half of 1893, Herzl developed much more elaborate plans, which are of course well-known.[2] With the help of the Austrian Catholic hierarchy, he would visit the Pope, requesting his help in the fight against antisemitism, and initiating in turn a movement aiming at "a free and honest conversion" of Austria's Jews to Christendom. The leaders of this movement, above all Herzl himself, would remain within the Jewish religion, propagating the conversion of their co-religionists to the religion of the majority—Catholicism. On Sundays at twelve o'clock should the conversion take place—in Vienna's St. Stephen's cathedral.

---

[*] First published in *Simon Dubnow Institute Yearbook*, vol. III (2004), 49–70. The permission to reprint was gracefully granted by Vandenhoeck & Ruprecht, Göttingen.

1. Alex Bein et al. (eds.), Theodor Herzl, *Briefe und Tagebücher*, vol. 1, Berlin 1983, 507–508 (letter undated, written in Paris after 27 December 1892). Literally: ". . . damit seine Ersitzungszeit im Christenthum möglichst früh zu laufen beginne." Figuratively spoken the time needed to be recognised (and respected) as a "full" Christian. This was, of course, no formal, but a psychological requirement—the longer the time of conversion lay in the past, the better.

2. Alex Bein, *Theodore Herzl: A Biography*, New York 1970, 94–95.

Herzl put great weight on his idea that conversions should take place in the full light of the day—not furtively, as individuals had hitherto done it, but "with a proud gesture"—"mit stolzen Gebärden." The leaders, remaining Jewish, would accompany their people only to the threshold of the church; this should enhance the "great sincerety" of this act. The leaders would remain the "borderline generation"; they would retain the faith of their fathers. Yet our sons, Herzl said, we would make Christians before they would reach the age of independent decision-making, when conversions would look like cowardice or careerism ("Feigheit oder Streberei"). Herzl somewhat incongruously shifted between two images—on the one hand, the leaders and their people, and on the other hand, fathers and their not yet grown up sons. He did not speak of daughters. Moriz Benedikt, to whom he conveyed these ideas, discouraged him. For a hundred generations had the Jewish people retained its jewishness. You cannot and must not change this, he told Herzl. Besides, the Pope would not receive him.[3]

Robert Wistrich has justly said of Herzl's idea of a dramatic mass conversion in St. Stephen's cathedral that it reveals that "his own assimilationism was much more than skin deep."[4] All the more dramatic was the breakthrough to the idea of Zionism about two years later.

Yet as we all know, Zionism—or, for that matter diaspora or *galut* nationalism—remained a minority position among the Jews of Vienna. Zionist groups would gain the majority in Vienna's "Kultusgemeinde" only in 1932. On the other hand, conversion to Christianity, be it Catholic or protestant, remained a minority position as well. Cultural assimilation to German literary culture plus loyalty to the Habsburg monarchy plus continuing membership in the "Kultusgemeinde" remained the mainstream position.[5] It also has to be said that leaving the Kultusgemeinde did not automatically imply conversion to a Christian denomination, since the status of "konfessionslos" (without denomination or religious affiliation) was possible. In Vienna around the turn of the 19th to the 20th century and in the early 20th century, approximately three fourths (or slightly more) of those leaving the "Kultusgemeinde" went on to join the Catholic or

3. Alex Bein et al. (eds.), Theodor Herzl, *Briefe und Tagebücher*, vol. 2, Berlin 1983, 46–48 ("Zionistisches Tagebuch," erstes Buch).

4. Robert S. Wistrich, *Socialism and the Jews: The Dilemmas of Assimilation in Germany and Austria-Hungary*, London 1982, 212.

5. The "Kultusgemeinde" by 1890 had obtained a new and stable legal status by virtue of the Austrian law "on the settlement of the external legal relations of the Jewish religious community" ("Gesetz über die Regelung der äußeren Rechtsverhältnisse der jüdischen Religionsgesellschaft"), of 21 March 1890. Detailed information in Ernst Mischler and Josef Ulbrich (eds.), *Österreichisches Staatswörterbuch*, vol. 2, Vienna 1906, 974–81 (article by Rudolf Herrnritt).

protestant churches,[6] about one fourth to one fifth chose to remain "konfessionslos."[7] Betweeen 1888 and 1937 (the last year before the "Anschluss") 34,455 persons left the "Kultusgemeinde." The relation of those leaving to those remaining was as follows: in 1890 1:382, in 1900 1:232, and in 1910 1:293.[8] These figures have to be seen against the background of the general proportion of the Jewish population (members of the "Kultusgemeinde") in Vienna in relation to the number of inhabitants of Vienna.

In 1890, the number of inhabitants was 1,363,578, of whom there were Jewish 118,495 persons (=8.69%).

In 1900, the number of inhabitants was 1,675,325, of whom there were Jewish 146,926 persons (=8.77%).

In 1910, the number of inhabitants was 2,020,309, of whom there were Jewish 175,318 persons (=8.63%).[9]

In 1923, the number of inhabitants was 1,865780, of whom there were Jewish 201,513 (=10.80%).[10]

The average number of persons leaving the "Kultusgemeinde" between 1890 and 1899 was 420 persons per year, from 1900 to 1913 640 persons per year, and in the war years 1914 to 1918 620 persons per year.[11]

Austrian statistical and legal terminology, incidentally, provided a term less emotionally charged than "conversion": the simple more neutral word "Übertritt." This signified changing or passing over from one religious denomination to another one. The "Übertritt" was preceded by the

6. Slightly more than one half joined the Roman Catholic church (tendency decreasing), about one quarter joined one of the two Protestant churches in Austria (Lutheran and Reformed/Zwinglian/Calvinist); a very small number joined the "Old Catholics" (Altkatholiken), a group which split away from the Roman Catholic church after the first Vatican Council of 1871. George Clare has written that the "Altkatholiken" were a group to which some Jews found it easier to convert to. George Clare, *Letzter Walzer in Wien*, Vienna 2001, 49–50. Addition 2006: As a result of current research by Anna Staudacher, Vienna, the relative proportion of persons passing from Judaism to Catholicism, Protestantism or a status of no religious affiliation may have to be revised.

7. An excellent and more detailed discussion of the "Konfessionslosen" is to be found in the University of Vienna Ph.D. dissertation of Philomena Leiter, *Assimilation, Antisemitismus und NS-Verfolgung. Austritte aus der jüdischen Gemeinde in Wien 1900–1944*, Vienna 2003, 282–88.

8. Figures taken from Leiter, *Assimilation*, 153. Detailed figures for the whole period 1884 to 1944 are also supplied ibid., 148–60, based on the "Austrittsbücher" of the "Kultusgemeinde," which are extant for this whole period.

9. The comparative figures for Berlin for the year 1910 are as follows: The number of inhabitants was 3,734,258, of whom there were Jewish 144,043 (=3.9%). Leiter, *Assimilation*, 249.

10. The figures refer to the resident ("ortsansässige") population, and are taken by Leiter, *Assimilation*, 146, from Leo Goldhammer, *Die Juden Wiens. Eine statistische Studie*, Vienna 1927, 9.

11. Leiter, *Assimilation*, 153.

"Austritt"—the "withdrawal" or exit from one religious commuity—again a term less emotionally charged than terms like "apostasy" or "renegades." A remarkable feature of the administrative procedure of "withdrawal" was that it became effective by a simple declaration (orally, or in writing) made not to the religious community to be abandoned, but to a secular authority, a state or municipal office (in Vienna the Magistrate's Dictrict Office), who in turn notified the religious community in question.

Now, as Stephen Beller has said, the number of converts was never particularly large in proportion to the whole Jewish community, "but there is the awkward fact that many of the most famous 'Jewish' figures in Vienna were either baptized at birth, or later converted." [12]

Perhaps the most famous of Vienna's *fin de siècle* converts was Gustav Mahler. Born in 1860 in Bohemia, he converted to Catholicism in Hamburg on February, 23, 1897 in the "Kleine Michaeliskirche" in the parish of Saint Ansgar. The function of god-father was assumed by Theodor Meynberg, of whom Mahler's most meticulous biographer Henry Louis de La Grange says that one knows virtually nothing about this individual except that he was a member of the "Sankt-Rafaels-Verein" in Hamburg.[13] This association had been established in 1871 as a Catholic organisation to protect and help persons emigrating from Germany overseas; it was to play a notable role after 1933 in helping Catholic "Non-Aryans" to leave Nazi Germany, until it was dissolved by the Gestapo in 1941.[14]

Mahler's conversion to Catholicism in February 1897 was closely connected with his energetically pursued efforts—or better his strategically planned campaign [15]—to obtain the direction of the Vienna Imperial Opera, the "Hofoper." There was general agreement that passage to Christianity was one of the unspoken, or rather unwritten, prerequisites of Mahler's appointment. Mahler actually had asserted his passage from Judaism to Christianity some time before it took place. In a letter of December 21, 1896, to a Hungarian friend and well-wisher, Ödön von Mihalovich, requesting the latter's intervention on his behalf in Vienna, Mahler told

12. Steven Beller, *Vienna and the Jews 1867–1938. A Cultural History*, Cambridge, England 1989, 11.

13. Henry Louis de La Grange, *Mahler*, vol. I, Garden City, NY 1973, 411 and 905, note 59.

14. The exact date of its foundation is 13 September 1871 (during the German "Katholikentag" in Mainz), the interdiction by the Gestapo took place on 25 June 1941. Cf. Jana Leichsenring, *Gabriele Gräfin Magnis. Sonderbeauftragte Kardinal Bertrams für die Betreuung der katholischen "Nichtarier" Oberschlesiens: Auftrag—Grenzüberschreitung—Widerstand?* (Arbeiten zur schlesischen Kirchengeschichte 9), Stuttgart 2000, 28, 65. In this monograph there are more details about the activities of the Sankt Rafaels-Verein during the Nazi period.

15. Cf. Jonathan Carr, *The Real Mahler*, London 1997, 81–87.

him "in case he should not already know it" that he had carried out his "Übertritt zum Katholizismus"—his "passage to catholicism"—soon after his departure from Pest (where he had been director of the Royal Opera from 1888 to 1891).[16] This did not correspond to truth—yet it illustrates the significance of the striving for an "Ersitzungszeit," of which Herzl had spoken to Moriz Benedikt.[17] In another letter, dated December 23, 1896, presumably directed to one of Mahler's well-wishers and promoters within the Opera administration, Hofrat Eduard Wlassack, Mahler also wrote that "according to an old plan, I have some time ago turned to Catholicism."[18] His biographer La Grange suggested that some people in Vienna close to the opera administration or even part of it may have advised Mahler to tell the untruth since some documents in the opera administration did refer to Mahler as Christian—the word even having been underlined—, surely an indication that those pushing Mahler's appointment were aware that the "Christianity factor" was all-important.[19] Mahler's ascension to the "Hofoper" ensued in three steps, quickly following one upon another. On 8 April 1897, his conductorship at the Hofoper was announced. On 13 July Mahler was given the temporary directorship, in view of the absence of the ailing director Wilhelm Jahn, and on 8 October Mahler was appointed "artistic director" of the Opera.

So far, so good—or perhaps not so good. The biographer La Grange has noted that Mahler in later times never referred to his conversion.[20] The career factor in a passage from Judaism to Christianity, in that case to Catholicism, has rarely been revealed as directly or even as blatantly as in the case of Mahler's appointment to the Vienna Opera. And yet this is only one dimension of the story. There is another one as well.

Mahler once told the journalist Ludwig Karpath:

"What particularly offends and angers me is the circumstance that I had to have myself baptized to get an engagement, that's what I cannot get over . . . I do not deny that it cost me a great deal of effort to take

16. Quoted in Herta and Kurt Blaukopf (eds.), *Gustav Mahler. Leben und Werk in Zeugnissen seiner Zeit*, Stuttgart 1994, 118.

17. See supra note 1.

18. ". . . daß ich vor geraumer Zeit einem alten Vorhaben gemäß zum Katholizismus über getreten bin." Quoted by Kurt Blaukopf, *Gustav Mahler oder der Zeitgenosse der Zukunft*, Kassel 1989, 137.

19. La Grange, *Mahler* I, 411 and 905, note 60.

20. Ibid.

an action for what one may justifiably call self-preservation and which one inwardly was not at all disinclined to take."[21]

Mahler had not been born into a traditional or conservative Jewish home. His father Bernhard, striving toward German assimilation, moving from a Czech rural community to a German-speaking bigger town (from Kalischt to Jihlava/Iglau), had no objections to contacts with the non-Jewish world. This should be seen against the backdrop of the apparently good relationship between the non-Jewish and Jewish communities in Iglau, including excellent relationships between the parish priest of the parish of St. James, where the young Mahler sang in the church choir, and the Rabbi of Iglau, J. Unger. Between the ages of 10 and 14, Gustav Mahler was exposed to or even participated in the performance of some important works of Christian music in addition to singing in the church choir at mass, including Beethoven's "Christ on the Mount of Olives," Rossinis's "Stabat Mater" and Haydn's "The Seven Last Words on the Cross," as well as Mozart's Requiem.[22] Thus there were no "Berührungsängste"—no being scared of getting in touch with Catholic surroundings.

The details of the life of young Mahler during his first Vienna years cannot be presented here. One close friend (and benefactor) was Victor Adler, eight years his senior, the assimilated medical doctor, baptized (in 1885) a protestant, subsequently the towering figure of Austrian Social Democracy. Yet there is the impact on Mahler of one person who merits closer attention, Siegfried Lipiner, like Adler and Mahler a member of the "Pernerstorfer circle," a group of friends strongly attracted to Wagner and Nietzsche.[23] Four years Mahler's senior, Lipiner[24] was one of Mahler's

21. Quoted in English translation in Carr, *The Real Mahler*, 84, from Ludwig Karpath, *Begegnung mit dem Genius*, second edition, Vienna 1934, 102. The last sentence deserves to be quoted fully in the original German: "Ich leugne nicht, daß es mich große Überwindung kostete, man darf ruhig sagen aus Selbsterhaltungstrieb eine Handlung zu begehen, d e r m a n j a i n n e r l i c h g a r n i c h t a b g e n e i g t w a r" [emphasis in the original]. No date of this conversation is given.

22. La Grange, *Mahler* I, 15 and 840, note 9.

23. The intellectual and artistic history of this group, with emphasis on Lipiner and Mahler, is to be found in William J. McGrath, *Dionysian Art and Popular Politics in Austria*, New Haven 1974.

24. For Lipiner, his friendship with and impact on Mahler cf. Constantin Floros, *Gustav Mahler I: Die geistige Welt Gustav Mahlers in systematischer Darstellung*, Wiesbaden 1977, 72–83, and McGrath, *Dionysian Art*, notably 100–119. La Grange, Mahler I, 68–70, has a disparaging judgment of Lipiner, including the erroneous statement that after his first work, Lipiner did not publish anything anymore.

closest friends for decades. He also assisted at the time of the fight for
Mahler's Vienna Opera appointment. Their friendship was interrupted
through Mahler's marriage to Alma, née Schindler, in 1902. Alma objected
to Lipiner, since Lipiner had been outspokenly sceptical about Mahler's
engagement to Alma. As late as 1909 a reconciliation between Mahler and
Lipiner took place, helped along, it seems, by Bruno Walter, to Mahler's
very great relief.[25] Lipiner, born in 1856 in Jaroslav in Galicia, went to
school first in Tarnow and from 1871 to 1875 to the Leopoldstädter Gymnasium in Vienna where we has an oustanding student. He went on to
study philosophy, literature and other fields at the University of Vienna
and for one semester (1876) in Leipzig. In 1881 Lipiner was appointed Librarian in the Library of Parliament, the Reichsrat, a position which he
held until his death in 1911, the year of Mahler's death as well. In 1885 he
withdrew from the Kultusgemeinde, only to reenter it in 1890 (possibly
in connection with a divorce) and to leave it again in 1892, when he converted to Protestantism.[26]

Lipiner was a young, perhaps premature, poet. While still in the last
years of the Gymnasium, he wrote part of his epos "Prometheus Unchained"—"Der entfesselte Prometheus," published in 1876 in Leipzig—
when its author was 20 years old. "Prometheus Unchained" was sent to
Nietzsche through the intermediary of Erwin Rohde, Professor of Classical Philosophy in Jena and a friend of Nietzsche's. Nietzsche commented
on Lipiner's epos in the most enthusiastic terms; Richard Wagner also
made flattering comments.

Now the important point about Lipiner is that in a time of "Freidenker-
tum" ("free thinking" in the sense of anti-religious and particularly anti-
Church discourse) as well as of Nietzschean anti-Christianism, he spoke out
in search of religious renewal,[27] though outside any dogmatic or orthodox
bounds. In his "Prometheus Unchained," the Promethean topos of mens'
liberation is connected with the Christian topos of redemption through
suffering and love, the great reconciliation of Promethean and Christian
promises ending in the invocation of eternal joy. Lipiner's eclectic religi-

---

25. Floros, *Gustav Mahler* I, 81.

26. I owe these detailed informations to the kindness of Frau Dozentin Dr. Anna Staudacher, whose book *Judisch-protestantische Konvertiten in Wien 1782–1914* (Frankfurt/Main
2004) I was allowed to consult prior to publication; see ibid., vol. II, 438. I am also grateful to
Dr. Staudacher for additional verbal information.

27. In 1878 Lipiner held and published a lecture "Über die Elemente der Erneuerung re-
ligiöser Ideen in der Gegenwart" (on the elements of a renewal of religious ideas in the present
times).

osity had a strong pantheistic—more precisely perhaps panentheistic—bent.[28] In Leipzig Lipiner had met the philosopher Gustav Theodor Fechner, a "Naturphilosoph," several of whose books were favorite readings of Gustav Mahler, whose interest in Fechner was probably awakened by Lipiner.[29] In a volume of Lipiner's poetry, "Buch der Freude" (book of joy) of 1880, Mahler scholars have found some poems very close to the program of Mahler's third symphony.[30] Also, the first movement of the second, the "Resurrection"-Symphony, originally entitled "Todtenfeier" (the memorial to the dead on All Souls Day) was suggested to Mahler by Lipiner's translation from Polish of the drama "Todtenfeier" ("Dziady") by the great polish writer Adam Mickiewicz.[31] In the decade of the nineties, Lipiner planned a cycle of four dramatic plays with biblical themes: Adam—as prologue, the only play completed, and then a trilogy "Christ," consisting of the plays "Mary Magdalen," "Judas Ischarioth," and "Paul in Rome." There is information about a meeting of Mahler with Lipiner in the summer of 1896 in Berchtesgaden, where Lipiner explained to Mahler his work in a long conversation, during a torrential rainfall.[32] The fact that Lipiner also wrote a poetic "Nachdichtung" of Saint Paul's praise of love suggests that the theme of the Jew turned Christian may have played a greater role in Lipiner's thought than has been seen so far.[33] I shall presently refer to the problem of the Jew turned Christian, as far as Mahler was concerned.

Two occurrences in Mahler's life a few years prior to his passage to Christianity seem worth recording. In 1894 in Hamburg, Mahler was moved to the innermost depths of his being by the words "Auferstehen wirst Du" ("You will be resurrected") from Klopstock's "Messias," sung on the occasion of the funeral rites for the conductor Hans von Bülow. This experience inspired him to write the last movement of his second symphony, the "Resurrection Symphony." Mahler has recorded in writing—a rare occasion!—the creative process that led from the hearing of the

28. Floros, *Gustav Mahler I*, 120.

29. Ibid., 112.

30. Ibid., 82–83.

31. Ibid., 82. Lipiner's translation was published in Leipzig in 1887. The first movement of Mahler's second symphony, originally entitled "Todtenfeier," was completed in September 1888.

32. La Grange, *Mahler* I, 378. The source is a report by Nathalie Bauer-Lechner, who had accompanied Mahler to visit Siegfried and Clementine Lipiner in Berchtesgaden on August 1, 1896. See Herbert Kilian, *Gustav Mahler in den Erinnerungen von Natalie Bauer-Lechner*, revised edition Hamburg 1984, 68.

33. Under the title "Paulus' Liebesgesang"; published in Natalie Bauer-Lechner (who was a great admirer of Lipiner as well as of Mahler), *Fragmente. Gelerntes und Gelebtes*, Vienna 1907, 31–32.

chorale to the first drafts of the Finale of the symphony.[34] From the following year 1895 we have the testimony of Bruno Walter of how deeply Mahler loved Dostoyevsky's "Brothers Karamasov."[35]

To the extent to which Mahler displayed a somewhat eclectic religiosity not quite unlike that of Lipiner, uniting pantheistic or panentheistic ideas with Christian themes of redemption through suffering and love, Mahler can indeed be said, as he said of himself, to have been "inwardly not at all disinclined" to take the action he took in 1897 by his conversion to Catholicism. Alma Mahler on various occasions has said that her husband, the "Juden-Christ" as she called him, was a believer in Christ ("christgläubig").[36] Alma Mahler has described the paradoxocal situation that she herself, though educated in the Catholic faith, under the influence of Nietzsche and Schopenhauer had become more and more a free thinker, "while a Jew zealously took the party of Christ" ("daß ein Jude einer Christin gegenüber sich heftig für Christus ereiferte").[37] Perhaps one should also consult the reminiscences of Ludwig Karpath who thought that Mahler felt Christian, "particularly Catholic," as long as no one reproached him his "Jewishness," yet he felt Jewish when the antisemites pestered him.[38]

Mahler's religiosity remained undogmatic. I say "religiosity" rather than "religion" on purpose, because I think that to Mahler applied a distinction which Martin Buber has once suggested: Religiosity is the creative, religion the organising principle—". . . religiosity implies activity—finding an elemental relationship of the self to the absolute, religion implies passivity—acceptance of the burden of the transmitted law."[39]

The decisive question was put to Mahler by Alfred Roller, the famous scene-painter closely associated with Mahler in the Vienna Opera, and it

34. La Grange, Mahler I, 294–95.

35. Bruno Walter, Thema und Variationen, Frankfurt 1960, 115. Many years later, in 1909, Mahler was to advise Arnold Schönberg: "You should read Dostojewskij, this is more important than counterpoint:" "But we have Strindberg"; replied Anton von Webern, who was also present. H. H. Stuckenschmidt, Schönberg: Leben—Umwelt—Werk, Zürich 1974, 213.

36. Alma Mahler, Gustav Mahler, Erinnerungen und Briefe, 2nd edition, Amsterdam 1949, 129.

37. Ibid., 30–31. This comment is, to say the least, not very tactful, having in mind that Mahler, when he met and subsequently married Alma Schindler, had left the Jewish community and had converted to Christianity. It raises a problem to which I shall come back in the conclusion.

38. Karpath, Begegnung mit dem Genius, 102 (. . . "hatten ihm aber die Antisemiten arg zugesetzt, so meldete sich doch sein Rassegefühl").

39. Martin Buber, Vom Geist des Judentums, Munich 1916, 51–52, quoted in translation by Alexander L. Ringer, Arnold Schoenberg—The Composer as Jew, Oxford 1990, 2.

called forth a revealing reply. Why did Mahler not write a mass, Roller asked him? Mahler seemed to be taken aback. "Do you think that I could do this? Well, why not? Oh, rather not. There is the 'credo' in the text" ("Da kommt das Credo vor"). Mahler began to recite the credo in Latin, yet added: "No, I cannot do this." Some time later, on the occasion of a rehearsal of Mahler's Eight Symphony in Munich—the "Symphony of the Thousand," uniting two great texts, the hymn "Veni creator spiritus" and the last scenes of Goethe's Faust, Second Part (Faust's redemption)—, Mahler told Roller: "You see, this is my mass." [40] And this indeed is the last word to be said on that issue.

Turning now to Karl Kraus, we encounter a very different story, and in-spite of the glaring clarity of Kraus' language, partly shrouded in mystery. Kraus, born in 1874, was 14 years younger than Mahler. He was born into a considerably more affluent familiy than Mahler; the passage from Bo-hemia (from the Czech town of Jičin) to Vienna took place early in Kraus' childhood. The assimilationist path was not a difficult one for Kraus to take. Kraus' development is not specially characterized by assimilation-ism as such, but rather by its radicalism. At the age of 25, in April 1899 Kraus not only founded *Die Fackel (The Torch)*, but on 12 October of that year he also left the "Kultusgemeinde." Incidentally, Arnold Schönberg, like Kraus born in 1874, had taken this step a year and a half earlier (in March 1898) and had entered the protestant (Lutheran) church almost im-mediately.[41] He would return to the Jewish community 35 years later, in 1933, in Paris, but this is not part of my story.[42] Kraus, however, would re-main "konfessionslos" for almost twelve years, before receiving Catholic baptism on 8 April 1911.[43]

Around the time of his withdrawing from the Kultusgemeinde, Kraus

40. Reported in Floros, *Gustav Mahler I*, 123–24.

41. Stuckenschmidt, *Schönberg*, 33, indicates March 21, 1989 as the date of his "Austritt." This date has now been corrected to March 3, 1898 by Staudacher, *Jüdisch-protestantische Konvertiten*, 639. The date of Protestant baptism was March 25, 1898.

42. On Schönberg's reentry into the Jewish community in Paris on July 24, 1933, see the facsimile of the pertinent declaration in Ringer, *Arnold Schoenberg*, 135. This interesting book is marred by some serious misstatements of fact. Ringer states that the Austrian govern-ment organized "a most humiliating event," the so-called "Judenzählung": "On 11 October 1916 the Austrian government ordered a precise count of all Jews in the armed forces . . ." (ibid., 123). Actually, this took place in Germany, not in Austria! See Werner T. Angress, The German Army's "Judenzählung" of 1916—Genesis—Consequences—Significance, in *Year-book of the Leo Baeck Institute*, vol. XXIII, 1978, 131.

43. Ringer, *Arnold Schoenberg*, 16–17, mistakenly states that Kraus at the turn of the cen-tury had turned Protestant.

extolled a program of radical assimilation in *Die Fackel:* "Durch Auflösung zur Erlösung."[44]

"Through assimilation to redemption" is the rendering given to this
phrase by Edward Timms in his great work on Kraus.[45] However, "Auflösung" seems to me more radical than assimilation, it is more than "Angleichung," it truly points to a dissolving process, a dissolution.

In 1899, Kraus' program contained two important points: first, passage ("Übertritt") to Christianity. In a preceding issue of "Die Fackel"
in July 1899, Kraus published an article by an "anonymous" author, yet
presumably enjoying Kraus' approval.[46] The writer expressed considerable
sympathy for Protestantism and pointed to the element of rational, if not
rationalistic approaches to metaphysical questions both in Judaism and
the main Protestant denominations—Lutheranism, Calvinism and Angli-
canism. Religious Judaism "had fulfilled its mission of enlightenment;" it
had completed it in the sense that from now on further reforming forces
would emanate from Protestantism. The article referred to Schopenhauer
who had spoken of "Protestant-Jewish rationalism."[47]

Die Fackel thus recommended turning to Christianity. Baptism was
not a humiliating bending under a yoke, if it was the result of a free decision, not made in favor of personal relief and material well-being, but—
and these a crucial words that now follow!—"in the love of future generations."[48] One ought to secure "the peace of future generations." For this
goal, the decision for the change of religion was worth it; a surprising argument follows: "What is the difference between a religion whose com-
mands one does not keep, and a faith in which one does not believe?"[49]

44. *Die Fackel*, No 23, middle November 1899, 7 (article entitled "Auf Anfragen aus
Böhmen").

45. Edward Timms, *Karl Kraus, Apocalyptic Satirist. Culture and Catastrophe in Habsburg Vienna*, New Haven/London 1986, 237.

46. In the first published version of this paper in 2004 I had written ". . . by an 'anonymous'
author, yet with virtual certainty written by Karl Kraus himself"—on the strength of indications submitted by an expert on Kraus in the Austrian Academy of Sciences. On the strength
of arguments communicated to me by Professor Edward Timms in December 2004, after the
paper had gone to press, I now tend to support the view of Professor Timms that the article in
question was not written by Kraus, but by a so far unidentified author.

47. *Die Fackel*, No. 11, middle July 1899, 3–4 (article on the Jewish question without title, ibid. 1–6). The great number of distinguished intellectuals and artists who converted to
Protestantism is now abundantly documented in the new book by Anna Staudacher, *Jüdisch-
protestantische Konvertiten in Wien 1782–1914* (see supra note 26), vol. I, 255–86.

48. *Die Fackel*, no. 11, 4.

49. "Denn welcher Unterschied ist zwischen einer Religion, die man nicht hält, und
einem Glauben, den man nicht glaubt?" Ibid., 5.

Yet there was a second recommendation: mixed marriages. People would find themselves in a foreign and even hostile posture vis-à-vis one another, if through generations they walked side by side without any attempt to unite. The author recommended the *connubium* of men and women of Jewish and non-Jewish origin, but he held that in practice this would work only if the Jewish side would opt for "the free and mature passage" (". . . jene Wahl des freien und reifen Übertritts") from Judaism to Christianity.[50] Gustav Mahler, incidentally, had also pleaded for the "mixing" or "amalgamationg" of Christians and Jews. In the long run, this would lead to a "refinement" ("Veredelung") of humanity.[51] The very important question of mixed marriages will be examined in the conclusion.

The radicalism of Kraus' attacks on Jewish journalists, bankers, people in foreign exchange etc. is known, though Kraus' anti-Jewish polemics never attained the depth of the fundamental condemnation of Jewry in Otto Weininger's *Geschlecht und Charakter*, for example.[52] Yet I agree with Edward Timms that it was not "Jewish self-hatred," so-called, but "the desire to liberate the self from compromising affiliations,"[53] that was operative here.

In 1913 Kraus wrote what I consider perhaps his most profound comment on Judaism, in an article entitled "Er ist doch e Jud"—I translate imperfectly "And still, he is a Jew," leaving uncommented the innuendos of the colloquial German. Here I must somewhat depart from the interpretation of Edward Timms who has said that this article is Kraus' "most vehement repudiation of Jewish identity."[54] In what I believe to be the key sentence of a very long piece, every sentence of which bears close inspection, Kraus says:[55]

"I believe I can say about myself, that I go along with the development of Jewry as far as Exodus, but I quit at the point where the dance around the golden calf begins, and that from that point on I have a share in those

50. Ibid.

51. Karpath, *Begegnung mit dem Genius*, 101–102. The conversation on this theme took place during a walk in the "Hauptallee" of the Vienna "Prater," but no date is given.

52. In 1905 Weininger converted to Protestantism. See Jacques Le Rider, *Der Fall Otto Weininger. Wurzeln des Antifeminismus und Antisemitismus*, Vienna/Munich 1985, 33f.

53. Timms, *Karl Kraus*, 237.

54. Ibid., 239.

55. For what follows: Karl Kraus, "Und er ist doch e Jud," in *Die Fackel*, No. 386 (October 1913), reprinted in his book *Untergang der Welt durch schwarze Magie*, (Karl Kraus, *Werke*, vol. 8, H. Fischer ed.), Munich 1960, 331 ff. (here quoted from this edition). All translations are mine.

qualities only, which also were part of the defenders of God and avengers of a people gone astray"[56] (my translation).

Here I see an identification of Kraus with the Jewish prophets. I would say that Kraus has put himself into the line of succession of the prophets. Kraus rejects what he thinks are qualities widespread among contemporary Jews—he hates these qualities which he would seek in vain in that stage of Jewish history in which Jewry ("die Judenheit") had not yet emancipated itself from God.[57] And most movingly Kraus went on: "I do no merely believe, I feel as if shaken by an experience of revelation, that I do not share all those qualities of the Jews, which according to the present state of things Jewish we consensually wish to determine [as Jewish]."[58] Kraus goes one step further: he expressly says that negative qualities considered as Jewish qualities, like greed for power and money are equally distributed among all peoples of the western world ("des Abendlandes") according to the resolve of infernal justice ("nach dem Ratschluß teuflischer Gerechtigkeit") This is prophetic language suddenly emerging out of the polemics of the satirist.

In the same piece, Kraus violently attacked the posture of those renegades, i.e., baptized Jews, whose motive force was the striving for immediate social prestige—and not something more arcane and mysterious: whose motive force was not "that secret altruism, which has an impact on (future) times and facilitates the life of future generations."[59]

Before attempting to explain these somewhat mysterious words on "secret altruism," it is necessary, however, to sketch more broadly the context of the debate on conversion, baptized Jews and their motives anno

---

56. Ibid., 333. "Ich glaube von mir sagen zu dürfen, daß ich mit der Entwicklung des Judentums bis zum Exodus noch mitgehe, aber den Tanz um das Goldene Kalb nicht mehr mitmache, und von da an nur jener Eigenschaften mich teilhaftig weiß, die auch den Verteidigern Gottes und Rächern an einem verirrten Volk angehaftet haben." In a more recent paper, Professor Timms has somewhat modified the interpretation of this article in his book of 1986 and now also points to the significance of this passage. Edward Timms, "True Believers." The Religious Vision of a Jewish Renegade, in Gilbert J. Carr/Edward Timms (eds.), *Karl Kraus und Die Fackel. Aufsätze zur Rezeptionsgeschichte/Reading Karl Kraus. Essays on the Reception of Die Fackel*, Munich 2001, 74–87, here 77. I am grateful to Professor Timms for having brought this paper to my attention.

57. "Und so ist es mir auch wohl möglich, Eigenschaften zu hassen, die ich auf jenem Stand der Judenheit, wo sie sich noch nicht von Gott selbständig gemacht hatte, vergebens suchen würde." Ibid., 332.

58. ". . . daß ich nicht nur glaube, sondern wie aus der Erschütterung eines Offenbarungserlebnisses spüre, daß mir nichts von allen den Eigenschaften der Juden anhaftet, die wir nach dem heutigen Stand der jüdischen Dinge einvernehmlich feststellen wollten:" Ibid., 332–33.

59. Ibid., 333. ". . . ein Renegatentum, dessen Beweggrund nicht jener heimliche Altruismus ist, der in die Zeiten wirkt und kommenden Geschlechtern das Leben erleichtert . . ."

1913. Three points need to be made, two of a more general nature, the third one concerning Kraus' personal stance and opening a way to understand his opaque reference on the secret altruism of (some) conversions.

First: The movement away from the Jewish Kultusgemeinde either to the Christian denominations or to the status of "no religious preference" was not endangering the Jewish community in terms of numbers, but to some extent the loss of members of upper social strata was a painful experience. Striving for social prestige in Imperial Austria was by no means chiefy connected with the goal of economic affluence, rather with the attainment of non-economic rankings in the bureaucracy, the universities and even the army. Franz Borkenau, a sociologist with Jewish bourgeois roots and a brief communist past, has pointed out two important aspects of the conversion movement in Austria. First, Borkenau pointed to Imperial Austria as a borderland between Western and Eastern Europe and the relevance of this position in terms of the Jewish question. Though there is some over-generalisation in the passage I am about to quote, it is worth consideration verbatim:

> "In the west no strong incentive to conversion exists, for there the Jews enjoy equality. The incentives for conversion were hardly stronger in the East. For in the east social equality would not have been granted even to the convert. [. . .] Vienna was perhaps the one place in the world where equality was granted conditionally, under the condition, namely, of conversion. [. . .] Conversion offered itself to the ruling group as a means of selection of the Jews it was ready to admit. De facto, though not in law, it was the first condition for every higher career." [60]

The story of Gustav Mahler's accession to the directorship of the Vienna Opera certainly is a case in point.

The second aspect pointed out by Borkenau is the following: the very fact that the number of prominent converted Jews was growing made it imperative to the antisemites to move from religious antisemitism to racialism. As Borkenau noted:

> "The problem for the anti-semites was: Who must be regarded as a Jew? And the answer, on account of Jewish mass conversions to Christianity, could only be: Those who by their blood belong to the Jewish

---

60. Franz Borkenau, *Austria and After*, London 1938, 114 (written and published a few months after the "Anschluss").

community even if by conversion to Christianity they had severed
their ties with the Jewish religious body."[61]

This observation was certainly true as far as first generation converts were
concerned, particularly when they were prominent and the object of envy.
Again Gustav Mahler is an eminent case in point, and once more, Herzl's
comment on the "Ersitzungszeit" comes to mind. This observation would
gradually lose its strength in so far as several generations of baptized persons would follow one another and/or in the cases of intermarriage with
non-Jewish families, a very frequent phenomenon among converted Jews
and often the motive for conversion.

Second: The departure from the Jewish community of those planning
to convert certainly produced bitter reactions. For years, well-established
Jewish periodicals like *Bloch's Wochenschrift* contained a regular heading: "The following have left Judaism," followed by the names of those
who had withdrawn from the Kultusgemeinde. If these were businessmen,
lawyers or doctors, the possibility of boycott by former clients could not
be excluded. A particularly acerbic, if not vitriolic attack was contained
in a brochure published in 1904, written by Fritz Wittels, entitled *Der
Taufjude*.[62] Wittels (1880–1950), Doctor of Medicine, first an admirer, then
a hater of Karl Kraus, and a member of the Vienna psychoanalytical association (with conflict-laden interruptions), defined "Taufjuden" as Jews
who had committed perjury by swearing that they believed something
which the Church commanded to be believed. Wittels was willing to grant
a milder judgment to certain categories among baptized Jews, though the
listing of these exceptions bristled with bitter irony. One exception, so
Wittels, was the artist. He gave an example. The conductor who needs a
whole apparatus and as Jew is not in a position to find one worthy of him.
It seems clear that Gustav Mahler was the target of his description. For
the common man, Wittels said, his worth consists in his honor. Yet for the
artist, his art is his honor. He did not need to spell out his conclusion.Wit-
tels poured his contemptuous irony on baptized Jewish scholars at the universities, on allegedly pious believers in Christianity of whom he says that
he never has seen one among baptized Jews,[63] and on various other groups.

61. Ibid., 110.

62. For the following, Fritz Wittels, *Der Taufjude*, Vienna 1904, passim.

63. The number of devout Christians among converts was far from negligible, though individual persons will not be mentioned here. Reference should be made however to the interesting cases of two very well-known writers of a somewhat younger generation, Joseph Roth
and Franz Werfel, both of whom never entered the Catholic Church, though increasingly and

The "Taufjude" in his sense is a person who will be baptized—according to Wittels thereby committing perjury—in order to gain immediate economic or social advantage. The "Taudfjude," Wittels said, "is a scoundrel." Concluding, Wittels' irony turns into wrath. Every Jew leaving the Jewish community is thus weakening the Jews' struggle for their rights. Wittels invoked the title of a then famous book by the German jurist Rudolf von Ihering, *Der Kampf ums Recht.* It was the Jews' fight for their right, or rights, which was impeded by the baptized Jews.

It is virtually certain that Karl Kraus knew Wittel's pamphlet, and that Kraus' attack on converts by dint of low motive, followed by the emphatic rejection of any imputation that his own anti-Jewish polemics might be guided by low motives, was written in knowledge of this pamphlet.

And now the third and most important point—on Kraus' own position. When Kraus wrote his piece "Er ist doch e Jud" in October 1913, he had been a baptized Catholic for one year and a half. Baptism had taken place on April 8, 1911, in the parish of the Vienna Karlskirche, the famous architect Adold Loos being the godfather. However, no one knew about Kraus' conversion, which he kept secret. We know next to nothing about the circumstances of Kraus' entering the Catholic Church, eleven and a half years after he had quit the Kultusgemeinde in 1899. There seems to have been no immediate private motive—his meeting and falling in love with Baroness Sidonie Nádhérny-Borotin took place only in September 1913. There are no indications that his close friend and godfather Adolf Loos may have had anything to do with Kraus' decision.[64] Edward Timms rightly has called Kraus' conversion perhaps "the most surprising event in his career." Timms refers to the Catholic revival prior to the First World War in several countries, to Belloc and Chesterton in England, to Claudel, Péguy and Barrès in France. Claudel's Catholicism had been commented upon in *Die Fackel.* Timms sees Kraus turning to Catholicism within this broader framework, including Kraus' more conservative tendencies in the years preceding the outbreak of the First World War. Kraus, for instance, had disapproved of the introduction of general male suffrage in 1907, and

---

greatly attracted by Catholicism. "A Catholic with Jewish Brains" was a self-characterisation of Joseph Roth. Werfel again, in spite of his immersion in Catholicism, regarded conversion as desertion of the Jewish people for several, including complicated theological reasons. See the interesting monograph by Frank Joachim Eggers, "*Ich bin ein Katholik mit jüdischem Gehirn.*" *Modernitätskritik und Religion bei Joseph Roth und Franz Werfel*, Frankfurt/Main 1996, notably 60 (on Werfel) and 240 (quote from Roth in a letter to Benno Reifenberg of 1926).

64. Loos, incidentally, was not Jewish, as has erroneously been stated by Wilma Iggers, *Karl Kraus. A Viennese Critic of the Twentieth Century.* The Hague 1967, 177.

his increasing admiration for the conservative Archduke Franz Ferdinand was visible after 1910.[65] All this might explain, incidentally, why Kraus finally did not turn to Protestantism which he may have favored in 1899. But there is a connection, so far not recognised, I think, between Kraus' arguments in favor of Christianity of 1899 and those of 1913, after his conversion to Catholicism.

Back in 1899, it has been shown before,[66] *Die Fackel* had argued in favor of farreaching assimilation, literally dissolution of Jewry through acceptance of Christianity and inter-marriage in order to avoid hostility in the future and to make life more acceptable to future generations. Now the worry about future generations of 1899 recurs in 1913, after his conversion, in the peculiar sentence about "secret altruism which has an impact on [future] times and facilitates the life of future generations." This is decidedly the reaffirmation of ideas first expressed 14 years earlier. Thus there seems to be, in Kraus' decision to convert to Christianity—even though it turned out to be Catholic rather than protestant Christianity—a fulfillment of his program of 1899: "Through Dissolution to Redemption"—"Durch Auflösung zur Erlösung." There has emerged no evidence that Kraus' conversion might have been the result of some sudden shattering experience. Nor was he provided with "a specificically Catholic faith," as he avowed retrospectively when leaving the Church again in 1922.[67] Yet "secret altruism" on behalf of future generations was a noble motive for conversion—and secret indeed did he keep it.[68]

Nonetheless, a number of more immediately plausible reasons for Kraus' secrecy have been suggested. He surely wished to avoid the likely reproach that he had converted for opportunistic reasons; he may not have wished to be compared to his literary arch-enemy Hermann Bahr, who at that time publicised his return to the Church. Considerably more

65. Timms, *Karl Kraus*, 241; also Gerald Stieg, *Der Brenner und die Fackel. Ein Beitrag zur Wirkungsgeschichte von Karl Kraus*, Salzburg 1976, 237–38.

66. See supra at notes 43–46.

67. ". . . der speziell in die katholische Richtung gewandte Glaube": See Kraus' article "Vom großen Welttheaterschwindel," in *Die Fackel*, nos. 601–607, November 1922, 3.

68. Edward Timms refers to Karl Kraus calling his conversion an act of "secret altruism," yet does not, as far as I see, suggest a connection between this "altruism" and the conversion program of 1899. Timms, *Karl Kraus*, 242. Professor Timms also refers to the "secret altruism" of Kraus' conversion in the forthcoming second volume of his great work on Kraus, "Karl Kraus, Apocalyptic Satirist—The German-Jewish Dilemma between the World Wars." I am most grateful to Professor Timms for having privileged me to see this chapter prior to publication.—Addition 2006: This work has now been published: Edward Timms, *Karl Kraus, Apocalyptic Satirist: The Post-War Crisis and the Rise of the Swastika*, New Haven/London 2005.

important, it seems to me, are Edward Timm's reflections on the structural problem of a "Christian satirist" as a "homo duplex"—the incompatibility of satire with Christian devotion.[69] Yet by renouncing satire, Kraus would have abandoned his innermost self.

One also may turn to more practical aspects and examine to which extent the status of "no religious affiliation," in which Kraus had persisted for twelve years, could be felt to be unsatisfactory. It was unsatisfactory at a time—difficult to visualise for today's younger generation—when denominational membership was noted in every conceivable document, in passports, student application forms at universities, or in school certificates. It has been argued that Victor Adler "became a convert to Protestantism so that his children should not have to suffer the consequences of non-denominational, *konfessionslos*, status at school."[70] There were also the "Meldezettel," as they were called in Austria,—documents unknown in Great Britain or the United States, yet in continental countries required by the police as proof that one's residence—permanent or temporary—had been duly registered with the police. Kraus has once been referred as a "Jude dem Meldezettel nach"—and this was meant as a compliment, though it came from a dubious person, Lanz von Liebenfels.[71]

Yet twelve years after having entered the Catholic Church, Kraus left it—precisely on 7 March 1923. If the entry had been quiet, the exit was spectacular. In a long article in *Die Fackel* in November 1922, Kraus turned his wrath on the misdoings of the Catholic Church. The experience of the First World War was uppermost in Kraus' mind, the blessing of arms and poison gas by priests and other gestures of Catholic support for the war led Kraus to speak of a Church which God seemed to have already quit—"eine Kirche, aus der Gott schon ausgetreten sein dürfte." The final straw that broke the camel's back was the permission of the archbishop of

69. Ibid., 243–46. I am perhaps a bit more reserved than Edward Timms (ibid., 247) as regards "glimpses of his devotional life"; one reference to attending the nativity midnight-mass on December 24/25 1914 seems scant evidence of devotional life; extended excerpts from the letters of Saint Paul might also suggest that Kraus may have compared his own fate to that of Paul of Tarsus—the convert prophet!

70. Michael Pollak, Cultural Innovation and Social Identity in fin-de-siècle Vienna, in Ivar Oxaal, Michael Pollak, Gerhard Botz (eds.), *Jews, Antisemitism and Culture in Vienna*, London 1987, 69.

71. In a letter of Lanz, editor of the ill-reputed teutonic "Ostara"-leaflets, to Ludwig von Ficker, editor of "Der Brenner," quoted by Sigurd P. Scheichl, Aspekte des Judentums im "Brenner" (1910–1937), in Walter Methlagl et al. (eds.), *Untersuchungen zum "Brenner." Festschrift für Ignaz Zangerle*, Salzburg 1981, 70–184, here 82.

Salzburg to have Hofmannsthal's "Das große Welttheater" performed in a
church, the Kollegienkirche.[72] Kraus vitriolically attacked Hofmannsthal,
the stage director Max Reinhardt and the main actor, Alexander Moissi,
for having virtually desecrated the church's altar.[73]

This was only the prelude to his announcement of leaving the church:

"So I declare [. . .] that I once left the Jewish community in which I had
found myself through the unfortunate accident of birth in order to let
a devil seduce me, after a period of comfortable and never sufficiently
valued non-affiliation, into the bosom of the true Church. One may
condemn me because I did this without a compelling reason, such as
specifically Catholic faith[74] or the more frequent motive of political or
social climbing might have been. Why I did this is a private matter to
an even greater extent than religion itself usually is."[75]

Perhaps this "private matter" was "secret altruism" on behalf of future
generation of Jews.

On Kraus' religiosity—not religion!—much more may be said—and
will be said in the forthcoming second volume of Edward Timms' magisterial work on Kraus. Kraus' moral rigorism or purism no doubt had a religious dimension: Kraus, as he once rhymed, did not deny God, but he denied those who denied God—and if God should will it, everything would
be wonderful.[76] Let it suffice here to cite this magnificent aphorism: "Es
ist halt ein Unglück, daß mir zu jedem Lumpen was einfällt. Aber ich
glaube, daß es sich immer auf einen abwesenden König bezieht" ("It is a
pity that to every scoundrel something occurs to me; but I believe that it is
always related to an absent king").[77]

72. Cf. Michael Steinberg, *The Meaning of the Salzburg Festival*, Ithaca, NY 1990, 72–74,
203–205.

73. *Die Fackel*, Nos. 601–607, November 1922, 2.

74. ". . . ohne einen zwingenden Grund, sei es der speziell in die katholische Richtung
gewandte Glaube . . ." Full text extensively quoted in German and in English translation in
Iggers, *Karl Kraus*, 215–16.

75. Ibid., translation taken from Iggers, *Karl Kraus*, 215–216. Actually, it took another few
months and one more reason (or pretext—the use of the cross to mark a paid advertisement),
until Kraus found the time to legalise his "Kirchenaustritt." "Was den letzten Anstoß gegeben
hat," in *Die Fackel*, Nos. 613–21, 9–11.

76. "Nicht Gott, nur alles leugn' ich was ihn leugnet, und wenn er will, ist alles wunder-
bar." "Vor dem Schlaf," quoted in the remarkable work by Caroline Kohn, *Karl Kraus*, Stuttgart 1966, 309.

77. Karl Kraus, *Schriften*, ed. by Christian Wagenknecht, vol. 8: *Aphorismen*. Frankfurt/
Main 1986, 290.

In my conclusion I would like to approach a theme fraught with difficulties—the theme of "mixed marriages."[78] As has been shown, both Mahler and Kraus were in favor of "Mischehen" or mixed marriages, of the *connubium* between persons of Jewish and non-Jewish origin. Mahler's marriage with Alma Schindler was a case in point. Yet prior to any further discussion of "mixed marriages" one point of capital importance, and often ignored or neglected by scholars, needs to be stressed.

Austrian law prohibited marriages between Christian and non-Christians. The relevant article of the Austrian Civil Code ("Allgemeines bürgerliches Gesetzbuch") of 1811 provided that marriage contracts between Christians and person without Christian confession could not validly be concluded.[79] This meant that marriages between Christians and "Konfessionslose," or and even more important, between Christians and persons belonging to the Jewish faith were not possible. In Austria, the religious authorities—priests, ministers, or Rabbis—were charged by the state with the registering of marriages and in this function, quite apart from the religious marriage rites, acted as commissioners of the state. They were held responsible by the state for the correct keeping of registry records. Only for persons not belonging to any legally recognised denomination (Konfessionslose, members of sects) was a civil marriage possible.[80] Civil marriage as an alternative for religious marriage or obligatory civil marriage in addition to a religious wedding—as it existed in Germany since 1876 and in the Hungarian part of the Habsburg Monarchy after 1894—did not exist in Austria (with the small exception just mentioned) prior to 1938.[81] As a consequence, if a Christian and a Jewish person wished to get married, some kind of change of the religious status was inevitable. Either the Jewish partner left the Jewish community and joined a Christian church; or the Christian partner left his or her church and either joined the Jewish community or remained "konfessionslos" (the latter being an alternative in so far as the marriage of a Jewish with a "konfessionslos" person was not prohibited by law and could be accepted by the Jewish authorities).

This situation had two important consequences. First, "mixed mar-

78. See also the discussion of this theme in the preceding essay, in this volume pp. 213–15.

79. Art. 64, Allgemeines bürgerliches Gesetzbuch: "Eheverträge zwischen Christen und Personen, welche sich nicht zur christlichen Religion bekennen, können nicht gültig eingegangen werden."

80. The so-called "Notzivilehe," introduced by law in 1870.

81. For Austrian marriage legislation and its social consequences in the early 20th century (no divorce for Catholic marriages, and attempts to circumvent this prohibition) see Ulrike Harmat, *Ehe auf Widerruf? Der Konflikt um das Eherecht in Österreich 1918–1938* (Studien zur Europäischen Rechtsgeschichte 121), Frankfurt/Main 1999.

riages" in the frequently used sense of a Jewish partner (member of the
Jewish community) and a Christian partner did not exist in Austria. Thus
it is impossible to draw up the statistics of mixed marriages by looking
for "Jewish-Christian" couples.[82] Gustav Mahler, Catholic, married Alma
Schindler, Catholic—period.[83] Second, it means that many passages from
the Jewish to the Christian religion (frequent) or from the Christian to the
Jewish religion (less frequent) or simply withdrawals from one religious
community have to be seen in the context of marriage planning. And this
is no doubt one important reason for the fact that around the turn of the
19th to the 20th century, as Marsha Rozenblit has said, Vienna's conversion rate was the highest in Europe.[84]

One caveat, however, is called for. The legal prohibition of marriages
of Christians with non-Christians was valid for the whole non-Hungarian
part of the Habsburg Empire. Yet it has been shown that withdrawal rates
from the Jewish communities in other parts of Imperial Austria (Bohemia,
Moravia, Galicia, Bukovina) were considerably lower than in Vienna.[85]

82. Thus the research situation in Germany is easier, though in Germany too the situation of "Christian-Christian" weddings, preceded by the passage of one partner from Judaism to Christianity, occurred, something which presents great difficulties for statistically
interested research. See Kerstin Meiring, *Die Christlich-Jüdische Mischehe in Deutschland,
1840–1933*, Hamburg 1898.

83. The entry for Gustav Mahler in a recently publish handbook of Austrian authors of
Jewish origin does not even mention Mahler's passing from Judaism to Catholicism. This ambitious publication is marred by arbitrary omissions and mistakes. References about denominational "Übertritte" are more often than not omitted, as in the cases of Arnold Schönberg
(neither his turning Protestant nor his return to Judaism), Victor Adler, Siegfried Lipiner, or
the writer Hermann Broch,who soon after his conversion contracted a Catholic marriage (see
Paul Michael Lützeler, *Hermann Broch. Eine Biographie*, Frankfurt/Main 1985, 51). References
are not omitted in the cases of Karl Kraus or Otto Weininger. In the case of the writer Peter
Altenberg, his withdrawal from the Kultusgemeinde is noted, not however his entry into the
Catholic Church. Neither in the case of Karl Popper nor in the case of the art historian Ernest
Gombrich is there a reference that they were born as Protestant children of converted par-
ents. The handbook has an entry to the great Hungarian writer Baron József Eötvös, fervent
advocate of Jewish emancipation,—yet he is not of Jewish origin. Cf. the entries mentioned in:
Österreichische Nationalbibliothek (ed.), *Handbuch österreichischer Autorinnen und Autoren
jüdischer Herkunft. 18. bis 20. Jahrhundert* (ed. Susanne Blumesberger, Michael Doppelhofer,
Gabriele Mauthe), 3 vols., Munich 2002.

84. Marsha Rozenblit, Jewish Assimilation in Habsburg Vienna, in Jonathan Frankel and
Steven Zipperstein (eds.), *Assimilation and Community· The Jews in Nineteenth Century Europe*, Cambridge 1992, 225–45, here 237.

85. Valuable indications are furnished in the excellent study by Wolfdieter Bihl, Die Juden,
in Adam Wandruszka and Peter Urbanitsch (eds.), *Die Habsburgermonarchie 1848–1918*,
vol. III: *Die Völker des Reiches*, Vienna 1980, 908–10. The most detailed figures for the Austrian lands, for Hungary and also in comparison with Germany, notably Berlin, are given bei
Leiter, *Assimilation*, 230–58.

This means that in addition to the legal situation, other factors have to be kept in mind. Jewish communities in other parts of Imperial Austria were more traditional than that of Vienna. As is well known, the phenomenal growth of the Jewish community in Vienna in the last decades of the 19th century was the result of thousands of new arrivals, people "on the move," who had left their more traditional communities (particularly in Bohemia and Moravia, but also Galicia and Bukovina, not to forget Hungary), people among whom there was proportionally a greater willingness to assimilate—and to marry outside their traditional surroundings.

Thus Vienna in the course of the later nineteenth and early twentieth centuries was a city with a high incidence of marriages—most of them "Christian-Christian" marriages—of persons of Jewish origin and persons on non-Jewish origin.[86] Direct statistical evidence does not exist; research combining denominational withdrawals and entries, followed by subsequent weddings (with very varied time spans between an entry into a religious community and a wedding within this community, keeping in mind decentralised wedding registers, sometimes also change of names) will be extremely difficult, but perhaps some day it will be done. There is one peculiar statistical evidence which should not be overlooked. This is the census organised by the NS authorities in May of 1939, differentiating between religious affiliation and affiliation according to the Nurenberg laws. According to this census,[87] there lived in Austria (at that time the "Ostmark" of Greater Germany) on May 1, 1939 16,938 persons who had two Jewish and two non-Jewish grandparents;[88] additionally 7,392 persons[89] had one Jewish grandparent. The overwhelming majority of these persons lived in Vienna (14.858, respectively 5.955 persons).[90] The awareness of the existence of mixed marriages in no small number may perhaps lead to a

86. Ivar Oxaal has convincingly argued that the number of mixed marriages in Vienna, if one takes into account the Christian marriages contracted after the "Übertritt" of one marriage partner, has been as high or higher than mixed marriages in Berlin. Ivar Oxaal, The Jews of young Hitler's Vienna, in Oxaal/Pollak/Botz (eds.), *Jews, Antisemitism and Culture in Vienna*, 32; Oxal's arguments also in Ivar Oxaal and Walter Weitzmann, The Jews of pre-1914 Vienna, in *Leo Baeck Institute Yearbook* 30, 1985, 395–432.

87. The results are reproduced and commented upon by Jonny Moser, *Demographie der jüdischen Bevölkerung Österreichs 1938–1945* (Schriftenreihe des Dokumentationsarchivs des österreichischen Widerstands zu Geschichte der NS-Gewaltverbrechen, 5), Vienna 1999.

88. Of whom 1,422 were members of the Kultusgemeinde and therefore "Geltungsjuden," ibid., 31.

89. Of whom 90 were members of the Kultusgemeinde and therefore "Geltungsjuden," ibid.

90. Ibid., 31. Specialists in the field will note that I avoided in the text using the horrific Nazi-terminology of "Mischlinge 1. und 2. Grades."

revision of stereotypes of an all-pervasive antisemitism. The children and grandchildren of mixed marriages, during the Nazi era afflicted with various discriminations and threatened by worse ones to come (sterilization was much discussed by the Nazi leadership), present a sociological group which, with one recent exception, has not been a theme of socio-historical research.[91] If we reflect that the great majority of these persons were able to escape the destruction of European Jewry, and again that most of these survived into post-1945 Austria, chiefly Vienna, we encounter a cultural "ingredient" of Vienna's post-World War II population that has carried into the present some of the heritage of the pre-1938, not to say pre-1914 assimilationist-liberal component of fin-de-siècle Vienna.

The final point is a delicate one; it is one of terminology, yet with far-reaching emotional and even moral ramifications. "Conversion" of "converts" are terms which seem to favor the receiving religious groups. Those who were "converts" for one side were "apostates" for the other side. "Apostasy" and "apostates" are terms to be encountered in the scholarly literature on the subject.[92] On the other hand, "apostates"—when they have been famous—not infrequently continue to be referred to or claimed to as Jews—tendency increasing.[93] An eminent scholar like the late Sir Ernest Gombrich, having left Vienna for London in 1936, has rather emphatically protested against this trend, arguing that in the last analysis the broad, non-religious application of the term Jewish, even if employed by authors whose philo-semitic sympathies are clear, uses criteria which approach those of the Nurenberg laws.[94]

In view of these delicate matters, touching on painful memories, readers may wish to ponder the following terminological suggestion. One might try to use in scholarly discourse more neutral terms than either "conversion" or "apostasy"—rather sober words as suggested by the statisticians: "Austritt," "Eintritt," "Übertritt"; the english equivalents "withdrawal," "entry," "passage," are as yet less familiar, but they may perhaps be put to more frequent use in scholarly discourse.

91. The exception, covering the whole of the Greater German Reich, is the monograph by the American historian Bryan Mark Rigg, *Hitler's Jewish Soldiers: The Untold Story of Nazi Racial Laws and Men of Jewish Descent in the German Military*, Lawrence, KS 2002.

92. E.g. Marsha L. Rozenblit, *The Jews of Vienna*.

93. E.g. Steven Beller, *Vienna and the Jews*. Malachi Haim Hacohen, with a fine sense of paradox, speaks of "a subgroup of an ethnic minority who posed for a short time as a social and cultural elite: Vienna's non-Jewish Jews," in his book *Karl Popper, The Formative Years 1902–1945*, Cambridge, England, 2000, 52.

94. Ernst H. Gombrich, *Jüdische Identität und jüdisches Schicksal. Eine Diskussionsbemerkung*, Vienna 1997, particularly 34–39 and 45–46.

There is a "lieu de mémoire" in Vienna, where the problems discussed in this paper have found a most poignant expression. In Vienna's largest Jewish cemetery, called "gate IV" ("Tor IV") of the "Zentralfriedhof" (Central Cemetery), there are, dating back to the Nazi years between 1941 and 1945, a number of Christian tombstones, with crosses. In October 1941, the Nazi administration of the city of Vienna ordered the compulsory burial of all persons of non-Jewish faith, Christians and persons without religious affiliation ("Konfessionslose"), considered Jewish according to the Nurenberg laws, in the Jewish cemetery. In November 2003, in the presence of the Chief Rabbi of Vienna, Paul Chaim Eisenberg, the Cardinal Archbishop of Vienna, Christoph Schönborn, the Lutheran bishop of Austria, Herwig Sturm, and the Greek-Orthodox Metropolite of Austria, Michael Staikos, a memorial stone was unveiled. Its text invokes the community of suffering of those who, separated by religion, yet united in dying, were all victims of national socialist racist delusion:[95]

"All those buried here are members of the community of suffering of the victims of National Socialist racial madness, separated by religion but united in death. May they rest in peace!"

95. "Alle hier Bestatteten gehören der Leidensgemeinschaft religiös getrennter, im Sterben vereinter Opfer des nationalsozialistischen Rassenwahns an. Sie mögen in Frieden ruhen!" The text also gives some information on the number of the persons of non-Jewish faith buried between 1941 and 1945 (approximately 800), and on the fact that many of these persons had set an end to their lives in order to escape imminent deportation. In greater detail cf. Leiter, *Assimilation, Antisemitismus und NS-Verfolgung*, 605–31.

CHAPTER ELEVEN

The Origins of Austrian Neutrality *

The purpose of this paper is to sketch the major developments which led to the recovery of Austrians full sovereignty after World War II by virtue of the State Treaty of May, 1955, and notably to the enactment of Austria's permanent neutrality by constitutional law on 26 October of that year. I shall discuss various options or contingencies that were conceivable as Austria emerged from the Second World War, liberated from Nazi rule by the USSR, the USA, Great Britain and France—but also subject to military occupation by those four powers who soon were to grow into two mutually hostile power blocks, confronting one another right across the territory of Austria. Chiefly, this paper will dwell on the emergence of permanent neutrality for a country that, during the first post-war decade, was militarily controlled in approximately two thirds by the U.S., Great Britain and France. Finally, the much discussed question of possible Soviet motives for Soviet withdrawal in 1955 also will receive attention.

The Background to the State Treaty

The point of departure for the reestablishment of Austria after World War II was the Declaration on Austria, issued in Moscow on 1 November 1943, by the Conference of Foreign Ministers of the USA, the United Kingdom, and the USSR. In this Declaration, the governments of the three powers (to be joined by France a few weeks later) regarded the annexation imposed on Austria by Germany in March 1938 as null and void and expressed

---

* First published in *Neutrality: Changing Concepts and Practices*, ed. by Alan T. Leonhard, Lanham, MD, 1988. The permission to reprint was gracefully granted by University Press of America, Inc.

their wish to see reestablished a free and independent Austria. The three powers added, however, a reminder to the effect that Austria could not avoid a certain responsibility for participation in the war. This "responsibility clause" was of British origin, had been concurred by the State Department, yet was considerably tightened through a Soviet amendment which the Western powers, "while not liking" it, accepted. A clause to that effect also was subsequently inserted into the preamble of the Austrian State Treaty; it was eliminated from the treaty text on Austrian request and by unanimous consent of the four powers on the eve of the signing of that Treaty during the Vienna Conference of Foreign Ministers of 14 May 1955.[1]

Preparing for Austria's liberation from Nazi rule, the Allied powers in 1944/45 discussed and drafted agreements for the temporary allied control and occupation of Austria—envisaged as measures of transition from the war situation to the definitive establishment of an independent and democratic Austria. Austria was divided into four zones of occupation: Soviet in the East, though also stretching to the North, and covering all of Austria's frontier lines with Hungary and Czechoslovakia; British in the South; American in the Northwest; and French in the West. In addition, the city of Vienna (surrounded by the Soviet zone, thus similar to the situation of Berlin!) was divided into five sectors: one for every occupying power, and an international sector in the center of the city, thus making partition, incidentally, more difficult than in Berlin where no such international sector existed.

Originally, hopes for an early withdrawal of allied forces and the conclusion of a "State Treaty" were high. Austria, as a country which had been liberated from Nazi rule, was not considered an enemy nation, and thus no Peace Treaty could be concluded with her. Austria was indeed something of a special case, as was recognized on several occasions.[2] The

1. The theme of the present paper is discussed in greater detail in Gerald Stourzh, *Geschichte des Staatsvertrages, 1945–1955, Osterreichs Weg zur Neutralitat* (Graz, Styria, 3rd enlarged edition 1985); earlier publications in English, on which parts of this paper are based, include Gerald Stourzh, "Towards the Settlement of 1955: The Austrian State Treaty Negotiations and the Origins of Austrian Neutrality" in *Austrian History Yearbook* 17/18 (1981/82), 174–87; idem, "Austrian State Treaty, 1955" in *Encyclopedia of Public International Law*, 3rd installment (1982), 41–44. In the following notes, references to archival materials are mainly limited to select documents that have been released in the last few years and that have not been made use of in the author's earlier publications.

2. James Byrnes and Vyacheslav Molotov agreed that Austria was in a special position at the Council of Foreign Ministers Meeting on 25 April 1946. Stourzh, *Geschichte des Staatsvertrages*, 10–11; Soviet Deputy Foreign Minister Andrei Vyshinsky said on 17 August 1946 that Austria was neither "an enemy of our enemies—nor [is] she an enemy herself." Quoted

allied powers originally prepared drafts for a treaty entitled "Treaty for the Reestablishment of an Independent and Democratic Austria." The Austrians, however, had developed a terminology of their own since the post–World War I period: the Austrian Republic in 1919 had denied legal succession to the Austro-Hungarian Monarchy, and therefore had refused to recognize the Peace Treaty of Saint-Germain as a peace treaty, instead merely enacting it in the statute book as Staatsvertrag—State Treaty. The Austrian government now applied this term—with better reason—to the draft treaty prepared after the Second World War, and gradually the allied powers accepted the Austrian term "State Treaty."

The outbreak of the Cold War and the escalation of the East-West conflict dimmed expectations of an early conclusion of the treaty and the departure of the foreign military forces. A compromise seemed in sight in the summer of 1949, because two major difficulties seemed to have been overcome. First, Yugoslavia originally had presented large territorial claims to the amount of 2,600 square kilometers. The Soviet Union at first had supported these claims at least in principle, though there is evidence that it applied pressure on Yugoslavia in 1947 to reduce these claims drastically. In 1949, about a year after the break between Stalin and Tito, the Soviet government withdrew support from the Yugoslav claims (which already had been somewhat reduced). A compromise was struck: Yugoslavia got neither territory nor reparations from Austria, yet it did receive Austrian property in Yugoslavia, and an article protecting the rights of Slovene and Croatian minorities in Austria was inserted into the draft treaty. The second major difficulty concerned German assets, real or alleged, in Austria. At the Potsdam Conference of Heads of State in 1945, it had been agreed that German assets outside of Germany were to be divided among the powers. German assets in Austria were large, and the Soviet Union asserted her rights under the Potsdam agreement on a large number of properties, including important industries, assets of the Danube Steam Shipping Company, and particularly rights and interests in the petrol producing area of Eastern Austria. Again a compromise was struck in June 1949 between the Soviet Union and the Western powers, according to which the Soviet Union was to turn over to Austria German assets upon payment by Austria of a lump sum of 150 million U.S. Dollars, with two important exceptions: Danube Shipping Company properties in Eastern Austria (as well as in Eastern Europe) were to be retained by the Soviet

by Audrey Kurth Cronin, *Great Power Politics and the Struggle for Austria. 1945–1955* (Ithaca, NY: Cornell University Press, 1986), p. 41.

Union, and rights and interests in the field of oil exploitation and exploration were to be given to the Soviet Union for a period of approximately thirty years. To give an estimate of the importance of the oil production in the Soviet zone of Austria, be it sufficient to indicate that in the decade from 1945 to 1955, the Soviets extracted more than 20 million tons of crude oil, of which more than half was exported from Austria without any profit at all for Austria.

The Five Options for Austria

The evolution of world politics in the second half of 1949, however, led to a renewed stalemate. The balance of power changed in various respects. In China, the communists scored final victory and the People's Republic of China was proclaimed. On the other hand, the deepening Soviet-Yugoslavia rift, the establishment of NATO, and the creation of the Federal Republic of Germany (followed by that of the DDR) strengthened the West. American hesitations were followed by Soviet delaying tactics and Austria remained occupied. After the outbreak of the Korean War in June 1950, the Austrian issue was put into a "deep freeze," as it were. If we look at post–World War II Austria, occupied by Soviet as well as Western forces, five options or contingencies were in principle conceivable.

(1)   The "Eastern" option—Austria turning into a "people's democracy" like her Eastern neighbors. This did not correspond to the wishes of the overwhelming majority of the Austrian people, and it also might have touched the security interests of the Western powers. Four milestones, as it were, of Austria's avoiding the "Eastern" solution should be mentioned: first, the national elections of November 1945, in which the communists obtained only 4 of 165 seats of the Austrian Parliament; second, a new Allied Control Agreement of June 1946, which abolished the veto power of a single occupation power for the majority of Austrian legislation as well as for bilateral agreements between Austria and the Allied powers, thus vastly reducing the nuisance value of Soviet veto possibilities; third, Austria's early option for the Marshall Plan in 1947 which made Austria the only partly Soviet-occupied country of Europe to profit from the European Recovery Program; fourth, the successful defeat of a communist led general strike movement in the fall of 1950 with the help of Western oriented Social Democratic workers and trade union groups.

(2)   An all-out "Western" option, going beyond Austria's undoubted devotion to parliamentary democracy and her participation in the European

Recovery Program, to include incorporation into the NATO alliance. Though a number of Western military spokesmen stressed the strategic importance of the alpine area of Western Austria for NATO (French General Emile Béthouart was particularly outspoken in this respect), the West was reluctant about a possible Austrian NATO membership. A confidential inquiry by Austrian Foreign Minister Gruber in February 1949—a couple of months prior to the signing of the Atlantic Pact—arguing in favor of Austria's inclusion into the Pact once the Austrian Treaty was concluded met rather with a rebuff by British Foreign Secretary Ernest Bevin. During the planning of the Atlantic Pact, Austria's future possible membership was once considered in passing; a provisional report said that Austria's "position as the gateway to the Po Valley makes Austria an important outpost of Western civilization." Yet, in the final planning stages of the Pact, Austria played no role. In June 1949, Austria's Foreign Minister Gruber declared that Austria did not wish to join NATO.[3]

The relation of Austria to Western military defense in the first decade after World War II is a complicated one and defies easy generalization. Discussing the problems of an "all-out" Western option for Austria, the following four points, at least, deserve special consideration.

First, the Western military estimate of Austria's strategic importance for the West was not constant. It varied over time, it varied among the main Western powers, and it varied occasionally even within the American military establishment itself. In October 1949, General Omar Bradley, heading the American Chiefs of Staff, in a statement published here for the first time, wanted to see the occupation of Austria "ended because of our militarily untenable position there," though Bradley did not think "we should make every concession just to get out, especially in view of the danger of subsequent Soviet Control."[4] But at that time and even earlier, the American Military Commander and High Commissioner in Austria, General Geoffrey Keyes, had taken a different position, stressing the need

3. On Gruber's approach to Bevin, see the excellent doctoral dissertation by Robert G. Knight, *British Policy Towards Occupied Austria. 1945–1950* (London, London University, London School of Economics,1986), p. 229; the quote on the Po Valley is from a Washington Security Talks—Working Party provisional report of 12 August 1948, also quoted by Knight, *British Policy*, p. 213; on the NATO-membership issue ibid., p. 213–14, on Gruber's statement in June,1949, ibid., p. 229.

4. Harry S. Truman Library, Independence, Missouri, Harry S. Truman Papers, President's Secretary file, "Memorandum for the President," October 20, 1949, on 47th Meeting of the National Security Council on October 20, 1947, at which Secretary of State Acheson presided, p. 3. Cronin, *Great Power Politics*, p. 87–88, refers to this meeting without reference, however, to Bradley's comment.

of American military presence in Austria in view of increasing East-West tensions. The latter view tended to prevail in the subsequent years, and the general trend of Western military planning has well been summed up by British historian Robert G. Knight: "What had begun as contingency plans for the evacuation of Austria in the event of a Soviet invasion became—especially after the signature of the Atlantic Pact—an argument for not abandoning a forward position, which—if a general European war ever did break out—would be a strategically important one."[5] To this, one ought to add that perhaps more important than the signing of the Atlantic Pact was the outbreak of the Korean War and the rapprochement between Yugoslavia and the West in the early fifties.

Second, there existed all along differences between British and American estimates of Austria's position; the British generally were prone to discount military possibilities in Austria more than the Americans (and the French), apparently connected with the fact that the British zone in Austria was the easternmost and least defensible of the Western zones in Austria.[6] Looking back in the spring of 1955 on the previous years, in a document released in 1986, a high ranking British diplomat wrote: "In the past, the Americans have favoured a 'forward strategy' in Austria. They would have liked Austria, after the Treaty, to join the Western military club. We have doubted the practicability of this, both on military and political grounds. But we had hoped they might join our political club. Even this now looks doubtful . . . ."[7]

Third, it seems important to point out that what this British diplomat called joining "the Western military club" did not necessarily mean NATO membership, but could also imply close cooperation through special arrangements or agreements. On one occasion in October 1949, an American diplomat spoke of "harmonizing" the Austrian army with the armed forces of the Atlantic Pact after the notification of the Austrian Treaty.[8] In connection with the allotment of funds under the Mutual Defense Assistance program, President Truman in 1952 indicated his readiness to determine, after the conclusion of an Austrian Treaty and as required by the Mutual Security Act, that Austria was a country "of direct

5. Knight, *British Policy*, p. 215.

6. Ibid., p. 212–13.

7. Public Record Office, Kew, Surrey (henceforth cited PRO), F. O. 371/117818, RR 1091/2 (Memorandum, "Austria: Neutralisation," quoting Harrison's minutes of 23 March 1955).

8. Col. Henry Byroade to a member of the French Embassy in Washington, as reported by Ambassador Henri Bonnet to the Quai d'Orsay on 28 October 1949. Archives diplomatiques du Ministère de relations extérieures, Paris, serie EU, Autriche, 1949–55, Vol. 80.

importance to the defense of the North Atlantic area and whose increased
ability to defend itself . . . is important to the preservation of the peace
and security of the North Atlantic area and to the security of the United
States."[9] At the latest in January/February 1954, as will be shown below,
the United States was ready to accept a neutral status for Austria if volun-
tarily chosen like that of Switzerland.

Fourth, it must be pointed out that beginning in the late forties and culminating in the early fifties (particularly 1951 and 1952), Austria, though
partly occupied by the Soviets, became something like a secret ally of the
West. In the Western zones, Austrian special Gendarmerie battalions,
American equipped, were secretly established to be the nucleus of a future
Austrian army. Even more, for the contingency of war in Europe while
the occupation lasted, prospective "auxiliaries" to the Western armies
were envisaged—in the utmost secrecy. By 1954, lists of up to 90,000 able-
bodied male Austrians living in the Western zones who had served in
World War II were drawn up.[10] It has to be added that the Western occupation forces in Austria, while not subject to the Commander of NATO
forces in Europe in peace time, were to be put under the command of
S.H.A.P.E. and, more particularly, under the Command for Southern Europe upon the outbreak of war.[11] Thus, for a country one-third of which
was occupied by Soviet forces, Austria's ties with the West were close
indeed—a situation unique in Europe. Though one high ranking Austrian
politician publicly favored Austria's joining NATO after the conclusion of
the Treaty, and though other prominent Austrian leaders confidentially

9. Harry S. Truman Library, Independence, Missouri, Harry S. Truman Papers, Confidential file, Memorandum for the President by W. A. Harriman, January 18, 1952, approved by the
President January 29, 1952.

10. See Stourzh, *Geschichte*, p. 321. See also for a report on the early stage of that program
of registering "able-bodied men willing to take up arms in case of an emergency" the letter of
the British High Commissioner Sir Harold Caccia to W. D. Allen in the Foreign Office dated
Vienna, 15 October 1951. PRO, FO 371/93621, CA 1192/20.

11. See Stourzh, *Geschichte*, p. 321, and particularly PRO, FO 371/93622, CA 1201/5/G.
Further sources on this in Cronin, *Great Power Politics*, note 3, pp. 193–94. Also, a new additional protocol to the North Atlantic Treaty of 27 May 1952 provided in a new Art. 6, para.
2 that the protection of the alliance also covered territory of non-member states if a member
state maintains occupation troops on that territory. A suggestion by the American Joint Chiefs
of Staff of 16 August 1950 concerning the inclusion "of Austria in the protective interest of
NATO and the best possible uses of her resources in the common defense" (quoted by Cronin,
Great Power Politics, p. 121) does not necessarily aim at NATO membership, but foreshadows
the inclusion of the territory of the three Western zones of Austria as implied by the additional
protocol of May,1952 just mentioned, as well as various possibilities of "harmonising" and
coordinating military contingency planning.

seem to have held similar views in certain periods of the post-war decade,[12] it appears in retrospect highly unlikely that the Soviets would ever have completely released the hold they had on parts of Austria on the expectation of the whole of Austria joining NATO. Increasingly, this unlikelihood struck Western diplomatic observers as well as Austrian government leaders, as will be shown below.

(3) Partition might have been not an option, but a possibility of post-war developments for Austria as it became a reality for Germany, Korea, Trieste (and, temporarily, Vietnam). This most undesirable contingency was much feared in Austria in the years after World War II. In Western, particularly American, records, speculating and contingency planning for the case of partition play a considerable role.[13] Yet no specific intentions or plans on the part of the Soviets have become known so far. In view of the smallness of the country, in view of the fact that Austria's Soviet zone bordered on linguistically completely different nations (Czechoslovakia and Hungary), partition would have created difficulties for the Eastern part. Even more important seems the reflection that, in case of partition, the larger part of Austria would have inevitably been driven into a closer relationship (under American auspices) with West Germany; and, assuming a

---

12. A public pronouncement of State Secretary Ferdinand Graf in July 1949 remained isolated. Stourzh, *Geschichte*, p. 108. Among those favoring, for a while at any rate, inclusion of Austria into the Western military system, was the leader of the Social Democrats Adolf Schärf, see ibid., p. 320. In a report of 10 May 1950, Walter Dowling, then Counselor of Legation in Vienna, wrote to Washington:

> "As for the Atlantic Pact, everyone seems to agree that until Austria has a state treaty it is too soon to talk about it. A very few People's Party politicians will privately admit that if a treaty is ever ratified, adherence to the Atlantic Pact will be necessary to protect Austrian independence. The Socialist Party maintains absolute silence on this point. . . . As long as Soviet troops occupy eastern Austria it is obviously inadvisable for responsible Austrians to advocate closer ties with the West."

This report contains interesting comments on Austrian attitudes toward "neutrality." National Archives, Washington, DC (henceforth cited NA), Record Group (RG) 59,663.0021/5-1050. While Dowling in May 1950 rather seems to have discounted the relevance of neutrality feelings, the British High Commissioner Caccia early in 1952 took this more seriously: "As with the citizens of most small countries, the unthinking wish of the vast majority is to become a second Switzerland. . . ." Caccia thought that one should bear in mind "the appeal which neutrality inevitably has to Austrian public opinion." Report to the Foreign Office, 1 January 1952. PRO, FO 371/98090, CA 1192/3.

13. On the fear of partition, cf. inter alia, a Memorandum by Charles Yost of 30 January. NA, RG 59, 663.001/1-3050. Addendum 2006: In 2005 Soviet sources were published showing that in 1948 the Soviet leadership was firmly set against a partition of Austria. Wolfgang Mueller, Die Teilung Österreichs als politische Option für KPÖ und UdSSR 1948 in *Zeitgeschichte*, 32 (2005), 47–54.

minimum of rationality, a new edition of "Anschluss" was certainly what Soviet policy wanted to avoid most assiduously.

(4) The fourth option was the continuation of the Four-Power-regime. Though the Allied Commission for Austria (and the quadripartite supervision of Vienna, symbolized by the "Four in a Jeep") was able to function even during some of the worst crises of the Cold War, the continuing occupation, quite apart from the financial burden, weakened the moral fiber of the country. Members of the Austrian government time and again implored the powers West and East to understand the moral dangers that were produced by a mood of continuous hopelessness and resignation.[14] Above all, Four-Power-occupation constantly implied the latent danger of partition, not so much out of any design of one of the powers, but rather in the eventuality of an international crisis defying management and getting out of hand. In addition, Austria's position as a secret ally of the West, in spite of Soviet occupation of a part of the country, was unique and exceptional in Europe. This is particularly true in view of the fact that large parts of the Western zones presumably would have been evacuated by the West in case of conflict, limiting possible defenses to the alpine area or parts of it.

(5) The option that finally emerged was that of Austria as a nation steering clear of military alliances, allowing no foreign military bases on her territory, and finally following the example of Switzerland as a permanently neutral nation. This option had been envisaged on various occasions, if rather vaguely and unspecifically, during the early years of the occupation, and sometimes even during the peak period of Austria's pro-Western commitments in the early fifties. It gained ground around 1953 and in the following two years. Increasingly, it had become clear that the Soviet Union might be willing to withdraw only on condition that Austria would not become part and parcel of the Western system in Europe. Archival materials released within the last few years reveal that, in 1951/52, extensive speculations among Western diplomats concerned with the Austrian situation took place, provoked both by diplomatic conversations with Soviet diplomats and by various propaganda moves of communist or fellow travelling spokesmen. "The crux of the business," the British High Commissioner and Ambassador Sir Harold Caccia wrote to London in November 1951, would seem to be "that the Russians, before they sign any State Treaty, may try to obtain some undertaking that Austria would not assume any military obligations after

---

14. E.g., a draft letter of Austrian Foreign Minister Gruber to Dean Acheson in the fall of 1949; see Stourzh, *Geschichte*, p. 67–68.

the Treaty and that, for instance, Austria would not join the Atlantic Pact."[15] In the Foreign Office, reaction varied. One high ranking diplomat responded very critically. "Even if we thought we could buy an Austrian Treaty at that price," Geoffrey Harrison replied to Ambassador Caccia, "we should on no account accept the neutralisation of Austria."[16] At that time, it should be added, a term like "neutralisation" was used rather indiscriminately without regard for its technical meaning (imposition by international treaties). Objections against "neutralisation" included the fear that it might serve as a precedent for Germany, and military objections were said to be strong. The (British) Chiefs of Staff had given their opinion "that an Austrian Treaty would only be to our advantage provided that we could be assured that an independent Austria would cooperate with the West and would not remain neutral in case of war. The existence of a neutral Austria, possibly under Soviet influence, would be a serious embarrassment to our military position in that part of Europe and would outweigh the advantage of securing the withdrawal from the Soviet zone."[17] Other British diplomats reacted differently. It was argued that it was "inconceivable that the Russians would sign an Austrian Treaty if there was any sure prospect of Austria becoming a formal ally of the Western Powers." The same diplomat argued—realistically—that it was "indeed more than likely that Austria would adhere to a policy which would in fact amount to neutrality" and he added: "It is arguable that such a policy would be in the interests of the Western Powers."[18] Another British diplomat added a note which is all the more interesting in that it prophetically anticipates, in January 1952, what actually was going to happen in 1955: "A freely chosen neutrality, under which a fully sovereign Austria elected to join no exclusive alliance, might be difficult for us to resist and not incompatible with our vital strategic requirements."[19]

The Diplomatic Path to Neutrality

In the autumn of 1952, certain signals—on a low diplomatic level—were given from the Soviets to the Austrians to the effect that if Austria "were

15. Sir Harold Caccia to Geoffrey Harrison, Vienna 26 November 1951. PRO, FO 371/93594, CA 1010/3.

16. Geoffrey Harrison to Sir Harold Caccia, London 21 December 1951. PRO, FO 371/93594, CA 1016/4.

17. Ibid.

18. Memorandum, "Neutralisation of Austria" by L. M. Minford (Foreign Office), 4 January 1952, and Minutes by Minford, 5 January 1952. PRO, FO 371/9806161, CA 107/3.

19. Minute by Denis Allen, 5 January 1952, ibid.

to defend herself" rather than let herself be defended by Western powers, if Austria were to become a nation like Sweden or Switzerland, the Soviet Union might consider withdrawal from Austria.[20] In Austria, responsible statesmen had repeatedly pointed to Austria's unwillingness to join a military alliance, and the example of Switzerland was mentioned on various occasions. Pronouncements of Karl Renner, First President of Austria after 1945, may be mentioned, as well as a very pointed statement by Theodor Körner, Renner's successor, published in February 1952 in a Geneva newspaper, to the effect that Switzerland would be a model for a free Austria. In June 1953, the Austrian Foreign Minister Karl Gruber visited Indian Prime Minister Jawaharlal Nehru in Switzerland, on the Bürgenstock near Lucerne. On this occasion, Gruber explained Austria's international position, an explanation that included a reference about Austria's unwillingness to participate in military alliances.[21] Gruber asked Nehru to lend his good offices in explaining to the Soviet government Austria's views. In a paper handed over to the Indian minister in Vienna a few days later, and jointly agreed to by Gruber and by Bruno Kreisky (then State Secretary in the Foreign Office), the Austrians stated that they would not be willing to join military alliances, and that the military neutralisation of the alpine region (of both Austria and Switzerland) would keep this area out of military speculations. The Indian Ambassador to Moscow, K.P.S. Menon, at the end of June 1953, told Soviet Foreign Minister V. Molotov that he thought that Austria might be willing to take a neutral position. Molotov's reply was rather evasive at that time, though there is evidence that in June 1953 Soviet diplomacy did indeed posit a connection between neutrality and the possible signing of the Austrian Treaty.[22]

Foreign Minister Gruber's initiative in the direction of Moscow via Indian diplomacy caused a major stir among the Western powers. Sources as to Western indignation, particularly British and American, are abundant. Western representatives in Vienna impressed on the Austrian leaders the need for prior consultation with the West.[23] Secretary of State Dulles stated that such one-sided indications of what Austria would be prepared

20. Stourzh, *Geschichte*, p. 81–82. The State Department was informed by the Austrians of this Austro–Soviet conversation that took place in Washington. See NA, RG 59, 663.001/9–2652.

21. Telegraphic report by the American High Commissioner and Ambassador Llewellyn Thompson about his talks with Gruber on the latter's conversations with Nehru on 25 June, 9 July and 1 August 1953. NA, RG 59,663.001/6–2553, 663.001/7–953, and 663.001/8–153.

22. Detailed description of the above in Stourzh, *Geschichte*, p. 86–88.

23. Cf. particularly Thompson conversations with Raab, Schärf and Gruber on 9 July 1953, NA, RG 59,663.001/7–953.

to do meant a weakening of the West's bargaining position.[24] In the ensuing period, one gathers the impression of increased Western-Austrian
consultations. In 1953, partly as a result of the signs of a certain emancipation of Austria's diplomacy from a tutelage that was at times close indeed,
the Western powers and particularly the Americans concerned themselves
with the possibilities of a future connection between the Treaty negotia-
tion and the issue of neutrality or neutralisation. Among American diplomats, there were also varied reactions; some were quite negative, like
the view of Walter Dowling, Deputy American High Commissioner in Vienna. He suggested that if certain economic provisions of the draft treaty
"and some form of neutrality were to go into effect, Austria would be lost
to the West."[25] There were skeptical memoranda in the State Department,
as well as cautious and well informed ones from the American Embassy in
Vienna, the latter stressing the great attraction neutrality would have for
the Austrian population.

A State Department position paper on "Austrian Neutrality" of September 1953 drew a gloomy picture. It did say that Austria enjoyed an "en-
viable reputation in the United States because of its staunch resistance to
Communism. $1.4 billion in aid and close diplomatic support have been
extended to Austria in the expectation it would side unalterably with the
West." The paper added: "Should Austria attempt to be neutral between
East and West, American criticism of Austria may be bitter." The paper
also argued that even if Austria were to declare that it would not join any
military alliance, there still could be expected "the possibility of covert
defense planning between NATO and Austria." Arrangements which
would "prevent Austria's participation in Western military planning"
were thought to be "highly objectionable." In addition to the importance
of the Austrian alpine mass for the defense of Western Europe, Austria
might "become a key link in future military connections between NATO
and Yugoslavia." The paper was also very doubtful of Austrian capacities
to practice neutrality: "That Austria could really practice neutrality is an
unsound concept. It lacks the will, the resources and the internal stability
to follow Switzerland's example. It lies in too exposed a position to follow
Finland's example." This paper is of interest for two reasons. First, there is
hardly sufficient awareness that the country in question, Austria, at that
time was occupied in about one third of its territory by the Soviet Union

24. Tel. Dulles to American Embassy Vienna, 7 July 1953. NA, RG 59, 663.001/7–753.
25. Walter Dowling to Assistant Secretary of State Livingstone T. Merchant, London
19 May 1953. NA, RG 59,663.001/5–1953.

and that at that very time the Soviet Union was exploiting some of Austria's most precious natural resources. In other words, the aim of finding ways and means to end Austria's occupation was an overriding one of the Austrian government. Second, the paper unknowingly pointed to one of the most difficult general problems facing any nation that contemplates—for important and legitimate reasons—a status of keeping free of military alliances or of neutrality. Elsewhere I have described that problem as the "affinity paradox" facing neutral nations. The "affinity paradox" means that powers, with whom for whatever reasons close ties of sympathy (e.g., ideological sympathy) exist, may be disappointed or even irritated that a neutral state "merely" pursues a neutral attitude. In most outspoken terms the "affinity paradox" has been formulated in Machiavelli's *The Prince*, Chapter XXI, where it is said that "it will always happen that the one who is not your friend will want you to remain neutral, and the one who is your friend will require you to declare yourself by taking arms." The predicament of America's attitudes toward Austria—as Austria, in order to recover its substantial unity, was slowly moving from a position of America's secret ally to that of a nation militarily, though certainly not ideologically, neutral—is enlightened, I believe, by pointing to the existence of that "affinity paradox" in Austro-American relations.[26]

Toward the end of 1953, a British-French-American working group in Paris set up the following recommendations in case of Soviet suggestions on "neutralisation":

"Any Soviet proposal to neutralise Austria to the detriment of Western and Austrian security should be resisted at once. The Austrian Government has already declared their unwillingness to join post-treaty military alliances. We would argue that this should be sufficient to allay Soviet fears but if the Austrians themselves should insist on further making a formal declaration, the Western Powers must ensure that such a declaration would leave Austria free to enter into associations compatible with the principles and purposes of the United Nations. It is

26. Vienna Embassy Memorandum 26 August 1953. NA, RG 59, 663.001/8–2653. Position Paper "Austrian Neutrality" by R. B. Freund, 21 September 1953, based on a preceding tentative paper by Peter Rutter, 15 September 1953. NA, RG 59,663.001/9–2153,663.001/ 9–1553; an earlier paper by Rutter on Neutrality of 22 April was also very critical. NA, RG 59, 663.001/4–2253. For the "affinity paradox" see Gerald Stourzh, "Some Reflections on Permanent Neutrality," in *Small States in International Relations*, edited by August Schou and Arne Olav Brundtland (Stockholm, Almquist & Wiksell,1971), 96. The quote from *The Prince* is taken from Niccolò Machiavelli, *The Prince and The Discourses*, (New York: Modern Library Ed., 1950), p. 83.

important that such a declaration should not in any way be annexed to the treaty. Although the cases are not parallel, we should also have to bear in mind the possible consequences in Germany and elsewhere of Austrian neutralisation. Moreover, it would increase the difficulties of the West in aiding in the development of an adequate post-treaty Austrian army and of defence planning between the West and Austria."[27]

In view of these skeptical views, a new development occurred in January 1954 when President Eisenhower, in a discussion with Secretary of State John Foster Dulles, took a more positive view. In a "Breakfast Conference" between Eisenhower and Dulles on January 20, 1954, the President said with reference to the Austrian Treaty, "he could see no objection to the neutralisation of Austria if this did not carry with it the demilitarization. If Austria could achieve a status somewhat comparable to Switzerland, this would be quite satisfactory from a military standpoint."[28]

The "green light" given by President Eisenhower in the direction of a neutrality somewhat on the pattern of Switzerland had important effects on the deliberations of the Berlin Conference of Foreign Ministers in February 1954. In a private conversation with Molotov on 13 February 1954, the records of which have been published only in 1986, Dulles told Molotov, "if Austria wants to be a Switzerland, the U.S. will not stand in the way, but this should not be imposed."[29] This was Dulles' first indication of how he was going to react on a proposal put forth by Molotov at that Conference to the effect of inserting a new neutralisation article into the draft Treaty with Austria. This the West opposed strongly, above all because it wanted to avoid that Austria might serve as a precedent for Germany, the Soviets having presented neutralisation proposals for Germany as early as March 1952, which had made a certain impact on public opinion in West Germany. Thus, the Swiss model, mentioned by Eisenhower a few weeks earlier, served Dulles to deflect the neutrality issue away from Germany to the level of smaller countries.

27. Here quoted from a British brief "The Neutralisation of Austria" without date, obviously prepared for the Berlin Conference of Foreign Ministers. PRO, FO 371/109361, CA 1071/178. Foreign Secretary Anthony Eden wrote in handwriting on the margin a comment on the recommendation that an Austrian declaration should not be annexed to the treaty: "The Russians may well ask, & I don't see how we could refuse, if Austrians agreed."

28. Dwight D. Eisenhower Library, Abilene, Kansas, John Foster Dulles Papers, 1953–1959, White House Memoranda Series. Stourzh, *Geschichte*, p. 322, also Cronin, *Great Power Politics*, p.134.

29. *Foreign Relations of the United States, 1952–1954,* Vol. VII, *Germany and Austria* (Washington, DC: U.S. Government Printing Office, 1986), Part 1, 1081.

Immediately after his private talk with Molotov, there followed a ple-
nary session of the Foreign Ministers Conference, and Dulles' statement
there included the following important passage:

> "A neutral status is an honorable status if it is voluntarily chosen by
> a nation. Switzerland has chosen to be neutral, and as a neutral she
> has achieved an honorable place in the family of nations. Under the
> Austrian State Treaty as heretofore drafted, Austria would be free to
> choose for itself to be a neutral state like Switzerland. Certainly the
> United States would fully respect its choice in this respect, as it fully
> respects the comparable choice of the Swiss nation."[30]

This highly positive statement is all the more interesting in view of
Dulles' widely publicized disapproval of neutrality on other occasions. In
fact, it seems that Dulles even at that time had considerable misgivings
about Austria going it alone, as it were. In a conversation with Austrian
Foreign Minister Figl and State Secretary Kreisky only three days later,
Dulles, as quoted in the recently published Memorandum of Conversation, "went on to point out the dangers and disadvantages for Austria in
staying out of collective security arrangements and becoming a vacuum,
stressing the importance of raising an Austrian Army." Dulles noted "that
Austria could become an inviting invasion route to the South comparable
to Belgium in 1914." Dulles "reiterated that the U.S. would not wish to
stand in the way of an Austrian policy in favor of military neutrality, but
said that the cost to Austria would be heavier and that the Western Powers and, he supposed, the Austrian Government would not wish to leave a
vacuum in Austria."[31]

It should perhaps be observed in passing that Dulles' often quoted public criticism of neutrality, from his Iowa State College speech of 9 July 1956,
was made after the United States had recognized the neutrality of Austria.
He referred to "exceptional circumstances," obviously keeping in mind
both Switzerland and Austria as special arrangements.[32]

30. Stourzh, *Geschichte*, p. 121; also Cronin, *Great Power Politics*, p. 131.

31. *Foreign Relations, 1952–1954*, vol VII, Part 1, 1133. There is a curious intervention by
Bruno Kreisky in this discussion: "Dr. Kreisky speaking on behalf only of his own party in
the coalition, considered the neutrality declaration just a device for obtaining a treaty, and expressed a wish to have the security of NATO if that were possible. He felt that it is not." Ibid.

32. The Iowa State College speech is published in *Department of State Bulletin*, 34 (1956),
999–1004.

Dulles' Berlin statement on Swiss neutrality and the possibility for Austria to follow this example is important for a special reason: Dulles' statement was to be taken up during the Austro-Soviet negotiations in Moscow in April 1955. At that time, Molotov extensively quoted from Dulles' Berlin statement as evidence that the Western powers would have no objections to Austrian misgivings about the term neutrality and its acceptability to the West.

The Berlin Conference also presented an occasion for Austria's Foreign Minister Leopold Figl to go on record that Austria would not join any military alliance nor admit any foreign military base on its territory. Though there had been various earlier statements to that effect, as has been shown above, and though even the Main Committee of the Austrian Parliament had in September 1953 accepted a similar declaration by Figl's predecessor Gruber, Figl's statement in Berlin, at the conference table of the Foreign Ministers' Conference, was Austria's most formal commitment so far.[33]

No agreement on Austria was reached in Berlin. Molotov had insisted that, even if the Treaty were signed, the Soviet Union wished to continue to station some troops in Austria until a Peace Treaty with Germany were signed. Everyone knew that a German Peace Treaty was not in sight; thus Molotov's condition was unacceptable to the Austrians as well as to the West. Molotov made it clear enough that he wished to link the Austrian to the German question and particularly to the issue of the European Defense Community. The EDC was defeated in August 1954 in the very country that had given birth to that project, France. Yet very speedily, the Western powers found an alternative solution to the problem of integrating West Germany into NATO—the Paris Treaties of October 1954. After their ratification had been secured in the French National Assembly at the end of 1954 and a few months later in the German Bundestag and the French Conseil de la République, the entry of the Federal Republic of Germany into NATO had become a certainty; its admission to NATO took effect in May 1955.

These events in Western Europe were followed, and party accompanied, by several fairly spectacular Soviet initiatives in Central and Eastern Europe. On 8 February 1955, Foreign Minister Molotov publicly indicated a new departure concerning the Austrian Treaty, and on 15 May 1955, the State Treaty was signed in Vienna. Only one day earlier, the Warsaw Pact had been signed. Toward the end of May, the two leading Russian

---

33. Stourzh, *Geschichte*, 90, 121–22.

statesmen of the epoch, First Secretary Khrushchev and Prime Minister Bulganin, arrived in Belgrade to heal the appalling breach between Soviet Russia and Yugoslavia that had been provoked by Stalin in 1948. Only a few days later, on 7 June 1955, the Soviet Government publicly invited Chancellor Adenauer to visit Moscow and suggested the establishment of diplomatic relations between West Germany and the Soviet Union. It is important to view the final phase of the Austrian Treaty negotiations and the emergence of Austria's status of permanent neutrality within that international context.

In a series of bilateral Soviet-Austrian contacts from February to April 1955, culminating in negotiations of a top government delegation from Vienna consisting of Chancellor Julius Raab, Vice-Chancellor Adolf Schärf, Foreign Minister Figl and State Secretary Kreisky, with a Soviet delegation headed by Molotov and Anastas Mikoyan in Moscow from 12 April to 15 April 1955, the following main agreements emerged (leaving a number of details aside): Most importantly, it emerged that the real guarantee against dangers of an "Anschluss" desired, and indeed insisted upon, by the Soviets was Austria's neutrality on the model of Switzerland. Chancellor Raab, leader of the Austrian People's Party, and strongly supported by Austria's Ambassador to Moscow, Norbert Bischoff, was willing to accept this more readily than his Social Democratic coalition partner in the government, Adolf Schärf. Schärf, leader of the Social Democrats, as well as others in his party, preferred a formula of "steering clear of alliances" to the term "neutrality." Why? It seems that the Social Democrats had misgivings about the Communists' year-long campaign in favor of neutrality, as long as the Soviets stayed in parts of Austria. The Communist Party had denounced the overwhelmingly pro-Western attitude of the Austrian press during the peak of the East-West confrontation in Europe as "not neutral." Also, the term "neutrality" no doubt was less flexible than a minimum commitment about merely steering clear of military alliances and admitting no foreign military bases—which had been the original Austrian formula presented to the Berlin Foreign Ministers' Conference.

Of course, the Austrians were aware of Western skepticism about neutrality. The British documents released in 1986 give ample evidence of the fears expressed in London.[34] It would not be surprising if, after the release of the American Department of State papers, similar apprehensions will become evident. In Austria in 1955, the Socialists were somewhat more willing to heed Western advice than Chancellor Raab, who had made up

34. See particularly PRO, FO 371, files 117789 and 117790.

his mind that the withdrawal of foreign, and particularly Soviet, forces from Austria was to be accomplished only under the primary condition insisted upon by Molotov that the permanent neutrality of Austria be based on the model of Switzerland. It must be added, though, that reference to the model of Switzerland, a staunchly Western country even though militarily neutral, was advantageous for Austria. The Swiss model contained more favorable conditions for Austria than the Finnish model, which in previous conversations sometimes had been mentioned. The Soviets' reference to the Swiss model, citing in support of their wishes declarations of John Foster Dulles in Berlin (as shown above) and of Austria's President Theodor Körner, a Socialist, relating Austria's position to the exemplary status of neighboring Switzerland, was obviously designed to overcome hesitations in the Socialist part of the Austrian delegation. It was also designed as a consensus formula because, after John Foster Dulles' Berlin statements both in private conversation with Molotov and in his published statement at the Conference table, it was virtually impossible for the United States, and thus for the other Western powers as well, not to accept an Austrian settlement explicitly based on the formula suggested by Dulles in Berlin.

In the negotiations of April 1955, the Soviets made very tangible concessions. Their oil production rights in Eastern Austria, which were to extend over a period of approximately thirty years, were instead to be transferred to Austria within two months from the entering into force of the Treaty. Austria was in turn to ship ten million tons of oil to the Soviet Union for a ten year period. These shipments subsequently were reduced to six million tons. The Soviet Union also declared its readiness to return to Austria the holdings of the Danube Shipping Company in Eastern Austria against a lump sum payment of two million U.S. dollars. As for the transfer to Austria of all other property, rights, and interests held as German property or war booty, the sum of 150 million U.S. dollars agreed upon in 1949 was maintained. It was to be paid—and was indeed going to be paid—by Austria within a six year period, but in commodities and not in cash; the commodity payments had been agreed upon in principle by the Soviets one year earlier at the Berlin Conference. Commodity payments were essential in order to keep going many productions that were turned over from the Soviet Union to Austria in a rather run-down fashion.

These various transfers to Austria finally were to eliminate what Dr. Schärf called the "Soviet enclave" in Eastern Austria. Indeed, it has not been sufficiently appreciated that the earlier drafts of the Austrian treaty had envisaged the maintenance of such enclaves in Eastern Austria—for example, in the oil production business for about thirty years; and along the Danube, in the properties of the Danube Steam Shipping Company, for time unlimited. Only gradually, in the early fifties, had both Austrians (in particular the Socialist leadership) and the West come to realize to what extent the future of the country was mortgaged by these provisions; Schärf in 1955 was particularly keen on wresting from the Soviets these "enclaves," though the return of the oil fields had also been requested by Foreign Minister Figl. No concessions were made by Molotov concerning the prohibition of various special weapons in the draft treaty, including the prohibition of self-propelled or guided missiles. Though Molotov conducted the talks with the Austrians with great skill and command of details (in the economic fields the negotiations were led by Anastas Mikoyan), it later became known that Molotov was executing a policy of the new leadership under Khrushchev of which he did not approve. Molotov seems to have opposed the withdrawal from Austria.[35]

The results just outlined were embodied in the "Moscow Memorandum" of 15 April 1955.[36] In this paper, the four members of the Austrian Government mentioned above undertook to initiate various measures of the Austrian Government and the Austrian Parliament which were to culminate in the declaration of the permanent neutrality of Austria by Parliament. In the "Moscow Memorandum," the model of Switzerland is mentioned on two occasions. First, there is a reference that the Austrian Government delegation would undertake steps leading to the adoption by Austria of a neutrality of the kind exercised by Switzerland. Second, there is a reference concerning Soviet willingness to support a guarantee of Austria's territorial integrity and inviolability to be granted by the Four Powers "according to the model of Switzerland." That guarantee, a territorial guarantee, not a guarantee of neutrality, had been suggested, in fact, by the Austrians who had modeled their suggestion on the pattern of the Great Power guarantee given to Switzerland's territorial integrity and inviolability after the Napoleonic wars in 1815. This proposed Four Power guarantee for Austria's territorial integrity and inviolability did never materialize. The Western powers, supported in this by some of the smaller NATO powers like Belgium, had doubts about the wisdom of such a guarantee. Since none of the three Western signatories of the Austrian Treaty bordered on

35. On this see particularly Sven Allard, *Russia and the Austrian State Treaty* (University Park, PA: Pennsylvania State University Press, 1970).

36. English text available in *The Austrian State Treaty: An Account of the Postwar Negotiations Together with the Text of the Treaty and Related Documents*. Department of State Publication No. 6437 (Washington, DC: U.S. Government Printing Office, 1957), 79–82.

Austria, it is indeed true that in case of the guarantee having to be backed up by military intervention, some other NATO powers would be involved. Thus, though in 1955 the Chancelleries examined that issue thoroughly and gave it a great deal of thought, as is apparent from the recently released British and French documents, the guarantee issue was allowed to lapse; and the Soviets did not insist. The Moscow Memorandum was initialed by the Austrians Raab, Schärf, Figl, and Kreisky; it was signed by Molotov and Mikoyan on behalf of the Soviet government. The majority of Austrian international lawyers stress the fact that the Moscow Memorandum is not a treaty, but rather a declaration of intent, an obligation on the part of those government members who initialed the Memorandum to see that the points enumerated in the Memorandum be fulfilled by the appropriate Austrian authorities.

After the breakthrough in the bilateral Austro-Soviet talks, the Western Powers had to be called in again. A Four Power Conference of Ambassadors opened in Vienna on 2 May. The Soviets were at first unwilling to incorporate the economic concessions granted in Moscow into the Austrian Treaty. It took considerable Western pressure, including a threat by John Foster Dulles to cancel his announced trip to Vienna, to get these undertakings included in the treaty by way of an annex and a reference to this annex in one clause of the Treaty. The Soviet Union also secured a provision according to which oil production and oil exploration rights to be turned back to Austria must not be passed on to former foreign owners. Also, the return of most former German properties to German claimants was prohibited, with certain exceptions chiefly concerning smaller private properties. Simultaneously with the Ambassadors Conference, the Western powers conducted negotiations with the Austrian Government on restitution and compensation, embodied in two Memoranda initialed on 10 May 1955 in Vienna.[37] On the basis of these agreements, Western oil firms received considerable compensation payments, and five firms in the field of oil refining and distribution that had been nationalized by Austria in 1946 were denationalized in favor of their former Western owners.

On the eve of signing the Austrian State Treaty, a Foreign Ministers Conference in Vienna on 14 May endorsed the principle of Austria's future neutrality. After approving the Treaty on 7 June, the Austrian Nationalrat (lower House of Parliament) passed a resolution on neutrality and requested the government to submit a neutrality bill to Parliament.

37. Ibid., 83–90.

The Austrian Treaty entered into force on 27 July 1955, having duly been ratified not merely by Austria but by the four other signatories as well. From that day, a 90-day period began to be counted, within which the withdrawal of the Allied forces was to take place. Only after the expiration of this period and after the last foreign forces had left Austria (they were British) did Parliament pass the Constitutional Law on Austria's permanent neutrality, on 26 October 1955. Its operative article is worded as follows:[38]

(Art. I)

1. For the purpose of the lasting maintenance of her independence externally, and for the purpose of [maintaining] the inviolability of her territory, Austria declares of her own free will her perpetual neutrality. Austria will maintain and defend this with all means at her disposal.

2. For the securing of this purpose in all future times Austria will not join any military alliances and will not permit the establishment of any foreign military bases on her territory.

The Four Powers recognized Austria's perpetual neutrality as embodied in this Law in simultaneous and identically worded notes on 6 December 1955. The principle of simultaneous and identical notes had been agreed upon by Soviet and Western powers alike at the time of a meeting in San Francisco in June 1955 commemorating the tenth anniversary of the UN. On 14 December 1955, Austria was admitted to the United Nations. The Four Powers had agreed as early as 1947 on recommending Austria's admission to the UN and had inserted a text to that effect into the preamble of the Treaty. When the issue of neutrality finally arose on the occasion of the Austro-Soviet talks of April 1955, the Austrian delegation specifically inquired of the Soviet delegation whether it saw any problems in UN membership for neutral Austria. The Soviets saw no difficulties, nor did, subsequently, the three Western powers. It is important to note that the Security Council of the United Nations recommended to the General Assembly the admission of Austria after four of the five permanent members of the Security Council had recognized the neutrality of Austria. Thus, admission was recommended with the full knowledge of Austria's new status.

---

38. Text in English in Stourzh, *Geschichte*, p. 239. Cronin, *Great Power Politics*, 167, omits the date when the neutrality law was passed and merely gives the date when it entered into force (5 November 1955).

Conclusions

It remains to ask about the reasons that may have impelled the Soviet government to withdraw so quickly, in 1955, from a country that had been kept under allied control for ten years.

Five considerations may be mentioned:

First, as a result of West Germany's joining NATO by virtue of the Paris Treaties of October 1954, the strategic value of communication lines between the old NATO member Italy and the new NATO member West Germany was enhanced. A newly neutral Austria, and its neighbor toward the West, traditionally neutral Switzerland, jointly formed a belt separating the new NATO member from the old, NATO's central tier from its southern tier.

Second, the ideal of neutral belts seems to have had even wider connotations. As has been said above, the Soviet leadership's reconciliation with Tito's Yugoslavia followed the Austrian settlement very closely. There is an interesting report among the Austrian diplomatic records, from the Austrian Ambassador to Moscow, Norbert Bischoff, dated late February 1955. Following a conversation with Vice-Foreign Minister Semyonov,[39] Bischoff reported that the Soviet view held that, through a well-secured neutralisation of Austria, the "tearing apart of Germany" would not be carried into Austria. Austria should fulfill a function similar to that of Sweden, Finland, Switzerland and Yugoslavia. In other words, there clearly emerged the intention of creating or enlarging neutral belts between NATO and Eastern bloc nations. One was to emerge in Scandinavia, and it is important to be aware of the fact that the Soviet Union in September 1955 announced its readiness to give up its naval base in Porkkala, Finland, the withdrawal to be effected by the end of the year. A second belt of neutral, or at any rate alliance-free, nations was to emerge in central and east central Europe. It is interesting to note Switzerland and Yugoslavia mentioned in one breath, as it were, together with Austria. This suggests an attention being paid to smaller states which is lacking, one sometimes feels, in American political thinking, which has a tendency to concentrate on the German problem and perhaps to underrate the role of smaller European nations outside a bloc.

Third, there is the question of Germany. It has often been suggested that the Soviets' Austrian policy was made with a view to Germany. Austria was to serve as bait, as it were, for German public opinion to be im-

---

39. Stourzh, *Geschichte*, p.139. Full text in the collection of Austrian archival documents, *Österreich und die Großmächte. Dokumente zur österreichischen Außenpolitik*, edited by Alfons Schilcher (Vienna, Edition Geyer, 1980), 241.

pressed with the advantages of not belonging to a power bloc. There is no question that various pronouncements of Soviet spokesmen support that thesis, last but not least Molotov's speech in the Belvedere Castle on 15 May 1955 on the occasion of signing the Austrian Treaty. However, a rational analysis of the timing in that momentous year 1955 shows that, by the time the Austrian question was seriously negotiated and settled, West Germany's entry into NATO was irreversible. That the Soviet leadership recognized this as a *fait accompli* is shown by its very early invitation to Chancellor Adenauer, who had just barely presented his country in the Council of NATO when he received the invitation to travel to Moscow. That seems to indicate that the concentration on smaller neutral states in Europe was the consequence of the existence and acceptance of two German states integrated in two different military blocs, not the attempt to prevent the integration of one of the two German states in the Western bloc.

Fourth, and briefly, we need to remind ourselves that the new Soviet leadership under Khrushchev very keenly strove for a new summit, which indeed was to take place in Geneva in July 1955. And the Western powers, particularly the Eisenhower administration, frequently had referred specifically to an Austrian settlement as an indication of good will.

Fifth, and also briefly, it should be pointed out that in 1955 the Soviet Union launched a worldwide initiative toward attracting non-aligned Third World countries. Nehru's visit to the Soviet Union in the late spring of 1955 should be mentioned, as should subsequent visits by Khrushchev and Bulganin to India, Burma and Afghanistan. And 1955 was also the year of the Bandung Conference.

For the West, though the military were not too happy about having to withdraw from Austria, the Austrian settlement meant an important chance. In central Europe, amid neighboring communist nations, a small, yet free, democratic and soon prosperous nation was allowed to develop. Austria soon was to prove the liberality of its disposition by receiving tens of thousands of refugees from Hungary in 1956 and from other countries in subsequent years. The "first détente," as the events of 1955 including the Austrian settlement have aptly been called,[40] has stood the test of time remarkably well.

---

40. Vojtech Mastny, "Kremlin Politics and the Austrian Settlement," in *Problems of Communism* 31 (July–August 1982): 38.

Postscript 2006

Reference is made in this paper to the third edition of my history of the Austrian State Treaty and the origins of Austria's neutrality, *Geschichte des Staatsvertrags 1945–1955*. *Österreichs Weg zur Neutralität* (1985; the first edition was published in 1975 under the title *Kleine Geschichte des Österreichischen Staatsvertrages*). In 1998, a considerably enlarged and partly rewritten fourth edition, for the first time making use of Soviet archival material, was published under a new title: Gerald Stourzh, *Um Einheit und Freiheit. Staatsvertrag, Neutralität und das Ende der Ost-West-Besetzung Österreichs 1945–1955* (Vienna, Böhlau-Verlag 1998, 831 pp.). The fifth edition, basically identical to the fourth edition, but with the addition of a new bibliographical essay covering the period 1998–2005, was published under the same title in 2005 (Vienna, Böhlau-Verlag, 848 pp.).

The English version of a new article by the author, "The Austrian State Treaty and the International Decision Making Process in 1955," is being published in the *Austrian History Yearbook* 38 (2007).

PART III

The Tocquevillian Moment:
From Hierarchical Status to Equal Rights

CHAPTER TWELVE

Equal Rights:
Equalizing the Individual's Status and
the Breakthrough of the Modern Liberal State*

1. Gradations of Status in the Societies of the Ancien Régime

Paul of Tarsus was about to be questioned under torture—so the Acts of the Apostles tell us—and preparations had begun. "The chief captain commanded him to be brought into the castle, and bade that he should be examined by scourging." Yet as the Roman soldiers "bound him with thongs, Paul said unto the centurion that stood by, 'Is it lawful for you to scourge a man that is a Roman, and uncondemned?' When the centurion heard that," so the story goes on, "he went and told the chief captain, saying, 'Take heed what thou doest: for this man is a Roman.'" The Latin Vulgate puts it even more precisely: *hic enim homo civis Romanus est*.

> Then the chief captain came, and said unto him, "Tell me, art thou a Roman?" He said, "Yea." And the chief captain answered, "With a great sum obtained I this freedom." And Paul said, "But I was free born." Then straightway they departed from him which should have examined him: and the chief captain also was afraid, after he knew that he was a Roman [*quia civis Romanus esset*] and because he had bound him.[1]

This is a timeless account of the relevance of Status. I shall give a second example—making an immense jump in time, from the first to the eighteenth century AD, and an immense jump in place, from Jerusalem to

*First published in *The Individual in Political Theory and Practice*, ed. by Janet Coleman (series "The Origins of the Modern State in Europe," ed. by the European Science Foundation), Clarendon Press, Oxford 1996, 303–27. The permission to reprint was gracefully granted by the European Science Foundation, Strasbourg.

1. Acts 22: 22–29.

Mexico City. In 1752, a jurist in colonial Mexico, by the name of Dr. Tembra, examined the question as to whether a man, having seduced a girl under promise of marriage, could be judicially obligated to marry her. His arguments on that question ran as follows:

> If the maiden seduced under promise of marriage is inferior in status, so that she would cause greater dishonour to his lineage if he married her than the dishonour that would fall on her by remaining seduced (as if for instance a duke, count, marquis, or gentleman of known nobility were to seduce a mulatto girl, a *china*, a *coyota*, or the daughter of a hangman, a butcher, a tanner) he must [not] marry her because the injury to himself and his entire lineage would be greater than incurred by the maiden by remaining unredeemed, and at any rate one must choose the lesser evil . . . for the latter is an offence of an individual and does no harm to the Republic, while the former is an offence of such gravity that it will denigrate an entire family, dishonour a person of pre-eminence, infame and stain an entire noble lineage and destroy a thing which gives splendour and honour to the Republic. But if the seduced maiden is of only slightly inferior status, of not very marked inequality, so that her inferiority does not cause marked dishonour to the family, then, if the seducer does not wish to endow her, or she justly rejects compensation in the form of endowment, he must be compelled to marry her; because in this case her injury would prevail over the offence inflicted upon the seducer's family, for they would not suffer grave damage through the marriage whereas she would were she not to marry.[2]

This text illustrates the nature of a socio-politico-legal order that is based on a gradation of status. Status, as dealt with in this chapter, does not refer to the frequent present-day usage of "status" in a merely sociological sense. It does not refer to mere "social status" indicated, for example, by the display of conspicuous consumption (T. Veblen) or the lack of it, or other symptoms open to empirical sociological analysis. Status as a central term and theme of this chapter refers to status as a legal quality of the individual, as an inescapable quality of every individual that defines his or her position *vis-à-vis* and within the socio-political-legal order called the "state."

---

2. "Dictamen de Dr. Tembra" concerning "los matrimonios entre consortes desiguales," Madrid, Biblioteca National, Manuscritos de America, in Verena Martinez-Alier, Elopement and Seduction in Nineteenth-Century Cuba, in *Past and Present*, No. 55, (May 1972), 91–129, here 91.

The "Dictamen" has also the advantage—though I shall not dwell on this aspect—of illustrating elements of status hierarchy that are not always thought of in connection with the concept of the *ständisch* (estates) order of the society of the *ancien régime*—the racial elements particularly vividly present in colonial or ex-colonial offshoots of Europe, and also the interesting category of "infamous" occupations—that is "outcast" occupations—such as executioners, comedians, or occupations associated with the remains of dead animals such as butchers, flayers, or tanners.[3]

The gradated nature of the politico-legal order of *ancien régime* society was embedded within a gradated, hierarchical notion of the universe. That notion included for centuries, and well into the early modern period, under God, spirits good and evil surrounding the world of humans. Angels were imagined to exist in a hierarchy of gradation, and hell was imagined as an intricately gradated system of retribution, as grandiosely depicted by Dante. Spiritual beings were seen to impinge on human lives in ways unimaginable in a secularized world, as the work of Jean Delumeau has shown: positively, in the protective power of patron saints and guardian angels;[4] negatively, in its most dreadful manifestation in late medieval and early modern history, in the denunciation of human beings, chiefly women and Jews, as agents of Satan, culminating in the witchcraft craze from the sixteenth to the eighteenth centuries.[5]

The universe and within it the world of humans as a never-broken "Great Chain of Being," to evoke the title of a celebrated work of Arthur Lovejoy: this was the worldview that informs classic texts of European literature, such as Dante's *Divine Comedy*, or the monologue of Ulysses in Shakespeare's *Troilus and Cressida*, "O, when degree is shaked, which is the ladder to all high designs, the enterprise is sick" (Act 1, scene iii). As the long course of the idea of the Great Chain of Being was approaching its end, shaken by new views of nature and the universe, Alexander Pope's *Essay on Man* (1733/34) provided a last summing-up of traditional thought:

Nor let the rich the lowest slave disdain,
He's equally a link of nature's chain;

---

3. See the excellent study by Werner Danckert, *Unehrliche Leute. Die verfemten Berufe* (Bern 1979).

4. Jean Delumeau, *Rassurer et protéger. Le sentiment de sécurité dans l'Occident d'autrefois*, (Paris 1989), 179–247, 293–339.

5. Jean Delumeau, *La peur en occident (XIVe-XVIIIe siècles)*, (Paris 1978), 273–388 (chs. 9–12).

Labours to the same end, joins in one view,
And both alike the will divine pursue.[6]

The notion of the gradated socio-political order, supported by attitudes of deference as well of the obligation "of one's station"—how often genuinely felt, how often not, no one can tell—has been analysed and documented too often to be sketched once more here. Charles Loyseau's *Traité des ordres et simples dignités* of 1610 has been invoked time and again as demonstrating a cross-section of an order based on gradation of status.[7] The most interesting evocation of the model of gradated status as an issue that came to a head in France, occurred on the occasion of the clash between Turgot and the *Parlement* of Paris in March 1776. The traditional constitution "composed of a number of distinct and separate estates" was threatened by Turgot's plan of a conversion of the *corvée royale:*

> Any system which, under a seeming humanity and beneficence, would tend, in a well-ordered kingdom, to establish between men *an equality of duties* and to destroy these necessary distinctions would soon bring about disorder, *the inevitable consequence of absolute equality,* and accomplish the overthrow of civil society, the harmony of which is maintained only *through* this gradation of powers, authorities, preeminences, and distinctions which keeps everyone in his place and safeguards all estates against confusion.[8]

Thirteen years later, the protest against "that unfortunate distinction between orders *which can be regarded as our nation's original sin*" and the postulate that against this distinction be set "an equality of right and power"[9] led to the events of June, July and August 1789. "Indeed, if everything was abolished together in 1789 it was because everything had been defended together at least as early as 1776," Robert Palmer has rightly commented.[10] The minute attention to the hierarchy of titles and privileges—

6. Quoted, with comments, in Arthur O. Lovejoy, *The Great Chain of Being* (Cambridge, MA 1936), 207.

7. Roland Mousnier, *The Institutions of France under the Absolute Monarchy 1598–1789* (Chicago 1979), 4–16; Georges Duby, *The Three Orders* (Chicago 1980), 1, 114, 355. An important study on the notion of gradated (and therefore unequal) orders independent of Duby's work is Tilman Struve, *Die Entwicklung der organologischen Staatsauffassung im Mittelalter* (Stuttgart 1978).

8. Mousnier, *Institutions*, 37–38; see also Robert R. Palmer, *The Age of the Democratic Revolution*, vol. I (Princeton 1959), 451.

9. Deputy's letter, 10 May 1789, quoted in Mousnier, *Institutions*, 38.

10. Palmer, *Age of Democratic Revolution*, 453.

la minutieuse appréciation des rangs (Cournot)—applied not merely to the nobility, but to what Garaud calls the *Tiers-état hiérarchisé* (hierarchized third estate). Cournot wrote that a "cascade of contempt more than anything else has provoked the revolutionary movement."[11]

The exacerbation of differences of legal privilege, though in economic terms largely obsolescent, mattered greatly in mental terms, as Tocqueville has brilliantly shown in his *L'ancien régime et la Revolution* (1856).[12] This kind of exasperation led the upper echelons of the Third Estate to rally around the type of anti-privilege rhetoric symbolized by Sieyes's *Qu'est-ce que le Tiers État?* The enormous success of this anti-privilege rhetoric is to be explained by the bitterness provoked among leading third estate members by the decision of the *Parlement* of Paris of September 1788 that the Estates General meet in the form it had taken in 1614, preceded by the decision of the Estates of Provence late in 1787 to reconvene in the form of their last meeting in 1639.[13]

The status revolution of 1789 was, of course, most clearly expressed in Article 6 of the Declaration of the Rights of Man and the Citizen:

> The law is the expression of the general will. All citizens have the right to join personally or, through their representatives, in its formation. It must be the same for all, whether it protects or punishes. All citizens, *being equal in its eyes,* are equally admissible to all its honours, positions, and public offices according to their ability and without any other distinction than that of their own virtues and talents.[14]

The clash of two worlds brought about by the French Revolution is instructively illustrated by an episode that took place in 1798 in the city of Berlin. In the Prussia of 1798, the *geburtsständisch* (inherited status) world of an *ancien régime* was still functioning. A Prussian aristocrat, Friedrich Ludwig von der Marwitz, recounted how on July 6, 1798 the estates

11. Marcel Garaud, *Histoire générale du droit privé français de 1789 à 1804: La Révolution et l'égalité civile* (Paris 1953), 104, 105, quoting from the *Souvenirs* of Cournot.

12. Tocqueville, *L'ancien regime et la Revolution* (collection Folio-Histoire, Paris 1985), 159–90 (Bk II, chs. 9, 10).

13. Colin Lucas, Nobles, Bourgeois and the Origins of the French Revolution, in *Past and Present*, No. 60 (August 1973), pp. 84–126, here 120–24.

14. "La loi est l'expression de la volonté générale. Tous les citoyens ont le droit de concourir personellement ou par leur représentants à sa formation. Elle doit être la même pour tous, soit qu'elle protège, soit qu'elle punisse. Tous les citoyens, *étant égaux à ses yeux*, sont également admissibles à toutes dignités, places et emplois publics selon leur capacité et sans autre distinction que celle de leurs vertus et de leur talents" (emphasis added).

of Brandenburg did homage to their new Elector and King, Friedrich Wilhelm III. The nobility was admitted to the White Hall of Berlin Castle, the burghers outside in the *Lustgarten*. The diplomatic corps was invited; when the minister of the French Republic, none other than Emmanuel Sieyes, appeared, with an enormous tricolour sash and with black hair (the Prussian aristocrats had powdered hair), he provoked considerable commotion. Marwitz spoke of Sieyes as a "chap with a real scoundrel's face" ("Kerl mit einem wahren Kanaillengesicht"); it was an "evil omen of the times that we would go through eight years later," that is, in 1806.[15]

It might be possible now to go on to a variety of questions that are posed by terms like "status revolution" or "equality," or also by what Mousnier has called the transition from the "society of orders" to a "class society," to "an open class society, whose members, free and equal before the law, should no longer be distinguished from one another except by wealth, talent, and mode of life."[16]

Two major questions need to be examined, however, before proceeding further. First, there is the question as to where, in a hierarchically structured society—part of a hierarchically imagined universe—"reservoirs of equality" or perhaps even traditions of equality might be identified, able to supply patterns of thought to political societies in Europe and North America in the late eighteenth century. Secondly, there is the phenomenon pointed out, a long time ago, by the distinguished German historian Otto Hintze: "The basic principles, on which the modern state rests, appeared, theoretically and practically, in England and America, prior to the French Revolution."[17]

2. "Reservoirs of Equality" before the "Status Revolution"

As to the first question, I shall single out five "reservoirs of equality" with relevance—some controversial, others less so—for the transitions from a society of orders to a society based on equal rights.

1. There was the emergence in city-states of ancient Greece, most notably Athens, of a state of affairs originally called *isonomia* and later *demokratia*. Notions of "equality" have often to do with the quest of

---

15. Otto Brunner, *Neue Wege der Verfassungs- und Sozialgeschichte* (2nd ed., Göttingen 1968), 131.

16. Mousnier *Institutions* (supra note 7), 45.

17. Otto Hintze, *Staat und Verfassung. Gesammelte Abhandlungen zur Allgemeinen Verfassungsgeschichte* (2nd ed., Göttingen 1962), 503.

(originally) weaker or oppressed groups of people against rule considered oppressive, tyrannical, and unjust. It was empirical evidence that led Aristotle to generalize that "the weaker are always asking for equality and justice, but the stronger care for none of these things" (*Politics*, 1318b 4). Isonomy, literally suggesting a regime of "equal laws," was apparently most often invoked and directed against tyranny, against arbitrary rule. A well-known historian of antiquity has noted that isonomy denotes expectations or demands akin to the *Rechtsstaat* (rule of law) or *Verfassungsstaat* (constitutional state) of the nineteenth century, expectations that institutions offer protection against arbitrary rule.[18] The state of affairs called *isonomia* came to be referred to more often (after the mid-fifth century AC) as *demokratia*, a word laying stress on prevalence of might (*kratos*) rather than on law (*nomos*). Johan Huizinga has expressed his regret that those cultures built on the foundations of Greek antiquity have not taken over, instead of the word "democracy," the word "isonomy"; the meaning of isonomy—equal laws—Huizinga suggested, expressed the principles of liberty and of the rule of law better than the word 'democracy.'[19]

Without going into the development of democracy in the Greek polis, and without discussing the extension of the idea of the polis to the—apolitical—"cosmopolis" of the Stoics, two reminders should be sufficient within the context of the theme of this chapter.

First, the equality of political rights to which the *polites* of ancient Greek democracy was entitled, was the equality of one clearly distinguished group of people—of men—on top of a legally stratified population including those living within the *oikos*, including the large group of the *metoikoi*, and including of course slaves. This is important for our theme, because even in the late eighteenth and the first half of the nineteenth centuries, a regime based on the equality of political rights of a part of the population, excluding (originally) even people without sufficient property qualifications, indentured servants, native Americans, and of course slaves, not to speak of women, regarded itself and was considered by others as a democracy.

Secondly, the reception of Aristotle's *Politics* from the second half of the thirteenth century to the eighteenth century—the first English translation only appeared in 1776—transmitted models of political structure including those of the *polis* created by citizens with equal rights, with vast consequences for late medieval and early modern political thought.

18. Christian Meier, Drei Bemerkungen zur Vor- und Frühgeschichte des Begriffs Demokratie, in *Discordia Concors. Festgabe für Edgar Bonjour* (Basel 1968), 10–16, and *idem, Entstehung des Begriffs "Demokratie"* (Frankfurt/Main 1970), 36–41.

19. Johan Huizinga, *Wenn die Waffen schweigen* (Basel 1945), 95.

2. A second "reservoir of equality" was supplied by the Roman civil law. The civil law was the law regulating relations among the *cives Romani* (Roman citizens). Again, Roman citizens were only one, though a growing, group of the population. In a legally stratified society—including, again, slaves as *res* (things)—the *cives Romani*, though themselves hierarchically differentiated,[20] were one group within which there was established the equal use of one kind of law, the civil law. The law of obligations, and there perhaps particularly the law governing the formation of a *societas* as one of *obligationes consensu contractae* (contractual obligations by consent) shows the individuality and equal independence of those entering into a contractual obligation.[21] The saying, *societas nil nisi paribus* (society is nothing except among equals), suggests an element of equal independence of the parties entering into a society. The Roman law model of forming *societates* thus suggests an important figure of thought for the contractualist elements of late medieval and modern natural law thinking.

3. A third "reservoir of equality," vast indeed, must now be examined—Christianity. Alexis de Tocqueville, in his correspondence with Arthur de Gobineau, was very outspoken. "Christianity has placed in a radiant light human equality, unity, and fraternity," Tocqueville wrote to Gobineau in 1843.[22]

> The revolutions which have reversed the old European hierarchy, the progress of wealth and of enlightenment that has rendered individuals very similar to each other, have given immense and unexpected developments to that principle of equality which Christianity had placed rather in the immaterial sphere than in the order of things visible.[23]

This transition from "the immaterial sphere" to the order of "things visible," Tocqueville had explained as follows: "Our society has distanced itself more from Christian theology than from Christian philosophy. Our religious beliefs having become less firm and the sight of the other world more obscure, morality must show itself more indulgent towards material

---

20. Peter Garnsey, *Social Status and Legal Privilege in the Roman Empire* (Oxford 1970); Claude Nicolet, *Le métier de citoyen dans la Rome républicaine* (Paris 1976).

21. Max Kaser, *Römisches Privatrecht* (7th ed., Munich 1972), 153–54. Incidentally, capital societies for commercial purposes developing in the later republic were not limited to Roman citizens; ibid. 45–47.

22. This and the immediately following quotations are from Tocqueville, *Oeuvres complètes*, IX, ed. Mayer et al. (1959), 45–47 (the translations are mine).

23. Ibid.

needs and pleasures."[24] Fourteen years later, in 1857, Tocqueville passionately rejected Gobineau's racist theories. Tocqueville discerned a "distinct
trait" of Christianity, the will to make "one . . . human species of which
all members should be equally capable of perfecting themselves and re-
sembling each other,"[25] and he added: "Christianity has evidently tended
to make of all men brothers and equals."[26]

At the basis of this vision of Christianity, there is, of course, the notion of all men and women being children of God and therefore brothers
and sisters. This notion transcended pre-existing barriers of religious, legal, and social status, as was seen at a very early date, and by no one more
clearly than by St Paul in his Letter to the Galatians: "There is neither Jew
nor Greek, there is neither bond nor free, there is neither male nor female:
for ye are all one in Jesus Christ" (Galatians 3:28). It has been observed, incidentally, in a most interesting discussion on the transition from a *ständisch* society (a society of estates) to *bürgerlich* equality held in 1979, how
the idea of equality was familiar in the European tradition, as shown by
the continuous use of the quotation from Paul's Letter to the Galatians.[27]
Yet there were vast impediments inhibiting the transformation of this
kind of equality to produce the dismantling of hierarchical status differences, replacing these by status equality. Four of these impediments need
to be enumerated:

A. The very idea of respecting existing secular status differences, while
at the same time making status differences look unimportant with regard
to men's relation to God, the hope of redemption, and eternal life, emerges
from Paul's Letter to Philemon, which is concerned with the sending back
of a runaway slave. There is no attack on the status of slavery or of this
particular slave, but this runaway slave is regarded as a brotherly being.
One should not forget, however, that there were occasions when the status
of servitude was held to run against man's creation by God in his image
and when the only origin of servitude was seen in coercion, imprisonment
and unjust violence. This is, at any rate, the remarkable message, or rather
outcry, written c.1230 by Eike von Repgow, author of the law book, *Der
Sachsenspiegel*.[28]

24. Ibid.

25. Ibid., 277.

26. Ibid.

27. Clausdieter Schott, Contribution to the discussion, in *Von der ständischen Gesellschaft zur bürgerlichen Gleichheit* (Beiheft 4 of *Der Staat*, Berlin 1980), 38.

28. Eike von Repgow, *Der Sachsenspiegel*, ed. by Claustdieter Schott (Zürich 1984), 189–91
("Landrecht," III, 42).

B. The entry of Neoplatonic speculations into Christian thought enhanced immeasurably a worldview based on gradation and hierarchy.[29] The hierarchy of earthly conditions, as said before, was only part and parcel of a hierarchical view of the creation visible and invisible, as evidenced by the notions of a hierarchical order of the angels as well as a hierarchical order of hell—immortalized by Dante's *Divine Comedy*.

C. The acceptance of legal and social hierarchies is part and parcel of Church history well into modern times (with possibilities for withdrawal from the world for those following the counsels of perfection in monastic communities or as hermits). Cases in point abound. One, particularly telling, occurs in 1727. The bishop of London was urging slave owners in English plantations overseas to baptize slaves; there was no suggestion of freeing them:

> Christianity, and the embracing of the Gospel, does not make the least alteration in Civil Property, or in any of the Duties which belong to Civil Relations; but in all these Respects, it continues Persons just in the same State as it found them. The Freedom which Christianity gives, is a Freedom from the Bondage of Sin and Satan, and from the Dominion of Mens Lusts and Passions and inordinate Desires; but as to their outward Condition, whatever that was before, whether bond or free, their being baptiz'd, and becoming Christians, makes no manner of Change in it . . . And so far is Christianity from discharging Men from the Duties of the Station and Condition in which it found them, that it lays them under stronger Obligations to perform those Duties with the greatest Diligence and Fidelity.[30]

In traditional status society, equality was found in death, as the topos of the *danse macabre* and similar emblematic representations demonstrate. The reversal of earthly fortune and earthly station through divine justice at the Last Judgement was a consequence of the favouring of the poor in the New Testament, making their prayer important for the redemption of the rich and powerful (thus injecting energy into charitable care for the poor).

D. The notion of equal brotherliness found its limits in attitudes toward heretics, Jews, and infidels. A modern thought like that expressed

---

29. For this see Lovejoy, *The Great Chain of Being* (supra note 6).

30. Quoted from Edmund Gibson, *Two Letters from the Bishop of London* (London 1727), in Winthrop D. Jordan, *White over Black* (Chapel Hill, NC 1968), 191.

by Mr. Justice Holmes on "Freedom for the thought that we hate" was incompatible with the claim that truth was known and therefore entitled to a position of monopoly.

Running counter to these tendencies to undo the possibilities of Christian equality in this world, I shall single out two developments that have indeed paved the way for notions of "equal rights" in the modern sense:

a. The development of the individual's "liberty of conscience"—a liberty of conscience not merely as "tolerance" imposed by external forces, but as a spiritual force, and as a subjective right, deserving respect and recognition by the powers that be.[31] It is, as the work of Hans R. Guggisberg and others has shown, a development not antedating the sixteenth century.[32]

b. The withdrawal of the State—the modern State—from its association with one belief system. Beyond the developments provoked by the Reformation and the establishment of various (often unequal) balances for toleration or mutual recognition, the emergence of the first religiously neutral state, the United States of America, is an event of monumental significance for the breakthrough of the "modern" State. An early and significant illustration of the United States' neutrality was the way in which, in 1790, President Washington addressed a Jewish congregation in terms of equality rather than of mere "tolerance": "It is now no more that *tolerance* is spoken of, as if it was by the indulgence of one class of people, that another enjoyed the exercise of their inherent natural rights."[33]

The fundamental importance of the American constitution's prohibition on Congress from making any laws concerning the establishment of religion, preceded by the fight of James Madison and Thomas Jefferson to disestablish the Episcopalian state church in Virginia, has been underestimated by many scholars working in the field of the history of human rights. In the first volume of *De la démocratie en Amérique* (*Democracy in America*), Tocqueville was to observe that as long as priests entered society as an established, ruling power and came "to place themselves there in the midst of the social hierarchy," using religious influence to assure

31. Martin Kriele, *Einführung in die Staatslehre* (Reinbek 1975), 116–19.

32. Hans R. Guggisberg, Wandel der Argumente für religiöse Toleranz und Glaubensfreiheit, in Heinrich Lutz, ed., *Zur Geschichte der Toleranz und Religionsfreiheit* (Darmstadt 1977); *idem*, The Secular State of the Reformation Period and the Beginnings of the Debate on Religious Toleration, in Janet Coleman, ed., *The Individual in Political Theory and Practice* (Oxford 1996), 79–98.

33. George Washington to the Hebrew Congregation of Newport, Rhode Island, 18 Aug. 1790, in *Writings of George Washington*, XXI, 93n.

the endurance of a political order, Catholics would be partisans of the aristocracy "as a result of their religious mentality." In the United States, on the other hand, where priests "were distanced from or distanced themselves from governments," Catholics were quite disposed "to transfer the idea of the equality of conditions to the political world."[34]

4. Natural law as a "reservoir of equality." There is no question that natural law writing, particularly in the early modern period from the sixteenth to the eighteenth centuries, supplies important sources for the development and final breakthrough of the idea of equal rights. The liberty of man in the "state of nature" consists in his independence. This independence he shares equally with other independent persons, whether strong or weak. Equal independence means an equal right to enter into contracts, particularly into the social contract, as was shown at a fairly early date (1514) by the Roman writer Mario Salamonio.[35] It is indeed an equality of right, not an equality of material or physical strength or possession.[36] It has been persuasively observed that the *libertas naturalis* of early modern natural law theories is chiefly and lastly the liberty of entering into a contract—of most varied contents, possibly including far-reaching or even complete losses of the *iura connata* of the original "state of nature."[37] As Samuel Pufendorf put it: "Thereafter, equality through civic status was taken away."[38]

One additional point on natural law teaching with respect to "equality" seems relevant: it must be stressed that the abstract character of natural law writing on man in the "state of nature" has an important individualist consequence. Abstract man in the "state of nature" appears in a more individualistic guise than in the post–contractual civil state. The various communities within the *societas civilis cum imperio* (civil society with empire) are post–contractual, not pre–contractual realities. However,

34. "s'y s'asseoir au milieu de la hierarchie sociale;" . . . "par esprit de religion;" . . . "sont écartés ou s'écartent du gouvernement;" . . . "à transporter dans le monde politique l'idée de l'égalité des conditions." Tocqueville, *De la démocratie en Amerique* (1951), I, 302.

35. Quentin Skinner, *The Foundations of Modern Political Thought*, 2 vols. (Cambridge 1978), ii, 132.

36. Diethelm Klippel, *Politische Freiheit und Freiheitsrechte im deutschen Naturrecht des 18. Jahrhunderts* (Paderborn 1976), 163.

37. Ibid., 45. On medieval natural law theory and rights: Janet Coleman, The Individual and the Medieval State, in *idem*, ed., *The Individual in Political Theory and Practice*, 1–34. For 17th century British discussions: Iain Hampsher-Monk, The State and the Individual: Seventeenth-Eighteenth Centuries: Theorizing the Challenge of Subjective Individualism in Britain, in ibid., pp. 243–67.

38. "Aequalitas deinde per statum civilem fuit sublata." Pufendorf, *De iure naturae* (3. 2. 9).

this presentation not infrequently forgets, as it were, man's pre–civil contractual possibilities: the *societas conjugalis* (conjugal relationship), the
societas paterna (patriarchal family), the *societas herilis* (the master's domain), the society, in other words, of the "entire house" or *domus* as *societas composita ex coniugali, paterna et herili* (society composed of marriage partners, father and family, and master and servants).[39]

Man entering by contract into civil society is thus man standing on
top of the pyramid of pre-civil and therefore pre-public *imperium priva-
tum* (private authority). Ambiguities of social contract terminology sometimes betray this, for example, when John Locke in one and the same
paragraph speaks first of "the individuals that enter into or make up a
commonwealth," and then goes on to speak of the "consent of any number
of freemen capable of majority" who unite and incorporate into a political
society (*Second Treatise*, § 99). Some authors have very clearly expressed
the fact that persons contractually entering into and thus forming civil society carry with them persons of dependent (and therefore unequal) status.
Bodin in his *Six livres de la Republique* had spoken of the uniting of *plusieurs ménages* (several households) forming civil society. Pufendorf sees
only the *patresfamilias* concluding the social contract.[40]

Though early modern natural law theory turns out to be more flexible than sometimes assumed, it seems important, for the purpose of our
theme, to point to one important difference among natural law theorists.
While Grotius, Pufendorf, and the tradition following them down to Christian Wolff are inclined to accept the (explicit or tacit) contracting away of
one's personal freedom, there is another line of thought that stresses the
immutability,[41] or, even more sharply expressed, the inalienability of fundamental natural rights. Thomas Hobbes, radical egalitarian in his diag-
nosis of man's basic motivating forces, stated that "the right men have by
nature to protect themselves, when none else can protect them, can by no
covenant be relinquished" (*Leviathan,* pt 2, ch. 21). John Locke stated that
"a man, not having the power of his own life, cannot by compact or his
own assent enslave himself to anyone, nor put himself under the absolute,
arbitrary power of another to take away his life when he pleases" (*Second*

39. Wolff, *Jus naturae*, pt 7, "De imperio private," quoted in Klippel *Politische Freiheit*
(supra note 36), 36.

40. Pufendorf, *De jure naturae* (2. 2. 4.), quoted in Klippel *Politische Freiheit* (supra note
36), 37.

41. The Spanish lay jurist, Fernando Vasquez, in 1563, spoke *of iura naturalia . . . quasi
immutabilia*, in the Preface to the Second edition of *Controversiae illustres*; quoted in Ernst
Reibstein, *Johannes Althusius als Fortsetzer der Schule von Salamanca* (Karlsruhe 1955), 139.

Treatise, § 22). A line of thought stressing the inalienability of certain rights[42] was bound to thrive when enlisted in the cause of resistance to authority considered arbitrary or tyrannical.[43] Inalienability thus became the battle cry of declarations of natural rights from America to France; men cannot, as was stated with particular precision in the Virginia Bill of Rights, "by any compact deprive or divest their posterity" of the inherent rights of "the enjoyment of life and liberty, with the means of acquiring and possessing property and pursuing and obtaining happiness and safety." Some sophistry went into the making of the Virginia Bill of Rights in view of the fact that slave-owners were the drafters of that document.[44]

5. There is a fifth "reservoir of equality," deserving attention. The centralizing tendencies of the State in the age of absolutism worked in favour of creating, vis-à-vis the ruler, the great mass of "subjects," of *Untertanen,* as the German word suggests more forcefully than the English one (in view of the fact that the English word "subject" is so closely connected with the notion of the "liberties of the subject" which was exactly what was missing in continental absolutist states). Depending on the extent to which all "nationals" of a particular state were subject to the sovereign ruler, and more particularly on the extent to which the ruler's administration or system of justice established more direct relations between "the state" and the individual, a general "association of all subjects" (*allgemeiner Untertanenverband*) could be imagined which was—theoretically—characterized by an equality of submission to the sovereign ruler.[45] A German legal theorist of the mid-nineteenth century thus felt justified to speak of a *Gleichheit des Unterthanenverhältnisses*—an equality of the

42. On this theme, see the suggestive reflections by Blandine Barret-Kriegel, *Les droits de l'homme et le droit naturel* (Paris 1989), 58–60. See Coleman, *op. cit.* (supra note 37) on medieval discussions of inalienable rights.

43. Even Blackstone on occasion—when referring to the Glorious Revolution—would adopt this line of argument, as I have shown in "William Blackstone: Teacher of Revolution;" in this volume, Chapter 2. On rights to resist unjust government in 16th-cent. Dutch discussions, see Martin van Gelderen, Liberty, Civil Rights, and Duties in Sixteenth Century Europe and the Rise of the Dutch Republic, in Coleman, ed., *The Individual in Political Theory and Practice*, 99–122.

44. Gerald Stourzh, *Wege zur Grundrechtsdemokratie. Studien zur Begriffs- und Institutionengeschichte des liberalen Verfassungsstaats* (Vienna 1989), 159.

45. Rolf Grawert, *Staat und Staatsangehörigkeit. Verfassungsgeschichtliche Untersuchungen zu Entstehung der Staatsangehörigkeit* (Berlin 1973), 165; Reiner Schulze, Statusbildung und Allgemeinheit der Bürgerrechte in Verfassungstexten und Staatslehre des frühen deutschen Konstitutionalismus, in Gerhard Dilcher et al., eds., *Grundrechte im 19. Jahrhundert* (Frankfurt/Main–Bern 1982), 111n. 28.

condition of subject vis-à-vis the ruler.[46] There is, of course, a problem of perspective: historians of the absolutist State and its administrative reforms inevitably stress the element of growing uniformity and therefore "equality"; historians of social structure, particularly those of rural society, are bound to stress the status hierarchies of "the world we have lost" (to use Peter Laslett's phrase).

3. Principles of the Modern State in England and America

Let us now turn to the second question mentioned above: we are confronted with the fact that the basic principles on which the modern State rests appeared prior to the French Revolution in England and America. Otto Hintze, already referred to, has pointed to the unique structure of the House of Commons among the corporate estates of Europe. Another distinctive characteristic was the mingling of the gentry with non-gentry freeholders and the well-to-do elements of corporate boroughs: such a mingling of the different orders was not to be found elsewhere; it was characteristically English.[47] Status rights—as distinct from property rights—from very early times have been of lesser significance in the English legal tradition than on the continent of Europe.

The unique structure of the Commons—and of course their electorate—in early modern England enabled the category of "free born Englishmen" to make an early appearance in England, without to my knowledge finding a terminological equivalent in continental countries, not even those with a strong contribution from or even prevalence of bourgeois or peasant elements. The distinction between free and unfree ("villain") was pronounced obsolete in early modern times.[48]

The constitutional struggles of the English seventeenth century led, of course, to an emphasis on these liberties and rights of Englishmen, finding their early and most significant expression in the Petition of Right of 1628. The Petition of Right is a more significant document with regard to individual rights than the Bill of Rights of 1689, because the latter is above all a document embodying guarantees of corporate rights, while the Petition of

46. Karl Mittermaier, "Bürgerstand," in *Staatslexikon*, ed. C. Rotteck and C. Welcker (1845–), quoted in Schulze (supra note 45), 111n. 28.

47. Hintze, *Staat und Verfassung* (supra note 17), 28.

48. Sir Matthew Hale, *The Analysis of the Law. Being a Scheme or Abstract, of several Titles and Partitions of the Law of England, digested into Method* (London 1713), preface, fol. A 3, and ch. II, 5.

Right of 1628 concentrates on safeguarding the rights of individuals. How popular these notions were becoming is illustrated, among other sources, in an unofficial catalogue of the rights of Englishmen appearing (1669) in the work *Angliae notitia* of Edward Chamberlayne. There the transition from a socio-politico-legal structure based on the three orders to a more modern structure may be seen very precisely. It was said: "As the Clergy and Nobility have certain Priviledges peculiar to themselves, so they have Liberties and Properties common to the Commonalty of England . . . The Commons of England for hereditary fundamental Liberties and Properties are blest above and beyond the Subjects of any Monarch in the World."

There follow eight "liberties and properties" of the commons of England, that I have published elsewhere. Let me merely add that as early as 1670 there appeared a German translation in the *Diarium Europaeum* in Frankfurt that I have also published elsewhere.[49]

Yet there is an additional dimension of English thought where a paramount place was assigned to individual rights: the realm of legal theory, of legal systematizing. Sir Edward Coke's four *Institutes* of the laws of England were written along pragmatic rather than systematic lines. Yet the first ambitious and the most consequential modern effort to encompass the laws of England in a theoretical System, "digested into method," Sir Matthew Hale's *Analysis of the Law,* written prior to 1676, published in 1713, 37 years after his death, resulted in a different system. In his *Analysis,* Hale discarded the distinction between common law and statute law and based his system exclusively on the matter of law: he distinguished only between two large matters of law: "Civil Rights" (including the remedies pertaining thereto), and "Crimes and Misdemeanors." Constitutional and administrative laws (never mentioned as such) were subsumed under the "civil part of the law." Under the heading "Of the Rights of the People or Subjects," Hale first distinguished between "Rights of Duty, to be perform'd" and "Rights of Privilege, to be enjoy'd." This terminology is notable, because it reveals that "Rights" were understood to mean "legal relationships" among persons. For "Rights of Privilege," Hale also employed the better known term "liberties." Hale—remarkably, prior to John Locke—then noted:

The *Rights and Liberties* to be enjoy'd by the People, both in relation to the King, and all his *subordinate* Magistrates, are, That they be protected by them, and treated according to the Laws of the Kingdom, in relation to,

---

49. Stourzh, *Grundrechtsdemokratie* (supra note 44), 34–35.

1. Their Lives.
2. Their Liberties.
3. Their Estates.[50]

William Blackstone, under the influence of Hale according to his own acknowledgement, similarly subsumed constitutional law under his treatment of the "Rights of Persons."[51] Rights and liberties, "a number of private immunities," that had been formerly the rights of all mankind, but "in most other countries of the world being now more or less debased and destroyed," might be said "to remain, in a peculiar and emphatical manner, the rights of the people of England." These rights, Blackstone continued, "may be reduced to three principal or primary articles; the right of personal security, the right of personal liberty; and the right of private property."[52]

Even more interesting, and certainly more surprising, are the implications deriving from the need to secure these "principal absolute rights." To secure them, the constitution had established certain other auxiliary subordinate rights of the subject, "which serve principally as barriers to protect and maintain inviolate the three great and primary rights of personal security, personal liberty, and private property." These "auxiliary and subordinate rights of the subject" were five in number:

1. The "constitution, powers, and privileges of parliament";
2. The "limitation of the king's prerogative, by bounds so certain and notorious, that it is impossible he should exceed them without the consent of the people";
3. The right of every Englishman "of applying to the courts of justice for redress of injuries";
4. The right of "petitioning the king, or either house of parliament";
5. The right of "having arms for their defence" as allowed by law.[53]

Systematizing the competences of Parliament or the king's prerogative as "auxiliary and subordinate rights of the subject" is an extraordinary feat which is scarcely paralleled in continental states. One may compare Blackstone's system of the laws of England to the system presented by a legal

50. Hale, *Analysis* (supra note 48), 42–44.
51. Stourzh, *Grundrechtsdemokratie* (supra note 44), 76–84.
52. William Blackstone, *Commentaries on the Laws of England* (Oxford 1765–69), I, 125.
53. Ibid., 136–39.

writer in one of the freest countries of the European continent, the Netherlands. This was Ulric Huber, who taught at the University of Franeker
in Friesland; in 1682 Huber published his vast work on the jurisprudence
of his time.[54] Huber, who was of course a civil lawyer, divided rights into
public or State rights on the one hand, and private or individual rights on
the other. Huber also included in his work a book devoted to "The State,
and the Officers of Justice," and in special chapters he treated such matters
as the State, sovereignty, and government. These are features absent from
Hale's and Blackstone's system. That there remain basic and unresolved
conflicts with regard to Blackstone's doctrine of legislative sovereignty is
obvious, but not a matter to be discussed here.

The tradition represented by Hale and Blackstone was continued by
Albert Dicey who very clearly expressed the gist of the matter. The law of
the constitution, wrote Dicey, "the rules which in foreign countries naturally form part of a constitutional code, are not the source but the consequence of the rights of individuals, as defined and enforced by the courts";
the "principles of private law," he continued, "have with us been by the
action of the courts and Parliament so extended as to determine the position of the Crown and of its servants; thus the constitution is the result of
the ordinary law of the land."[55]

No less a figure than Frederick Maitland has observed that "constitutional law" was no technical term of English law.[56] The fact that matters
of constitutional law were systematically subsumed under the "Rights of
Persons" was evidence of a strong presumption in favour of the central and
primary place of individual rights in the English legal mind.

There was, then, in England a strong tendency in legal discourse as well
as in political and constitutional rhetoric, to put individual rights ahead of
categories such as sovereignty or the State. This sort of development I have
characterized with the term "fundamentalizing" individual rights in England. I am distinguishing the process of "fundamentalizing" individual
rights from the process of "constitutionalizing" individual rights.[57] "Constitutionalization" refers to a process of entrenching individual rights on a

54. Ulric Huber, Heedensdaegse Rechtsgeleertheyt (1682), English translation: *The Jurisprudence of my Time* (Durban 1939).

55. Albert V. Dicey, *An Introduction to the Study of the Law of the Constitution* (10th ed.)
(London 1965), 203.

56. Frederic W. Maitland, *The Constitutional History of England* (Cambridge 1908), 527.

57. Gerald Stourzh, *Fundamental Laws and Individual Rights in the 18th Century Constitution* (Claremont, CA 1984), 11–12.

level of constitutional norms that are above the power and competence of the normal legislator to change or abolish.

The constitutionalization of individual rights first began in the North American colonies. Of particular significance is the Charter or Fundamental Laws of West New Jersey in 1676. The eleven articles of this "Charter" chiefly embody rights with reference to criminal procedure, including habeas corpus. The most important aspect of there eleven articles, however, was the fact that they were entrenched, as it were, and put beyond the reach of the legislative power of West New Jersey. These fundamental individual rights were agreed upon "to be the foundation of the Government which is not to be altered by the Legislative Authority or free Assembly hereafter mentioned and constituted."[58] The idea of entrenching—beyond and above the reach of legislative power—individual rights is what is meant by "constitutionalizing" individual rights. This process came to full flowering after the breaking-away of the colonies from Great Britain, in the years of constitution building from 1776 to 1787 and 1789.[59] The impact of the American Bills of Rights, particularly of that of Virginia, on the French document of 1789 has been discussed so frequently, the controversy between Georg Jellinek and Emile Boutmy being the most famous, but by no means the only discussion of this issue, that a more detailed exposition in this paper is not needed.[60]

4. The New Social Language and the Process of Status Equalization

It has well been said that the French Revolution may be seen

> as the destruction of one social language and its replacement by a new and radically different one, a language which put nature in the place of God and contract in the place of religious oath, and which reduced the vast and varied collections of *états*, *corps* and *ordres* to a single *État* with a unified general will.[61]

58. Ibid., 13. See also the immediately following chapter, notably pp. 314–18.
59. Gerald Stourzh, "Constitution: Changing Meanings of the Term from the Early Seventeenth Century to the Late Eighteenth Century," supra Chapter 3, notably pp. 95–99.
60. Stourzh, *Grundrechtsdemokratie* (supra note 44), 155–74.
61. William H. Sewell, État, Corps and Ordre: Some Notes on the Social Vocabulary of the French Old Regime, in Hans-Ulrich Wehler, ed., *Sozialgeschichte heute. Festgabe für Hans Rosenberg zum 70. Geburtstag* (Göttingen 1974), 65.

Among the key words of the new social language—to be precise the new
socio-politico-legal language—there are, of course, "Man" and "Citizen,"
"Liberty" and "Equality." This radically new social language had roots
and precedents in what had gone on before in England and particularly
in North America, and in the vocabulary of natural law writers in many
countries, including France. Among the key words of this radically new
social language, I shall concentrate on two, "man" and "equality," because
they are apt to demonstrate the profound change from the older ways of
Status gradation to new ways of Status equalization.

In what follows, I use 'man' in the sense of *Mensch*, not *Mann*. It is
one of the incomprehensible weaknesses of French and English, that these
languages have not developed a word for human beings that would encompass both man and woman. In 1781, there appeared in Berlin a book by
Christian Wilhelm Dohm, *Über die bürgerliche Verbesserung der Juden*.
The occasion for the writing of this book, as Robert Badinter has recently
shown, went back to the Jewish community in Alsace, whose head, Théo-
dore Cerf-Berr, had enlisted the help of Moses Mendelsohn in Berlin to
reply to an anti-Jewish pamphlet, and Mendelsohn in his turn had enlisted
the writing talent of the Prussian professor and writer Christian Wilhelm
Dohm.[62] "Der Jude ist noch mehr Mensch als Jude"—"the Jew is even
more a human being than a Jew"—this is perhaps the key sentence of the
book.[63] In view of this human rights argument, Dohm pleaded that reason
and justice demanded that the Jews be accorded civil rights. The book was
very quickly translated into French, appearing in 1782 under the title *De
la reforme politique des juifs*. A second part, taking issue with some of
the reactions provoked by the book of 1781, followed in 1783. One main
concern of Dohm's book was to advocate what I should like to call the
equalization of the Jews' legal status. A full reading of the passage where
the key statement appears—"the Jew is even more man than Jew"—con-
firms this interpretation:

> The Jew is even more man than Jew, and how should it be possible that
> he should not love a State, in which he could acquire and enjoy free
> property, in which his taxes would not be greater than those of the
> other citizens, and where he, too, could acquire honour and respect?

62. Robert Badinter, *Libres et égaux . . . L'émancipation des Juifs 1789–1791* (Paris 1989),
67–71.

63. Christian Konrad Wilhelm Dohm, *Über die bürgerliche Verbesserung der Juden*,
2 vols. (Berlin and Stettin 1781–83), I, 28 (reprint in one volume Hildesheim and New York
1973); Reinhard Rürup, *Emanzipation und Antisemitismus* (Frankfurt/Main 1987), 18.

Why should he hate people, who would no longer be separated from him by grievous privileges, with whom he would share equal rights and equal duties?[64]

The Jews were, of course, a group that had lived under a special status, often regulated by the *privilegia odiosa* of special orders issued by the territorial sovereign under whose protection they happened to live. The sentence, "Der Jude ist noch mehr Mensch als Jude" appropriately expresses—symbolically and vicariously, as it were—the claim of all groups of people living under a status of limited legal capacity, or sometimes virtually nonexistent legal capacity, living, in other words, under the disabilities of special status. The slave is more man than slave. The serf is more man than serf.[65] The comedian—to name another group of people with limited rights in the gradated structure of the *ancien régime*—is more man (or woman) than comedian. Woman, finally—thinking of Condorcet's *De l'admission des femmes au droit de cité* or of the *Déclaration des droits de la femme et citoyenne* of Olympe de Gouges—woman is more a human being than a woman.[66] Also, one may add—and this status distinction remains one of the most important to the present—the stranger is more man than stranger.[67] Jews, slaves, serfs, comedians, non-believers in the established religion, women, strangers—all of them were groups characterized by peculiar traits of inferior legal status. On the other hand, there were of course the privileged orders of the *ancien régime*. All of them were to be drawn into an equalizing process best described as a process of equalization of legal capacities. "To the extent to which conditions were equalized"—"à

64. "Der Jude ist noch mehr Mensch als Jude, und wie wäre es möglich, dass er einen Staat nicht lieben sollte, in dem er ein freyes Eigenthum erwerben, und desselben frey geniessen könnte, wo seine Abgaben nicht grösser als die andrer Bürger wären, und wo auch von ihm Ehre und Achtung erworben werden könnte? Warum sollte er Menschen hassen, die keine kränkende Vorrechte mehr von ihm scheiden, mit denen er gleiche Rechte und gleiche Pflichten hätte?" Dohm, *Verbesserung* (supra note 63), I, 28.
65. On slavery and serfdom, respectively, reference should be made to five outstanding volumes. On slavery and the anti-slavery movement: David Brion Davis, *The Problem of Slavery in Western Culture* (Ithaca, NY 1966): idem, *The Problem of Slavery in the Age of Revolution* (Ithaca, NY 1975); Thomas Bender, ed., *The Antislavery Debate. Capitalism and Abolitionism as a Problem of Historical Interpretation* (Berkeley, CA 1992). On serfdom: Jerome Blum, *The End of the Old Order in Rural Europe,* (Princeton, NJ 1978); Peter Kolchin, *Unfree Labor. American Slavery and Russian Serfdom* (Cambridge, MA 1987).
66. Joan B. Landes, *Women and the Public Sphere in the Age of the French Revolution* (1988), 112–17, 124–27.
67. Particular reference is made to *L'Étranger. Recueils de la société Jean Bodin*, 2 vols. (Brussels 1958).

mesure que les conditions s'égalisent," as Tocqueville said—modern individualism as a democratic phenomenon has emerged.[68]

There is no doubt that the transformation from aristocratic to democratic society that is the central theme of Tocqueville's work and that is
characterized by Tocqueville's stress on the emergence of what he calls
égalité des conditions, goes beyond the equalizing of legal status; however,
it does not go as far as to include material equality, equality of fortunes,
and this may present a major difficulty in understanding Tocqueville's
égalité des conditions which certainly includes great varieties in the rise
and fall of individual fortunes; yet the lifting or disappearance of status
discrimination was both a sign of social transformation and an indispensable precondition for the further development of the *conditions d'égalité* of
modern liberal democracy.[69]

There is a profound truth in the use of the term "emancipation" to refer to the processes of lifting disabilities of legal status and thereby equalizing the rights of persons. This term, derived from the Latin *emancipatio,*
applied to the process of lifting the disabilities of those subject to the Roman *patria potestas,* of persons *alieni iuris* becoming persons *sui iuris,* in
their own right. One meaning of Henry Sumner Maine's famous observation of the shift from status to contract was precisely to indicate a process
when "the subordinate members of the family ceased to be entirely subject
to the paterfamilias and came to acquire an independent legal capacity of
their own."[70]

Terms current in modern and contemporary history, such as "Jewish
emancipation," the "emancipation of slaves," "Catholic emancipation" (in
England), the "emancipation of women" may be understood on a new level
of comprehension if the background of status disabilities and the purpose
of status equalization are fully grasped. This process of status equalization—within the context of the history of the modern State—has been im-

---

68. Tocqueville, *De la démocratie en Amerique* (1951 ed.), II, 106 (2, 2). It is interesting
that the phrase "à mesure que les conditions s'égalisent" occurs twice in the same brief chapter. For more details, see the essay on Tocqueville in this volume, Chapter 14.

69. In 1867 the Swiss historian Jacob Burckhardt compared the *ancien régime* with his
own times in categories not unlike those of Tocqueville; he stressed legal equality, the free dis-
ponibility of real property, the equalization of inheritance laws, and the "beginnings of absolute
political equality." Commenting on the disappearance of the privilege of birth, he argued that
money, the successor to birth and now "the great measure of things;" was more just than birth
because it did not remain long with incompetent heirs. Burckhardt, *Historische Fragmente,* ed.
Dürr (1957), 261–62, quoted in Stourzh, *Grundrechtsdemokratie* (supra note 44), 364.

70. Geoffrey MacCormack, Status: Problems of Definition and Use, in *Cambridge Law
Journal,* vol. 43, No. 2 (Nov. 1984), 361–76, here 362–63.

mensely expedited, if not triggered, by the breakdown of the old order of gradated status hierarchies and the new discourse on the rights of man and citizen in the second half of the eighteenth century, though it is a process that was to continue through the nineteenth and, in various forms, through the twentieth century as well.

The significance of the discourse on the rights of man, from the time of its passage from the writings of natural law theorists into public opinion, and even more particularly from the moment of its transition into constitutional and legal documents—what in German is called *Positivierung des Naturrechts*—lies precisely in two points.

First, the quality of man—*Mensch*, not *Mann*—as a quality equally pertaining to all human beings now becomes a *tertium comparationis* of vastly greater importance than ever before. To treat equal things equally, unequal ones unequally, is a time-honoured principle of justice. Let us return for a few moments to Dohm's ringing phrase, "The Jew is even more a man than a Jew." Comparing Jews and non-Jews, the *tertium comparationis*—the quality of being human—now becomes the common denominator at the basis of the postulate that both Jews and non-Jews be accorded equal rights, because the quality of being human belongs both to Jews and non-Jews.

Secondly, the quality of man that now becomes the *tertium comparationis* or yardstick to be applied to the task of assessing men's place in society, is an essentially legal quality. The human being who is the subject matter of natural law teaching now enshrined in a constitutional text like la *Déclaration des droits de l'homme et du citoyen* of 1789 is essentially a legal being. No one seems to have seen and expressed this more clearly than the German-French philosopher Bernhard Groethuysen. Even if he wished to, Groethuysen has written, man cannot renounce his natural rights. Man cannot renounce being human and thus rid himself of his legal status. It suffices to be human in order to possess rights: Groethuysen has summarized the essence of the natural rights philosophy. It is the recognition of men's humanity as a legal quality that accounts for the increase of the relevance of that *tertium comparationis*: the humanity common to Jews and non-Jews, to bond and free, men and women, and so on.[71]

The discourse on the rights of men and citizens, then, has enabled claims for the equalizing—the French *égaliser* used by Tocqueville sounds less artificial—of status differences. Thus it is perfectly justified that

---

71. Bernhard Groethuysen, *Philosophie der Französischen Revolution* (Neuwied 1971), 118–25. For the following Jacques Godechot, *Les institutions de la France sous la Révolution et l'Empire*, 2nd ed. (Paris 1968), 48–58.

Jacques Godechot, in his magisterial work *Les institutions de la France sous la Révolution et l'Empire* under the heading "Equality" deals with the special status groups of women, comedians, serfs, Protestants, Jews, and people of colour. As we know, the right of suffrage (Robespierre's motion notwithstanding) was not granted, but on 20 September 1792, the day of the victory at Valmy, the Legislative Assembly granted women equality of civil status, including the right to be a witness in civil actions. As for comedians, they benefited from the secularization of the *état civil* in September 1792. The end of servitude came of course officially in the night of 4 August, de facto in March 1790. The Protestants, enjoying the support of Malesherbes, had seen important disabilities removed in the last years of the *ancien régime* (*état civil* given to Protestant ministers in 1787–88); the National Assembly in 1790 returned those properties still in national hands that had been confiscated under Louis XIV. As for the Jews, their emancipation occurred in two stages, whereas in the case of people of colour those in mainland France were freed, those (virtually all of them) in the colonies were left to the devices of colonial assemblies, that is, to the devices of their masters. . . .

There has to be added an important observation. The natural rights enthusiasm of the political language of the American and French Revolutions, as well as the revival of the language of the rights of man since the end of the Second World War, documented by the Universal Declaration of Human Rights of 1948, the European Convention on Human Rights and Fundamental Liberties of 1950, and numerous additional documents, has tended to obscure an important fact. In terms of legal development, the rights of the citizen have proved to be a more important catalyst of the forces in favour of equal rights than the rights of man. The territorial imperative of political organization, as well as the replacement of natural rights thinking by other schools of legal thought, historical or positivist, was, during the nineteenth century, to channel guarantees of general rights into the framework of citizens' rights: the Belgian Constitution of 1830 evokes the "Rights of Belgians"; the German Revolution of 1848 produces a catalogue of the fundamental rights of the German people, and so on.

Thus the "normal person" of modern law is, in the first place, the citizen. If "status" has been defined by a legal writer as "a special condition of a continuous and institutional nature, differing from the legal position of the normal person,"[72] the status of the stranger, whether foreign citi-

---

72. MacCormack, Status (supra note 70) 368, quoting from Ronald H. Graveson, *Status in the Common Law* (London 1953).

zen or—even worse—"stateless," continues to be a special and precarious one. In spite of important equalizing developments concerning the status of strangers—sometimes, as in the Napoleonic Code, on the basis of reciprocity—the "foreigner" will retain a "special" status and will become, with the disappearance of many other status inequalities toward the end of the twentieth century, the most important single category of persons subject to legal disabilities of various kinds.

With the definition of man as a legal being by nature, with the emergence of citizenship as a vast category full of promises of equal rights, and, it has to be added, with the emergence of economic and social circumstances that put a premium on general rights at the expense of specific status rights, a double tendency in direction of the *generalization* and equalization of legal capacity was unleashed. There was unleashed a trend towards what has been called, in the felicitous words of Geoffrey Sawer, "a regime of equal capacity,"[73] or, as one might say perhaps even more accurately, a regime approximating, though never fully attaining, equal capacity. Why this qualification? Because "pockets" of certain disabilities—concerning children and minors, criminals, the insane, and "foreigners"—are likely to remain even in those political societies that grant rights and freedoms to the utmost without any distinction of "race, colour, sex, language, religion, political or other opinion, national or social origin, property, birth or other status"—to employ the words of the Universal Declaration of Human Rights of 1948.

The transition from a society based on status hierarchies to a society based on a "regime of equal capacity" calls to mind, of course, the celebrated phrase on the transition from status to contract, already referred to. Without going into the controversies that have been caused by Maine's famous statement,[74] and without commenting on "the rise and fall" of the freedom of contract and new limitations on the freedom of contract that have arisen through social policy legislation, one important point needs to be made. The major transition from societies of the *ancien régime* type to societies of the liberal democratic type has not been the transition from "status to contract"; it has been the transition from societies based on a hierarchy and multiplicity of status positions to societies where the category of citizenship—as has brilliantly been shown by T. H. Marshall in his

73. G. Sawer, *Law in Society* (Oxford 1965), 66, quoted in R. C. J. Cocks, *Sir Henry Maine. A Study in Victorian Jurisprudence* (Cambridge 1988), 178.

74. Sir Henry Sumner Maine, *Ancient Law*, (5th ed.) (London 1874) 170, and comments by Cocks, *Sir Henry Maine*, 169–80.

lectures on 'Citizenship and Social Class'[75]—has been able to level former status differences—privileges as well as disabilities. Men are not equal by nature, as a great sociologist of the law and a social reformer at that, who had grown up in the age of Social Darwinism, said, but the law makes them—may make them—equal.[76]

It is, of course, easy to find fault with the process of equalization and to point to the various ways in which the emergence of a bourgeois class society was favoured. Take as an example the rhetorical genius of the Abbé Sieyes distinguishing between *citoyens actifs* and *citoyens passifs*, a distinction thrown into relief even more sharply by Kant's theory of the *Staatsbürger* as distinguished from the mere *Staatsgenosse* (best translated perhaps as 'associate' of the State), though Kant's distinction is grounded in older traditions of the Aristotelian *oikos* and the Roman law teaching on the *status familiae*.[77] Take as another example the guild-destroying power of the *loi Le Chapelier* preventing for decades the formation of employees' or workers' unions which could confront employers with the collective bargaining power of unions. Take as a third example, the Napoleonic Code discriminating, in its infamous Article 1,781, against the employee in favour of the employer by stating: "The master is believed on the basis of his own affirmation for the amount of wages and the payment," an article revoked only in 1868 as incompatible with equality before the law.[78] We must not ignore "the majestic equality of laws, which prohibits the rich as well as the poor from sleeping beneath bridges, from begging in the streets, or from stealing bread" (Anatole France, *Le lys rouge*).

Yet two important considerations have to be kept in mind: first, liberal political thought, because of the very generality of its most important terms, such as "freedom," "equality of individuals before the law," "rights of men and citizens"—thus in striking contrast to the specificity of status categories in the old gradated *société des ordres*—has been and continues to be peculiarly adept at adjusting to changing social conditions; the democratization of liberal societies that were not, at the outset, democratic at all is a striking illustration of this adaptability.

75. Included in T. H. Marshall, *Class, Citizenship and Social Development* (Garden City, NY 1964).

76. Karl Renner, *Das Selbstbestimmungsrecht der Nationen in besonderer Anwendung auf Österreich, I: Nation und Staat* (Leipzig 1918), 148.

77. Gerhard Luf, *Freiheit und Gleichheit. Die Aktualität im politischen Denken Kants* (Vienna–New York 1978), 160–63; Schulze, Statusbildung (supra note 45) 115n. 66.

78. "Le maître est cru sur son affirmation pour la quotité des gages et le paiement": Stourzh, *Grundrechtsdemokratie*, 343.

Secondly, the very notion of equality has proved exceptionally adaptable. Many status groups originally considered to be unequal have finally successfully pleaded the argument that what is equal among human beings of different religion, property, colour, or sex, is more important than what is unequal among them. New situations and new claims have been tackled with the rule of "equal protection of the laws," to use the American formula.[79] What in German legal usage is referred to as the *Gleichheitssatz* has become, in the modern liberal State, one of the central and one of the most often invoked principles of constitutional guarantees.[80] The principle of equality has an inherently radicalizing tendency, as the German jurist Gerhard Leibholz has perspicaciously observed.[81] At the root of this radicalizing tendency Leibholz sees "the abstract basis of the idea of equality."[82]

It is easy to be skeptically inclined towards the idea of equal rights, when faced with vast inequalities of a material nature that often seem offensive to our sense of justice. Yet it would be difficult to deny the historical force of claims for equal rights in the history of the last two centuries (and sometimes earlier); the claims for equal suffrage rights and the claims for equal rights put forward by disadvantaged linguistic or ethnic minorities fill the records of modern and contemporary history. One should also remind oneself that a successful effort to undo the legal emancipation of one group that had suffered for centuries under the *privilegium odiosum* of a special Status—the Jews—led to most horrible consequences. Anyone ignoring the impact of the legal discrimination against the Jews under Nazi rule—powerfully described in such works as Ernst Fraenkel's brilliant book on the "Dual State"—does so at his peril. As early as 1936, the German Supreme Court (*Reichsgericht*) in the Charell case limited the legal capacity of a Jewish person, explicitly rejecting the "former liberal notion" of the equal personality rights of human beings, and affirming "older thoughts" that distinguished between persons of full legal capacity and persons of inferior rights, a distinction now to be applied according to racial criteria.[83] As early as 21 October 1938, the supreme judge of the German Nazi party, Buch, wrote: "The Jew is no human being."[84]

79. J. R. Pole, *The Pursuit of Equality in American History* (2nd ed.) (Berkeley, CA 1993), 172–73 and passim.

80. There is a brilliant discussion in Konrad Hesse, Der Gleichheitssatz im Staatsrecht, in *Archiv des öffentlichen Rechts*, vol. 77 (1951/52), 167–224.

81. Gerhard Leibholz, *Die Gleichheit vor dem Gesetz* (2nd ed.) (Munich–Berlin 1959), 25.

82. Ibid.

83. Ernst Fraenkel, *Der Doppelstaat* (Frankfurt/Main 1974) 126–27.

84. "Der Jude ist kein Mensch;" quoted from the periodical *Deutsche Justiz*, 100 (1938), no. A/42, 1660, in Stourzh, review essay in *Vierteljahrshefte für Zeitgschichte*, vol. 38 (1990), 501.

At the turn of the eighteenth and the beginning of the nineteenth centuries a fundamental change took place from a society based on a hierarchy of legal status, expressed in a great variety of legal capacities or the
lack of them—that is, legal disabilities. The late eighteenth and the early
nineteenth centuries witnessed a fundamental change towards general
and tendentially equal legal capacities.[85] The new principle of general legal capacity found an impressive and succinct formulation in § 16 of the
Austrian Civil Code of 1811 (*Allgemeines Bürgerliches Gesetzbuch*): "Every man has inborn rights, evident by nature, and therefore is to be considered as a person. Slavery or serfdom and the exercise of a power based on
these is not admitted in these lands."[86]

A society based on the principle of general and tendentially equal legal
capacity—based on the principle of "equal rights"—is radically different
from a society based on a hierarchy of gradated status rights or status disabilities, even if important "pockets" of legal disabilities have lingered on
well into the twentieth century. As an illustration, it may be noted that in
a legal system as egalitarian as that of France, domestic servants were entitled to jury service only as late as 1932;[87] as another, the phenomenon that
in Switzerland women obtained general suffrage rights as late as 1971.

The criteria of "modernity," particularly as far as the State is concerned, may vary. For the early modern period of European history, the
centralizing tendencies in the fields of taxation, military organization, the
administration of justice, and so on are often evoked as hallmarks of modernity. Yet to anyone convinced of the profundity of the change of paradigm of which Tocqueville is the unsurpassed analyst—the change from
aristocratic societies to democratic ones, the change from one type of society to another one so "prodigiously different" that Tocqueville went so far
as to speak of "two distinct humanities"[88]—*ancien régime* societies with
their systems of status differentiation are bound to look "pre-modern."

85. Eugen Ehrlich, *Die Rechtsfähigkeit* (Berlin 1909), 61–91. The developments in Germany, notably Prussia, in the early 19th cent. are well summarized in Otto Dann, *Gleichheit
und Gleichberechtigung. Das Gleichheitspostulat in der alteuropäischen Tradition und in
Deutschland bis zum ausgehenden 19. Jahrhundert* (Berlin 1980), 164–71.

86. "Jeder Mensch hat angeborne, schon durch die Vernunft einleuchtende Rechte und ist
daher als Person zu betrachten. Sklaverei oder Leibeigenschaft und die Ausübung einer sich
darauf beziehenden Macht wird in diesen Ländern nicht gestattet." On the limitations of the
Austrian Civil Code vis-à-vis the remaining feudal/corporate structures in Austria cf. Dieter
Grimm, Das Verhältnis vom politischer und privater Freiheit bei Zeiller, in *Forschungsband
Franz von Zeiller (1751–1828)*, ed. by W. Selb and H. Hofmeister (Vienna 1980), 102–103.

87. Georges Ripert, *Le régime démocratique et le droit civil moderne* (Paris 1984), 100.

88. See above all the concluding chapter of Tocqueville, *De la démocratie en Amérique*,
vol. II.

In any case, the breakthrough of equal rights, the breakthrough of political ideas and purposes associated with "Human Rights," or, to express it more technically, the tendency towards the generalization and equalization of legal capacities, provide fundamental criteria for distinguishing the modern liberal State (and society) from other types of State (and society). Perhaps it is not sufficient simply to seek the origins of the modern State. It is necessary to inquire into the more specific question of the origins of the modern liberal State. In any enquiry into the relationship of the individual to the modern State, the question of the origins and breakthrough of the notion of "equal rights" is bound to loom large. To the extent to which the enquiry into the origins of the modern State is connected with interest in the roots of modern liberal democracy, the emergence of general and generally equal rights of individual persons lies at the very core of the questions addressed in this essay.

CHAPTER THIRTEEN

Liberal Democracy as a Culture of Rights: England, the United States, and Continental Europe*

I

"The Commons of *England* for hereditary fundamental Liberties and Properties are blest above and beyond the Subject of any *Monarch* in the World." Thus wrote Edward Chamberlayne in 1669, in his highly successful work *Angliae Notitia*, that was to run through no less than thirty-eight editions until 1755, and very soon was translated into German and other languages.[1]

Chamberlayne did not mean the members of the House of Commons; he had in mind free Englishmen who did not belong to Clergy and Nobility, and he proceeded to enumerate, in what may be considered an early, though unofficial catalogue of the rights of Englishmen, these liberties and properties in eight points. I shall mention only a few of them. The first point: "No Freeman of England ought to be imprisoned or otherwise restrained, without cause shewn for which by Law he ought to be so imprisoned." In

*First published in *Nordamerikastudien. Historische und literaturwissenschaftliche Forschungen aus österreichischen Universitäten zu den Vereinigten Staaten und Kanada*, ed. by Thomas Fröschl, Margarete Grandner and Birgitta Bader-Zaar (*Wiener Beiträge zur Geschichte der Neuzeit* vol. 24) (Vienna–Munich 2000), 11–27; reprinted in *Bridging the Atlantic: The Question of American Exceptionalism in Perspective*, ed. by Elisabeth Glaser and Hermann Wellenreuther (New York 2002), 11–41. The permission to reprint was gracefully granted by Professor Wolfgang Schmale, University of Vienna.

1. Edward Chamberlayne, *Angliae Notitia* (London 1669), 446–48, reprinted in Gerald Stourzh, Vom aristotelischen zum liberalen Verfassungsbegriff. In idem, *Wege zur Grundrechtsdemokratie* (Wien–Köln 1989), 34–35. An early version of this paper was presented orally at a symposium honoring the memory of Erich Angermann, "Transatlantic History and American Exceptionalism," held in June 1995 in Washington, DC at the German Historical Institute. I would like to thank Dr. James Hutson and Dr. Vera Nünning for their thoughtful comments on the occasion of the lecture in Washington, as well as my friends Ralph Lerner in Chicago, and Jack Pole in Oxford, for their critical reading of the manuscript.

point two, the Writ of Habeas Corpus was mentioned; in point four, it was stated: "No soldiers can be quartered in the House of any Freeman in time of Peace, without his will." In point five, the Englishmen's property rights were extolled: "Every Freeman hath such a full and absolute property in Goods, that no Taxes, Loans, or Benevolences ordinarily and legally can be imposed upon them, without their own consent by their Representatives in Parliament." Chamberlayne went on to describe the unrestricted freedom to bequeath one's property, "which other Nations governed by the Civil Law, cannot do." Those familiar with the Petition of Right of 1628 will recognize, in points four and five, various similarities in content and partly even in wording. Point six stated that no Englishman could be compelled (unless bound by his tenure) to fight in wars abroad.

Reflecting on this catalogue of rights of 1669, two observations are called for: First, there is an awareness, a proud one at that, that things in England are different from, and better than the situation in other countries; a contrast is drawn to the civil law countries, which meant most continental countries, but partly Scotland as well. The English, or to be exact their "Commonalty," those belonging to the third estate, are blessed with fundamental liberties and properties "above and beyond" the subjects of any monarch in the world—thus proclaiming an English "exceptionalism"! The Common law/Civil law distinction is certainly an important element of setting England apart from the rest of Europe—as has rightly been stressed by Hermann Wellenreuther in his contribution to the Festschrift for Erich Angermann.[2]

Second, notwithstanding an awareness of *ständisch* (corporate) differences—the "Commonalty" set apart from Clergy and Nobility—there is an almost imperceptible identification of the "Freemen of England" with "Englishmen." And indeed, what Chamberlayne referred to as the liberties and properties of the Commons of England was, already in the course of the 17th century, often referred to as rights of Englishmen or English subjects, without bothering to refer to any order or estate. The Petition of Right of 1628 had enumerated "divers rights and liberties of the subject"; in 1646, the issue was raised in Massachusetts whether "our due and naturall rights, as freeborne subjects of the English nation" were respected.[3] In 1675 William Penn summed up "those rights and privileges which I call

2. Hermann Wellenreuther, England und Europa. Überlegungen zum Problem des englischen Sonderwegs in der europäischen Geschichte. In Norbert Finzsch & Hermann Wellenreuther (eds.), *Liberalitas. Festschrift für Erich Angermann zum 65. Geburtstag* (Stuttgart 1992), 97–98.

3. Quoted in Stourzh, *Verfassungsbegriff*, 27.

English, and which are the proper birthrights of Englishmen," and in 1687 Penn caused the first printing of Magna Charta in America—in Phila-delphia—in a publication entitled *The Excellent Priviledge of Liberty & Property Being the Birth-Right of the Free-born Subjects of England.* In the early 1680s, there appeared the very popular collection of Henry Care, entitled *English Liberties: or, the Free-Born subjects inheritance,* fre-quently reprinted, including two American editions in Boston 1721 and in Providence, Rhode Island, in 1774.[4] In other words, in the course of the 17th century, references to liberties or rights had lost or were about to lose, their relation to a specific order or estate; they had become, in an un-translatable German word, *standesunspezifisch.*

Rights—those of the people of England—were the primary concern of the most celebrated attempt to present a system of the laws of England, Wil-liam Blackstone's *Commentaries on the Laws of England* (1765–1769). The rights of the people of England were summarized by Blackstone in three "principal or primary articles"—first, the right to personal security, sec-ond, the right of personal liberty, and third, the right of private property.[5] These three "principal absolute rights" were to be protected by "auxiliary subordinate rights of the subject." The first of these auxiliary and subordi-nate rights consisted in "the constitution, powers, and privileges of parlia-ment," the second in "the limitation of the king's prerogative"; the third was the right to apply to the Courts for the redress of injuries; the fourth was the right to present petitions to the king or to parliament, and the fifth was the right to bear arms for one's defense "such as are allowed by law."[6]

In view of this system of the primary and the auxiliary rights of Eng-lishmen it has been rightly observed—by Sir Ernest Barker—that for Black-stone, the constitution was "a body of rights belonging to the subject, and vested in the subject."[7] We may also remind ourselves that Blackstone, according to his own word, was greatly influenced by Matthew Hale's *Analysis of the Law,* written prior to 1676, who built his entire system of law, including public law, on a system of legal relations or "rights" and not

---

4. For the preceding, cf. ibid., 29–30.

5. On the impact of three absolute rights in revolutionary America cf. James H. Hutson, The Bill of Rights and the American Revolutionary Experience. In Michael J. Lacey & Knud Haakonssen (eds.), A *Culture of Rights: The Bill of Rights in Philosophy, Politics, and Law— 1791 and 1991* (Cambridge/UK 1991), 62–97, here 78–79.

6. William Blackstone, *Commentaries on the Laws of England,* 4 vols. (London 1765–1769) vol. I, 125–39.

7. Sir Ernest Barker, Blackstone on the British Constitution. In idem, *Essays on Govern-ment* (2nd ed.)(Oxford 1951), 142.

on a fountain or top of sovereign power.[8] One hundred and twenty years after Blackstone, Albert Dicey said that with the English, constitution was not the source, but the consequence of the rights of individuals.[9]

Now to an observer from the European continent, used to the traditional primacy of the state or its ruler and its highest organs—a primacy respected even in the freest of the Civil law countries, in the Netherlands, as the writings of the Dutch jurist Ulric Huber show in contrast to Hale or Blackstone—to an observer aware of the Roman law tradition of the *princeps legibus solutus*, a conception like Blackstone's explaining the limitations of the king's prerogative as "auxiliary and subordinate" rights of the people, is utterly astonishing. Yet this conception is truly expressive of the English Common law tradition that ignored, as Maitland once observed, the term "constitutional law" as a technical phrase.[10] This conception is also expressive, I submit, of the fact that the politico-legal culture of England may justly be called a "culture of rights"—taking this felicitous phrase from the well-known volume published in 1991 by Michael Lacey and Knud Haakonssen on the occasion of the Bicentennial of the Federal Bill of Rights.[11]

This phenomenon is something which, I repeat, set England apart from the European continent, and which linked it with the emerging political societies of English—I say English rather than British!—origin across the Atlantic ocean. "Rights were taken seriously in the eighteenth-century British Empire"—John Phillip Reid, obviously alluding to Ronald Dworkin's celebrated book title, says at the opening of his *Constitutional History of the American Revolution*, of which the first volume is dedicated to "the authority of rights."[12] I stress this phenomenon now because it is apt, of course, to put a question mark around the juxtaposition of "Europe" and "America." I stress it also because in a suggestive discussion of English and American differences with respect to "rights," Alan Ryan has too one-sidedly minimized, I think, the relevance of "rights" in England. He observes that the "common law is based less on rights than on rules, forms of

8. On Hale see the immediately preceding chapter, pp. 290–91.

9. Albert V. Dicey, *Introduction to the Study of the Law of the Constitution* (10th ed.) (London 1965), 203 (see also the preceding chapter, p. 292).

10. Frederick W. Maitland, *The Constitutional History of England* (Cambridge/UK 1908), 527.

11. Lacey & Haakonssen (eds.), *A Culture of Rights*, particularly the introduction by the editors, 1–18.

12. John Phillip Reid, *Constitutional History of the American Revolution*, 4 vols. (Madison, WI 1986–1991) vol 3.

action, and procedures for arriving at right decisions [. . .]."[13] Yet this means
nothing else than the basic principle "no right without remedy," as valid in
America as in England. John Adams, at the time of the Stamp Act crisis,
noted from Coke's *First Institutes*: "Want of right and want of remedy is all
one; for where there is no remedy there is no right."[14] Ryan also observes,
rightly, that the purpose of the English Declaration of Rights of 1689 "of restricting the freedom of the sovereign was much more evident than any notion of liberating the 'individual,'"[15] and indeed the 1689 document is more
concerned with protecting parliamentary privileges than individual persons. Yet Ryan omits any reference to the Petition of Right of 1628, which
was more "person-centered" than the Bill of Rights of 1689. One also ought
not to forget the powerful halo surrounding "that second *magna carta*,"
the Habeas Corpus Act of 1679.[16] Furthermore, I would like to refer to the
tremendous significance surrounding the issue of the freedom of the press,
at least from the time of Milton's *Areopagitica*, and particularly after the
last Licensing Act ran out in 1695 and was not renewed.[17]

I submit that in 17th and 18th century England, a process of "fundamentalizing" the rights of persons took place, and that some important
phases of this process, apparently neglected by Ryan, had taken place prior
to the Declaration of Rights of 1689. This process was not matched by any
contemporary parallel development in continental Europe. England was
different. Seventeenth century England, as Tocqueville observed in one of
his masterpieces of comparative juridico-socio-political analysis, was already a truly modern state, *"une nation toute moderne,"* some feudal remnants nothwithstanding.[18] Speaking of the equalization of rights across
fading differences of orders or estates, one ought to be mindful of other
restrictions of legal capacity like those hitting the indigent or, under the
common law doctrine of the *feme covert*, married women.[19]

13. Alan Ryan, The British, the Americans, and Rights. In Lacey & Haakonssen (eds.),
A Culture of Rights, 378.

14. Cf. Gerald Stourzh, The American Revolution, Modern Constitutionalism, and the
Protection of Human Rights. In Kenneth Thompson & Robert Myers (eds.), *A Tribute to Hans
Morgenthau* (Washington, DC 1977), 169, quoting from *The Works of John Adams* (Boston
1850–1856) vol. 2, 159.

15. Ryan, *The British*, 384.

16. Blackstone, *Commentaries* vol. 1, 133.

17. Gerald Stourzh, Die Entwicklung der Rede- und Meinungsfreiheit im englischen und
amerikanischen Rechtsraum. In idem, *Wege zur Grundrechtsdemokratie*, 175–81.

18. Alexis de Tocqueville, *L'ancien régime et la Revolution* (Paris "folio" ed. 1967) book I,
ch. iv, 78.

19. On the latter point, see Lee Holcombe, *Wives and Property: Reform of the Married
Women's Property Law in Nineteenth-Century England* (Toronto 1983), 25–31. For early

What did not happen in England, and what was happening across the Atlantic Ocean in North America, as will be shown in due course, was the process of "constitutionalizing" the rights of persons. There were times when the lack of rules or procedures binding the legislator was bitterly felt and expressed by Opposition writers—like Daniel Defoe in 1701, or Opposition politicians critical of the Septennial Act of 1716, when a Parliament elected for three years prolonged its own term of office for another four years, and opposition speakers argued that this measure violated "the constitution."[20] The case of the Septennial Act was to be noted and commented upon decades later in America, as shall be shown below.

There was, then, no procedural way, no legal way, no easy way out of the dilemma between the primacy of the rights of Englishmen, so forcefully proclaimed by Blackstone or Dicey, and the absolute sovereignty of Parliament (to be precise the King-in-Parliament or the Queen-in-Parliament), also forcefully expressed in Blackstone's and Diceys's writings. There was, however, a difficult—and risky—way out of that dilemma, once the contradiction became too burdensome, as long as legal and constitutional thinking was pervaded by natural law thinking—which was the case with Blackstone (though not, more than a century later, with Dicey). For cases of extreme emergency Blackstone had this to say: "Indeed, it is found by experience, that whenever the unconstitutional oppressions, even of the sovereign power, advance with gigantic strides and threaten desolation to a state, mankind will not be reasoned out of the feelings of humanity; nor will [they] sacrifice their liberty by a scrupulous adherence to those political maxims, which were originally established to preserve it." To future generations—thus Blackstone concluded a remarkable passage—was left, "whenever necessity and the safety of the whole shall require it, the exertion of those inherent (though latent) powers of society, which no climate, no time, no constitution, no contract, can ever destroy or diminish."[21] The message was heard and understood, in America, at the appropriate time.[22]

America, cf. Marylynn Salmon, *Women and the Law of Property in Early America* (Chapel Hill, NC 1986). An illuminating discussion with reference to an extremely interesting case is presented by Linda K. Kerber, The Paradox of Women's Citizenship in the Early Republic: The Case of *Martin vs. Massachusetts*, 1805. In *American Historical Review* 97 (1992), 349–78.

20. For details cf. Gerald Stourzh, Vom Widerstandsrecht zur Verfassungsgerichtsbarkeit. In idem, *Wege zur Grundrechtsdemokratie*, 42–49.

21. Blackstone, *Commentaries* vol. l, 238. Cf. also David Liebermann, *The Province of Legislation Determined: Legal Theory in Eighteenth-Century Britain* (Cambridge/UK 1989), 52–53.

22. For details cf. Gerald Stourzh, *William Blackstone: Teacher of Revolution*, above, Chapter 2.

In spite of the fundamental place of the rights of persons in the English public mind, then, the legislator was entitled to suspend such rights, including the hallowed one of habeas corpus, and did so on various occasions.[23] Yet it was precisely the legislative, and not the executive power alone, that was entitled to suspend habeas corpus, as Blackstone was eager to point out.[24] As almost instinctively critical as one is inclined to be in view of our overwhelmingly "constitutionalist" perspective—not merely in the United States but in most European continental nations as well—one ought not to forget that the sovereign legislator of England, Parliament, by the 17th and 18th centuries was a remarkable institution, including by far the strongest "Third Estate" of any of the major European states. This Parliament, for generations of European observers the very epitome of "representative government," of a "free government," was gradually widening the franchise rights required to elect representatives. The years 1832, 1867, 1884, 1918, and 1928 were landmarks on the way from "representative government" to a "representative democracy," though phases between these landmarks, be it the Chartist or the Suffragette movements, must not be forgotten. But even the democratically elected Parliament of the 20th century (I refrain from commenting on the decline plus reforms of the House of Lords during the 20th century) has remained as sovereign as described by Blackstone or Dicey in the preceding centuries. The most telling symbol of this legislative sovereignty remains for me the Emergency Powers (Defense) Act of 1940, passed at a time when German invasion seemed imminent. It provided "for requiring persons to place themselves, their services, and their property [!] at the disposal of His Majesty." The bill to this effect passed through all its stages in both Houses of Parliament and received the royal assent within one single day! A perspicacious observer has commented that this law "put into a legal formula the 'blood and tears and sweat' that Mr. Churchill had promised as the British contribution to the war effort."[25]

II

Which were the major transforming elements that contributed to the growth in parts of North America—out of a rich heritage of English legal

23. For details, Sir David Lindsay Keir, *The Constitutional History of Modern Britain since 1485* (8th ed.) (London 1966), 398.

24. Blackstone, *Commentaries*, vol.1, 132.

25. O. Hood Phillips, *Constitutional and Administrative Law* (5th ed.) (London 1973), 321, quoting from Sir Ivor Jennings, *Law and the Constitution* (3rd ed.) (London 1943), xxv–xxvi.

and political traditions—of a different type of "free government," of liberal constitutional democracy, American style, of a liberal democracy expressing itself indeed in a more intensive way than in Britain as a "culture of rights"?

I shall single out the four following points:

1. Republican government,
2. Federalism,
3. The rise of a paramount law above the ordinary legislator, and
4. The constitutionalization of individual rights.

I shall deal with points one and two rather briefly, with the interrelated points three and four at greater length.

Ad 1. Breaking away from the British monarchy produced the sudden and simultaneous rise of the powerful notions of republican government and of the constituent power of the people (of the latter more in point 3). So much has been written about the "paradigm of republicanism" within the last 25 years that I shall limit myself to a few very brief observations.

As far as the historiographical attention given to the meaning of republican government and "republicanism" is concerned, to which I contributed myself a quarter of a century ago,[26] it seems that the exaggerated juxtaposition of the "republican" and "liberal" paradigms has given place to more balanced interpretations.[27] John Pocock himself, whose great work on the "Machiavellian Moment" had done so much to unleash the "republicanism vs. liberalism-debate," has admitted that his account of "civic humanism" was a "tunnel history" which "pursued a single theme, that of the *vivere civile* and its virtue, to the partial exclusion of parallel phenomena."[28] Among these parallel phenomena the most important was and is what Pocock rightly calls the "law-centered paradigm."[29]

26. Gerald Stourzh, *Alexander Hamilton and the Idea of Republican Government* (Stanford, CA 1970); see the review article by J.G.A. Pocock, Virtue and Commerce in the Eighteenth Century. In *Journal of Interdisciplinary History* 1 (1972–1973), 119–34.

27. Among recent interpretations, the work of Paul A. Rahe, *Republics Ancient and Modern* (Chapel Hill, NC 1992) stands out.

28. J.G.A. Pocock, The Machiavellian Moment Revisited: A Study in History and Ideology. In *Journal of Modern History* 53 (1981), 53.

29. Idem, *Virtue, Commerce and History* (Cambridge/UK 1985), 37. Among the vast amount of scholarly discussion produced by the "republican paradigm" and its critics, I would like to single out, for reference, the collected contributions by Joyce Appleby in her volume *Liberalism and Republicanism in the Historical Imagination* (Cambridge, MA 1992).

There is no question that in an inquiry about a "culture of rights," the "law-centered paradigm" assumes a priority of place, as it does in this paper. Yet the question has to be asked whether, and if so, in which way, the "republican paradigm" contributes to enlighten us about certain roots of enduringly strong elements of a "culture or rights."

It seems to me that the notion of "citizens," replacing in America the English notion of "subjects"—even freeborn subjects of King or Queen!—is the most important element that the republican paradigm has contributed to the American "culture of rights." Citizenship in a republic implies rights, particularly rights of participation, though in the republican tradition, as Rousseau made very clear, citizenship was by no means bound to reach all classes of the population.[30] It certainly was a republican manner of speech that impelled Noah Webster to associate citizenship with suffrage. A citizen for Webster was a person, native or naturalized, "who has the privilege of exercising the elective franchise, or the qualifications which enable him to vote for rulers, and to purchase and hold real estate."[31] It was the republican association of the idea of citizenship with the franchise that inspired the women who drew up the Seneca Falls Declaration of 1848 on women's rights to speak "of the first right of a citizen, the elective franchise," and to denounce man who had deprived woman of this first right, "thereby leaving her without representation in the halls of legislation [. . .]."[32] Yet though the "participatory connotations" of citizenship had their origins in classical republicanism,[33] the dynamics of the extension of suffrage to groups hitherto excluded, like people without property qualifications, colored people, or women, was due to the—modern—tendency to equalize legal capacities, connected with modern natural rights thinking and also, though not exclusively so, with the rise of modern democracy.

The notion of citizenship and the rights pertaining to it, after independence tied to the individual States, nationally defined and entrenched

30. Cf. Rousseau's note on the meaning of the word "citoyen" in book 1, ch. vi, of the Social Contract. Cf. Rogers Brubaker, *Citizenship and Nationhood in France and Germany* (Cambridge, MA 1992), 42.

31. Quoted in the magnificent work by Don Fehrenbacher, *The Dred Scott Case* (New York 1978), 615 note 55, from Noah Webster, *An American Dictionary of the English Language*, 2 vols. (New York 1828). The last words echo section 6 of the Virginia Bill of Rights, in which it was stated that "all men, having sufficient evidence of permanent common interest with, and attachment to the community, have the right of suffrage [. . .]." Henry Steele Commager, *Documents of American History*, 2 vols. (7th ed.) (New York 1963) vol.1, 104.

32. Commager, *Documents*, vol. I, 315.

33. Brubaker, *Citizenship*, 50.

only in the 14th Amendment of 1868, were however frequently discussed without reference to the franchise question, and women were held to be citizens without having the right of the franchise.[34] The central issue of early discussions of citizenship was the status of the free persons of African descent—particularly in connection with the Missouri compromise—, and later, with Chief Justice Taney's Dred Scott decision, the question whether the status of citizenship was accessible to colored persons at all.[35] The final answer, after years of bloodshed, were the 14th and 15th Amendments to the Constitution, the latter affirming the right of citizens of the United States to vote, not to be denied or abridged on account of race, color, or previous condition of servitude. I will return to the relevance of status for the theme of this paper later on.

Ad 2. Federalism, as it emerged from the work of the Philadelphia Convention and was embodied in the Federal Constitution, is relevant for the development of a "culture of rights" on two counts:

First, federalism, as Dicey rightly said, "means legalism." A federal system cannot work with an unspecified sovereign "power"—singular; it needs specified "powers"—plural. In other words, federalism necessitates the attribution of powers in the specific sense of competences. The transformation of "power" into "powers" inevitably produces an additional network of legal norms, unknown and unnecessary in unitary states. The need to settle possible differences of interpretation as to the meaning and extent of respective "powers" enhances the role of the judiciary, and it has been rather well said that particularly during the first century of American constitutionalism (under the Federal constitution), the theme of powers was its central motif: "the extent of the authority of each branch and level of government and their relationship to each other and to the people."[36] Federalism, Dicey also rightly said, means "the prevalence of a spirit of legality among the people."[37]

Second, and more specifically, we have to remind ourselves that American federalism injected a new element into "federal" relationships: The powers of the federal—i.e., national—government were to extend "to certain enumerated objects only," as Madison phrased it carefully. Yet within

34. Fehrenbacher, *Dred Scott Case*, 65 and 615 note 56. Cf. also the discussion by Kerber, *Women's Citizenship*, particularly 376–78.

35. Fehrenbacher, *Dred Scott Case*, 64–68, 340–50.

36. Morton Keller, Powers and Rights: Two Centuries of American Constitutionalism. In *Journal of American History* 74 (1987–1988), 675–94, here 676.

37. Dicey, *Law of the Constitution*, 175.

these confines, the government of the Union was empowered, again in Madison's words, to operate "on the individual citizens, composing the nation, in their individual capacities."[38] This was the truly new departure of the Federal Constitution of 1787, and this was the important wedge with the help of which individuals and their claims would be connected with federal jurisdiction—for instance, concerning interstate commerce—and that jurisdiction's competence to adjudicate conflicting claims of state legislation and the rules of the Federal Constitution—a vast field for developing a "culture of rights."

Ad 3. The emergence of the "written constitution" as the "fundamental and paramount law of the nation"—to employ John Marshall's phrase in *Marbury vs. Madison*—was a process that began in North America long before independence. The dissociation of legislative and sovereign power—a phenomenon central to American constitutionalism—set in during the colonial period. This was indeed an important departure from the English system; it was also a departure from one of the main tenets of early modern political thinking, from Bodin to Hobbes to Rousseau or to Blackstone: the legislator is the sovereign. In colonial America, the colonial assemblies did indeed legislate for their respective colonies; they passed laws, they were considered to carry out legislative acts, they imitated—increasingly—the Parliament at Westminster in the style of proceedings—and yet they were not by any means sovereign, being subject to various superior norms—frames of government, charters and grants, the disallowance powers of the Privy Council and finally, if not unequivocally, to the legislative authority of Parliament itself.

An important experience that separated colonials from Englishmen in the mother country was the experience of founding a political community—an experience of contemporary or at any rate recent memory. Conscious founding necessitates conscious organization, and in several cases, the foundational documents emphasized the "fundamental" or "paramount" character of the rules laid down in them vis-à-vis the "ordinary" legislature. The "Fundamental Orders" of Connecticut (1639), the "General Fundamentals" introducing the revised code for New Plymouth of 1671, the "Charter or fundamentall Laws of West New Jersey agreed upon" of 1676, Penn's "Frames of Government" for Pennsylvania with a provision of a qualified majority for amending procedures are some cases in point. Thus

---

38. Jacob E. Cooke (ed.), *The Federalist* (Middletown, CT 1961) No. 39, 256 and 255. Cf. also Gerald Stourzh, Il "Federalista." Teoria politica e retorica della persuasione. In Guglielmo Negri (ed.), *Il Federalista: 200 anni dopo* (Bologna 1988), 271–90, here 282.

Americans, unlike Englishmen in the mother country, had become accustomed to being governed by a hierarchy of legal norms, of which the Laws passed by the assemblies held by no means the highest rank.[39]

The Americans' polemics—in the 1760s and 1770s—against what they considered the "unconstitutional" deeds of Parliament in London further encouraged the dissociation of legislative from sovereign power. I have shown in an earlier publication how the use of the word "unconstitutional" suddenly spread in North America, once it had first been used in 1764/65 in Rhode Island.[40] Theoretical awareness that the legislator was inferior to the constitution was greatly helped by the very clear presentation of this subordination in the work of Emmerich de Vattel, *Le droit des gens ou principes de la loi naturelle*, published in 1758.[41] It was immediately translated into English, very soon used and quoted by James Otis in Boston, and unmistakably echoed in the Massachusetts Circular Letter of 1768, in which it was stated that "in all free States the Constitution is fixed; & as the supreme Legislative derives its Power & Authority from the Constitution, it cannot overleap the Bounds of it, without destroying its own foundation."[42]

With the breaking away from Britain in 1776, the need for new fundamental frames of government or (with a more recent name) constitutions produced the first sustained and successful coming into action of the "constituent power of the people" in Western history.[43] Anticipating the Abbé Sieyes in France by twelve years, Thomas Young of Pennsylvania spoke of the "supreme constituent power" of the people, distinguishing it from the delegated powers of the representatives.[44] The process of constitution-making in the States from 1776 to 1780, with increasing procedural

---

39. Cf. Stourzh, *Wege zur Grundrechtsdemokratie*, 25–34.

40. Ibid., 52–53.

41. Gerald Stourzh, Naturrechtslehre, leges fundamentales und die Anfänge des Vorrangs der Verfassung. In Christian Starck (ed.), *Rangordnung der Gesetze (Abhandlungen der Akademie der Wissenschaften in Göttingen*, phil.-hist. Klasse, 3. Folge, No. 210) (Göttingen 1995), 24–25.

42. Gerald Stourzh, *Constitution: Changing Meanings of the Term from the Early Seventeenth to the Late Eighteenth Century.* See above, Chapter 3, p. 96.

43. For the "constituent power of the people" see in particular Robert R. Palmer, *The Age of Democratic Revolution: A Political History of Europe and America, 1760–1800*, vol. 1: *The Challenge* (Princeton, NJ 1959), 213–35. Cf. also for this and some of the following, Gerald Stourzh, *Fundamental Laws and Individual Rights in the 18th Century Constitution* (Claremont, CA 1984), 18–25. Reprinted in J. Jackson Barlow, Leonard W. Levy, & Ken Masugi (eds.), *The American Founding: Essays on the Formation of the Constitution* (Westport, CT 1988), 159–93, here 176–83.

44. Willi Paul Adams, *The First American State Constitutions: Republican Ideology and the Making of the State Constitutions in the Revolutionary Era* (Chapel Hill, NC 1980), 65.

sophistication, culminating in the Massachusetts Constitution of 1780,[45] remains a memorable chapter in the history not merely of constitutional democracy in North America, but in the history of liberal democracy *tout court*.[46] In what was one of the earliest uses of a modern expression, Alexander Hamilton in 1777 spoke of the new form of government as a "representative democracy."[47]

The "written constitution" as paramount law: the decisive quality of the "written constitution" did not consist in its quality as a written document, but in its rank as paramount law vis-à-vis legislature-made law. The awareness that this was so, and that this was the great innovation of the American system of government was not the discovery either of Alexander Hamilton—in *Federalist* no. 78—or of John Marshall in *Marbury vs. Madison*. This awareness was widespread and antedated the Federal Constitution, though it certainly was vastly enhanced by the work of the Philadelphia Convention and by the ratification debates accompanying the adoption of the Federal Constitution. Merely a few examples will be given. As early as May 1776 the town of Pittsfield, Massachusetts, had asked for "the formation of a fundamental Constitution as the Basis and ground work of Legislation."[48] This indeed was done, within a period of less than fifteen years, both on the state level and on the level of the Union.

Among those who grasped and articulated what was new in the American system, the North Carolina jurist James Iredell, subsequently nominated to the Supreme Court of the U.S., stands out. As early as 1783, he pointed out that an independent judiciary was "a point of the utmost moment in a Republic where the Law is superior to any or all the Individuals, and *the Constitution superior even to the Legislature*, and of which the Judges are the guardians and protectors."[49] In an article published in the summer of 1786, Iredell extolled the new chance of protecting individual rights, with the help of the courts, against unconstitutional legislation, thus protecting the constitution itself. In North Carolina something was possible which did not exist in England, where the principle of unbounded legislative power was prevailing. And Iredell pointed to an event which

---

45. Oscar Handlin & Mary Handlin (eds.), *The Popular Sources of Political Authority. Documents on the Massachusetts Constitution of 1780* (Cambridge, MA 1966).

46. Cf. Adams, *The First American State Constitutions*.

47. Stourzh, *Hamilton* 49 and 223 note 36.

48. Handlin-Handlin, *Popular Sources*, 90.

49. Don Higginbotham (ed.), *The Papers of James Iredell* (Raleigh, NC 1976) vol. 2, 449 (my emphasis).

had happened in England seventy years before: in England, a Parliament elected for three years had prolonged its own duration for another four years; this was not possible in North Carolina. People in England were less free than in North Carolina![50] A year later, Iredell considered the judges' obligation "to hold void laws inconsistent with the constitution" unavoidable, "the Constitution not being a mere imaginary thing, about which ten thousand different opinions may be formed, but a written document to which all may have recourse, and to which, therefore, the judges cannot wilfully blind themselves."[51]

The contrast to England, even with reference to the same dreadful event seven decades earlier—the Septennial Act of 1716—was expressed by eminent authors. In 1788, James Madison, in *Federalist* no. 53, proudly wrote: "The important distinction so well understood in America between a constitution established by the people, and unalterable by the government; and a law established by the government, and alterable by the government, seems to have been little understood and less observed in any other country." And Madison went on to denounce the "dangerous practices" demonstrated by the British Septennial Act, to wit, the possibility of changing by legislative acts, some of the most fundamental articles of the government.[52] For Thomas Paine, writing in *The Rights of Man*, the Septennial Act was proof that "there is no constitution in England."[53]

The most artful of all comparisons between the British and the American system of government, embellished with all kinds of rhetorical flourishes, came from the pen of James Wilson. His "Lectures on Law" delivered in Philadelphia in 1790/91—the inaugural lecture was held in the presence of President Washington and Vice-President Adams!—are a monument of American "exceptionalism." Wilson made very clear the dissociation of legislative from sovereign power in America, as opposed to the English doctrine; in America, there existed a guard against "legislative despotism": the superior power of the constitution, the judges called to decide under

---

50. "To the Public," August 17th, 1786. In Griffith J. McRee (ed.), *Life and Correspondence of James Iredell*, 2 vols. (New York 1858) vol. 2, 147–48.

51. Iredell to Richard Spaight, August 26, 1787, ibid., 174. I have discussed Iredell extensively in "The American Revolution" (supra note 14), 170–72, and in *Wege zur Grundrechtsdemokratie* 60–64. The great significance of Iredell, long neglected by American authors, has now been duly emphasized by Sylvia Snowiss, *Judicial Review and the Law of the Constitution* (New Haven, CT 1990), 45–53, although I cannot share all of her interpretations.

52. *The Federalist*, 360–61.

53. As quoted by Charles H. McIlwain, *Constitutionalism Ancient and Modern* (Ithaca, NY 1958), 2.

the constitution. Above the constitution, retaining the right of abolishing, altering or amending the constitution, there stood the sovereign power of the people. Concluding his "parallel between the pride of Europe—the British constitution—and the constitution of the United States," Wilson threw out his challenge: "Let impartiality hold the balance between them: I am not solicitous about the event of the trial:"[54]

To return from "exceptionalist" rhetoric to reality: The pattern of the written constitution as paramount law and the practice of judicial review were to become the most characteristic features of the American culture of rights—both on the relatively neglected level of the state constitutions and on the superior level, in the limelight of public attention and controversy, of the Federal Constitution.[55] Yet this development might not have moved so much into the center of public interest, if it had not been inseparably intertwined with another phenomenon to which I now turn.

Ad 4. The constitutionalization of individual rights.

I distinguish between two kinds of processes—"fundamentalizing" and "constitutionalizing" individual rights. The first term, which I have used in the first part of this paper referring to England, relates to a process that leads to the recognition of certain imperatives or prohibitions—e.g., habeas corpus—as fundamental Laws of the land without thereby creating a special category of legal norms. By "constitutionalizing" I refer to a process whereby certain imperatives or prohibitions become part of the higher law or paramount law in the technical sense that it cannot be abrogated or changed by normal legislative procedure. This process also could be described as a process of entrenching certain rules—protecting individual rights for instance—above and beyond the license of simple legislative majorities—the term entrenching being taken from public law discussions in South Africa and in Canada.

Constitutional developments in North America in the 17th and 18th centuries added a new dimension to the securing of individual rights. To the dimension of rights secured by the law of the land and considered fundamental, though changeable by the legislator (example habeas corpus), the dimension of "entrenched" guarantees was added. A remarkable example of this process in colonial times is a document entitled "Charter or funda-

54. Robert G. McCloskey (ed.), *The Works of James Wilson*, 2 vols. (Cambridge, MA 1967) vol. l, 77, 185–88, 329–30, 333.

55. The significance of judicial power in the United States was soon recognized in Europe, e.g. as early as 1824 by the young Robert von Mohl, *Das Bundes-Staatsrecht der Vereinigten Staaten von Nord-Amerika* (Tübingen 1824), 298–302. Cf. also Erich Angermann, *Robert von Mohl 1799–1875. Leben und Werk eines altliberalen Staatsgelehrten* (Neuwied 1962), 26.

mental laws" of West New Jersey of 1676.[56] It is part of the "Concessions and Agreements of the Proprietors, Freeholders and Inhabitants of the Province of West New Jersey" of that year. The eleven articles of that "Charter" were alternatively called "the common law or fundamental Rights" of West New Jersey. They chiefly embodied rights with reference to criminal procedure, including habeas corpus. These fundamental rights were agreed on "to be the foundation of the Government which is not to be altered by the Legislative Authority or free Assembly hereafter mentioned and constituted. But that the said Legislative Authority is constituted according to these fundamentals to make such Laws as agree with and maintain the said fundamentals and to make no Laws that in the least contradict, differ, or vary from the said fundamentals under what pretence or allegation soever."

The clarity of distinguishing between fundamental law (in which various individual rights were "entrenched") and legislative-made law is extraordinary; it would not be surpassed by statements made more than a century later like Hamilton's *Federalist* no. 78 or John Marshall's dictum in *Marbury vs. Madison.*

With American independence, the tendency of entrenching individual rights in the fundamental—or paramount—law of the Constitution was vastly enhanced. One reason was the appeal to natural rights that pervaded the movement for independence and many of the documents drafted in and around 1776, Jefferson's preamble to the Declaration of Independence and Mason's Virginia Bill of Rights merely being the two outstanding and best known examples.[57] Another reason was the firm determination to protect the rights of persons from legislative arbitrariness, as the activities of Parliament in London had come to be felt. The protection of rights emerged in America as the very *raison d'être* of a constitution: This was unsurpassably well said in the Concord town meeting's resolution of October 21, 1776: "[. . .] we Conceive that a Constitution in its Proper Idea intends a System of Principles Established to Secure the Subject in the Possession and enjoyment of their Rights and Privileges, against any Encroachments of the Governing Part."[58] This is, in a nutshell, the liberal idea of a constitution, and it is, if connected with the idea of the constituent power of the people

56. For the following cf. Julian P. Boyd (ed.), *Fundamental Laws and Constitutions of New Jersey 1664–1964* (Princeton, NJ 1964), 71 ff. (spelling modernized).

57. Cf. extensive source materials presented in Hutson, *Bill of Rights*, 62–80, and, with more emphasis on the moral and public opinion-related aspects of rights, the chapter on "Rights" in Jack N. Rakove, *Original Meanings: Politics and Ideas in the Making of the Constitution* (New York 1996), 288–338.

58. Handlin-Handlin, *Popular Sources*, 153 (original spelling preserved).

and a democratic franchise, the central idea of liberal democracy. In Europe, the central place of rights—of "subjective" rights, as French and German legal terminology has it[59]—in a liberal constitution will be aptly expressed thirteen years later in Article 16 of the Declaration of the Rights of Man and Citizen: "Any society in which the guarantee of rights is not assured, nor the separation of powers determined, has no constitution."[60]

Many, though not all, state constitutions included bills of rights. There are examples, like the well known North Carolina case of *Bayard vs. Singleton* of 1786/87, that judicial review, weighing the constitutionality or unconstitutionality of legislation, measured legislation according to the criterion of an individual right entrenched in the constitution (in that particular case, the right to trial by jury).[61]

What happened in the United States beginning in 1776 was a process of "constitutionalizing" individual rights that worked, as it were, from two directions. On the one hand, natural rights were reduced, if one may put it this way, to the level of constitutional rights—what German authors have called *Positivierung des Naturrechts*.[62] A classic application of this process of transforming natural rights into legal (constitutional) rights is supplied by the well-known "Quok Walker" case in Massachusetts. In 1783, the Chief Justice of Massachusetts, William Cushing, instructed a Jury to the effect that the natural freedom of all men, as asserted in Article I of the Massachusetts Bill of Rights (a part of the Constitution of Massachusetts), was incompatible with the idea of slavery. Subsequently, the institution of slavery, which to be sure never had been strong in Massachusetts, vanished in the Commonwealth.[63] On the other hand, the process of "constitutionalizing" individual rights also included the raising of various rights of English common law or of parliamentary origin, particularly procedural rights, to the level of constitutional rights.

---

59. On the significance of the notion of "subjective" rights and its applicability to English and American notions of rights, cf. the suggestive study by James Hutson, The Emergence of the Modern Concept of a Right in America: The Contribution of Michel Villey. In *The American Journal of Jurisprudence* 39 (1994), 185–224.

60. "Toute société, dans laquelle la garantie des droits n'est pas assurée, ni la séparation des pouvoirs déterminée, n'a pas de constitution."

61. For details, cf. Stourzh, *Wege zur Grundrechtsdemokratie*, 60–64.

62. Jürgen Habermas, Naturrecht und Revolution. In idem, *Theorie und Praxis* (Neuwied 1967), 52–88 (often lacking historical precision), quote p. 55; also Dieter Grimm, Europäisches Naturrecht und Amerikanische Revolution—Die Verwandlung politischer Theorie in politische Techne. In *Ius Commune* 3 (1970), 120–51.

63. Henry Steele Commager (ed.), *Documents*, vol. 1, 110. Cf. also Arthur Zilversmit, *The First Emancipation: The Abolition of Slavery in the North* (Chicago 1970).

The early existence of a "culture of rights" in the United States—awareness of the centrality of rights in a political System, awareness of the various levels on which rights were located—is excellently expressed in an essay published in December 1787: "Of rights, some are natural and unalienable, of which even the people cannot deprive individuals: Some are constitutional or fundamental; these cannot be altered or abolished by the ordinary laws; but the people, by express acts, may alter or abolish them. These, such as the trial by jury, the benefits of the writ of habeas corpus, &c. individuals claim under the solemn compacts of the people, as constitutions, or at least under laws so strengthened by long usage as not to be repealable by the ordinary legislature—and some are common or mere legal rights, that is, such as individuals claim under laws which the ordinary legislature may alter or abolish at pleasure."[64]

The story of the advocacy of a Federal Bill of Rights and of the adoption of the first ten amendments has been told too often to be repeated.[65] Also, the qualitative change of the constitutional protection of individual rights resulting from the passing of the 14th Amendment, making the Supreme Court the ultimate arbiter of the individual states' respect for "the equal protection of the laws," shall not be attempted here. Again, it cannot be a theme of this paper to give an account how the most important provisions of the Federal Bill of Rights became applicable to the states—a process that has been described as the "nationalization of the Bill of Rights."[66]

Constitutional litigation involving the protection of rights has become, in the twentieth century, the major feature of America's "culture of rights." As constitutional adjudication during (roughly) the first century of U.S.

---

64. "Letters from the Federal Farmer" (abbreviated title; anonymous) in Herbert J. Storing (ed.), *The Complete Anti-Federalist*, 7 vols. (Chicago 1981) vol. 2, 261 (Letter VI; the authorship by R.H. Lee, often claimed, has been drawn in doubt by several scholars; arguments for the authorship of Melancton Smith, an important, moderate Anti-Federalist from New York have been put forward by Robert A. Webking, "Melancton Smith and the Letters from the Federal Farmer." In *William and Mary Quarterly*, 3rd series 44 (1987), 510–28; they are shared by Rakove, *Original Meanings*, 228–29).

65. Most recent interpretations of this process in Hutson, *Bill of Rights*, 80–97, and, with a subtle analysis of James Madison's views and motives, Rakove, *Original Meanings* 330–38.

66. Cf. Richard C. Cortner, *The Supreme Court and the Second Bill of Rights: The Fourteenth Amendment and the Nationalization of Civil Liberties* (Madison, WI 1981); Michael Kent Curtis, *No State Shall Abridge: The Fourteenth Amendment and the Bill of Rights* (Durham, NC 1986); very suggestive, and with ample references, Robert J. Kaczorowski, To Begin the Nation Anew: Congress, Citizenship, and Civil Rights after the Civil War. In *American Historical Review* 92 (1987), 45–68. Cf. also the radically egalitarian interpretation by Judith A. Baer, *Equality under the Constitution: Reclaiming the Fourteenth Amendment* (Ithaca, NY 1983).

constitutionalism has (chiefly) been a constitutionalism of "powers," the
second century of U.S. constitutionalism has been marked by "a new constitutionalism of rights." Especially since 1945, "the civil rights of racial
and other groups have taken center stage in what has become a vigorous
constitutionalism of rights."[67] Thus one encounters the striking phenomenon that in an age of increasing relativism, particularly "cultural relativism,"[68] in an age in which generally recognized moral obligations seem to
be weakening or waning, "rights talk" persists. "The Curious Persistence
of Rights Talk in the 'Age of Interpretation'" is the title of a thoughtful
article,[69] and it is indeed a phenomenon that calls for comment.

I suggest two answers, one obvious and one perhaps less obvious, both
limited to the specifically U.S. American "culture of rights." I shall return
to this problem in my conclusion, where I shall attempt to suggest an additional answer applying both to Europe and America.

As far as the United States are concerned, the obvious answer would
be: The Enlightenment project of the American system of government, as
expressed in the Declaration of Independence and the Federal Constitution, rededicated in the Gettysburg Address and the 14th Amendment,
including a considerable potential of conflict resolution through constitutional litigation and adjudication, has generated very strong institutional
and emotional (patriotic) support, strong enough to defy intellectual fashions and even more slowly changing moral currents.

A less obvious answer would be this: The "culture of rights" of the
United States draws its peculiar intensity and poignancy from the fact
that in no other liberal democracy in the North Atlantic world, the affirmation of human rights and their denial have been as closely adjacent to
each other as in the United States. As you see, I am developing Edmund
Morgan's "American Slavery, American Freedom" theme.[70] Joyce Appleby
has written that the most radical achievement of the American Revolution
was "the abolition movement that brought northern slavery to an end and
turned the surveyors' line of Mason and Dixon into the most conspicuous

67. Keller, *Powers and Rights*, 686, 688.

68. Cf. the challenging reflections by David A. Hollinger, How Wide the Circle of the
"We"? American Intellectuals and the Problem of the Ethnos since World War II. In *American
Historical Review* 98 (1993), 317–37, particularly 326.

69. Thomas L. Haskell, The Curious Persistence of Rights Talk in the "Age of Interpretation." In *Journal of American History* 74 (1987–1988), 984–1012.

70. Edmund Morgan, Slavery and Freedom: The American Paradox. In *Journal of American History* 59 (1972–1973), 5–29, and idem, *American Slavery, American Freedom: The Or-
deal of Colonial Virginia* (New York 1975).

ideological divide in the world."[71] I agree with Hendrik Hartog who has said that for the past two centuries, "American understandings of constitutional rights have changed as understandings of the interrelated meanings of slavery and of political freedom have changed." Hartog rightly adds: "The long contest over slavery did more than any other cause to stimulate the development of an alternate, rights conscious, interpretation of the Federal Constitution."[72]

In no other liberal democracy has the postulate of equal rights been taken as seriously and at the same time has encountered utter denial as directly as in America.[73] One may compare the Declaration of Independence's proposition that all men are created equal with Chief Justice Taney's denial that citizenship might ever be accessible to the black person, whether slave or free. In no other liberal democracy have varieties of legal capacity ranging from the fullest capacity of the male citizen "having sufficient evidence of permanent common interest with and attachment to the community"[74] to the denial of active legal capacity pertaining to the status of slavery, been as great as in America.[75] Think of status issues arising out of the fugitive slave movement and the personal liberty laws in antebellum America,[76] or arising out of transit through or residence in free territory, culminating in the *Dred Scott* case.[77] I believe that the intensity of the pre-civil war struggle on the status of persons, free/unfree, equal/unequal, continues to provide an ever-present foil for the subsequent debates on inequality of status and its remedies, on discrimination negative and positive, in other words, on rights. After the abolition of slavery, status discrimination concerning colored people, whether de jure in the South ("grandfather laws") or de facto in many places, and more recently status

71. Joyce Appleby, The Radical Recreation of the American Republic. In *William and Mary Quarterly*, 3rd series 51 (1994), 679–83, here 682 (contribution to a forum discussing Gordon S. Wood's *The Radicalism of the American Revolution*).

72. Hendrik Hartog, The Constitution of Aspiration and "The Rights That Belong to Us All." In *Journal of American History* 74 (1987), 1013–34, here 1017.

73. Cf. the very thoughtful work by J. R. Pole, *The Pursuit of Equality in American History* (revised ed.) (Berkeley CA 1993).

74. Virginia Bill of Rights of 1776, section 6.

75. Robert von Mohl, in 1824, divided his chapter on the personal rights of the inhabitants of the United States into three sections: rights of the "free whites," of the "free colored," and of the "slaves"—the latter amounting to a list of rights denied, and of the rights of the masters. Mohl, *Bundes-Staatsrecht*, 385–418.

76. William M. Wiecek, *The Sources of Antislavery Constitutionalism in America, 1760–1848* (Ithaca, NY 1977); Paul Finkelman, *An Imperfect Union: Slavery, Federalism, and Comity* (Chapel Hill, NC 1981).

77. On this issue see the masterly work by Don Fehrenbacher (supra note 31).

discrimination concerning other groups, notably women, have continued to throw into relief, though with uneven spells of intensity, the issue of status inequalities. Hartog has rightly stressed that the history of "rights consciousness" has received an enormous impulse since the end of the Civil War and emancipation. He has emphasized: "All the varying meanings that have been derived from the phrase 'equal protection of the laws' are rooted in contending views of what it was that was overthrown by the end of slavery."[78] All this has supplied an impetus to civil rights or equal rights litigation that is probably not found anywhere else in the North Atlantic world and indeed characterizes America's "culture of rights."

III

The constituent Power of the people, which had been exercised in America since 1776, re-emerged on the continent of Europe, in France, in 1789 as the *pouvoir constituant de la nation*. Its most important advocate was Emmanuel Sieyes, whose booklet "What is the Third Estate?" played a powerful role early in 1789, similar to that played by Tom Paine's "Common Sense" early in 1776.[79] The constituent Power of the nation found its institutional expression in the National Assembly, also often referred to as the "constituent" National Assembly or *constituante*. The name "National Assembly" employed in Paris in 1789 was to reverberate through the subsequent history of the constituent Power of the people in Europe— in Frankfurt on Main in 1848, in Weimar and Vienna in 1919, in Paris again or in Rome after the Second World War. The history of the United States has never known—on the level of the union—such an assembly issued from a nationwide election, uniting the representatives of the whole nation for the task of drawing up the constitution as fundamental law of the nation, but at the same time legislating as well. Such bodies reflected and felt themselves to be in the legitimate possession of the sovereignty of the people.

The French National Assembly of 1789 adopted, as we all know, the Declaration of the Rights of Man and Citizen. Much has been written on the impact, present or absent, of the American states' declarations of rights on the French Declaration. I would agree with Georg Jellinek and

78. Hartog, *Constitution of Aspiration*, 1017.

79. The best critical edition is Emmanuel Joseph Sieyes, *Qu'est-ce que le Tiers état?*, ed. Roberto Zapperi (Geneva 1970).

Robert R. Palmer, among others, that such an impact indeed existed.[80] Yet
it is also important to see differences between the type of bills of rights
prevailing in the United States and the French Declaration of 1789 and its
many successors. The French text of 1789 contained in no less than seven
out of seventeen articles express invitations or rather authorizations addressed to the legislator, to settle matters *par la loi*, by law. The law (*la loi*)
was explicitly declared to be the "the expression of the general will" (Article 6); in the Constitution of 1791 it was also stated expressly that "there
is in France no authority superior to that of the law." Thus *la loi* assumed
a central significance, and so did consequently the maker of the law, the
legislator, assumed to be the mouthpiece of the nation's sovereign will.[81]
In the American declarations, there are more statements about what existing law prescribes, in the French Declaration, more is said about what the
law will be supposed to settle. In America the declarations had to do with
legislative restraint; the French declarations (of 1793 no less than of 1789),
quite apart from their function as a kind of revolutionary "catechism,"
became guideposts for legislative action rather than legislative restraint. It
also has been observed that the French (unlike the English and the Americans) "are more sensitive to grand principles than to the procedures which
guarantee them."[82] The consequences of this disposition will be discussed
shortly.

Finally, in France no less than in America, a "written constitution" was
drawn up and adopted in 1791; the end of the monarchy and the proclama-
tion of the republic in 1792 necessitated a new constitution, more democratic (with strong Rousseauian overtones) in theory; it never was allowed

---

80. Jellinek's little book, first published in 1895, is conveniently found, together with a
number of more recent studies, partly critical, partly revising and developing Jellinek's theses, in Roman Schnur (ed.), *Zur Geschichte der Erklärung der Menschenrechte* (Darmstadt
1964). A parallel printing of the corresponding articles of the Virginia Bill of Rights and the
French Declaration of 1789 has been assembled in Robert R. Palmer, *The Age of the Democratic Revolution.*, vol.1, 518–21. Among the vast literature published around the bicentennial
of 1789, I would like to draw attention to Stéphane Rials (ed.), *La déclaration de 1789* (Special
issue of *Droits. Revue française de théorie juridique* No. 8 1988, and to Wolfgang Schmale, article "Droit." In Rolf Reichardt and Hans-Jürgen Lüsebrink (eds.), *Handbuch politisch-sozialer
Grundbegriffe in Frankreich 1680–1820*, vol.12 (München 1992), 65–87, particularly 78–84.

81. For the following cf. Gerald Stourzh, The Declarations of Rights, Popular Sovereignty
and the Supremacy of the Constitution: Divergencies between the American and the French
Revolutions. In Claude Fohlen and Jacques Godechot (eds.), *La Révolution américaine et
l'Europe* (Colloques internationaux du Centre National de la Recherche Scientifique No. 577)
(Paris 1979), 347–64, particularly 355.

82. Professor Georges Vedel in *Le Monde*, November 10, 1977, 1.

to operate. As we all know, the number of constitutions in France was to multiply in the years and decades to come. In revolutionary France, the halo surrounding the notion of "constitution" was even stronger than in America; the relevance of an almost deified "constitution" in the context of dechristianization and revolution in France has been the object of thoughtful recent discussion.[83]

Yet in spite of the exalted place of the constitution, a logical consequence of the constitution as paramount public law did not develop in France: mechanisms to control the constitutionality of legislation, notably judicial review. In 1791, a project for a special *assemblée de revision* was worked out; this special assembly was to be empowered to investigate whether the "constituted powers" had stayed within the limits prescribed by the constitution. The plan came to nothing. In 1795, under the Directory, someone who grasped the logic of the constitution as higher law and who asked for a kind of special constitutional court was Emmanuel Sieyes; yet his proposal of a *jury constitutionnaire* was not taken up either.[84] An excellent expert on French public law has commented that the reason for the failure of Sieyes' plan is to be found "in the concept of the absolute power of the legislative body as representative of the general will."[85]

Certainly, the primacy of legislative sovereignty in France in spite of the existence of written constitutions had various sources. In France, as distinct from America, the Revolution was not directed against the "despotism" of a sovereign Parliament, but against absolutism (and against the *société des ordres*). In France, opposition against the existing judicial organization was strong, since it was regarded to be part and parcel of the *ancien régime*, while in America the judiciary, from the time of the Stamp Act, had sided with the "patriots."

Now the concept of the primacy of the legislative assembly as expression of the sovereign will of the nation had far-reaching consequences. It prevented, for a very long time indeed, any kind of judicial review of legislation. Only in 1958 did the constitution of the Fifth Republic create the Conseil Constitutionnel, empowered to exercise a control of the constitutionality of legislation. But it was not and is not a court *stricto sensu*, since suits by individual citizens cannot be addressed to it; specific complaints as to the unconstitutionality of certain laws or legal provisions

83. Wolfgang Schmale, *Entchristianisierung, Revolution und Verfassung. Zur Mentalitätsgeschichte der Verfassung in Frankreich, 1715–1794* (Berlin 1988).

84. Stourzh, *Declarations of Right*, 361–62.

85. Georges Burdeau, *Traité de Science politique*, vol. 4 (Paris 1969), 374, also 408–10.

may be brought before the Conseil Constitutionnel by the Government, by the Presidents of the two Chambers of the National Assembly, and after a reform also by a minority group of deputies, but not by individuals. A proposal by President Mitterand in connection with the Bicentennial of the French Revolution, to entitle citizens to bring suits before the Conseil was not taken up by the National Assembly. Nevertheless, a constitutional "revolution" happened in 1971, when the Conseil Constitutionnel ruled for the first time that the Declaration of the Rights of Man and Citizen of 1789 had constitutionally binding character and that consequently ordinary law was to be measured by the standard of the legally superior Declaration of Rights.[86]

Thus three types of western democratic government were in the process of emerging and developing: in Great Britain, the primacy of a sovereign Parliament without a "written," i.e., paramount constitution, and without a constitutional protection of individual rights; in the United States, the primacy of the written constitution including an unequivocal subordination of legislation and the constitutional protection of individual rights; in France (at least until the onset of the Fifth Republic) a de facto sovereignty of the legislator in spite of the existence of a written constitution and (until 1971) no constitutional protection of individual rights. The "culture of rights" in these three nations obviously was influenced by this state of affairs. In a very general way, and with an awareness and due respect for differences in time and space among various countries, I would say that in other European nations developing towards liberal democracy, for a long time constitutional systems developed rather similar to the French type; a strong tendency in direction of the American type developed only in the second half of the twentieth century.

Prior to sketching this fairly new development, I need to turn to an aspect of the transformation of the legal landscape of Europe which has wholly altered the "culture of rights" in Europe. I refer to the process of the "equalization" (Angleichung) of individual rights—or technically speaking, of the individuals' legal capacity—that went on from the late eighteenth century well into the twentieth century. This process consisted not

---

86. For the breakthrough in a decision of July 16, 1971, see Louis Favoreu & Loïc Philip (eds.), Les grandes décisions du Conseil Constitutionnel (Paris 1975), 267–87. Cf. also Christian Starck, Der Schutz der Grundrechte durch den Verfassungsrat in Frankreich. In Archiv des öffentlichen Rechts 113 (1988), 636. For a general discussion of the French development cf. Gerald Stourzh, Verfassungsgerichtsbarkeit und Grundrechtsdemokratie—die historischen Wurzeln. In Verfassungsgerichtshof der Republik Österreich (ed.), 70 Jahre Bundesverfassung (Wien 1991), 26–28.

merely in the reduction or disappearance of the privileges, immunities and "liberties" of orders or estates or other "privileged" groups in the every-day understanding of the word "privileged." This process included, and in a major way, the lifting of the *privilegia odiosa*, of the special obligations and restrictions burdening most diverse groups of the population.

One passage from the celebrated book "On the Civil Improvement of the Jews" by the Prussian author Christian Wilhelm Dohm, published in 1781, explains what I would like to convey.[87] Dohm wrote: "The Jew is even more a human being than a Jew, and how should it be possible that he should not love a State, in which he could acquire and freely enjoy property, in which his taxes would not be greater than those of other citizens, and where he, too, could acquire honor and respect? Why should he hate people, who would not anymore be separated from him by grievous privileges, with whom he would share equal rights and equal duties?"[88]

Dohm's sentence "Der Jude ist noch mehr Mensch als Jude"—"The Jew is even more a human being than a Jew" is apt to explain—symbolically and vicariously, as it were—the claim of all groups of people living under a Status of limited, or sometimes virtually non-existent, legal capacity.[89]

The emancipation of serfs and peasants (*Bauernbefreiung*); the emancipation of slaves, not merely in the United States, but in territories under European domination; the emancipation of Catholics in England, e.g., or of Protestants in Catholic nations; the emancipation of the Jews—in France at the time of the French Revolution,[90] in a slower and halting process elsewhere in continental Europe; the legal equalization of the status of domestic servants; the legal improvement and final equalization of the status of woman—these and many other stages and chapters in the process of the equalization of legal capacity have had a profound impact on the character of "cultures of rights."

I stress this transforming process for three reasons: First, there is a vast difference between a society based on unequal legal capacity and a society based on equal legal capacity. A close reading of Tocqueville's writings shows how very great is the part of the transformation of legal capacity in his account of the progress of the *égalité des conditions*—the central

87. Christian Konrad Wilhelm von Dohm, *Über die bürgerliche Verbesserung der Juden*, 2 vols. (Berlin–Stettin 1781 and 1783, reprint in one volume Hildesheim–New York 1973), the following quote vol. l, 28. The book appeared in a French translation as early as 1782.

88. My translation. For more details see the immediately preceding paper, pp. 294–95.

89. The German legal term is "Rechtsfähigkeit."

90. Cf. particularly Robert Badinter, *Libres et égaux . . . L'émanicaption des Juifs 1789–1791* (Paris 1989).

term of Tocqueville's work describing the emergence, development and future tendencies of the vast socio-juridico-political system which he called "democracy."[91]

Second, the traditional story of human rights and of civil rights, particularly in Europe, has put a too one-sided emphasis on those rights which were entrenched in the catalogues and declarations of rights drawn up in the tradition of the French declaration of 1789.[92] By the same token, developments in private law, e.g. concerning property or inheritance legislation have long been neglected by historians,[93] and there is no question that feminist historical writing has been instrumental in calling attention to the significance of disabilities of legal status and capacity beyond the limited sphere of constitutionally entrenched rights.[94]

Third, attention to the role of legal capacity and legal status sharpens our awareness of threats to individual rights as harbingers of worse things to come. Under National Socialism, as early as 1936, the German Supreme Court (Reichsgericht) denied legal capacity to a Jewish person in a suit for damages, explicitly rejecting "the former liberal notion" of the equal personality rights of human beings, affirming "older thoughts" on the legitimate distinction between persons of full legal capacity and those of inferior right, a distinction now to be applied according to racial criteria.[95] This statement antedates the November pogrom of 1938 and further degradation and destruction to come. It shows how the reduction or denial of legal capacity is a signal for the destruction of any "culture of rights" previously existing.

The victory over National Socialism and Fascism in 1945 has produced a new thrust in the direction of the protection of human rights which has led, within the last 50 years, to a new level of the "culture of rights" in many European nations. The western world, in the United States no less than in Europe outside the remnants of fascism and the communist orbit,

91. For this see the immediately following chapter.

92. This is the case, e.g., in the widely used book by Gerhard Oestreich, *Geschichte der Menschenrechte und Grundfreiheiten im Umriss* (Berlin 1968).

93. Although there are as always exceptions to the rule, such as Elisabeth Fehrenbach, *Traditionale Gesellschaft und revolutionäres Recht* (Göttingen 1974).

94. See, e.g. the references supra note 19.

95. The "Charell case," brilliantly analyzed by Ernst Fraenkel in his classic study on the Dual State (New York 1940), here reference to the German edition: Ernst Fraenkel, *Der Doppelstaat* (Frankfurt/M. 1974), 126–27. On this case, as well as on the process of "Entrechtung" (taking away of previously held rights) which led to the genocide of the Jewish population under Nazi rule, I have written in greater detail in Gerald Stourzh, Menschenrechte und Genozid. In Heinz Schäffer et al., (eds.), *Staat—Verfassung—Verwaltung. Festschrift anläßlich des 65. Geburtstages von Prof. DDr.DDr.h.c. Friedrich Koja* (Wien 1998), 135–59, here particularly 147–56.

was swept by a renewal of the enlightenment tradition of the natural rights of mankind. The Universal Declaration of Human Rights of 1948 and the many international conventions on the protection of human rights (including the two Covenants on Human Rights of 1966) in general or of certain groups of people in particular are important cases in point. On the European level, the European Convention on Human Rights and Fundamental Liberties of 1950 has set a landmark for a new culture of rights in those European nations who adhere to that Convention. By creating procedures enabling individuals to apply for remedies against violation of human rights and appropriate judicial or semi-judicial institutions (the European Commission of Human Rights and the European Court of Human Rights), the European Convention did establish the most efficient transnational system of the protection of human rights anywhere in the world. During the year 1998, a major revision of the institutional system of the European protection of human rights took place. The European Commission of Human Rights as an intermediate institution between complaining individuals and the European Court went out of existence, and the European Court of Human Rights was transformed into a Court with full time judges—one judge for every member nation of the Council of Europe. By linking membership in the Council of Europe to adherence to the European Convention of Human Rights, this system has been extended to a large number of nations in Eastern and South Eastern Europe, including Russia and the Ukraine. It will be of very great interest to watch the impact of this "new" European Court of Human Rights (whose work started on 1 November 1998) on nations with a weak tradition of the protection of individual rights.

On the national level of the European democracies, the constitutional protection of human rights has made considerable advances by developing or extending procedures that first were suggested or tried, rather sporadically, in the 19th century. The German constitution of 1848, drawn up in Frankfurt's Paulskirche, provided that the Reichsgericht would be empowered to decide on suits of German citizens concerning the violation of rights guaranteed by the constitution.[96] Yet the constitution of the Paulskirche was never given the chance to be put into practice, and a provision

---

96. Cf. Hans Joachim Faller, Die Verfassungsgerichtsbarkeit in der Frankfurter Reichsverfassung vom 28. März 1849. In Gerhard Leibholz, Hans J. Faller, & Paul Mikat et al. (eds.), Menschenwürde und freiheitliche Rechtsordnung. Festschrift für Willi Geiger zum 65. Geburtstag (Tübingen 1974), 827–66, particularly 835, 839–40, 845. On the impact of the American constitutional principles on the deputies of the Paulskirche, cf. the excellent study by Eckhart G. Franz, Das Amerikabild der deutschen Revolution von 1848/49. Zum Problem der Übertragung gewachsener Verfassungsformen (Heidelberg 1958), 98–133. On American comments on the German constitutional projects of 1848, cf. Günter Moltmann, Atlantische Blockpolitik

corresponding to the one just mentioned had to wait until the "Grundgesetz" (Basic Law) of 1949. However, the liberal constitutional program of 1848, embodied in the Austrian "Kremsier" draft constitution as well as in the Frankfurt constitution, was taken up, by virtue of a peculiar political constellation when the Austrian Emperor needed the support of the Austrian liberals, in the liberal constitution of Imperial Austria of 1867.[97] Rights guaranteed under the Austrian fundamental law on the rights of citizens could be sued for in the Austrian Imperial Court (Reichsgericht), though some legal deficiencies impaired the effectiveness of this provision; the Imperial Court was a forerunner of the Austrian Constitutional Court created in 1919/20, where, with the significant participation of a legal theorist turned constitution maker, Hans Kelsen, the first efficient system for the constitutional protection of citizens' rights was created. It differed from the American system by separating the functions, united in the American Supreme Court, of a Supreme Court (for civil and criminal matters) and a special Constitutional Court.

Only after 1945 has there been a vast expansion of constitutional jurisdiction including the creation of special constitutional courts, and including the remedy of individual suit (*Verfassungsbeschwerde, Individualbeschwerde*). The Federal Republic of Germany has to be mentioned as the nation with the most developed post–World War II tradition of constitutional jurisdiction (beginning in 1951); yet Italy (1956), Spain (1980), Belgium (1984) also deserve special mention; the somewhat exceptional case of France has been referred to already.[98] More recently, constitutional courts have been created in Poland, Hungary, the Czech Republic, even in Russia (though conclusions as to impartiality and effectiveness in the latter case would be premature). Within the English speaking world, constitutional jurisdiction, though not located in separate courts, has increasingly included jurisdiction concerning "entrenched" provisions or bills of human rights. A notable example of a transition from the "British" system without an entrenched bill of rights to the "American" system of an entrenched bill of rights has been the creation and operation of the Canadian Charter of Rights.[99] It has been rightly said that the experience of the last decades shows that

---

im 19. Jahrhundert. Die Vereinigten Staaten und der deutsche Liberalismus während der Revolution von 1848/49 (Düsseldorf 1973), 213–35.

97. Gerald Stourzh, Die österreichische Dezemberverfassung von 1867. In idem, *Wege zur Grundrechtsdemokratie*, 239–58.

98. Cf. supra at note 86.

99. Cf. Anne F. Bayefsky, Parliamentary Sovereignty and Human Rights in Canada: The Promise of the Canadian Charter of Rights and Freedoms. In *Political Studies* 31 (1983), 239–63.

constitutional jurisdiction (in American parlance judicial review) has become the institutional protector for the preservation and development of
western democracy. This is particularly true of the function of protecting
individual rights.[100]

There remains Great Britain, without an entrenched bill of rights. The
case in favor of a bill of rights removed from Parliament's sovereign legislative will was reopened in 1974 by the eminent British judge Sir Leslie
Scarman (later Lord Scarman), it has been taken up most prominently by
Ronald Dworkin, and the case has also been persuasively argued by Alan
Ryan in a study mentioned earlier in this paper. One most interesting phenomenon needs to be noted: A kind of subsidiary bill of rights—and a subsidiary Court—have been operating for more than three decades. The European Convention of Human Rights, and the European Court of Human
Rights, and the impact of this institution and the "Strasbourg" cases on
public discussion in Britain has been considerable. The Queen's Speech of
14 May, 1997, embodying the legislative program of the new Labour Government, announced the "incorporation" of the European Convention of
Human Rights into British Law. This will enable British courts to apply
directly the provisions of the European Convention, though the exact way
in which possible clashes between the European Convention incorporated
as British law and other parliamentary enactments might be reconciled
still remains to be worked out.*

Looking back on the last half century, it can be said that in the liberal democracies of the western world, more than ever before the idea of a
liberal constitution expressed in 1776 by the Concord Town Meeting has
been fulfilled: "[. . .] a Constitution in its proper idea intends a system
of principles established to secure the subject in the possession and en-

100. Cf. for an early survey the chapter on judicialism in Carl. J. Friedrich, *The Impact of
American Constitutionalism Abroad* (Boston 1967), 71–96, and the excellent study by Alexander von Brünneck, *Verfassungsgerichtsbarkeit in den westlichen Demokratien. Ein systematischer Verfassungsvergleich* (Baden-Baden 1992), 151; for a comparative survey of the constitutional protection of individual rights, cf. ibid. 62–125; for the following paragraph, see ibid.,
150–51; also Sir Leslie Scarman, *English Law—The New Dimension* (London 1974), and Ronald
Dworkin, *A Bill of Rights for Britain?* (London 1990); Ryan, *The British* 416–20, 431–39.

* Special Note 2006: In fulfillment of this announcement in the Queen's Speech of 1997,
the Human Rights Act 1998 was enacted on 9 November 1998 (1998, Chapter 42). It entered
into force on 2 October 2000. Since then, rights contained in the European Convention on
Human Rights are enforceable in Courts of the United Kingdom. It makes it unlawful for a
public authority to violate convention rights, unless, by an Act of Parliament, it had no choice.
If persons feel that they are a victim of a non-compliance of a public authority with convention rights, they may avail themselves of the remedies set up by this act within the UK Court
system. If an incompatibility between British legislation and the European Convention on

joyment of their rights and privileges, against any encroachments of the governing part."[101] In the United States the background of slavery and slave emancipation and racial discrimination has given added intensity to the American culture of rights; in Europe, the horrors of genocide and the havoc brought on millions of persons by National Socialism have provided, in the years after 1945, a new impetus to the protection of human rights, indeed to a new culture of rights. By the end of the 20th century, not merely in the United States, but in many other states, particularly in Europe, a new and more intensive level of a "culture of rights" had been reached or was in the process of attainment.

IV

My conclusion is very brief and consists of two points only.

First, I would like to express—from the vantage point of the theme of liberal democracy as a culture of rights—my scepticism as to simply juxtaposing "America" and "Europe." What about England or Great Britain? What about Canada, so often forgotten in comparative discussions?[102] I have doubts about "exceptionalisms," American or European. If I may be allowed the pun, I take exception to the term "exceptionalism." In many countries there are certainly assertions of one's own special and providential task or burden.[103] There are certainly various types and even more numerous variants within the family of liberal democracies; there are numerous distinctions to make in that vast development which Alexis de Tocqueville described and analyzed as the development of those "conditions of equality" which are the core of modern liberal democracy. Yet "exceptionalism" as a category of historical and comparative analysis will not, I fear, open up

Human Rights is upheld by the Courts, it is up to Parliament to decide what action to take. Information on the British Human Rights Act and its application (including a list of incompatibilities claimed) is provided by the UK Department for Constitutional Affairs in the Internet at http://www.dca.gov.uk/hract/hrafaqs.htm, with additional links.

101. See supra note 58 (here spelling modernized).

102. For all too rare comparative volumes that consider both the United States and Canada, cf. Seymour Martin Lipset, *Continental Divide: The Values and Institutions of the United States and Canada* (New York 1990); Marian C. McKenna (ed.), *The Canadian and American Constitutions in Comparative Perspective* (Calgary, Alberta 1993); and the thoughtful review by Willi Paul Adams in *Reviews in American History* 23 (1995), 545–51, here 551, who writes that the latter volume can "serve to jolt students of American as well as Canadian constitutional law and history out of the ruts of the well-trodden paths of homonational historiography."

103. It is in the context of the Americans' consciousness of a special task or mission and its rhetorical implications that Erich Angermann has placed the term "exceptionalism": Erich Angermann, Was heißt und zu welchem Ende studiert man anglo-amerikanische Geschichte? In *Historische Zeitschrift* 256 (1993), 637–59, here 648f.

new insights. Carl Degler has stated the essential point years ago: "To ask what differentiates one people from another does not mean one has to insist on deviation from a norm, which is clearly implied in the term exceptionalism."[104] The recent restatement of the United States as exceptional and an "outlier" among nations by a distinguished believer in American exceptionalism has encountered manyfold critical comments.[105]

Second, I would like to refer once more to Tocqueville. Tocqueville has said that he knew of merely two methods of establishing equality in the political world. "Rights must be given to every citizen, or none at all to anyone." Tocqueville pointed to the decline of divine as well as moral notions of rights and concluded: "If, in the midst of this general disruption, you do not succeed in connecting the notion of right with that of private interest, which is the only immutable point in the human heart, what means will you have of governing the world except by fear?"[106] Fear, to a reader of Montesquieu like Tocqueville, was the principle animating the worst form of government, despotism. The "curious persistence of rights talk in the 'Age of Interpretation,'"[107] or to be more blunt, the care for a culture of rights in an age of increasing relativism, may indeed be the only way to stave off the threats of a new despotism.

104. Carl N. Degler, In Pursuit of American History. In *American Historical Review* 92 (1987), 4. Cf. also the thoughtful paper by George M. Frederickson, From Exceptionalism to Variability: Recent Developments in Cross-National Comparative History. In *The Journal of American History* 82 (1995), 587–604.

105. Seymour Martin Lipset, *American Exceptionalism: A Double-Edged Sword* (New York 1996), 17. Three critical review essays by experts on Canadian, Japanese and German history appeared in the following year: H.V. Nelles, American Exceptionalism: A Double-Edged Sword. In *American Historical Review* 102 (1997), 749–57 (with an interesting survey of the development of Lipset's exceptionalism in his earlier work); J. Victor Koschmann, The Nationalism of Cultural Uniqueness. In ibid. 758–68; and Mary Nolan, Against Exceptionalisms. In ibid., 769–74, with her devastating conclusion: "The repeated assertion of American exceptionalism masks the complex nature of American society and its similarities with and interconnections to other nations. It dismisses the ways the rest of the world sees the United States. In both Germany and America, exceptionalist arguments produce inadequate history, limited self-understanding and arrogant politics" (ibid., 774).

106. Alexis de Tocqueville, *Democracy in America,* ed. Phillips Bradley, 2 vols. (New York 1945) vol l, 53, 246 (vol. I, part i, ch. iii and part II, ch. vi [only in the Bradley edition numbered as ch. xiv]).

107. This is the title of the brilliant article by Thomas L. Haskell, referred to above, note 69. Addendum 2006: There is no question that fear is abroad in the western world in the first decade of the 21st century to a much greater extent than in 2000, when this essay was first published. And inroads on the respect for rights have been on the increase. The insistence on a culture of rights seems all the more justified at a time when increasing fears provoke the piecemeal reduction of the rule of law in favor of "security" or the "national interest." Democracy devoid of a culture of rights will not survive, even if succeeding types of rule may clothe themselves in the mantle of democratic notions.

CHAPTER FOURTEEN

Tocqueville's Understanding of "Conditions of Equality" and "Conditions of Inequality"*

This essay is dedicated to Ralph Lerner,
meticulous scholar, profound thinker
and trusted friend over almost five decades.

In a chapter notable for its brevity as well its density, Alexis de Tocqueville has explained the great transformation from aristocracy to democracy by the image of a broken chain. In this chapter in volume II of his *Democracy in America*, on "Individualism in democratic countries," Tocqueville characterizes the socio-political form of the past, typologically classed as "aristocracy," by the image of a "long chain" linking distinct groups of people in an ascending direction from peasant to king. The newly emerging society, typologically classed as "democracy," and developing "à mesure que les conditions s'égalisent"—to the extent to which conditions become equalized—does away with this chain: "Democracy breaks the chain and puts every link apart."[1]

---

*First published in *Enlightening Revolutions. Essays in Honor of Ralph Lerner*, ed. by Svetozar Minkov, Lanhan, MD 2006, 259–80.

1. *De la démocratie en Amérique*, Vol. II, Second Part, ch. II, in: Alexis de Tocqueville, *Oeuvres complètes*, ed. J.P.Mayer (et al.), Paris 1951–, I (2), Paris 1951, 105–106 (henceforth cited as OC). All references to Tocqueville's works will be to this edition, except when quoted from other secondary works. Translations are my own, except otherwise indicated. This chapter, incidentally, is given central significance in Louis Dumont's *Homo hierarchicus*, Paris 1966. Reference is also made to the two most thoroughly annotated editions of *De la démocratie en Amérique*: first, the *"Première édition historico-critique revue et augmentée,"* edited by Eduardo Nolla, 2 vols., Paris 1990 (henceforth cited as Nolla), and second, the edition in vol. II of Tocqueville's *Oeuvres* in the Bibliothèque de la Pléiade, edited under the direction of André Jardin and for vol. II with the collaboration of Jean-Claude Lamberti and James T. Schleifer, Paris 1992 (henceforth cited as Pléiade II).

Tocqueville's image of the chain from peasant to king is nothing else but a late reincarnation of the "Great Chain of Being"—an image encompassing the notion of a gradated, hierarchically structured universe, the story of which was brilliantly told by Arthur Lovejoy in his William James Lectures at Harvard in 1933.[2] Tocqueville's evocation of that image was a somewhat truncated one, since it limited itself to the gradation of human groups and omitted earlier, all-encompassing notions of the Great Chain of Being, including, under God, spirits good and evil surrounding the world of the humans. Dante's *Divina commedia* remains the most enduring testimony of that idea in its long course through Western history from (at least) the Neo-Platonism of Plotin through its christianization by Augustinus and Dionysius Areopagitica down to the 18th century. One of the great texts of the gradated order of things is, of course, Shakespeare's monologue of Ulysses in *Troilus and Cressida:* "O when degree is shaked, which is the ladder to all high designs, the enterprise is sick . . ." Alexander Pope's *Essay on Man* of 1733/4 is among the last (and more placid) expressions of what is one of the longest lasting theodicies in Western history:

> Nor let the rich the lowest slave disdain
> He's equally a link of nature's chain;
> Labours to the same end, joins in one view,
> And both alike the will divine pursue.[3]

Tocqueville, however, pronounces the end of this. The equalization of conditions leads to social organization of a new type, democracy—twice in the same brief chapter the phrase "à mesure que les conditions s'égalisent" occurs!—and "[d]emocracy breaks the chain and puts every link apart."[4] The result is the birth of individualism—a term whose novelty is stressed by Tocqueville[5]—and above all the birth of a society of individuals who have lost their former moorings in the smaller groups who had been part of the chain ascending "from peasant to king." These smaller groups To-

---

2. Arthur O. Lovejoy, *The Great Chain of Being,* Cambridge, MA 1936.

3. Quoted, with comments, in Lovejoy, *The Great Chain of Being,* 207.

4. The image of the chain is commented neither by Nolla nor in Pléiade II. On gradations of status in the societies of the *ancien régime* see Gerald Stourzh, *Equal Rights. Equalizing the Individual's Status and the Breakthrough of the Modern Liberal State,* in this volume, pp. 275–303.

5. Though the term was not invented by him. Cf. Jean-Claude Lamberti, *Tocqueville and the Two Democracies,* Cambridge, Mass., 168–73 (henceforth cited Lamberti).

queville describes with a word to which he obviously gives less precision than subsequent social thought—"classes." "The classes being quite distinct and immobile within an aristocratic people, each one of them becomes for those belonging to it a kind of little fatherland, more visible and more dear than the great one." However, as in aristocratic societies all citizens are placed in a fixed position ("à poste fixe"), the ones above the others, it results from this situation that everyone always perceives above him a man whose protection he needs, and further down he discovers another one whose help he may claim. The vertical structure of "aristocratic society"—or the vertical bend of the "chain from peasant to king" could not be described more drastically.[6]

Also, in aristocratic peoples according to Tocqueville, families remain for centuries within the same status, and often in the same place, and therefore the ties among generations are much closer. All this—relations among generations, and the relations of protection and support tying classes of different rank to one another—disappears with the approach of conditions of equality. The new individualism, "of democratic origin," "threatens to develop to the extent that conditions become equalized."[7] Thus democratic individualism cuts traditional ties, it throws people on their own resources, "it drives every man into isolation and it finally threatens to lock everybody in the solitude of his own heart"—"dans la solitude de son propre coeur." Thus the chapter ends with a touch of Pascal—whose anguished reader Tocqueville had been[8]—though Raymond Aron has rightly pointed out that the "Pascalian affinities of Tocqueville belong to his biography rather than his work."[9]

6. OC I(2) 106.

7. Ibid., 105.

8. Tocqueville read Pascal on various occasions, but notably in 1836, prior to writing volume II of *De la démocratie en Amérique*. See OC XVI, *Mélanges*, ed. by Françoise Mélonio, Paris 1989, 551, introductory note to Tocqueville's MS Notes on the *Pensées* of Pascal (ibid., 551–54). On the significance of Pascal for Tocqueville, see Luis Diez del Corral, Tocqueville et Pascal, in *Revue des travaux de l'Académie des sciences morales et politiques*, 1965, 2nd semestre, 70–83. By the same author in Spanish: *La mendalidad politica de Tocqueville con especial referencia a Pascal*, Madrid 1965; on Pascal and Tocqueville see now also Sheldon S. Wolin, *Tocqueville between Two Worlds: The Making of a Political and Theoretical Life*, Princeton 2001, 84–90 (henceforth cited Wolin).

9. Rayond Aron, in a discussion in the French *Académie des sciences morales et politiques* on 15 November 1965 on the occasion of a paper presented by Luis Diez del Corral on "Tocqueville et Pascal" (see preceding note), *op. cit.*, 81 speaks of the "anguish" accompanying Tocqueville through his life and asks whether this was "une angoisse pascalienne." He concludes that ". . . de toute manière, les affinités pascaliennes ressortissent à la biographie

Tocqueville's approach to the two types of society which he constantly compares is an ambivalent one. Let me first discuss his approach to aristocracy, omitting for the time being the often discussed biographical aspect of his aristocratic origin. Several of Tocqueville's comments on aristocracy do suggest a positive approach, like the passage just referred to, on the chances—in the vertical chain linking the status groups of an aristocratic society—to appeal to protection from above or to assistance ("concours") from below.[10] Also, in the well-known conclusion to volume II of *Democracy in America*, the evocation of the "very high virtues, very brilliant and very pure ones" of aristocratic society communicates a feeling of regret and nostalgia for past greatness.[11] The Age of Chivalry has gone. . . . Yet on the other hand, there are striking instances of a very harsh judgment on characteristic features of the gradated society of orders—or aristocracy, as Tocqueville simply put it. I believe that on balance, Tocqeville's critical attitude towards the hierarchical order of society prevails over his admiring or wistful references to that order. I shall single out three instances which seem quite revealing of his attitude.

First, I turn to Tocqueville's inquiry into the relations between servant and master, and how democracy modified these relations. One chapter of volume II of *Democracy in America* is devoted to this subject[12]—a theme well-known to the history of philosophy because of Hegel's section on it in his *Phenomenology of the Mind*—, though I see no evidence that Tocqueville may have known Hegel's treatment of it.[13] Tocqueville's chapter on master and servant is a key chapter to understand his views on a society based, as he explicitly states, "on a permanent inequality of conditions."[14] It is also a chapter particularly suggestive of Tocqueville's method—reaching highest perfection in volume II of the *Democracy*, which fundamentally was a phenomenological one: empirical/historical perception, often of a strikingly visual kind, generalized and combined with an extraordi-

plutôt qu'à l'oeuvre de Tocqueville." Tocqueville's intense interest in Pascal is variously expressed notably in volume II of the *Democracy*: e.g., OC I(2), 49 (cf. also Nolla II, 50), 81 (without mentioning Pascal's name, but cf. Nolla II, 77), 132 (on Pascal's famous "bet"; in a MS note Tocqueville found this not worthy of "Pascal's great soul"—Nolla II, 117), 252; it is an existential rather than a scholarly one.

10. OC I(2), 106.
11. OC I(2), 337.
12. Third Part, ch.V, OC I(2), 185–93.
13. Cf. the section on "Herrschaft und Knechtschaft" (mastery and servitude) in: *Phänomenologie des Geistes*, in Georg Wilhelm Friedrich Hegel, *Werke in zwanzig Bänden* (paperback edition ed. by E. Moldenhauer and K. M. Michel), Frankfurt/Main 1970, vol. 3, 145–55.
14. OC I(2), 187.

nary power of intuitive introspection.[15] The Tocquevillian "ideal types"[16] of aristocracy and democracy are, as it were, distilled from the "phenotypes" of two socio-political systems; they are so distinct from one another that Tocqueville refers to them as "two distinct humanities."[17] The chapter on master and servant is a remarkable case in point.

In aristocratic society, servants and masters are like two societies superimposed on one another.[18] There are hierarchies and ranks within the society of the servants as well as the society of the masters. There were "noble and vigorous souls" among the servant class, but there was also on the low end of the hierarchy the "lackey." The "permanent inequality of conditions" in aristocratic societies produces a situation in which the poor person is "equipped" as it were from infancy with the idea of obeying to commandments. In countries where the permanent inequality of conditions prevails, the master receives prompt, complete, respectful and easy obedience. Though in aristocracies master and servant are placed at an immense distance in the "ladder of beings,"[19] through wealth, education, opinions, rights, in the course of time a long community of shared memories brings them closer together. The master comes to look on his servants like "an inferior and secondary part of himself," and he interests himself in their fate "by an ultimate effort of egoism." Nevertheless, the subordinate position of the servant, the superior position of the master remain unchanged. "On one side, obscurity, poverty, obedience forever; on the other side, glory, riches, command forever."

In democratic society, there are also masters and servants. Yet their relation to each other is radically changed: "The equality of conditions makes of servant and master new beings, and establishes new relations among them." The decisive change is the fact that now master/servant relationships are concluded on a contractual basis. Tocqueville throws into relief the fundamental change: "In a democracy, the servant may at any

15. I agree with Jean-Claude Lamberti's great emphasis on the "génie intuitif" of Tocqueville: "Notice" to volume II of *De la démocratie en Amérique* (by Lamberti), Pléiade II, 914; cf also Lamberti, 17. Sheldon Wolin rightly observes: "The reliance on visual impressions became an abiding feature of Tocqueville's mode of theorizing." Nevertheless, I disagree with Wolin's reference to Tocqueville's theory as "political impressionism." Wolin, 140; also 146 on the importance of "visual representation" in Tocqueville's theorizing.

16. Cf. Nolla I, 16; also Lamberti, 25.

17. OC I(2), 338. The translator of Lamberti's book has rendered "deux humanités distinctes" by "two different branches of mankind" (Lamberti, 37); this is too weak a rendering. "Two distinct humanities" would seem more powerful as well as more precise.

18. For the following, see OC I(2), 187.

19. "échelle des êtres"—another allusion to the "Great Chain of Being"!

moment become master, and he aspires to become one; the servant therefore is not another human being than the master."[20] One should note the
emphatic language employed by Tocqueville: Master and servant become
"new beings." The servant is not anymore "un autre homme," another human being than the master. Gone is the "immense distance on the ladder
of beings." Now two human beings may be servant and master only within
the limits of a contract. Outside the contract, "they are two citizens, two
human beings."[21] The inequalities of bargaining positions (and as far as
contemporary France was concerned, the inequality of the legal positions
as well)[22] in early capitalist society did not deter Tocqueville from painting the contrast between "aristocracy" and "democracy" as sharply as he
did. He concluded that though riches and poverty—as well as commanding positions and obedience—may "accidentally" put great distances between two human beings, public opinion (in a democracy) creates among
them "a kind of imaginary equality in spite of the real inequality of their
conditions."[23] Tocqueville's message was clear in this chapter, as it was to
be in the concluding chapter of volume two: A society which had shaken
off the inherent and perpetual status inequalities of aristocratic society in
favor of the (at least potential or "imaginary") equality of human beings
and citizens was more just and therefore morally to be preferred.[24]

A second example: In his chapter on how *moeurs*—customs, habits,
ways of feeling and thinking!—become milder as conditions get equalized,[25] Tocqueville quotes extensively from a letter written in 1675 by
Mme. de Sévigné to her daughter. Mme. de Sévigné, then residing in Brittany, replied to her daughter who lived in the *Provence*; in fact her daughter was the wife of the governor of *Provence*, the comte de Grignan. After a few pleasant phrases she turns to the news from Rennes, the capital

20. In view of the emphatic sense in which Tocqueville uses the term "homme," I translate it by "human being."

21. OC I(2), 188–189.

22. The *Code civil* contained during Tocqueville's lifetime a glaring inequality in its
art. 1781, according to which in disputes on wages the "patron" was to be believed on his
word alone ("sur son affirmation"); this article was revoked in 1868 as being incompatible
with equality before the law. Cf. Gerald Stourzh, *Wege zur Grundrechtsdemokratie*, Vienna/
Cologne) 1989, 343. There is a manuscript comment by Toqueville on this chapter stating :
"The majority of remarks which I have made speaking of servants and masters may be applied
to masters and workers." Pléiade II, 1137.

23. OC I(2), 189 ("une sorte d'égalité imaginaire"—a striking phrase).

24. OC I(2), 337–38

25. OC I(2), 171–75. It would be wrong to render "moeurs" with "manners"; according to
Tocqueville, "manners" ("les manières") were only the "surface" of "moeurs." *L'ancien régime
et la révolution*, OC II(1), 146. For the full, extensive meaning of "moeurs" see OC I(1), 300.

of Britanny, about the suppression of a tax revolt by the "lower classes," as Tocqueville expresses himself.[26] Mme. de Sévigné describes the exemplary cruelty of punishments—the inhabitants of a large street banned and thrown out of the city—women who had just given birth to a child, old people, children, erring around and weeping without knowing where to go; the leader of the revolt had been quartered and the four parts of his body exposed on the four corners of the city; sixty burghers had been arrested, "and they will begin with the hanging tomorrow." Mme. de Sévigné added in an exhortatory manner that this province (Brittany) was a good example for the other provinces, above all to respect "les gouverneurs et les gouvernantes"[27]—and "not to throw stones in their garden." She then immediately turns to everyday conversation. In a later letter to her daughter, Mme. de Sévigné added that "la penderie"—the hangings—now seemed to her "a refreshment" ("un rafraîchissement"): she had quite another ideas of justice, she wrote, since she was "in this country" (in Brittany). "Your galley slaves seem to me a society of honest people who have withdrawn from the world to live an agreeable life."[28]

It would be wrong to believe, Tocqueville added, that Mme. de Sévigné was an egoistic and barbaric creature. But she "did not clearly perceive what it was to suffer if one was not a noble person."[29] Do we have a greater sensibility in our days, Tocqueville went on asking. He did not know: "but surely our sensibility reaches more objects." Tocqueville thought that with the coming of "equality," pity reached out to all those being encompassed within the circle of equality, in principle "all members of humankind."[30] As far as contemporary slavery was concerned—since equality then ceased to apply—the sufferings of slaves inspired little pity in their masters. This was another proof for Tocqueville that "douceur"—mildness, including feelings of compassion—was more closely related to equality than either to (the advance of) civilization or enlightenment.[31] It clearly emerges—and we shall come back to it—that differences of (legal) status (nobles/non-nobles, but also masters/slaves) represented "conditions of inequality," whereas the dichotomy rich/poor, not depending on permanent differences of legal

26. For the following OC I(2), 173 (third part, ch. I).

27. This refers to Mme. de Sévigné's daughter being the wife of the governor of *Provence*.

28. ". . . une vie douce." The reference to "Your galley slaves" is related to the fact that her daughter stayed in a region bordering the Mediterranean, where men condemned to galley slavery served their sentence.

29. ". . . ce que c'était de souffrir quand on n'était pas un gentilhomme." OC I(2), 173–74.

30. This is a strongly Rousseauian thought. Cf. comments in Pléiade II, 1133.

31. OC I(2), 174 and 175.

capacity, was possible in a democracy and thus compatible with at least a certain type of "conditions of equality."

The "message" of this chapter is quite unequivocal. Members of a "caste" do not have the same way of thinking and feeling as others outside it; they hardly believe to be part of the same humankind. Real sympathy was possible among "fellow-beings" ("des gens semblables"); and in the aristocratic centuries, only members of one's own caste were perceived as fellow-beings.[32]

My third example is taken from Tocqueville's *L'ancien régime et la révolution*. Tocqueville shows how towards the end of the ancien régime, the middle classes ("la bourgeoisie") and the nobility in most respects shared the same "moeurs" and also had come close to one another in terms of material possessions. "They did not differ anymore among themselves except by their rights."[33] The differences in rights—or more precisely, in privileges—is, however, for Tocqueville, the decisive point, the most powerful engine, we may say, that brought about the Revolution. Chapter IX of book II of *L'ancien régime et la révolution* is exclusively devoted to show the amount of envy, exasperation, hatred and desperation existing in France prior to the Revolution.[34] The chapter's long title tells the whole story: "How these people so similar to one another were more separated from one another than they had ever been, into small groups, foreign and indifferent to one another." The differences between privileged and non-privileged groups evoked by Tocqueville cover a wide range: They reach from the serious grievances provoked by the tax exemptions of the nobility and privileged corporations (particularly the royal *taille*)[35] to the

32. OC I(2), 172: "[C]ar il n'y a de sympathies réelles qu'entre gens semblables; et, dans les siècles aristocratiques on ne voit ses semblables que dans les membres de sa caste" (part III, ch. I). There is an interesting MS draft by Tocqueville pertaining to this passage, published by Nolla II, 146, note f: "Sympathie./ C'est un mot démocratique. On n'a de sympathie réelle que pour ses semblables et ses égaux." Cf. also the incisive observations on the significance of the dichotomy sembable/dissemblable in Pierre Manent, *Tocqueville et la nature de la démocratie*, Paris 1983, 74–75 (henceforth cited as Manent); cf. also Wolin, 368–69.

33. OC II(1), 146 (conclusion of book II, chapter VIII of *L'ancien régime et la révolution*).

34. OC II(1), 147–58. While ch. IX deals chiefly with the hatred of the "roturiers" against the gentilshommes, chs. I (particularly toward the end) and XII of book II depict the hate potential engendered among the "gens du peuple," notably the farmers. Cf. the new book by Robert T. Gannet, Jr.—a student of Ralph Lerner—, *Tocqueville Unveiled. The Historian and his Sources for "The Old Regime and the Revolution,"* Chicago 2003, notably 51–55.

35. The varieties of taxes and exemptions granted were much more complicated than sketched in Tocqueville's book; even the infamous *taille* was a less unified institution than sometimes supposed., Cf. the informative article "Impôts" by Gail Bossenga in François Furet

envy of the bourgois vis-à-vis their recently ennobled former equals, and on to the grotesque conflicts of "préséance" (precedence) among various corporations. The result is the picture of a society torn by a multiplicity of (sometimes very small) groups chiefly distinguished by the possession of privileges or the absence of it. For Tocqueville, French society on the eve of the Revolution consisted "of thousand small groups, thinking only of themselves." Tocqueville created for this state of affairs the term "collective individualism," which prepared the minds for the real individualism of modern times.[36]

Tocqueville's analysis of the status-ridden society of the late ancien régime was a harsh one, and his fundamentally critical stance did not change from the mid-thirties—when he was preparing volume II of the Democracy and published an article not yet referred to, on the "Social and Political State of France Prior and After the Revolution"[37]—to the early fifties, when he wrote L'ancien régime et la révolution. In contradistinction to the English aristocracy, the French nobility of the ancien régime had degenerated into a "caste," held together by the chief privilege of birth.[38] This caste held even the group of the recently ennobled persons, the "annoblis," at a distance.[39] The French nobility, by holding fast in particular to privileges connected with money—tax exemption—retained "from inequality what hurts most and serves least."[40] Tocqueville's contempt for this type of "conditions of inequality" provoked his exalted evocation of "89":

and Mona Ozouf, eds., *Dictionnaire critique de la Révolution française*, paperback edition, vol. II: *Institutions et créations*, Paris 1992, 259–74.

36. OC II(1), 158. The French historian Françoise Mélonio created a new word by referring to the society depicted by Toqueville as a "société . . . groupusculaire"! Françoise Mélonio, *Tocqueville: aux origines de la démocratie française*, in François Furet and Mona Ozouf, eds., *The Transformation of Political Culture 1789–1848* (vol. 3 of *The French Revolution and the Creation of Modern Political Culture*, ed. by Keith Baker and Colin Lucas), Oxford etc. 1989, 595–611, here 602. François Furet, in a lecture held at the Institute of Human Sciences in Vienna on 21 March 1997—one day after his election to the Académie Française!—on Tocqueville's *L'ancien régime et la révolution*, stressed the significance of this chapter with its emphasis on the multiplication of "differences of status" and on the "collective individualism" of groups simultaneously "similar to one another and isolated from one another" (notes taken by the author). Furet's lecture was held in English.

37. *État social et politique de la France avant et depuis 1789*, in OC II(1), 31–66 (published 1836 in the *London and Westminster Review*).

38. OC II(1), 37 (*État social*), and virtually identical twenty years later at the beginning of Book II, ch. IX of *L'ancien régime et la révolution*, OC II(1), 147.

39. The "annobli" could only from afar see "the promised land" where only his sons would enter (ibid.).

40. OC II(1), 41 (État social).

"It is 89, time of inexperience without doubt, but time of generosity, of enthusiasm, of manliness and greatness, time of immortal memory, to which will turn the views of men with admiration and with respect, when those who have seen it and ourselves will have disappeared a long time ago."[41]

Should this be "empty" rhetoric? Certainly not. Professor Ralph Lerner has given us a most sophisticated guide to the purpose and rhetoric of *L'Ancien régime et la révolution*.[42] He shows us how Tocqueville's appeals to the example of the men of '89 who, even though they were religious disbelievers, "had an admirable belief which we lack": belief in themselves.[43] I do take Tocqueville seriously on '89 for two reasons. First, "89" for Tocqueville is the turning point when "conditions of equality" prevail over "conditions of inequality," as he says a few lines later: The men of '89 "reduced to dust that obsolete legislation which [had] divided people in castes, corporations, classes and *made their rights even more unequal than their conditions*."[44] Second, the men of '89 also gave to France "free institutions," which they placed amidst "democratic institutions." The joining of equality and liberty, for a brief moment of fulfilment, and the enthusiastic and exalted account Toqueville gives of it, reveal his most ardent wishes for a less petty democratic society of the future, the prefiguration of which he had found in America. All this as well as his fears of democratic "despotism" of a new kind in the future shall be no further theme of discussion here—all the more so as one of the most thoughtful recent reflections on Tocqueville's notion of the possibilities of a democratic despotism has come from the pen Ralph Lerner.[45] I shall confine myself, in the remaining part of these reflections, to three questions. First, what dimensions of equality did Tocqueville have in mind when he spoke of the "état social" designated as "democracy"? Second, where are the most striking limits of Tocqueville's analysis of "conditions of equality"? Third and by way of conclusion, finally, I shall briefly comment on Toqueville's often discussed personal stand between aristocracy and democracy.

41. OC II(1), 247 (*L'ancien régime et la révolution*, book III, ch. VIII).

42. Ralph Lerner, Tocqueville's Political Sermon, in his volume: *Revolutions Revisited*, Chapel Hill, NC 1994.

43. Ibid., 126, with reference to the third book, ch. II–OC II(1), 207. Lerner concludes by pointing out how Tocqueville, fearing that democrats would relax into pettiness, attempted to mobilize human pride by the examples of '89. Ibid., 128 (with a reference to volume II of the *Democracy*, third part, ch. XIX, OC.I(2), 255).

44. OC II(1), 247. Italics mine.

45. Ralph Lerner, The Complexion of Tocqueville's American, in: Ralph Lerner, *The Thinking Revolutionary*, Ithaca, NY 1987, 174–91.

I would like to suggest five dimensions or elements of the "conditions of equality," characterizing the "état social" designated by Tocqueville as democracy.[46]

First, "conditions of equality" simply—but very importantly—refer to the elimination, or disappearance or, as in America (with the exception of slaves and Indians), to the non-existence of its opposite, "conditions of inequality." As the various cases in point presented previously show, "inequality" of conditions are chiefly unequal status conditions existing "perpetually" ("à perpetuité"). These status conditions may be connected with (great) inequalities of material conditions, but the distinguishing feature are status differences characterized by (legal) "privileges" or (unequal) "rights" of specific groups sometimes rather indistinctly referred to as classes, yet sometimes more precisely, and with the connotation of disapproval, characterized as "castes."[47] Tocqueville's code word for unequal status conditions—and for the abyss perpetually separating different groups of people—is "aristocracy." In manuscript notes written when preparing part III of volume II of De la démocratie en Amérique, the character of "aristocracy" and "aristocratic" as code words emerges with particular clarity. "In an aristocracy, the different classes being placed far one from another find themselves so to speak in the relation of foreigners" ("étrangers"); a few lines later Tocqueville illustrates the gulf separating the different classes in an aristocracy even more sharply by the analogy of foreign peoples: "When peoples are very different from one another, separated by opposite opinions, beliefs, and usages, they also seem to have left the common humanity." In addition, "aristocratic sentiments" are established between them, "they feel themselves not merely different, but superior to one another."[48]

The absence or disappearance of "aristocracy" thus understood produces "conditions of equality" or democracy. The great divide in French history, when the balance of the two opposite systems was tipped in favor of "democracy" was, of course, "89." A progressive equalization of conditions had gone on for seven centuries prior to "89," sketched in a majestic sweep of history introducing volume I of De la démocratie en Amérique.[49] Yet prior to "89," unequal "privileges" had prevented the breakthrough of

---

46. Tocqueville's original title for what became volume II of De la démocratie en Amérique was: "L'influence de l'égalité sur les idées et les sentiments des hommes!" Cf. James Schleifer, The Making of Tocqueville's "Democracy in America," Chapel Hill, NC 1980, 34.

47. Cf. particularly OC I(2) 172 (cf. above note 32).

48. Quoted in Pléiade II, 1132.

49. OC I(2) 1–5.

equality. Equality before the law, as proclaimed in articles I and VI of the French Declaration of 1789,[50] emerges as the fundamental breaking point between "aristocracy" and "democracy," between "inequality" and "equality" in Tocqueville's scheme of things.[51] His views on the fundamental change in the relation between master and servant discussed above strikingly demonstrate this point. "Conditions of equality," to sum up then, very importantly are created by the lack or disappearance of the structure of legal privileges of a hierarchically ordered society,[52]—a *"ständische"* society, as the German language puts it succinctly, but untranslatably.[53] In this context it is worth noting that *"condition"* in French has among its several connotations an important one in the sense of rank or status. *"Être de basse condition"* means "to belong to a lower rank/status"; *"être de grande condition, de haute condition"* means "to belong to an elevated rank/status." I suggest that our reading of Tocqueville's numerous references to equality or inequality of condition may be opened to new hues of meaning by having this connotation of *"condition"* in mind.

In spite of political backlashes in subsequent French history like the Restoration, the *"lois civiles"* initiated in 1789 were to prove strong enough to carry on the process of democratic equalization.[54]

The establishment or existence of civil liberty for all citizens—in French referred to as *"l'égalité civile,"* was a central dimension of the

50. Art. I: "Les hommes naissent et demeurent libres *et égaux en droits*" (emphasis mine); Art VI: ". . .Tous les citoyens, *étant égaux à ses yeux* [de la loi, emphasis mine, G. S.], sont également admissibles à toute dignités, places et emplois selon leur capacité et sans autre distinction que celles de leurs vertus et de leurs talents." In the "État social de la France avant et depuis 1789" Tocqueville wrote that conditions in France (on the eve of 1789) were more equal than elsewhere: "The Revolution has augmented [in another variant: developed] the conditions of equality and *introduced the doctrine of equality into the laws.*" (my emphasis). OC II(1), 65.

51. Cf. OC II(1), 247–48 (*L'ancien régime et la révolution,* book III, ch. VIII, see also above note 41).

52. Cf. Tocqueville on "aristocratically and hierarchically organized countries." OC I(2), 201 (*De la démocratie en Amérique,* volume II, third part, ch. VIII).

53. This point is convincingly emphasized in an excellent interpretation by the German historian Hans-Christoph Schröder: Alexis de Tocqueville. Ein Aristokrat als Analytiker der demokratischen Gesellschaft, in Peter Alter/Wolfgang Mommsen/Thomas Nipperdey, eds., *Geschichte und politisches Handeln. Theodor Schieder zum Gedächtnis,* Stuttgart 1985, 164–85, here 166.

54. In a letter of 29 June 1831 to Louis Kergorlay, Tocqueville commented that Louis XVIII with his "Charte" had created "aristocratic institutions" in the political laws, yet had left untouched in the civil laws an eminently active democratic principle (". . . laissait dans les lois civiles un principe démocratique tellement actif. . ."). OC XIII(1), 233, cited in the brilliant article by François Furet, Naisssance d'un paradigme: Tocqueville et le voyage en Amérique (1825–1831), in *Annales: Économies – Sociétés –Civilisations,* vol. 39, 1984, 225–39, here 234.

"equality of conditions."[55] I shall call it, against the backdrop of what just had been shattered, the *post-feudal* dimension of "conditions of equality," or to be more precise, the *legal* dimension of "conditions of equality." It did, incidentally, leave considerable leeway for inequalities among rich and poor.[56]

Yet Tocqueville did not stop there. Conditions of equality had—and this is the second dimension—a *socio-economic* connotation notably connected with changing distributions of property through inheritance. Changes in the possession or inheritance of estates in spite of the feudal laws of inheritance in France on the eve of the Revolution was noted by Tocqueville.[57] The voyage to America, however, occasioned Tocqueville's most extensive discussion of the significance of inheritance laws.[58] The transition from the privileged inheritance status of the elder son to free inheritance laws enabling the more equal distribution,[59] yet simultaneously the more frequent partition of real property had a double effect. It encouraged more rapid change in the possession of real property as well as its transformation into movable property, and it weakened or even destroyed what Tocqueville called "family spirit"—the care for the preservation of (great) property in the hands of one family from generation to generation. By destroying the "esprit de famille," free inheritance favors "individual egotism."[60] It was also, as Tocqueville put it somewhat grandiloquently, "the last step" towards equality.[61]

Yet there are still other dimensions of equality. In the third place, then, there is what I would like to call the *socio-anthropological* dimension of conditions of equality, the question of *connubium*—more simply put, the joining together of hitherto separate groups or classes of people in marriage and procreation. Travelling through the Ohio and then the Mississippi valley in November/December 1831, Tocqueville wrote down some notes "On Equality in America," comparing conditions in the United States and in

55. François Furet considers "l'égalite civile" as the essential content of his definition of "democracy"—"le contenu essentiel de sa définition de la 'democratie' "! See Furet's essay Tocqueville et le problème de la Révolution française, in his volume: *Penser la Révolution française*, Paris 1978, 190.

56. See e.g., OC I(2), 185, 189; OC III(2), 737. Cf. also Manent, 33–34.

57. OC II(1), 43 (État social, 1836).

58. First presented in a letter to Louis de Kergorlay dated (begun) 29 June 1831, OC XIII(1), 231–233, and fully developed in volume I, first part, ch. III of *De la démocratie en Amérique*. OC I(1), 1, 45–51.

59. The importance for democracy of the distribution of real property in small properties is stressed in the "État social . . . " of 1836: OC II(1), 52.

60. OC I(1), 49.

61. OC I(1), 46.

France. In France, "the prejudice of birth" still played a very great role, and the "classement" according to professions as well. This was not so in America. Different professions did not create any "radical inequality," because they did not prevent the "union of families." He concluded that to judge on equality among different classes, one ought to ask how marriages were made. This was the root of the matter ("*le fond de la chose*"). Equality, or a semblance of it, might exist for a variety of reasons—necessity, manners, politics. Yet if one were to practice equality by the union of families, one would put the finger into the wound (of a not truly existing equality).[62]

A fourth dimension of conditions of equality is the *Christian* dimension. "Christianity, which has rendered all human beings equal before God, will not resist seeing all citizens equal before the law."[63] Tocqueville has repeated the message of the equality of human beings according to the teachings of Christianity frequently. In notes written in preparing the section on religion as a political institution of volume I of the *Democracy*, Tocqueville also put down his view that "of all religious doctrines" Christendom is "most favorable to equality."[64] He even expressed the view that the catholics, once church and state were separate as in America, were more disposed than anyone else "to transport the idea of the equality of conditions into the political world."[65] Five years later, in the second volume of the *Democracy*, Tocqueville stressed that the greatest minds of Greece and Rome, limited by the acceptance of slavery as a natural phenomenon, were never able to reach the idea of the similarity of all human beings and of "the equal birthright of everybody to liberty."[66] It took the coming

62. OC V(1), 279, 280–81 (*Voyage en Amérique*).

63. OC I(1), 9 (*De la démocratie en Amérique*, volume I, first part, Introduction).

64. Pléiade II, 1014. In the section on religion considered as a political institution, and how it powerfully serves to maintain the democratic republic in America, OC I(1), 301–3, Tocqueville speaks in great detail on Catholicism, virtually ignoring the Protestants. There is no question that Tocqueville wishes to address the French public by extolling the separation of church and state and denouncing the negative consequences of the proximity of the church to the powers that be (the European union of "throne and altar"); Tocqueville regretted the conservatism of the Catholics in France and the anticlericalism of the liberals. Tocqueville, sceptical on dogma, yet full of the greatest respect (and in search for, as his notes on reading Pascal testify, OC XVI, 551–54) for Jesus Christ and His moral teachings, was indeed something of a "liberal catholic."

65. OC I(1), 302.

66. OC I(2), 22: "l'idée . . . de la similitude des hommes et du droit égal que chacun d'eux apporte, en naissant, à la liberté" (volume II, first part, ch. III). A finer differentiation as far as Greek writers are concerned, as well as further comments on the contribution of Christianity to morals in OC XVI, 224–25.

of Jesus Christ to make men understand that all members of humankind really were fellow-beings ("semblables") and equals. Tocqueville's view on the Christian roots of the idea of human rights emerges quite clearly.[67] The best known defense of the moral teachings of Christianity occurs in Tocqueville's correspondence with count Arthur Gobineau, the theorist of racism and author of a work on the inequality of the human races. It has been the greatness of Christianity to form "a human society outside of all national societies." Above all, the "principle of equality" which Christianity had placed in the "immaterial sphere rather than in the order of visible things" was being transformed in modern times, through the development of wealth and knowledge, into the idea that all human beings had a right to certain goods and certain enjoyments. While Christianity had preached charity as a private virtue, the idea of it as "a social duty, a political obligation and a public virtue," indeed a new "social and political morality" unknown to the ancients had developed out of "a combination of the political ideas of antiquity and the moral notions of Christianity."[68]

There is a fifth dimension of equality. I shall call it the *utopian*, or more sceptically expressed, the *mirage* dimension of equality. It is the desire for an ever more perfect equality that pervades the pursuits and lives of individuals in a democratic society. Tocqueville did not really think that any society, however equal conditions might be, would be without the distinction of rich and poor.[69] Yet in a society where the greater part of citizens had attained a condition of being more or less alike and where equality was an old and acknowlegded fact, public opinion so to speak ignores "accidental" differences between wealth and poverty, authority and obedience, and creates a kind of "imaginary equality."[70] "Égalité imaginaire" thus turns out be a kind of social norm in a democratic society in spite of existing inequalities.[71] This norm becomes a goal at least for those who feel themselves at a disadvantage.[72] In one of the profoundest—and saddest—chapters

67. Though Tocqueville passes over the acceptance of slavery in this world e.g., in the writings of Saint Paul. On Christian roots of human rights see also the comments by Jean-Claude Lamberti in Pléiade II, 909 and 1064.

68. OC IX, 46–47(*Correspondence d'Alexis de Tocqueville et d'Arthur de Gobineau*), letter to Gobineau of 5 September 1843; cf. also his letter to Gobineau of 24 January 1857, ibid., 277, very sharply criticizing Gobineau's racialism and stressing that Christianity evidently had tended to make all human beings brothers and equals.

69. OC I(2), 185.

70. OC I(2), 189. See above at note 23.

71. Cf. the perceptive observations of Françoise Mélonio, *Tocqueville et les Français*, Paris 1993, 104–105.

72. Cf. Aristotle, *Politics*, 1318b: "But, although it may be difficult in theory to know what is just and equal, the practical difficulty of inducing those to forbear who can, if they

of volume II of the *Democracy* Tocqueville has intuitively grasped the mirage character of the idea of equality.[73] Having destroyed the privileges of the few, those hoping that under conditions of equality the attainment of their goals may have become easier, now encounter the barrier of universal competition—"la concurrence de tous." And even if a society with "perfectly equal conditions" were achieved—if the misfortune of an "absolute and complete levelling" were achieved (!)[74]—, the inequality of intelligence, coming directly from God, would persist. Whatever the social state and the political constitution of a people, its citizens would always perceive certain points (factors) dominating them[75] and their attention would obstinately be fixed on these points. In an egalitarian society the smallest inequalities hurt more than great inequalities in a society based on the inequality of conditions. "Therefore the desire of equality becomes more insatiable to the extent as equality is greater."[76] The secret of envy as a psycho-social phenomenon of democratic societies has nowhere found a profounder explanation than in this chapter.[77] And there follows the celebrated paragraph on the mirage of equality: "Among democratic nations, people will easily attain a certain equality; yet they will never attain the equality they desire. This equality draws back from them, without however disappearing from sight. At every moment people think to grasp it, yet at every moment it escapes from their hold. They see it close enough to know its attractions, yet they never come close enough to enjoy them, and they die before having fully tasted its sweetness."[78] In these passages Tocqueville came close to touching an aspect of the idea of equality that has been put into relief, in the twentieth century, by the German jurist Gerhard Leibholz. He has observed that the principle of equality has an innate tendency to

---

like, encroach, is far greater, for the weaker are always asking for equality and justice, but the stronger care for none of these things" (Modern Library ed., New York 1943), 263.

73. Second part, ch. XIII, "Why the Americans are so restless in the midst of their prosperity," OC I(2), 142–45.

74. Cf. OC III(2), 742: "À vrai dire, l'égalité complète est une chimère. . . ." (Fragment of 1847).

75. OC I(2), 144; the translation of the French text is difficult: ". . . chacun de ses citoyens apercevra toujours près de soi plusieurs points qui le dominent . . ." The most satisfactory translation is offered in the new Mansfield /Winthrop translation: ". . . each of its citizens will always perceive near to him several positions in which he is dominated, and one can foresee that he will obstinately keep looking at this side alone." Alexis de Tocqueville, *Democracy in America,* translated, edited and with an Introduction by Harvey C. Mansfield and Delba Winthrop, Chicago 2000, 513.

76. OC I(2), 144.

77. See also the remarkable comments by Manent, 95.

78. OC I(2), 144–45.

radicalize itself,[79] to open itself to ever new domains of applicability, and he has detected the abstract character of the idea of equality as the root of what I would like to call the "protean" shape of the notion of equality.

Tocqueville's visionary genius intuitively grasped the mentality of restlessness in liberal western democracies, and his power of imagination seems limitless; yet he reached the limits of imagination, and of analysis, in some sectors of social life. His chapter on how a new and more dreadful aristocracy might emerge out of manufactures, though impressive (and incidentally tapping the same sources as Friedrich Engels!),[80] remains a rather solitary performance, unintegrated in—and in some ways contradictory to[81]—the other parts of volume II of the *Democracy*. Tocqueville did not come to grips with the hardening and hardened class structures of the European 19th century. Toward the end of the July Monarchy, in 1847, Tocqueville, with plans for a new party of the left in his mind, sketched a catalog of legislative measures on social policy, including i.e. tax exemptions for the poorest part of the population, no charges for schools, and laws restricting the duration of working hours.[82] He advocated the disappearance of all remaining inequalities in fiscal legislation. His proposals show Tocqueville as a socially committed thinker and politician, without however going beyond the limits of the prevailing economic system of private property. He summed up—possibly in retrospect—his position as follows: "In one word, to guarantee the poor person all legal equality and all well-being compatible with the individual right to property and the inequality of conditions which derives from it."[83] There is no question

79. Gerhard Leibholz, *Die Gleichheit vor dem Gesetz*, Munich/Berlin 1959, 25 (first published 1925).

80. Both Tocqueville and Friedrich Engels, the latter for his celebrated book on the situation of the working class in England, *Die Lage der arbeitenden Klasse in England*, first published in 1845, consulted the work of the British physician James Kay, *The Moral and Physical Condition of the Working Classes, Employed in the Cotton Manufacture in Manchester* (2nd ed. 1832); cf. OC V(2), 79. Cf. the excellent book by Jürgen Feldhoff, *Die Politik der egalitären Gesellschaft. Zur soziologischen Politik-Analyse bei Alexis de Tocqueville*, Köln/Opladen 1968, 167, note 171. Tocqueville actually met Dr. Kay: Seymour Drescher, *Tocqueville and England*, Cambridge, MA 1964, 66–67.

81. This is particularly the case concerning the relations between master and servant (volume II, third part, ch. v).

82. OC III(2), 742–44 [Fragments pour une politique sociale].

83. OC III(2), 737. "Question financière." The editing of this document (pp. 734–37, to be read with the two following documents pp. 738–44) is not satisfactory. The editor describes it as "a copy" made in November 1848 of a document originated in the fall of 1847; however, the style of this text shows that it was not just copied, but written in November 1848, though based on or referring to manuscripts of October 1847 and partly based on not anymore existing notes; one passage clearly refers to the text printed on pp. 742–43, without any proper indication. The

that the days of June 1848—the insurrection of the workers of Paris and its
bloody suppression—led to a considerable hardening of Tocqueville's position on social policies. He voted against the limitation of the working day
to ten hours, against the abolition of the tax on salt, against an amnesty of
the sentenced workers of the June insurrection.[84]

Tocqueville remains the great analyst of rather fluid individualistic/
egalitarian societies, where class conflicts never became congealed or
were supplanted by racial/ethnic conflict (the case of the United States),
or where these conflicts were softened, if not dissolved through the welfare state and the *embourgeoisement* of the former proletariat (the case of
western Europe in the second half of the 20th century). This explains, of
course, the extraordinary revival of interest in Tocqueville in the last decades of the 20th century.

A combination of profound insights with certain limitations of vision
also appears in the famous chapter on the three races in America at the
end of volume I of the *Democracy*.[85] With one stroke of genius did Tocqueville express the radical character of white superiority in the famous
account of a five years old white girl accompanied by a black and an Indian
woman, the little girl showing "by her slightest movements a sense of superiority which contrasted strangely with her weakness and her age," and
also receiving "the attention of her companions with a sort of condescension."[86] By including an Indian woman in this scene, Tocqueville showed
how the prejudice of color and its evil consequences, unconsciously poi-
soning even the behaviour of small children growing up in a society of
racial inequality, went beyond slavery. Among the strongest parts of his
chapter is Tocqueville's treatment of free blacks and the contempt poured
on them by white Americans, as well as his premonitions that the liberation of the black slaves would even increase race prejudice among white
Americans.[87] The perversion of the principle of equality through the doc-

question whether or to what extent the document written in November 1848 may show the
impact of the intervening events of June 1848 and the hardening of Tocqueville's position remains open. On his earlier "Mémoire sur le pauperisme" of 1835 and an unpublished continuation see André Jardin, *Alexis de Tocqueville 1805–1859*, (paperback) Paris 1984, 232–34.

84. Jardin, 396. See also Tocqueville's speech in the French constituent assembly on
12 September 1848 on his opposition to the recognition of a "right to work" in the constitution,
and his idea of aid to the poor derived from the principles of Christianity, OC III(3), 168–180.

85. Wolin, 603, note 23, comments that there are surprisingly few analyses of this chapter
by political theorists, an exception being Ralph Lerner in his book *The Thinking Revolutionary* (cf. supra note 45).

86. OC I(1), 335; here quoted from Ralph Lerner, The Complexion of Tocqueville's American, in his book *The Thinking Revolutionary*, 178–79.

87. OC I(1), 357–59.

trine of "separate and equal," endorsed by the Supreme Court in 1896 and revoked only 58 years later, proved Tocqueville right for a long time.[88] The integration efforts of the second half of the twentieth century—though they are an open-ended story—have demonstrated the resilience of the principle of equal rights[89] in a way not foreseen by Tocqueville. The limitation of the chapter on the three races—in so far analogous to the chapter on the possible emergence of a new aristocracy out of manufactures—is the lacking integration of its findings into the general thesis of the other parts of *De la démocratie en Amérique*, a thesis basically not including the impact of racial (or ethnic) prejudice on democracy.[90]

A third limitation of *De la démocratie en Amérique*—in a way the most astounding one—is the non-consideration of the rights of women. Tocqueville remains satisfied with the conventional wisdom of the "separate sphere." Women are the makers of the "moeurs,"[91] and "moeurs," as has been said before, means a great deal, not merely "the habits of the heart," but ideas and opinions, the "habits of the mind" in general.[92] The power of women, though not asserted in the public sphere, is great and important through the imprint they put on the mind and character of the family, notably through the education of children. Tocqueville's position on women is close to that of an eminent American jurist who spoke and wrote about this theme exactly fifty years earlier, though there is no evidence that Tocqueville may have known the text in question. I refer to James Wilson's inaugural lecture as Professor of Law at the College of Philadelphia in 1790. Wilson's rhetorical question: "What are laws without manners? How can manners be formed, but by a proper education" led him to present his views on the place of women and to expose the idea of the separate spheres.[93]

---

88. The classic cases are *Plessy v. Ferguson* (1896) and *Brown v. Board of Education of Topeka, Kansas* (1954).

89. Unfortunately, neither the English nor the French language have an exact equivalent for the German word "*Gleichberechtigung*"—and thus "equality" or "*égalité*" often are used when what is really meant are "equal rights"—i.e., *Gleichberechtigung*.

90. Cf. also Wolin, 364. A most thoughtful analysis of Tocqueville's chapter on the three races in America is Delba Winthrop, "Race and Freedom in Tocqueville," in *Tocqueville's Political Science: Classic Essays*, ed. by Peter A. Lawler, New York 1993, 171–96.

91. OC I(2), 206 (volume II, third part, ch. IX).

92. OC I(1), 300. (volume I, second part, ch. IX, section on the influence of the "moeurs" on the democratic republic in the United States).

93. *The Works of James Wilson*, ed. by Robert G. McCloskey, Cambridge Mass., 1967, vol. I, 85–86. Wilson's Inaugural Lecture "On the Study of Law in the Unites States" offered a particularly favorable occasion to address this subject, since exceptionally a part of his audience was female. It is reported that "President Washington, Vice-President Adams, and a

Tocqeville's chapters on American women are full of respect for the independence, energy and self-discipline of these women both prior to and subsequent of marriage.[94] Yet Tocqueville, for whom the word "semblable" (often used in the sense of "fellow-being," "alike human being")[95] plays an important role in the history of the equalization of conditions,[96] now juxtaposes "equal" and "alike." There are, he says, persons in Europe who, confounding the differences of the sexes, pretend to make of men and women beings not merely equal but alike ("non seulement égaux, mais semblables").[97] In order to stress differences between men and women, Tocqueville even recurs to "the great principle of political economy," the division of labour. He approvingly describes the self-confinement of (married) women, who never direct the external affairs of the family, conduct a business, or force their way into politics. Never did Americans think, so Tocqueville, that the consequence of democratic principles would be to tear down marital power (*renverser la puissance maritale*); they think that the man is the natural head of the conjugal association.[98]

Speaking of citizens rights in volume one, Tocqueville approvingly said that "democratic government lets the idea of political rights trickle down to the lowest of citizens"—yet *ex silentio* women are excluded.[99] Nowhere has Tocqueville even touched the idea of women's suffrage[100]—though in

galaxy of other republican worthies turned out, some with their ladies at their sides . . ." (Introduction by the editor, ibid., 37).

94. OC I(2), 206–22 (volume II, third part, chs. IX–XII).

95. Cf. OC I(2), 175: "Ainsi, le même homme qui est plein d'humanité pour ses semblables quand ceux-ci sont en même temps ses égaux, devient insensible à leurs douleurs dès que l'égalité cesse." Cf. also supra note 32.

96. Cf. OC I(2), 189: "Lorsqu'e la plupart des citoyens ont depuis longtemps atteint une condition à peu près semblable, et que l'égalité est un fait ancien et admis . . ."

97. OC I(2), 219.

98. OC I(2), 220 (ch. XII "How Americans understand the equality of men and women"—a title of unintended irony if one takes into account the contents of this chapter.

99. OC I(1), 249: ". . . fait descendre l'idée des droits politiques jusqu'au moindre des citoyens. . ."

100. There has been little comment coming from feminist discourse, as far as I can see. Jean Bethke Elshtain merely says that Tocqueville in the midst of his praise fo America's success in raising the moral and intellectual level of women "glossed over or lost" the fact that equal regard did not lead to social or political equality. Elshtain, *Public Man, Private Woman. Women in Social and Political Thought*, Princeton 1981, 129. Though (understandably) speaking disparagingly on Tocqueville's view of the status of women, there is no sustained analysis of Tocqueville's pertinent chapters in the interesting essay by Linda K. Kerber, "Separate Spheres. Female Worlds, Woman's Place: The Rhetoric of Women's History," in *Journal of American History* 75 (1988/89, 9–39, here 9–10. The most sustained analysis has been offered by Delba Winthrop, "Tocqueville's American Woman and 'The True Conception of Democratic Progress'," in *Political Theory* 14 (1986), 239–61, particularly 250–51, though I differ

an earlier generation, the Marquis de Condorcet had argued in favor of the admission of women to the rights of citizenship.[101] When another revolutionary of 1789, the abbé Sieyes, had sketched his well-known distinction of "active" and "passive" citizens and had put women into the category of "citoyens passifs," he had added the escape clause "at least in the present state"[102]—an interesting perspective for the future, not taken notice of, as far as I am aware, by the scholarly discourse on suffrage rights for women. Nothing of the kind in Tocqueville's writings—there is no trace of a discussion on women's suffrage, even in the future or hypothetically. Perhaps do we indeed find a clue in Tocqueville's curious separation, almost opposition, of "equal" and "alike," of "égal" and "semblable," which does not correspond to the proximity of these words elsewhere in his writings.[103] Women, it appears, were, in an important respect, not "semblables" to men. Democracy as an "état social" included women and children (though with all the limitations of the rights of the married women in Tocqueville's time). Democracy as a system of government based on voting rights remained, what it had been from antiquity onwards, reserved for adult male citizens, however small or however wide the circle of citizens might be drawn. This means that since the introduction and finally generalization of women's suffrage during the twentieth century, Tocqueville' use of the term democracy for a system of government (and the usage of numerous authors of the nineteenth and early twentieth centuries) as well has become dated.

To conclude. François Furet, the French historian, with close ties to the University of Chicago and its Committee on Social Thought, and with close ties of friendship to Ralph Lerner, has contributed a comment of great

---

from her by critically pointing to Tocqueville's logical *non sequitur*, declaring the equality of men and women, yet denying to women those political rights which democratic government makes "descend to the least of citizens. . ." (here quoted according to the Mansfield/Winthrop translation of *Democracy in America*, 228).

101. De l'admission des femmes au droit de cité; cf. Joan B. Landes, *Women and the Public Sphere in the Age of the French Revolution*, Ithaca, NY, 1989, 112–17. Comments on Tocqueville's refusal to consider women as voters or office holders in a democracy has, as far as I am aware of, drawn little comment from feminist writers.

102. Abbé Sieyes, Préliminaire de la Constitution. Reconnaissance et exposition raisonée des Droits de l'homme et du citoyen, lu les 20 & 21 Juillet 1789 au Comité de Constitution, Paris 1789, here quoted after the critical German edition in Emmanuel Joseph Sieyes, *Politische Schriften 1788–1790*, transl. and ed. by E. Schmitt and R. Reichardt, Munich/Vienna 1981, 251.

103. Cf. Pierre Manent, interpreting Tocqueville's discourse on democracy, describes "la convention démocratique . . . visant l'égal, le même, le semblable dans les hommes [in the sense of human beings]." Manent, 114.

insight to the ever ongoing debate on Tocqueville: Tocqueville set out to explain *one* phenomenon central to his thought since the age of twenty —the phenomenon of the equalization of conditions or the progress of democracy. His was an extraordinary concentration on one theme. This gave him *"une exceptionelle profondeur et une exceptionelle étroitesse"*—an exceptional profundity and an exceptional limitation.[104] Tocqueville remains the unsurpassed analyst of one of the greatest *caesurae* of modern history: the transition from the hierarchical, status- and privilege-oriented institutions of Europe's ancien régime[105] to institutions based on everybody's equality before the law—"l'égalité civile"[106]— briefly and in Tocqueville's own terminology, from "aristocracy" to "democracy." I therefore believe that of the five dimensions of "conditions of equality" sketched earlier in this paper, the first dimension of *post-feudal* or *legal* "conditions of equality" is the most important one in two respects: first, in contrast to the fallen institutions of hierarchical "conditions of inequality";[107] and second, as the basis from which further developments of the "equality of conditions" were to develop.[108] Tocqueville's "exceptional profundity" as analyst of the great transition from "pre-1789" to "post-1789" stems from three facts:

first, his existence as an aristocrat in a post–aristocratic society, yet through the history of his family and the nearness of events very close to "89";[109]

second, the stroke of genius to emancipate himself from the time-honored comparison France-England and to grasp "the future in the present" available in the United States;

third, his uncanny ability to transform empirical observation—with the help of a master idea—"we move toward a democracy without limits, pushed by an irresistible force"[110]—into his vast canvas of the mental structure of democratic/egalitarian individualism.

104. François Furet, *Naissance d'un paradigme*, (supra note 54), 228.

105. See particularly book I of *L'ancien régime et la révolution*, OC II(1), 79–96. "Institutions" for Tocqueville have an all-encompassing character, covering both the social and the political realm. Cf. also Furet, *Tocqueville et le problème de la Révolution française* (supra note 55), 183.

106. Furet, ibid., 190.

107. An example: the chapter on master and servant in volume II of the *Democracy* (third part, ch. V).

108. An example: the chapter on the restlessness of Americans in the midst of their well-being in volume II of the *Democracy* (second part, ch. XIII).

109. Tocqueville's system of thought is based "sur un socle qui n'est pas d'ordre intellectuel, mais purement existentiel." Furet, *Naissance d'un paradigme* (supra note 54), 231.

110. OC XIII(1), 233 (Letter to Kergorlay begun on 29 June 1831).

His "exceptional" narrowness stems from the fact, in no need of further discussion, that his was one great theme: "equality of conditions"—its advent, and its prospects.

There are, I once submitted, two concerns of political theory distinguishable according to their primary aim. One strand of inquiry searches into the principles of political obligation; a second strand investigates—comparatively in space and time—the domestic institutions, foreign policies and moral properties of societies.[111] Benjamin Rush explained this very clearly at the time of the American Revolution: "It is one thing to understand the *principles,* and another thing to understand the *forms* of government. The former are simple; the latter are difficult and complicated. . . . Mr Locke is an oracle as to *principles,* Harrington and Montesquieu are oracles as to *forms* of government."[112] There is no question that Tocqueville belongs to the second group of "oracles," and he has rightly and long ago been put into the "great empirical tradition within political philosophy" which "has its high points in Aristotle, Machiavelli, Montesquieu and Tocqueville."[113]

This tradition has included the comparative study of the "moral properties" of polities or societies, and it has also included moral judgment. He posed occasionally as the equidistant and detached observer of the two "social states" of aristocracy and democracy. Yet weighing these two types of societies on the scale of justice, this aristocrat by birth and life-style regarded the scales tipped in favor of the equality of conditions, because, as has been pointed out before, it was more just.[114] "Permanent inequality," he wrote to Gobineau in an impassioned letter which, if any, presents his moral "confession of faith," permanent inequality gives birth to arrogance, violence, the contempt of one's fellow-beings ("le mépris du semblable"!), tyranny and abjectness in all its forms.[115] The choice for the moral preference of conditions of equality must also be seen, it seems to me, in the

111. Gerald Stourzh, *Alexander Hamilton and the Idea of Republican Government,* Stanford 1970, 3.

112. Quoted ibid., 4, from Benjamin Rush, Observations on the Government of Pennsylvania (1777), in Dagobert Runes, ed., *The Select Writings of Benjamin Rush,* New York 1947, 78. "Forms of government" in this sense have to be seen, of course, in a less narrow way than later: they most importantly (vide Montesquieu) include the "moeurs"!

113. Quoted ibid., 213, note 3, from David Lowenthal, Review essay on B. Moore's *Social Origins of Dictatorship and Democracy* in: *History and Theory,* vol. VII (1968), 278, note 15.

114. OC I(2), 338 (*De la démocratie en Amérique,* volume two, concluding chapter).

115. OC IX, 203 (Letter of 17 November 1853). The entire letter bears close reading. It is also referred to by Lerner, *The Thinking Revolutionary,* 175, note.

light of what has been said above about Tocqueville's convictions on the
Christian dimension of these conditions.

This choice in favor of conditions of equality did of course not by any
means imply blindness to the threats and dangers of this type of "état social." These threats were to be countered, so Tocqueville hoped, by the
survival of liberty among conditions of equality. For liberty to survive,
the survival of two things, closely tied to one another, was necessary, of
rights, and of self-rule. There were only two ways to establish equality in
the political world: "Rights must be given to each citizen or to no one."
Tocqueville also said that rights—legal rights—were particularly important at a time when religious beliefs were on the decline, the divine notion
of rights disappeared, and with the changing of the "moeurs" the moral
notion of rights is fading away as well. "If in the midst of that universal
disturbance you do not come to bind the idea of rights to the personal
interest that offers itself as the only immobile point in the human heart,
what will then remain to you to govern the world, except fear?"[116] Yet
fear, to a reader of Montesquieu like Tocqueville, was the principle animating despotism. Rights and self-rule were to be based, then, in times
of the growing equality of conditions, on the doctrine of enlightened self-
interest. It was, for the people "of our time"—Tocqueville's time, our
time—"the strongest remaining guarantee against themselves."[117]

116. OC I(1), 52 and 249. I follow here the new Mansfield edition of *Democracy in America*, Winthrop 52 (vol. I, part I, ch. 3), and 228 (vol. I, part II, ch. 6).

117. OC I(2), 129 (*De la démocratie en Amérique*, volume II, second part, ch. II). See also
Lerner, *The Thinking Revolutionary*, 191.

PART IV

On the Human Condition

CHAPTER FIFTEEN

The Unforgivable Sin:
An Interpretation of Albert Camus' *The Fall**

> Wherefore I say unto you, All manner of sin and blasphemy shall be
> forgiven unto men: but the blasphemy against the Holy Ghost shall not
> be forgiven unto men.
> —*Matt. 12:31*

> . . . The holy innocence of those who forgive themselves.
> —Albert Camus, *The Fall*

There appeared in *The New Yorker*, some time ago, a widely noted article entitled "The Study of Something New in History." It discussed
the breakdown of prisoner-of-war morale in Korea as a consequence of the
Communists' systematic provocations designed to put men to shame in
front of their comrades, to make them lose face, to ridicule them; in other
words, to shatter their image of self. That report came as a rude shock to
the many among us who regard man (paradoxically) as a both fundamentally harmless and fundamentally dignified animal. The frightening effectiveness of the Communist technique was explained in *The New Yorker*
by the Communists' expert manipulation of "guilt—perhaps the most corrosive emotion that the human spirit has to wear."

That explanation, however, only serves to throw into relief the confusion in our discourse between guilt and shame. Strictly speaking, guilt
is not an emotion, though shame is. Guilt is the breach of standards of
conduct. Shame is the subjective reaction to the breach or non-fulfillment
of standards, moral, intellectual, or aesthetic, which we recognize as valid,
which we desire to live up to. Our inclination to speak of guilt when we

---

*First published in *Chicago Review*, vol. 15, No. 1, Summer 1961, pp. 45–57.

mean shame is all the more regrettable since in our time guilt has become a cheap commodity. In revolt against Puritan or Jansenist austerity, Romanticism has done away with guilt by proclaiming the primacy of "self-expression" and of "authenticity"; to exaggerated notions of universal depravity, the modern mind has reacted with the most comfortable, though not the most logical, of all deductions: "everyone guilty—no one guilty." A vulgar understanding of psychoanalysis has now made "guilt feelings" fashionable and "harmless." All these closely related trends have veiled from our awareness an emotion which, if it is the most corrosive one to which the human mind is exposed, may well reveal the moral predicament of man more strikingly than love or hate or fear: shame.

Albert Camus, at any rate, has put "shame, then, or one of those silly emotions that have to do with honor" into the center of *The Fall*. Camus' own report on the condition of modern man reads like an illuminating commentary on the grim tales of viciousness and degradation of *The New Yorker*'s "Study of Something New in History." *The Fall* is the story of the corrosion of a man's mind. At first view, that corrosion seems due to an act of cowardice—the protagonist's failure to come to the rescue of a young unknown woman who has jumped into the Seine. This is "the fall"—the woman's physical fall into the Seine, and the by-passer's moral fall from the heights of his vast self-love.

The fall from the innocence of his naive self-love dawns upon Jean-Baptiste Clamence with the recurring perception of laughter. At first, to be sure, it is "a good, hearty, almost friendly laugh" which engages his curious attention; yet gradually laughter pursues him until he feels the universe laughing at him. Indeed, the gates of hell resoundingly shut behind Clamence with the sound of laughter; there ensues the decline of his career as a brilliant and respected Paris lawyer and his final retirement to the murky job of legal counselor to the underworld of the port of Amsterdam.

Camus' understanding of laughter recalls Baudelaire's reflections on its satanic character. "The Incarnate Word," Baudelaire has observed, "was never known to laugh. For Him who knows all things, whose powers are infinite, the comic does not exist. And yet, the Incarnate Word was capable of anger, was capable even of shedding tears." Laughter, Bergson has noted, is incompatible with compassion. What Bergson has ignored, and Baudelaire recognized, is the contemptuous, rather than intellectually detached, character of laughing, as far removed from the radiant smile of affection as from joyful outbursts of discovery or invention. We are not always willing to admit that the comic and the ridiculous are synonymous terms, and that laughter is perhaps man's most constant violation of the golden rule.

Laughter may be borne if directed at some incident not beyond remedy. The ghastly character of the laughter which pursues Camus' hero derives from the fact that it aims at the very image of his being, an image shattered beyond hope of redemption, it seems to Jean-Baptiste, since involved in the death of a human being. The irrevocable deed, then, brings irrevocable damnation. Jean-Baptiste, indeed, finds himself in Inferno.

Yet it may be superficial to regard the weakness of a single fleeting moment as the prime and single cause of irremediable damnation. Perhaps that failure was but the straw which broke the camel's back. Evil, which visibly takes possession of Clamence as the sounds of laughter pursue him, may insidiously have entered his soul long before it was pushed to the surface. If this should be the case, though, it is not readily apparent. The protagonist's early innocence, as it emerges from his autobiographical account, is more real than he cares to admit in his later mood of bitter self-depreciation. There is in the make-up of the hero as a young man the intensity and immediacy of enjoyment of adolescence. He tells us what he used to dream of: "A total love of the whole heart and body, day and night, in an uninterrupted embrace, sensual enjoyment and mental excitement—all lasting five years and ending in death. Alas!"

His self-love and vanity, though considerable, are naive, unreflective, without self-consciousness, since they are grounded in the conviction of natural, inborn goodness and without any claim to merit. "I refused," Clamence comments on his early happiness, "to attribute that success to my own merits." There is even, without any formal religion, a sense of piety which keeps Clamence from believing that mere chance had endowed him with physical and mental attributes of high order; he had felt that his happiness "was authorized by some high decree." In fact, even after the "fall" and amidst corruption and putrefaction, memories remain pure and clean—like Milton's Lucifer, Clamence retains the vision of past beauty and goodness unimpaired. The mordant irony of presentation ceases suddenly in respect of lost purity when Clamence longs for the innocence of the past, for the blue Mediterranean—which Camus himself loves so passionately—for Paris at dusk, for places of bliss: "Oh, sun, beaches, and the islands in the path of the tradewinds, youth whose memory drives one to despair."

What is wrong with naive innocence? The price to be paid for it after childhood and adolescence are over, more exacting the longer the day of awakening is postponed. It is the price of self-deception and the evasion of responsibility. Self-deception—or wishful thinking—and the refusal of responsibility are the typical failings of infancy and immaturity. They are

the failings which prepare man's expulsion from Paradise in the story of
Genesis. They are the insidious channels through which evil enters. If not
detected in time, they push the corrosion of the mind to an unsuspected
degree. The slightest circumstance—"there are always circumstances,"
says Clamence—will suffice to cause the collapse of a hollow image of innocence, hollow, since it conceives of innocence as purity of thought rather
than as integrity of action. The result will be the sacrifice of integrity of
action to a fake purity—to a naivete purchased by increasing amounts of
dishonesty with oneself. "I had principles, to be sure, such as that the wife
of a friend is sacred. But I simply ceased quite sincerely, a few days before,
to feel any friendship for the husband."

Childlike egoism, as expansive as unreflective, has a peculiar way of
side-stepping the true intent of the rules of moral conduct. Exhortations to
be like children lest the Kingdom of God escape us, not to judge others lest
we be judged ourselves, are turned into the evasion of responsibility. Indeed,
the steady emphasis on the meaning of responsibility is one of the most remarkable features of *The Fall*. Camus' hero tells of his instinctive disdain
for judges, as if it were presumptuous for men to judge. In fact, he likens
judges to locusts, the scourge of God! Trained in jurisprudence, Clamence
employs his skill not in judgment, but in "doing good." He specializes in
hardship cases. As an attorney for the damned, the miserable Jean-Baptiste
Clamence appears as a do-gooder of the first order, as a modern Don Quixote. Don Quixote, we know, loosened the chains of sentenced galley-slaves
and set them free, since the dispensation of justice was for God alone. . . .

Carried on the crest of the wave of good intentions, unburdened by responsibility for judgments of integrity, Clamence finds it easy to be generous. Foregoing the judgment of others, he also finds it easy to avoid judging
himself. Man is innately good, after all . . . In a crucial passage, Camus has
summarized his indictment of modern man's infantile claims to natural
goodness and irresponsibility:

> You won't delight a man by complimenting him on his efforts by which
> he has become intelligent or generous. On the other hand, he will beam
> if you admire his natural generosity. . . . Yet there is no credit in being
> honest or intelligent by birth. Just as one is surely no more responsible
> for being a criminal by nature than being criminal by circumstance.
> But those rascals want grace, that is, irresponsibility. . . .

Corruptio optimi pessima. The claim of natural goodness gives way,
after intervention of damaging circumstances like cowardice, to the alle-

gation of universal corruption. Clamence, attorney for the damned, ends up by issuing "testimonials of bad character and habits" to everyone. The dream of total love gives way to the desperate denial that "real" love, like Tristan's and Isolde's, exists, except once or twice a century (*Liebestod* and *La vie en rose* become nauseating to the naive-turned-cynic). Good will and good intentions are replaced by malicious hatred, cynicism, and contempt. The naivete of self-deception with its rosy-colored view of the world is followed by willful destruction of self and others. In other words, the pride of naive innocence is followed by evil hundred-fold worse: by the abyss of self-abasement, giving birth to crime, lust of domination, indeed megalomania, and ultimately to the shadows of madness.

There is a point when Clamence feels to be standing in the innermost circle of Dante's Inferno. It is the circle reserved for those guilty of the most heinous sin, betrayal of those to whom they were bound by special ties. And has not Clamence also said that he has betrayed every single person whom he once loved? Yet madness has always been considered the characteristic punishment of treachery, and Dante has placed the souls of the insane in that innermost sphere of his Inferno. The fever which plagues Jean-Baptiste Clamence during the last and weirdest, most desperate and most cynical part of his confession gives expression to his pathological state of mind—though Camus does not fall into the modern trap of considering this as an absolution from responsibility. Clamence calms his interlocutor's disturbance at his mad ravings with the assurance that they are controlled. But does this mean more than the recognition that mental illness, sickness of the soul, is a disease of the will, based upon a distortion of moral judgment—that distortion which assumes the finality and totality of corruption?

Pursued by the laughter of self-contempt, cast out, Jean-Baptiste Clamence becomes a "false prophet in the wilderness" out of the direst need for fellowship. It is the fellowship of universal complicity, purchased by the bribe of public self-accusation, chaining masters to slaves as much as it chains slaves to masters. For Clamence, the world has become like Dante's Inferno where everyone is subject to someone else. For the corrupt, as for naive children, judgment and domination coincide. Like a child, the fallen Clamence wishes good and evil to be "arbitrarily, hence obviously, pointed out." But of course now he must be on the top. In his days of innocence, he scorned judges as locusts. Unable to shed his identification of judgment, domination and punishment, he turns into a locust himself; he creates a blight by understanding (or so he thinks) but *never* forgiving. Punish he must in order to judge; judge he must in order to dominate; and dominate he must lest he suffocate in the stupor of total despair. That is the ugly and ambiguous business of a "judge-penitent," as he calls himself. "Every man needs slaves as he needs fresh air. To command is to breathe—do you agree with me? And even the most destitute manage to breathe." In other words, people in glass houses, threatened with death by asphyxiation, may well choose to throw stones as their only chance of survival. . . .

The original claim of natural, inborn, goodness is accompanied by the idea of perfection. Albert Camus sees man as a natural perfectionist whose troubles begin when he realizes that he is less than perfect, that everyone is liable to be caught with his pants off, that cowardice is rather more natural than courage, as Adam and Eve demonstrated when they went into hiding before God. Camus has realized the terrible ambiguity of man's moral predicament: "Be ye perfect as our Father in Heaven is perfect"—yet to strive to achieve supreme perfection is tantamount to striving to be *sicut Deus*, to commit Lucifer's original sin of *hybris*! The "longing to be immortal" Camus calls the key to Clamence's, to man's nature. But what else is the longing for immortality but the desire to achieve what we have been endowed with perceiving—perfection? There is indeed immoderate pride in that longing, and pride without bounds, if unflattering circumstances intervene, turns into the abjectness of vengeful malice. In the tradition of Christianity, which has found its most powerful allegorical realization in Dante's *Divina Commedia*, Satan lacks the glamour which Milton and Romanticism have bestowed on the melancholy beauty of the magnificent crime. Dante, whom we may truly recognize as Camus' guide through the Inferno which our world has become, has Satan standing on his head, and his feet frozen in a pool of ice, out of which he vainly tries to liberate himself with bat-like wings. The mixture of ridicule and power of destruction, of helplessness and cruelty, of Dante's Satan is the most telling illustration of the Christian understanding of evil as a kingdom divided against itself: "Every kingdom divided against itself is brought to desolation" (Matt. 12:25). In the process of self-destruction, however, destruction is wrought unto others as well.

Camus has translated Dante's allegorical universe into the psychological realism of our time. There is, in the last pages of *The Fall*, a breathtaking succession of the most dreadful visions and desires which leave the reader in doubt whether Clamence determinedly talks in allegories or whether he is possessed by the demons of madness. The desire to be arrested by the police, even to be decapitated like the real John the Baptist, is followed by the wish to set himself up in supreme judgment like God the Father. There ensues finally the explicit identification with Satan, when Clamence feels himself grow "very tall" and when the desperate and wretched approach him from all corners of Europe to receive from his hands their final sentence of damnation. Only in those last pages do we fully understand Clamence's remark that at times he feels himself standing in the innermost circle of Dante's Inferno.

Critics of *The Fall* agree with the hero's preconception of his own lucidity and power of insight. Yet they also share, then, Clamence's ignorance of his main and decisive limitation: his ignorance of the existence and the conditions of integrity. Amidst his ravings from self-contempt to lust of domination, there occurs to Clamence the idea of putting himself at the top of a closed universe by getting ahead of the greatest spiritual power on earth, the greatest power visible to the unbeliever's naked eye: "My great idea is that one must forgive the Pope. To begin with, he needs it more than anyone else. Secondly, that's the only way to set oneself above him. . . ." Yet an error of calculation, due to ignorant condescension, upsets his much vaunted lucidity. There is someone who may forgive the Pope. The fact that every Pope is obligated to confess his sins to a confessor is largely ignored by a secularized world, though surely not by Albert Camus. The author of *The Fall*, with his uncanny gift for revealing situations which are scarcely ever thought of, has fastened upon the relationship of a Pope—symbol of supreme, infallible, and therefore irresponsible power—to his confessor in order to convey the central positive message of *The Fall*: the right to, and the conditions of, judgments of integrity, of responsible judgments, in other words. Clamence, we hear, hides in his chambers a famous stolen painting (which actually disappeared in 1934, and has never turned up) called *les juges intègres* or "The Judges of Integrity" (the usual English translation, "The Just Judges," falsifies its meaning). Clamence does not believe in the message of the painting which he guards at home; in fact, he enjoys despoiling and desecrating that message by the very act of keeping stolen property instead of returning it to its rightful owners. He glories in trampling on the idea of integrity. It's a big lie, he says, there is no such thing. Indeed, integrity, we often forget, is incompatible with naivete as well as with cynicism. Without the knowledge of temptation, there is no integrity. The naive-turned-cynic cannot grasp the meaning of responsible judgment, of a judgment aiming at atonement rather than punishment. He cannot see that the "Judges of Integrity" of Van Eyck's painting are sinners themselves and know it.

Beyond the antinomy of naive innocence and total depravity, of purity and corruption, Albert Camus attempts to illumine a third sphere: responsibility. Responsibility cannot be satisfied with good intentions alone;

it requires good judgment as well. Good judgment is impossible without the unique human—or divine—gift of making distinctions of degree. Camus has written in his recent essay on Capital Punishment that "man is not good; he is better or worse." Yet distinctions of degree are profoundly incompatible with those simplistic absolutes of modern times which, in truth, are nothing but regressions to immaturity and primitive tribalism. They are also features of Inferno: "Yes, hell must be like that: streets filled with shop signs and no way of explaining oneself. One is classified once and for all." One is either a good guy or a bad guy; either a true believer, or a heretic; either an elect, or damned soul; either a citizen, or an outlaw; either an Aryan, or a Jew; either a proletarian, or a capitalist. . . .

> . . . O, when degree is shaked,
> Which is the ladder to all high designs,
> The enterprise is sick.
>
> * * *
>
> Take but degree away, untune that string,
> And, hark what discord follows; each thing meets
> In mere oppugnancy; the bounded waters
> Should lift their bosoms higher than the shores,
> And make a sop of all this solid globe.
> Strength should be lord of imbecility,
> And the rude son should strike his father dead.
> Force should be right; or rather, right and wrong,
> Between whose endless jar justice resides,
> Should lose their names, and so should justice too.
> Then every thing includes itself in power,
> Power into will, will into appetite;
> And appetite, an universal wolf,
> So doubly seconded with will and power,
> Must make perforce an universal prey,
> And last eat up himself. . . .
>   —Shakespeare, *Troilus and Cressida, Act I, Scene 3*

The denial that every human being, at any particular moment, is better or worse than he was the moment before and than he will be the moment after, leads to terrible extremes: the judgment of final corruption is even more sinister than the presumption of innocence or perfection. That presumption of perfection is indeed the "original" sin of pride; yet the judgment or irremediable depravity is the final, the unforgivable sin of malice. It is what the Gospel calls the sin against the Holy Ghost.

Jean-Baptiste Clamence, the cynic, commits the one unpardonable sin, the sin against the Holy Ghost. It is said (Matt. 12:32): "Whoever speaketh against the Son of Man can be forgiven for it, but whoever speaketh against the Holy Ghost cannot be forgiven for it, either in this world or the next." Albert Camus, that master of unobtrusive presentation, in the last pages of *The Fall* leads us to the confrontation of the essence of evil—the persistence in corruption and self-contempt. Jean-Baptiste mentions that an old beggar once said to him, " 'Oh, sir, it's not just that I'm no good, but you lose track of the light.' Yes," Clamence adds, "we have lost track of the light, the holy innocence of those who forgive themselves." Then, as if there were no connection at all, Clamence looks out of the window where it has started snowing:

> See the huge flakes drifting against the windowpanes. Surely, they must be doves, who finally make up their minds to come down, the little dears; they are covering the waters and the roofs with a thick layer of feathers; they are fluttering at every window. What an invasion! Let's hope they are bringing good news. Everyone will be saved, eh?—and not only the elect.

Clamence sees the symbol of the Holy Ghost—yet he does not believe in it, since he considers himself corrupt beyond atonement, beyond redemption. The consciousness of one's own corruption, of being spoiled beyond repair, results in a deadly alliance of diffidence with complacent indolence. The final *fall*, the fall beyond remedy, the fall past redemption, the sin against the Holy Ghost, Clamence experiences or commits in the very last words of the book: It is the refusal of a second chance. The intimation of a second chance—"Oh young woman, throw yourself into the water again so I may again have the chance to save both of us!"—is followed by the ultimate self-deception that it will always be too late. Besides, the water would be so cold. . . .

The sin against the Holy Ghost emerges as the central theme of *The Fall*. Once we think of it, His symbol, the dove, appears in other parts of the book as well. There also emerges Camus' indictment of modern humanity which refuses salvation. The doves, Clamence notes, "wheel above the earth, look down" and would like to come down. But there is "nothing but the sea and the canals, roofs covered with shop signs [as in hell!], and never a head on which to light."

Yes, life now has become hell, and hell, as Dostoyevsky has said, is the inability to love. The full measure of love cannot be attained either by the childlike devotion of naive innocence or by the cynical sensuousness of the self-styled corrupt. It cannot be attained without a sense of respect. Self-deprecation and malice born of it prevent Jean-Baptiste Clamence from acquiring that measure of self-respect and self-confidence without which we cannot love, since like Satan we can only spread and communicate the evil we feel within us. If we betray ourselves, we shall go on betraying all others, God and men. And the sin against the Holy Ghost *cannot* be forgiven if first we are not ready to forgive ourselves, if we feel ourselves totally unworthy of forgiveness, if we deny that we have been made in the image of God. God is powerless to remedy man's malice against himself. If we remain untrue to the virtue within us, God cannot help us. Then we commit the truly diabolical sin, the final unpardonable sin against the Holy Ghost. That is Satan's own sin. Yet perhaps the devil himself could be forgiven, Camus suggests, if it occurred to him that under the stone-heap of fraud and malice there might be a spark of worth; even the devil might, with diligence, work out his salvation if it occurred to him that he might be worthy of forgiveness. But Satan thinks, of course, that the spark of worth has been extinguished long ago.

A sense of worth, of nobility, in other words, a sense of honor—these are the ideas on which Camus has staked his hope for man's salvation. Radical evil is perceived by Camus not in an excess of self-exaltation, though this is at the source. Radical evil is an excess of self-humiliation and self-degradation, defiling the image of God. In a sense of nobility Camus sees the best protection against the malignant double growth of self-abasement and lust of domination. Camus has given us the answer to the dismal story of Jean-Baptiste Clamence in his more recent short story "The Growing Stone" (*La pierre qui pousse*), which is significantly placed at the end of the volume *Exile and the Kingdom*. A French engineer has come on business to a Brazilian village. Surely not by accident, Camus has ascribed to him noble birth, while in *The Fall*, Clamence was very conscious of the humble birth and the plebeian features of himself. Like Clamence, the engineer d'Arrast had been responsible for the death of a human being in Europe, though no details are told. In Europe, there had been "shame and anger." Anger, not ridicule, will be the reaction of a man not devoid of nobility who has caught himself in a situation of shame. Anger at having been caught unawares. Anger will give him the determination and energy to look for a second chance. D'Arrast finds his second chance in this Brazilian village where perhaps the most superstitious distortions of Catholic worship to be found anywhere take place. D'Arrast witnesses the physical breakdown of a humble native man who had vowed to carry a large rock in a procession honoring St. George, the knightly killer of the dragon. Though d'Arrast knows that the man's breakdown has been caused by drinking and dancing the night before, he quickly decides to take up the rock. But instead of delivering it to the local church, he turns about and delivers it to the home of the original bearer.

A nobleman comes to the rescue of an humble, faltering fellow-being, and thereby rescues himself. The second chance having been grasped, there also dawns another kind of redemption from which Clamence had been barred. D'Arrast, in contrast to Clamence, is capable, perhaps again capable, of love. Not by accident, there occurs in "The Growing Stone" the figure of a young girl to whom d'Arrast finds himself attracted with more than mere sensuality while Clamence, sensuous though incapable of love, sadly progresses from one woman's bed to another without ever encountering the kind of girl whom Camus has chosen for the engineer d'Arrast to meet.

The English rendering of the title "The Growing Stone" does not do justice to the double meaning of *la pierre qui pousse*. In French, the Greek identity of *"Peter"* and *"the rock"* has been preserved. Already in *The Fall*, Camus is concerned with the "irony" that the faltering Peter, of all men, should have been called upon by Christ to be the rock upon which the Church was to be built. It is both permissible and sensible to recognize in "The Growing Rock" *corpus mysticum ecclesiae*. The fact that the "rock" is not delivered at the local church may mean two different things which do not, however, exclude one another: First, it may mean that Camus himself is not ready to enter the Church—indeed he has declared that he does not believe in the resurrection of Christ; therefore, he calls Jesus "my friend who died without knowing it"—a phrase which occurs both in *The Fall* and in his adaptation of Faulkner's *Requiem for a Nun*. There can be no doubt, though, as to Camus' new proximity to the moral teachings of Christianity, and in particular to Catholic Christianity as shown by his anti-protestant stress of freedom of the will, his devastating attack on the doctrine of predestination, and his sympathy for the ideal of the Christian knight—d'Arrast, St. George—with its admixture of the Greek heritage. Second, the symbolic refusal to deliver "the Growing Rock" to the local church may perhaps convey the view that the one true Church, *una sancta ecclesia*, is not accessible with the help of "shop signs."

It is not true, after all, that "guilt" or shame must inevitably be corrosive. Those who feel that in a shameful situation their "true" nature has been revealed, will fall into the abyss like Clamence; those who know that they did violence to their better self, to the image of God in themselves, those who like Peter denied God, will react with anger at themselves and with impatience to redeem themselves. In fact, those who believe that there is such a thing as a birthright might even, like Jacob, wrestle with God to extract His blessing. Albert Camus, I think, is one of those. Has he not written in *The Fall*: "'One doesn't talk back to one's father'—you know that expression? In a way, that is very odd. To whom should one talk back in this world if not to whom one loves? . . ."

It is unfortunate that the notion of Pride, in consequence of the Reformation in particular, has come to be identified with arrogance or *hybris*. There is also a meaning of pride in the sense of self-respect, informed by moderation, by a sense of proportion, and Camus has not abandoned his combat against *la démesure*, against excess of any kind. His story "The Renegade," also included in *Exile and the Kingdom*, illustrates Camus' loathing of the spirit of extremes. Utter self-mortification is all too often but lust of domination in disguise. The spiritual breakdown of a young man who looks for triumph in martyrdom, a "renegade" of a Catholic seminary who disregards the more moderate counsels of his superiors, occurs in the hour of physical defeat, when he turns to idolatry. Yet idolatry extorts the most horrible of all sacrifices, self-mutilation, visited upon the "renegade" in dreadful manner.

Among ideals such as love, reason, and justice, a principle has been obscured in modern times which yet seems best destined to keep us in balance between the extremes of sentimental fraternization and brutal domination—"honor, the virtue of the unjust ones," Camus has recently called it. In an interview with Jean Bloch-Michel (published in *The Reporter*), Camus has elaborated on this idea:

> I have never been able to make up my mind to spit, as so many have done, on the word "honor"—no doubt because I was and continue to be aware of my many human weaknesses and the injustices I have committed, and because I knew and continue to know instinctively that honor, like compassion, is the irrational virtue that carries on after justice and reason have become powerless. He whose passions, folly and faltering heart lead him into the most common weaknesses must surely turn to something for help so that he can succeed in gaining some measure of self-respect and thus become capable of respecting others.

Camus' earlier work has often been praised as that of a seeker for purity and sainthood in a world without God. Today, Camus seems more interested in decency than purity. As for sainthood, it hardly can be reached by the haughty extreme of self-mortification, but rather by modesty. If we reconsider our opinion of ourselves, Camus has written in *The Fall*, we might "go mad with suffering, or even become modest—for everything would be possible." Everything is possible. While in *The Plague*, Camus accused God of having betrayed the world, the fault now seems to be with the world's insistence, stubborn, desperate, and complacent, to perpetuate hell on earth.

♜

APPENDIX

Bibliographical Information

I. BOOKS AND INDEPENDENT PUBLICATIONS

Stourzh, Gerald. *Benjamin Franklin and American Foreign Policy*. Chicago: University of Chicago Press, 1954; 2nd ed. and paperback 1969.

———. *Alexander Hamilton and the Idea of Republican Government*. Stanford, CA: Stanford University Press, 1970.

———. *Vom Widerstandsrecht zur Verfassungsgerichtsbarkeit: Zum Problem der Verfassungswidrigkeit im 18. Jahrhundert*. Graz: Universitäts-Buchdruckerei Styria, 1974.

———. *Kleine Geschichte des österreichischen Staatsvertrages*. Graz: Verlag Styria, 1975. Second revised and enlarged edition under the title *Geschichte des Staatsvertrages 1945–1955. Österreichs Weg zur Neutralität*. Graz: Verlag Styria, 1980. Third edition under the same title, with a 1985 epilogue. Graz: Verlag Styria, 1985. Fourth edition, completely revised and considerably enlarged, under the title *Um Einheit und Freiheit. Staatsvertrag, Neutralität und das Ende der Ost-West-Besetzung Österreichs 1945–1955*. Vienna/Cologne/Graz: Böhlau, 1998. Fifth edition under the same title, with a bibliographical epilogue. Vienna/Cologne/Graz: Böhlau, 2005.

———. *Fundamental Laws and Individual Rights in the 18th Century Constitution*. Claremont, CA: Claremont Institute, 1984.

———. *Die Gleichberechtigung der Nationalitäten in der Verfassung und Verwaltung Österreichs 1848–1918*. Vienna: Verlag der Österreichischen Akademie der Wissenschaften, 1985.

———. *Wege zur Grundrechtsdemokratie. Studien zur Begriffs- und Institutionengeschichte des liberalen Verfassungsstaates*. Vienna/Cologne: Böhlau, 1989.

———. *Vom Reich zur Republik. Studien zum Österreichbewußtsein im 20. Jahrhundert*. Vienna: Edition Atelier, 1990.

————. *Begründung und Bedrohung der Menschenrechte in der europäischen Geschichte.* Vienna: Verlag der Österreichischen Akademie der Wissenschaften, 2000.

————. *1945 und 1955: Schlüsseljahre der Zweiten Republik.* Innsbruck: Studienverlag, 2005.

2. COEDITOR AND CONTRIBUTING AUTHOR

With Anna M. Drabek and Mordechai Eliav. *Prag–Czernowitz–Jerusalem. Der österreichische Staat und die Juden vom Zeitalter des Absolutismus bis zum Ende der Monarchie (Studia Judaica Austriaca* vol. 10). Eisenstadt: Edition Roetzer, 1984, including G. Stourzh, Galten die Juden als Nationalität Altösterreichs? 73–117.

With Margarete Grandner. *Historische Wurzeln der Sozialparterschaft* (Wiener Beiträge zur Geschichte der Neuzeit, vol. 12/13). Vienna: Verlag für Geschichte und Politik, 1986, including G. Stourzh, Zur Institutionengeschichte der Arbeitsbeziehungen und der sozialen Sicherung—eine Einführung, 13–37.

With Friedrich Koja. *Schweiz-Österreich. Ähnlichkeiten und Kontraste.* Vienna/Cologne/Graz: Böhlau, 1989, including G. Stourzh, Wandlungen des Österreichbewußtseins im 20. Jahrhundert und das Modell der Schweiz, 11–32.

With Erhard Busek. *Nationale Vielfalt und gemeinsames Erbe in Mitteleuropa.* Vienna/Munich: Verlag für Geschichte und Politik/Oldenbourg, 1990, including G. Stourzh, Der Anton Gindely-Preis für Geschichte der Donaumonarchie, 11–21, and Die Idee der nationalen Gleichberechtigung im alten Österreich, 39–47.

With Birgitta Zaar. *Österreich, Deutschland und die Mächte. Internationale und österreichische Aspekte des "Anschlusses" vom März 1938.* Vienna: Verlag der Österreichischen Akademie der Wissenschaften, 1990, including G. Stourzh, Die Außenpolitik der österreichischen Bundesregierung gegenüber der nationalsozialistischen Bedrohung, 319–46.

With Richard G. Plaschka and Jan Paul Niederkorn. *Was heißt Österreich? Inhalt und Umfang des Österreichbegriffs vom 10. Jahrhundert bis heute.* Vienna: Verlag der Österreichischen Akademie der Wissenschaften, 1995, including G. Stourzh, Erschütterung und Konsolidierung des Österreichbewußtseins: Vom Zusammenbruch der Habsburgermonarchie zur Zweiten Republik, 289–311.

With Barbara Haider and Ulrike Harmat. *Annäherungen an eine europäische Geschichtsschreibung.* Vienna: Verlag der Österreichischen Akademie der Wissenschaften, 2002, including G. Stourzh, Statt eines Vorworts: Europa, aber wo liegt es? ix–xx.

With Arnold Suppan and Wolfgang Mueller. *Der österreichische Staatsvertrag 1955/The Austrian State Treaty 1955.* Vienna: Verlag der Österreichischen Akademie der Wissenschaften, 2005, including G. Stourzh: Der österreichische

Staatsvertrag in den weltpolitischen Entscheidungsprozessen des Jahres 1955, 965–95.

3. COEDITOR

With Ralph Lerner. *Readings in American Democracy*. New York: Oxford University Press, 1959.

With Robert A. Goldwin and Ralph Lerner. *Readings in World Politics*. New York: Oxford University Press, 1959.

With Robert Goldwin and Ralph Lerner. *Readings in American Foreign Policy*. New York: Oxford University Press, 1959.

With Robert A. Goldwin and Marvin Zetterbaum. *Readings in Russian Foreign Policy*. New York: Oxford University Press, 1959.

With Karl Braunias. *Diplomatie unserer Zeit/Contemporary Diplomacy/La diplomatie contemporaine*. Graz: Styria, 1959.

4. CONTRIBUTIONS TO SCHOLARLY JOURNALS, COLLECTIVE VOLUMES, AND RELATED WORKS
(selection; contributions republished in the present volume are not included)

Ideologie und Machtpolitik als Diskussionsthema der amerikanischen außenpolitischen Literatur. In *Vierteljahrshefte für Zeitgeschichte* 3 (1955): 99–112.

Review of *Il pensiero politico degli Autori del Federalist* by Aldo Garosci, and *Il Federalista*, by A. Hamilton, J. Jay, and J. Madison, translated into Italian by Bianca Maria Tedeschini Lalli. *Political Science Quarterly* 71 (1956): 309–12.

Die tugendhafte Republik. Montesquieus Begriff der vertu und die Anfänge der Vereinigten Staaten von Amerika. In *Österreich und Europa. Festgabe für Hugo Hantsch zum 70. Geburtstag*, Graz/Vienna/Cologne: Böhlau, 1965, 247–67 (reprinted in *Wege zur Grundrechtsdemokratie*, 117–36).

Die deutschsprachige Emigration in den Vereinigten Staaten: Geschichtswissenschaft und politische Wissenschaft. In *Jahrbuch für Amerikastudien* 10 (1965): 59–77 (reprinted in *Wege zur Grundrechtsdemokratie*, 371–92).

Bibliographie der deutschsprachigen Emigration in den Vereinigten Staaten 1933–1963: Geschichte und politische Wissenschaft, with the collaboration of W. P. Adams and A. Lagois, parts I and II. In *Jahrbuch für Amerikastudien* 10 (1965): 232–66 and 11 (1966): 260–317.

Die politischen Ideen Josef von Eötvös' und das österreichische Staatsproblem. In *Der Donauraum* 11 (1966): 204–20 (reprinted in *Wege zur Grundrechtsdemokratie*, 217–37).

Some Reflections on Permanent Neutrality. In *Small States in International Relations*, ed. A. Schou and A. O. Brundtland, 93–98. Stockholm: Almquist and Wiksell, 1971.

The American Revolution, Modern Constitutionalism and the Protection of Human Rights. In *Truth and Tragedy: A Tribute to Hans J. Morgenthau*, ed. K. Thompson et al., 162–76. Washington, DC, 1977.

Staatsformenlehre und Fundamentalgesetze in England und Nordamerika im 17. und 18. Jahrhundert. Zur Genese des modernen Verfassungsbegriffs. In *Herrschaftsverträge, Wahlkapitulationen, Fundamentalgesetze*, ed. R. Vierhaus, 294–328. Göttingen: Vandenhoeck & Ruprecht, 1977.

The Declarations of Rights, Popular Sovereignty and the Constitution: Divergencies between the American and French Revolutions. In *La Révolution américaine et l'Europe: Colloques internationaux du Centre national de la recherche scientifique No. 577, 21–25 février 1978*, 347–67. Paris: Éditions du Centre national de la recherche scientifique, 1979.

Die Gleichberechtigung der Volksstämme als Verfassungsprinzip 1848–1918. In *Die Habsburgermonarchie 1848–1918*, vol. 3: *Die Völker des Reiches*, ed. A. Wandruszka and P. Urbanitsch, 975–1206. Vienna: Verlag der Österreichischen Akademie der Wissenschaften, 1980.

Grundrechte zwischen Common Law und Verfassung. Zur Entwicklung in England und den nordamerikanischen Kolonien im 17. Jahrhundert. In *Grund- und Freiheitsrechte im Wandel von Gesellschaft und Geschichte*, ed. G. Birtsch, 59–74. Göttingen: Vandenhoeck & Ruprecht, 1981 (reprinted in *Wege zur Grundrechtsdemokratie*, 75–89).

Towards the Settlement of 1955: The Austrian State Treaty Negotiations and the Origins of Austrian Neutrality. In *Austrian History Yearbook* 17/18 (1981/82): 174–87.

Alexander Hamilton (1755–1804). In *Encyclopedia of the American Constitution*, vol. 2, ed. L. W. Levy and K. L. Karst, 889–92. New York: Macmillan, 1986.

Il Federalista. Teoria politica e retorica della persuasione. In *Il Federalista: 200 anni dopo*, ed. G. Negri, 271–90. Bologna: Il Mulino, 1988.

Naturrechtslehre, leges fundamentales und die Anfänge des Vorrangs der Verfassung. In *Rangordnung der Gesetze*, ed. Ch. Starck, 13–28. Göttingen: Vandenhoeck & Ruprecht, 1995.

Some Reflections on International Conflict Resolution among Ethnic Groups in Historical Perspective. In *Wiener internationale Begegnungen zu aktuellen Fragen nationaler Minderheiten/Vienna International Encounter on Some Current Issues Regarding the Situation of National Minorities*, ed. F. Matscher, 17–30. Kehl/Strasbourg/Arlington VA: N. P. Engel Verlag, 1997.

Der Dualismus 1867 bis 1918. Zur staatsrechtlichen und völkerrechtlichen Problematik der Doppelmonarchie. In *Die Habsburgermonarchie 1848–1918*, vol. 7: *Verfassung und Parlamentarismus*, ed. H. Rumpler and P. Urbanitsch,

1177–1230. Vienna: Verlag der Österreichischen Akademie der Wissenschaften, 2000.

Reply to the Commentators. In historiography roundtable on Stourzh's *Staatsvertragsgeschichte*, with comments by V. Mastny, T. A. Schwartz, K. Larres, and A. Pelinka. In *Neutrality in Austria* (Contemporary Austrian Studies, vol. 9), ed. G. Bischof, A. Pelinka, and R. Wodak, 278–92. New Brunswick/London: Transaction, 2001.

Gleichheitsgebot und Benachteiligtenförderung. Der Fall *Regents of the University of California* vs. *Bakke* vor dem Supreme Court, 1978. In *Der Rechtsstaat vor neuen Herausforderungen. Festschrift für Ludwig Adamovich zum 70. Geburtstag*, ed. B.-Ch. Funk et al., 773–89. Vienna: Verlag Österreich, 2002.

"Égaux en droits:" The Place of Non-Discrimination in the History of Human Rights. *Human Rights Law Journal* 25 (2004): 2–10.

5. BIBLIOGRAPHIES

A complete list of scholarly publications 1951–1989 is to be found in *Geschichte zwischen Freiheit und Ordnung. Gerald Stourzh zum 60. Geburtstag*, ed. E. Brix, T. Fröschl, and J. Leidenfrost, 460–64. Graz: Verlag Styria, 1991. This list is continued for the years 1990–1999 in *Geschichte und Recht. Festschrift für Gerald Stourzh zum 70. Geburtstag*, ed. T. Angerer, B. Bader-Zaar, and M. Grandner, 433–38. Vienna/Cologne/Weimar: Böhlau, 1999. More recent publications are listed annually in *Almanach der Österreichischen Akademie der Wissenschaften*.

INDEX OF NAMES

Note: Names of authors or editors mentioned only in connection with bibliographical references are set in italics. Names of authors who are also discussed or quoted in the text or in amplified notes are set in roman type.